THE DAY THE DEVIL WEPT

To Richard and Elizabeth,
With my grateful thanks for your practical help and prayerful support that lies behind so much of this book,

The Day the Devil Wept

Peter Ramosa Green

JANUS PUBLISHING COMPANY
London, England

First published in Great Britain 2011
by Janus Publishing Company Ltd,
105–107 Gloucester Place,
London W1U 6BY

www.januspublishing.co.uk

British Library Cataloguing-in-Publication Data
A catalogue record for this book is available from the British Library

ISBN 978-1-85756-752-9

Cover Design: Scorch Media Design
http://www.scorchmedia.co.uk/

Printed and bound in India

Dr Peter Green MBE
Ramosa

Founder
Durham-Lesotho LINK
1986

Dedication

This book is dedicated to my wife, Pam,
and our children, Edmund and Rachel,
without whose loving support
neither the book nor the work it describes
would have started or developed
into the active witness it has become.

Contents

Foreword xi

A Biblical Paraphrase xiii

Preface xv

Acknowledgements xvii

Prologue: Before the Beginning? xix

Map of Durham xxii

Map of Lesotho xxiii

Chapter 1: In the Beginning was the Word 1

Chapter 2: 'Saddle Up!' 25

Chapter 3: Them and Us 53

Chapter 4: In the Jungle 81

Chapter 5: Trees of the Field 109

Chapter 6: Ha Popa 147

Chapter 7: Sing a New Song 187

Chapter 8: Suffering Little Children 223

Chapter 9: Ha Mohatlane 239

Chapter 10: Saddle-Sore 281

Chapter 11: Yap! Yap! Yap! 317

Chapter 12: Reflections in the Mountains 339

Index 355

A LINK Prayer 375

Foreword

The Kingdom in the Sky

Lesotho is a wonder of God's creation so it is not surprising that it is fondly called the Kingdom in the Sky. The majestic and rugged mountains with which it is blessed hide from the outside world the spiritual and gentle Basotho people who inhabit this beautiful, awe-inspiring country. This is the land, the people and their culture, which the author vividly opens up in this remarkable story. As few others have done he has ventured into the remote interior of the country, joined in the harsh life of the people and shared in their Christian faith.

This book tells the story of how, exercising his worldwide experience, professional knowledge and Christian faith, Ramosa, as he was named by the Basotho, brought together in the Durham-Lesotho LINK two diverse peoples living 6,000 miles apart. For over twenty-five years that LINK has provided people in both regions with an active, personal and modern-day witness to the word of the Gospel of Christ.

The Durham-Lesotho LINK has become a vibrant movement showing how mission can be developed to the benefit of the poor, and also the rich, and taken into the twenty-first century. Forging a link between peoples of different cultures is always a difficult and exciting journey. It should not be undertaken lightly or by the faint-hearted and this narrative describes how that difficult work was started and developed and what has been achieved despite inevitable disappointments and setbacks!

In the language of the Basotho 'Ramosa' means '*one who is endued with kindness*'. Such names are given only after a long period of observation by the host community or family and reflect the trust of the community in the person being honoured. This trust comes from a spiritual belief that a person who has journeyed sacrificially over land and sea, in order to forge a bond with another, must be a person of great vision, kindness and generosity.

The Lesotho-Durham LINK, now twenty-five years old, could only have survived and thrived through God's gracious blessing and on the basis of human understanding and mutual respect of all those many people involved as they have drawn ever closer together into one body under Christ's leadership. The churches of Lesotho and the determined spirituality of the Basotho people have sustained the Christian faith in Lesotho for many decades. That, with Ramosa's vision and leadership, helped to ensure that the LINK graphically described in this book did not collapse in the dark brutal days of southern Africa apartheid around the Kingdom of Lesotho. The Lesotho-Durham LINK truly worked within apartheid by which we were all surrounded.

In the Lesotho-Durham LINK people of faith, and sometimes of none, have found solace and encouragement in the common decency of men and women and the kindness, 'Mosa', of one believer unto another. As we, in Lesotho, look with immense joy and pride on what Dr Peter Green and others have done for our *'Kingdom in the Sky'*, on what the LINK has achieved and is still achieving, we must also recognise the challenges that still lie ahead. Some causes that were obvious in the early days are still there, others have mutated into different forms and some have been solved. Tackling these outstanding issues will need still more sacrificial, human and financial help.

What will endure, however, in the Durham-Lesotho LINK, is the kindness, the '*Mosa'* of people of faith, one to another, that has already sustained us for twenty-five years.

His Royal Highness Prince
Seeiso Bereng Seeiso

High Commissioner for the Kingdom of Lesotho,
to the United Kingdom.

January, 2011

A paraphrase of Paul's First Letter to the Corinthians Chapter 3 verses 4–9

When one of you says, 'I follow Lesotho,' and another, 'I follow Durham' are you not acting like worldly people?

After all, what is Durham? And what is Lesotho? We are simply God's servants, by whom you were led to believe. Each one of us does the work which the Lord gave him to do:

Durham sowed the seed, Lesotho watered the plant, but it was God who made the plant grow. The one who sows and the one who waters really do not matter. It is God who matters, because He makes the plant grow.

There is no difference between the Dunelmian who sows and the Mosotho who waters: God will reward each according to the work that has been done.

For we are working together for God, and you, Lesotho and Durham, are God's field.

Preface

This book is a personal narrative of one life lived in two cultures for one purpose. It is an account of how the Durham-Lesotho Diocesan LINK was founded in 1986 and how it has led the transition of mission in those two places from the twentieth into the twenty-first century. It is not claimed to be comprehensive as some events within the orbit of the LINK during the past quarter of a century have inevitably escaped record. My twofold hope is that it will serve as an accurate historical record of events in which I was involved and provide a useful guide, encouragement and pool of ideas for those who are engaged in, or contemplating an association with, other cultures, countries and communities. As we move into the twenty-first century I trust that our successes may be copied and our failures avoided.

This book straddles two cultures so there may be some aspects that seem unusual to the reader in the other region and with this in mind explanations may be found in extensive endnotes. As a historical account, evidence for statements and events has been sought and documented, but as a voluntary organisation precise records have not been kept so some information is unavailable to me. Much information has already been lost. My own personal daily journal, usually written at the end of each day, and my field notebooks have provided much of the detailed information, particularly about the early years. Statements and events have been carefully researched in Lesotho, Durham and elsewhere and evidence, if it exists, is provided. Furthermore, even though idioms may be commonplace in one of the two regions, for the benefit of the other, they have been amplified in the endnotes. In Lesotho it is rather silly to catch a cold, the cold always catches you! Likewise, where it has been judged that Basotho or Dunelmians would be interested in the expansion of a topic, although not directly concerned with the LINK, this has also been included in the endnotes.

I would like to take this opportunity to clarify two points: to describe people living in Durham city, county or diocese the word Dunelmian is used. This word is from Dunelmum, the Latin name for Durham.

Secondly, after an initial introduction I have avoided, wherever possible, the use of titles except to help clarity. This style has been adopted because of the plethora of diplomatic, academic and ecclesiastical designations, many of which are ephemeral and so quickly become obsolete. In no way does this approach indicate or imply any disrespect for the bearer of any title; it is used solely for the sake of simplicity and accuracy.

As will become clear in its reading this is not the story of a partnership. The concept of partnership, and the very word itself, contains an element of separation; separate parts coming together. Separate partners sooner or later involve the distinction of a senior and junior partner. All of this I wanted to avoid. I perceived those I was working with in both places not as two separate groups of people but as one group of Christians. I was not blind to differences in colour; I was not deaf to differences in language; I was not immune to differences in wealth. I was, however, conscious that people become what others perceive them to be. My conceptual analysis of the Durham-Lesotho LINK contained three persons: the Mosotho, the Dunelmian, the Christ. Without any one of those three the LINK becomes nonsense.

I hope that the following pages will be of value to those individuals and organisations that seek to become more effective in their wider ministry and work. Although my major objective was, and still is, rooted in the development of Christian lives, the account that follows could be useful to those many secular authorities in counties, cities and towns across the UK and elsewhere that have various forms of association with regions overseas. Secular and religious agencies were successfully brought together with people of all major denominations into one vibrant movement for the benefit of all people in both Lesotho and Durham.

Most of the Sesotho words that appear in the text are the names of places and English phonetics will give an adequate rendering of the word for the general reader's own satisfaction. There are two guiding principles: the stress is generally (you will not be surprised to learn that there are exceptions) on the penultimate syllable and a letter 'L' before an 'I' or a 'U' is pronounced as a 'D'. None of these linguistic hurdles need worry anyone who is simply reading for their own enjoyment and information but for those who may wish to learn the language works of reference are quoted in the endnotes.

I hope, in reading this book, you will experience the Wonder of Oneness.

Peter Green,
Durham,
England.
August, 2010

Acknowledgements

An Open Letter

Durham,
England.
August, 2010

Dear Reader,

Over the past twenty-five years countless numbers of people, whose names are unrecorded, have contributed to the Durham-Lesotho LINK in ways so numerous and varied as to be almost unbelievable. Even if not named it is their involvement sometime during the past twenty-five years that this book celebrates.

Those who have contributed to the writing of this book range from princes to kings; from archbishops to bricklayers; from collectors of pounds to the gatherers of stones; from various shades of white to different tints of black; from the tax-payer in Lesotho and southern Africa to their counterpart in Durham and Europe; from the young to the old (some of whom have now died). Some have helped voluntarily, others in their professional capacity; some I know but many are unknown to anyone except themselves.

It is they who have given freely of advice, money, wisdom, time in prayer, kindly criticism and encouragement, hospitality and, on rare occasions when it was necessary, supporting sympathy. Each one will know of their individual gift without reminder. However you may have given to the LINK, to each one I express my deep thanks and sincere gratitude in the knowledge that without your support there would be little to write about in a book of this type. Without any one of your contributions the LINK would have been weaker and less effective.

However you may have contributed you will be aware of your part in the story of the Devil's past twenty-five despondent years in Lesotho and Durham: in that we can all rejoice together and thank each other for our mutual support. Naming any one individual risks overlooking the very many. 'Thank you' to each and every one in whatever way you may have been involved.

Yours sincerely,

Peter Ramosa Green

Prologue

Before the Beginning?

Identifying the beginning of some things, where and how they started and even why, is notoriously difficult especially when those 'things' involve the thoughts and varied actions of many very different people. Where *do* you stop in the backward search for the beginning? The tree, cultivated by soil and rain, has numerous roots that feed the one trunk, that nurtures many branches, that produce countless seeds that germinate to produce new life. One of the seeds that brought Basutoland (as it then was) into my consciousness, and may possibly have stimulated the thinking that developed into new life, began its remarkable existence in the most unlikely and improbable of places: Pneumonia Bridge!

In the late 1940s three naval personnel were battling their way across the appropriately named bridge, not in some dramatic heroic naval action but simply to get 'ashore' from the large naval hospital in which they all worked. As they struggled against the 'strong breeze' that former naval officer Francis Beaufort[1] had much earlier categorised as 'force six', the waves in the Spithead were taking off their white caps seemingly to acknowledge the determined effort of the three young men to stay on the high arch of the open iron girder footbridge. As members of His Majesty's Royal Navy we had the privilege of using the toll bridge that spanned Haslar Creek without dipping into our four-shillings-a-day[2] naval pay. On the windswept bridge conversation between the three of us was difficult, but as it took us to the Gosport side of the creek and we reached Holy Trinity Church with its separate, rather unattractive brick tower, we began talking about the Naval Christian Fellowship[3] that Alan Edmonds and I, with others, were starting in the Royal Naval Hospital, Haslar. It was then we suggested to Fred Warren that he should join with us and it was then he surprised us both with the news that he couldn't because he was leaving the navy to become a medical missionary in Africa.

That night Africa seemed a long way away, but Fred's enthusiasm was infectiously heightened, no doubt, by the wild, boisterous weather, contrasting with our generalised misconception of weather in Africa. Expressing his faith in the 'higher' end of the ecclesiastical spectrum Fred, a red-headed Christian who worshipped at Holy Trinity Church, talked about his calling into what little he knew of the future. I cannot now remember and neither did I record at the time in which country he said he was going to serve, but I do recall, with clear precision (and I guess a twinge of envy), that he told us it was mountainous and not only did he have to know his Bible, which he did, but he also had to know how to ride a horse, which he didn't. He was certainly testing his nascent faith. By now we had reached the welcome comfort of a small café and as we sat talking about this stark change in his life, chalk and cheese seemed quite closely related compared to equestrian skills and biblical understanding bound together by medical knowledge. But my interest didn't linger – or so I thought. I was still to learn that in my life as scripture says:

> 'What no one ever saw or heard,
> what no one ever thought could happen,
> is the very thing God prepared for those who love him'.[4]

Our ways parted. Alan was tragically killed in a car accident and I lost touch with Fred who, from deep memory, I think lived in Christchurch, Dorset. Then, some fifty-four years later, I was sitting in my study in Durham reading a small book written by the first medical doctor to work at St. James' Hospital, Mantšonyane, Lesotho. Ken Luckman, writing about a lady who had served in a dispensary built by Fr. Clement Mullenger of the Society of the Sacred Mission that was the forerunner of the hospital, went on to say:

> 'Previous to her a male nurse, Fred Warren, had also worked at Ha Chooko for a short time in 1954'.[5]

That was all; no further mention. Now, there might be more than one male nurse with the name of Fred Warren but surely not another who, in early 1949, shared with his friends his call to be a medical missionary in a country of mountains where horsemanship was a necessary attribute and where the mode of worship accentuates the use of ritual and ceremony. Could it, I wondered, have been the same Fred Warren who walked across Pneumonia Bridge with Alan and me on that rough, force six, night all those years ago? Without any doubt, if he had worked at Ha Chooko, he most certainly would have had to learn to ride a horse in the mountains and if he had worshipped with Clement Mullenger,[6] the Oxford Movement[7] would have influenced their devotions. I paid my only visit to Ha Chooko on Tuesday, 6 May 1986, climbing and walking there from Mantšonyane without any thought that a long-lost friend might have preceded me. What was much more significant was whether or not he was the person (chosen by God?) to plant the seed that I then pushed into my subconscious, to lie there germinating for so many years. Was this 'the very thing God had prepared'?[4]

---

1. Royal Naval Commander Francis Beaufort, in 1805, devised the Beaufort scale that has been used ever since to categorise the state of the sea and wind speeds.
2. Four shillings in 1949 would have been equivalent to twenty pence in the future decimal coinage.
3. The Naval Christian Fellowship was started in 1948 at the Royal Naval Hospital, Haslar, by a group of Royal Navy Christians under the leadership of Surgeon Lieutenant James Watt and is still ministering to naval personnel from its headquarters in Portsmouth Dockyard. After a lifetime of Christian service in the Royal Navy, James Watt died on Monday 28th December 2009 aged 95. Obituary in *The Times,* Thursday, 21st January 2010 (p. 70).
4. 1 Corinthians 2:9 (Good News Bible: Today's English Version: The Bible Societies 1976).
5. Luckman, Kenneth, *Place of Compassion,* (UK, Authors OnLine Ltd, 2001) p. 9.
6. Clement Mullenger was an Anglican priest in the Society of the Sacred Mission who spent most of his life in Christian service in Ghana and Lesotho. In Lesotho he had a great love of Ha Chooko in the Mantšonyane valley. He was distressed when I showed him photographs of the church he built there after a gale had destroyed the roof. I saw him frequently during his latter years that were spent in Durham at the Society's St Antony's Priory, which was formerly the vicarage of St Nicholas Church. Clement was born in Norfolk on Thursday 16th July 1914 and, after many years of eccentric service to the Basotho, died in Sherburn Hospital, Durham, on Tuesday, 26th February 2008 aged 93 years.
7. The initiators of the Oxford Movement during 1833 to 1845, troubled by the spread of liberalism within the Anglican Church, attempted to introduce a higher, more formal, standardised form of worship in the Church of England by restoring seventeenth-century High Church practices. Although there are a few exceptions, most congregations in the Province of Southern Africa, within which Lesotho lies, contribute to this expression.

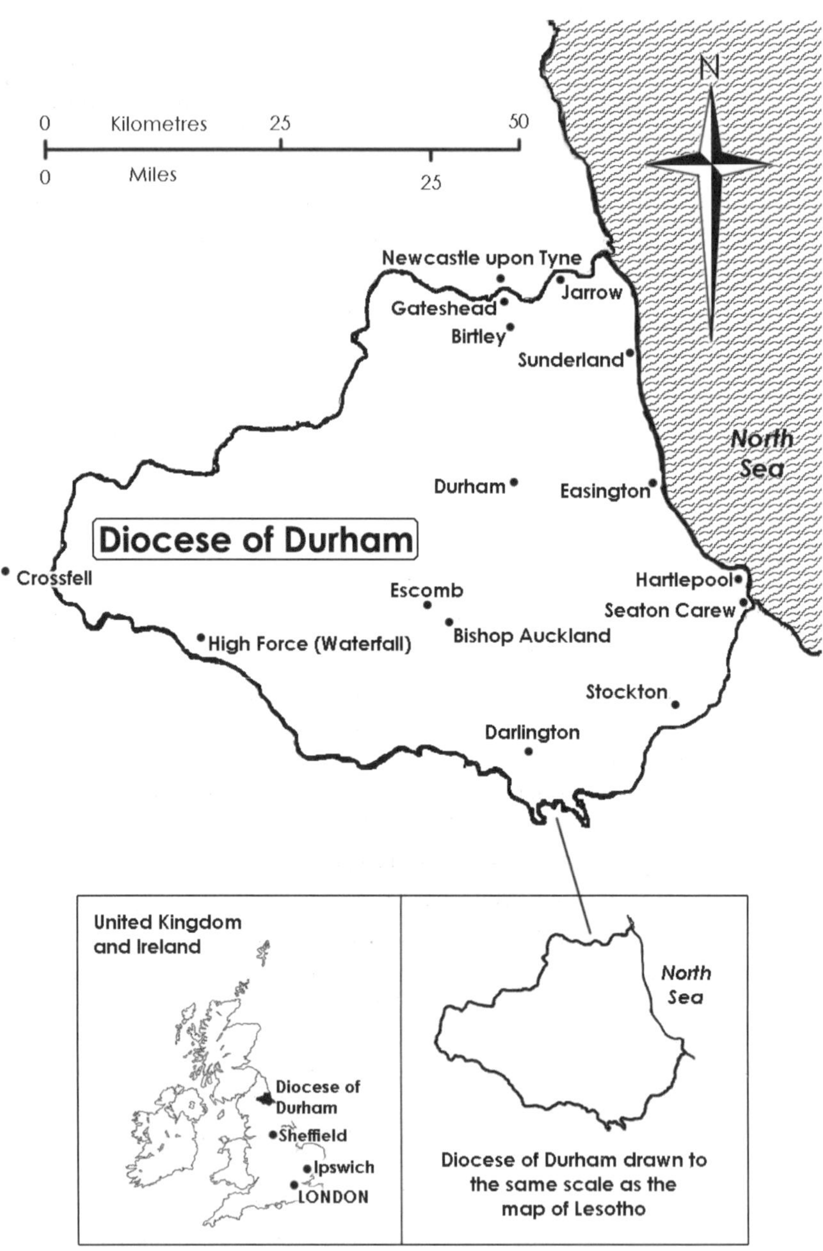
0
Kilometres
25
50
0
Miles
25
N
North Sea
Newcastle upon Tyne
Jarrow
Gateshead
Birtley
Sunderland
Durham
Easington
Diocese of Durham
Crossfell
Escomb
Hartlepool
Seaton Carew
Bishop Auckland
High Force (Waterfall)
Stockton
Darlington
United Kingdom
and Ireland
Diocese of
Durham
Sheffield
Ipswich
LONDON
North
Sea
Diocese of Durham drawn to
the same scale as the
map of Lesotho

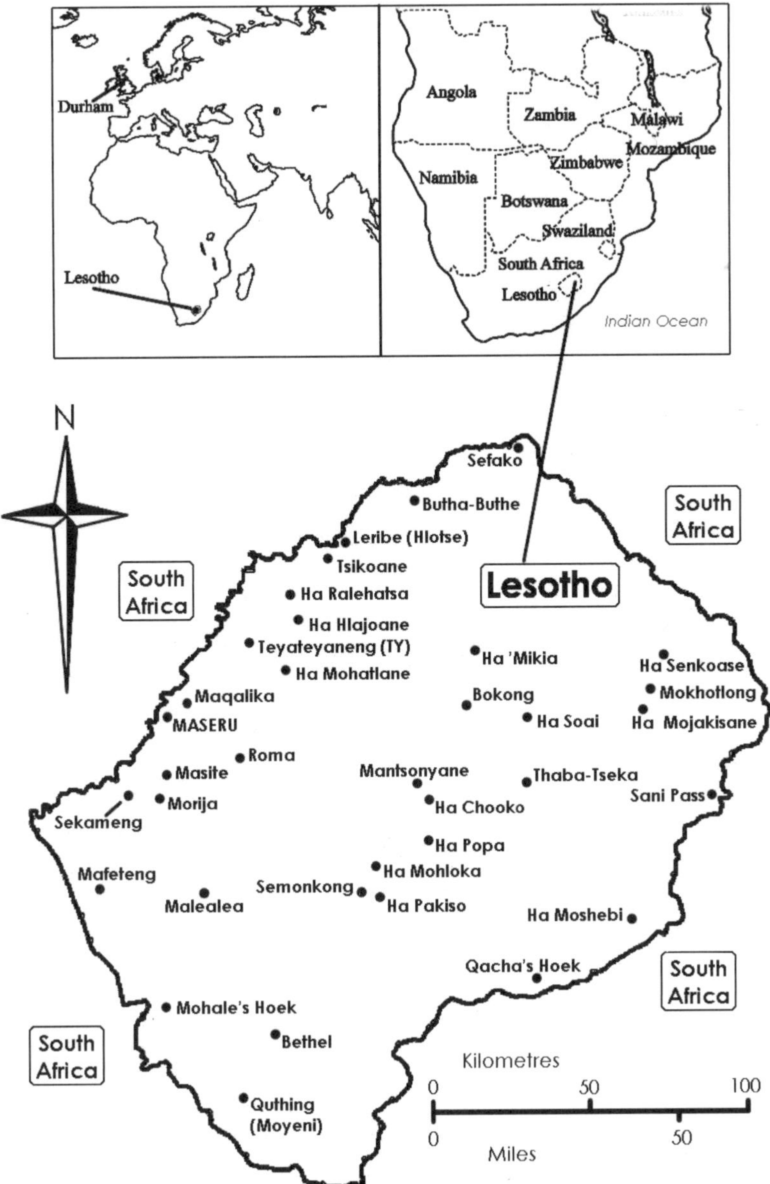

Durham
Lesotho
Angola
Zambia
Malawi
Mozambique
Zimbabwe
Namibia
Botswana
Swaziland
South Africa
Lesotho
Indian Ocean
N
Sefako
Butha-Buthe
Leribe (Hlotse)
Tsikoane
South Africa
South Africa
Lesotho
Ha Ralehatsa
Ha Hlajoane
Teyateyaneng (TY)
Ha 'Mikia
Ha Senkoase
Ha Mohatlane
Mokhotlong
Maqalika
Bokong
MASERU
Ha Soai
Ha Mojakisane
Roma
Masite
Mantsonyane
Thaba-Tseka
Sani Pass
Morija
Ha Chooko
Sekameng
Ha Popa
Mafeteng
Ha Mohloka
Semonkong
Malealea
Ha Pakiso
Ha Moshebi
Qacha's Hoek
South Africa
Mohale's Hoek
South Africa
Bethel
Kilometres
0
50
100
Quthing (Moyeni)
0
50
Miles

Chapter One

In the Beginning was the Word

It all began with an argument; at least, I think it did. It was not a serious argument but it was a disagreement about a serious issue made more significant as it took place between two strong personalities. The protagonists were good friends then, as they are now, and neither knew that their difference of opinion would have long-term implications for many people in two different countries of the world. In the late 1970s I was actively engaged in discussions with a future Archbishop of Canterbury, George Carey, about the necessary and costly refurbishment of St. Nicholas Church in the centre of Durham city.[1] In spite of the fact that this church had been described, somewhat liberally, as 'a spired and inspired Victorian masterpiece'[2] Gerald Blake, a mutual friend who was a far-sighted, decisive thinker, had presented a vision of a serving church that required a functional, well-designed building better suited to providing a wide range of facilities seven days a week in the Britain of Queen Elizabeth II. The initiative stimulated an enthusiasm that wanted to see the idea realised and realised quickly. Having worked and worshipped in the old building for some five or six years, surviving some of its leaks and draughts, I did not doubt the need to undertake the changes. I was as eager as anyone to see the proposal developed and to play my part as chairman of the church council that would have the final say as to whether or not the suggestion went ahead.

However, I did question the ethical position of spending an enormous amount of money to achieve an aim that contained quite a strong element of self-interest. It was my view that whilst undertaking the suggested redevelopment we should, simultaneously, mount a project for the benefit of some needy section of society. Unlike most of those involved I had not only seen, but also lived close to the abject poverty some experience day after every hopeless day. I wanted to bring a sense of balance into the thinking and to widen the vision but, such was the enthusiasm for Gerald's proposal, I found little support. George was adamant that we had to be 'single-minded' when dealing with a scheme as large, complex and costly as the one we were considering and that any other project, however worthy, could be mounted later. I had some wavering understanding of that position and did not press my point as vigorously as perhaps I should have done but, despite the stress and strain the church project spawned, I never once lost sight of my hope that there would be a parallel scheme and it remained alive and, often, kicking. After the splendid church refurbishment was completed, not surprisingly, nothing further was done about 'the other project' – everyone was exhausted!

Perhaps it was no coincidence that when the church in the market place was reopened in all its new-found splendour on Friday, 23rd October 1981, I was absent from the hundreds of people gathered on its carpeted, heated floor for the dedication service. Whether it was a twist of fortune I shall never know, but my professional work had sent me to the small country of Lesotho in the southern hemisphere well away from the celebrations. There, after a long search and many false and increasingly frustrating attempts, I managed to find a telephone that was rather more than decorative and actually worked and, somewhat to my surprise, managed to reach George in Durham to send my greetings to both him and those gathered for the gala evening.

We had worked closely together for many a long hour during the previous year and it was rather ironical that at this point we were now thousands of miles (kilometres) apart. Nevertheless there was, as we spoke, an ambivalent streak in my mood. I commented that it was appropriate for me not to be there as a church was a place in which Christians should not only gather but, more importantly, from which they should go out into the world.[3] George faithfully passed on my greetings and message during the service. Time has proved St. Nicholas Church in Durham to be a place from which many have left to travel around the world, which is perhaps most appropriate for a church dedicated to the patron saint of sailors.[4] Time has also proved the value of the costly renovation, but I was troubled about the enormous resources committed so tenaciously to the venture.

As a middle-aged academic I was never quite sure into which of the prophet Joel's two categories I came.[5] Was I simply a dreaming old man or was I still young enough to have a vision? Did it matter anyway since, as they are overlapping concepts, the boundary between the two is difficult, if not impossible, to distinguish.[6] Given the context in which I hoped 'the other project' would operate and the target at which, in my mind, it was aiming, I discovered that the difference was crucially important to some people. There were those who saw a vision as a God-given attraction, whereas a dream was nothing more than a human enticement; perhaps my motive contained a bit of both. What was very clear to me, and a position with which few could argue (although some did), was that biblical thinkers were not just that but were also people of action.[7]

Some years later I was to experience a rather bitter occasion when a small group of Christians were persuaded not to support 'the other project' because I was accused of not preaching the gospel. As this book will confirm, although that was a totally inaccurate perception of what I was doing it raised, in my mind, the constraining limitation of the concept of preaching as a means of proclaiming and communicating the gospel in the world and in the environment in which I was working. The command of Jesus 'to go into all the world and preach the gospel'[8] was given to eleven men who, at the time, were having grave doubts about what they had experienced; would it have been a step too far to command them to be even more practical in expressing their faith in Christ? Maybe my driving force was what Bertrand Russell described as 'intuitive knowledge',[9] but whatever the generative power the direction of my aim was towards the target of proclaiming Christ the King in word and work.

In any case if, as I believe, it all began with an argument, perhaps I could not claim to be either dreaming or visionary, just reactionary. Since I had been through the trauma, not exactly of Judah's locusts[10] but of Thatcher's politicians[11] and pseudo-educationalists devouring an education that had enthusiastically captured my professional encouragement for the past twenty years, perhaps I might qualify for one, or the other, or perhaps both, since they are not reciprocally destructive; especially in middle age! What would my critics do with a middle-aged man dreaming about the fulfilment of a vision? I never did ask them, for the crucial point I had to bear in mind was that, according to Joel, the spirit of the Lord would be poured out on everyone, young or old, men and women; the spirit of the Lord would not be withheld from anyone who had remained faithful to Him through the ordeal; and servants come in for a special mention.[12] I cannot claim to have had a vision as a command from God. All I *can* claim is that I had an argument that may have been the work of God; I just do not know. What I do know is that the disagreement was a spur to the thinking that stimulated my action, which is what I hoped God wanted of me. I had the energy and the time that (at a cost to other cherished activities) could be made available. It was, conceivably, a call to redirect those resources over which I had some element of control. What I had to do was to make them available to God or, alternatively, withhold them because He had given me the free will to make that choice and the consequent decisions necessary to implement that voluntary option.

At this stage there was no conscious decision on my part to start immediately another major enterprise. As vice-principal of an Anglican College of Education I had enough on my main course plate with professional upheavals in higher education causing fierce turmoil generated by politicians interfering with professional matters about which they knew little and, seemingly, cared even less. As Secretary of State for Education and Science Margaret Thatcher, with her eye on Downing Street,[13] gave no indication that she knew of any difference between instruction and teaching, let alone any distinction between training and educating. Indeed, she left professional educators to pick up the pieces, as they are still doing years later, of some educationally disastrous policies.[14–15] It was all very disheartening not only because it took an immense amount of time and energy that could have been used more effectively in the task of educating, but also since those who wanted to could quite clearly see the future harmful consequences.

Nevertheless, I had become infected by an idea that, because of these other events, was becoming increasingly virulent and potent; although it needed more time to incubate and become fully infectious. That was fortunate, very fortunate, because there were students to teach, books to write, meetings to attend, journals to be satisfied, contributions to government reports to be submitted, sermons to preach and arguments to pursue, as well as a college to run, research to complete and, with my wife, Pam, the care of a young family. Life was full, active and happy. As I grappled with these professional issues and personal concerns, some of which required extensive, time-consuming travel both in Britain and overseas, the notion persisted; the ideas danced an ungraceful jig in my mind; the concept was being refined and desperately needed an outlet!

Even if it was 'an ungraceful jig' I did, at least, know the tune. Almost twenty years earlier, just after I had completed my teacher education at Keswick Hall College of Education in 1963, I was awarded a bursary by the King George VI Commonwealth Memorial Fund and given the choice of going either to Hong Kong, Fiji or the Seychelles. What a choice! I had been to none of them and now I had to choose one. Since at that time few people had even heard of the Seychelles and the only way of getting there was by sea, via Zanzibar, I plumped for six weeks on some of the ninety-two islands scattered around the Indian Ocean. At least there were ninety-two before some were joined together to make a flat surface on which to land an aeroplane and thereafter alter the lives of the Seychellois. So, with the active encouragement of Pam, I took a Comet 4 Jetliner of East African Airways to Benghazi and on to Nairobi, changing there to a Friendship aircraft of doubtful years' service to land safely at Mombasa. After a wait of five days, I then embarked on the British India ship *Kampala* that took me to Zanzibar and on to the idyllic Seychelles, to run leadership courses for the Scout Association, the movement that first brought Pam and me together.

This marked the beginning of my international educational and development work that was to spread into thirty-six different countries of the world. Now, it helped to launch me into the Caribbean as four years later the Department of Education and Science sent me to Jamaica to study the educational background of the many immigrants that were arriving in Britain from that part of the world, with their confused mixture of psychological baggage as diverse as their mass of physical luggage. Whatever the emotional rhetorical statements of some politicians I was convinced that an increasingly rapid fusion of ethnic groups would take place in the world and that, in the field of education, we ought to increase our knowledge and understanding of the inevitable intermingling of minds. Subsequently, my research into the education of children who had emigrated from other countries[16] kept me in close touch with a wide array of differences and although I still had much to learn, I wasn't completely ignorant of other countries' cultures and conditions. In the early 1980s, as I continued to think about 'the other project', the score of the 'jig' became increasingly apparent and rather more melodic.

When colonial Basutoland reverted to independent Lesotho in October 1966, the college of which I was to become vice-principal, St. Hild's College, Durham, had, at the request of the British Council, started a British government-funded venture to conduct in-service courses for Basotho primary school teachers. This was a project, started by Nina Joachim, the then college principal, that was to run for eleven years during which time many Basotho teachers improved their professional skills and qualifications. The general pattern of the courses consisted of two weeks of lectures and activity workshops, held in the capital Maseru, followed by a further fortnight when the Durham tutors worked alongside the local participants in their schools around the country. During these four weeks two or three Basotho teachers on the course were selected to return to St. Hild's College where they were provided, usually for one academic year, with the opportunity to further their education. In the academic year 1974–1975, one of those teachers, Sister Magdalena Matsoso, a Roman Catholic nun from Holy Cross Primary School in the south-west of the country, was to make a practical contribution to my future work in Lesotho.

With little knowledge of her native country I arrived in Durham from Nottingham in August 1972, just two years before she did. A year later I was invited to join a team of tutors from Durham colleges that was going to Lesotho during the summer vacation under the calm, persuasive leadership of David Buchan, a lecturer in art and design. David had a stimulating concept of primary education and this project continued to make a constructive contribution to the post-colonial education of Basotho teachers until 1976. However, things were changing in Lesotho and having been asked to take over the leadership, I was then commissioned to bring the project to an end, transferring the work to the newly established Lesotho National Teacher Training College.

This was not a complete severing of the Durham contribution as for some months I had been involved in discussions about the college curriculum with an American, Dwight Allen, who had been charged with setting up the college soon to be restyled Lesotho College of Education. It was then that I was asked by the Lesotho Minister for Education to continue working with his team as a technical adviser, a request to which I agreed as I knew I would enjoy the challenge in trying to find solutions to at least some of the many obdurate problems facing education in Lesotho. I had not been back in my own college very long after I had received this invitation before Sister Magdalena came to see me to get the latest news from her home country.

Sitting in my comfortable study, which had one of the grandest of all views overlooking the River Wear towards the huge, magnificent Norman cathedral and its protecting castle, I had been sharing with her some of the many problems in Lesotho that I was grappling with at the time. We talked for a little while and then, wrapping her capacious black habit round her diminutive frame, she looked at me sternly and in her quiet, convincing manner mounted a plausible argument concluding with the spirited rejoinder, 'Peter, you will never get anywhere with anything until you learn their language!' The thought filled me with horror because apart from the need to find the time if I were to follow her advice, I doubted my ability to command a click-language and, despite my many Basotho friends by this time, I had still not tuned in to their indigenous speech. I was also very conscious of the fact that after living in the north-east of England for two years I was only just beginning to gain a superficial understanding of Newcastle Geordie and, unlike Sesotho, that didn't have any clicks! Anyway, I argued, the Basotho with whom I was most frequently in touch spoke fluent, well-constructed English. It was all to no avail. This little, determined nun maintained her position as I tried to convince myself she was wrong but gradually, and somewhat reluctantly, came to realise she wasn't.

The next time she came to see me I met her challenge with my own that was much more demanding: 'teach me'! Returning two days later she had recorded the first twelve lessons in the simpler of the only two books on the Sesotho language then available.[17] For the next three months I rarely went to sleep without listening to Sister Magdelena's recording of a Sesotho lesson from Sharpe's book. It was a real struggle, especially as I tried to get the clicks in the correct places at eleven o'clock at night; sweet dreams rapidly became cognitive nightmares.

Others were also coming to grips with their problems that were given some necessary revelation that carried with it unwelcome publicity. In the early 1980s, the Anglican Diocese of Durham received a rather unfavourable report[18] that was critical about its lack of missionary endeavour. A Partners in Mission team of observers considered the diocese to be 'introspective', a reprimand that stimulated an instruction to its mission committee to turn critical appraisal into constructive action. In the improbable setting of the ancient small town of Easington, County Durham, still nursing its own troubles after fifty-one miners and two rescue workers were killed in the local coal mine,[19] the committee under its chairman, Alan Piper, took a typically Anglican decision to set up a working party to consider how relationships might be established with an overseas diocese. The action moved slowly south-west across the county some 16 miles (or, for the metric-minded, 25 kms) to another ancient settlement, Escomb.

The church there dates from the seventh century but now, 1,300 years later, three clerics, Stephen Pedley, Nick Beddow and Ian Calvert, met to consider approaching four possible 'Partners in Mission'. It had taken four years to get this far, geographically and mentally, which did not seem to illustrate an urgency of purpose especially as Ian, the diocesan adviser for mission, now took the suggestion of the four possible partners to each deanery synod in the diocese for further discussion! I was no longer a member of the General Synod so I had no access to deanery meetings, but my wife was a member of the Durham Deanery Synod and took the opportunity to speak strongly in favour of establishing a relationship with Lesotho. Even though few people had any idea about who the Basotho were, or where Lesotho was on the globe, she was obviously persuasive as interest in this small African country and a possible future relationship was beginning to seep through the mesh of diocesan organisation to the people.

Whilst that was taking place a lot of other things were happening in 1984, almost six months of which was spent in southern Africa. Meanwhile, in the latter half of the year, David Jenkins was, thanks to the unlikely patronage of Margaret Thatcher, becoming Bishop of Durham, moving his somewhat controversial thinking and stimulating speaking from the ivory towers of academia to the rather less enclosed ramparts of Auckland Castle. Not long after he had pulled on his purple frontal we found the opportunity to talk together about our work and walking from his study (and perhaps, more importantly, away from his telephone) we adjourned for lunch at The Queen's Head, Bishop Auckland.

It was not long before he introduced into our vigorous discussion questions about connections I had with the Anglican Church in Lesotho and in the Province of Southern Africa where, so we discovered, we had a number of mutual friends. Taking another of his unusual, but often effective, decisions he circumvented the torturously slow diocesan debate, asking if I thought the Lesotho diocese would look favourably on some sort of association with Durham. I didn't know the answer to that question but I did know that I was determined not to impose, or expose, my ideas for 'the other project' that by this time were well advanced and included a strong reluctance to be constrained by dilatory ecclesiastical practices. My professional qualifications in cognitive psychology and philosophy were going to be useful and I was determined not to inflict my ideas but simply to present them as realistic possibilities. I knew where I was, where I hoped to go and who I wanted to come with me but the vehicle was, at this stage, undefined. Nevertheless, I undertook to investigate the prospect of some sort of diocesan association when I was next in Lesotho. Knowing the people who would be involved in any kind of relationship, I recognised the value of an early non-committal approach and assured David that I would raise the possibility when I was next in the country. My 'ungraceful jig' was taking on the proportions, manner and prospect of an elegant ball. I thought I might have discovered 'the other project', though I rapidly acknowledged that the concept was rather too large for a parish to handle: the diocese was to be the ballroom.

What then *was* the backdrop against which the LINK was eventually to be presented? In the early 1980s there was rarely a time when the possibility of some sort of association with another diocese was out of my mind. I still wanted to see my image of the 'other project' fulfilled as a complement to the refurbishment of my parish church, but the passage of time had expanded my thinking. I could now see the possibilities on a diocesan scale within which the parish church congregation could, and I still felt strongly should, participate. However, there were extensive demands upon my time and energy that took me, in addition to my frequent visits to Lesotho, to Burundi, Botswana, Swaziland, Zimbabwe, Zaire (as it then was) and four of the so-called 'homelands' of Bophuthatswana, Ciskei, Transkei and KwaZulu in apartheid South Africa.

During this time of terror in South Africa I was conducting research about the teaching and learning of indigenous languages and guiding local authors with their writing of children's books. This was all much to the concern of my family and close friends. This understandable anxiety was made even more acute when a parcel bomb, sent by an apartheid death squad on Tuesday, 17th August 1982, murdered a former lecturer of Durham University, Ruth First.[20] I never actually met Ruth face-to-face, we were both busy people and often out of the country, but we did have long telephone conversations and her death was a stark reminder of the vicious brutality within which I was sometimes working. This was compounded by an attack, from the same source, on Michael Lapsley, a priest in the Society of the Sacred Mission who had visited my wife and me in Durham during April 1983, seven years before he had both of his hands blown off by the same tactics. This did not make comfortable reading in *The Times*[21] as I flew home on Tuesday, 1st May 1990 on flight BA054.

I had been working in Namibia supervising a water project that was producing useful results, the people having dug 296 groundwater wells in the Owamboland region, but across the continent the fledgling Durham-Lesotho LINK was a mere 4 years old and still very susceptible to emotional disturbances. Other South African friends were under apartheid banning restrictions limiting their movements, contacts and speaking and, with only partial success, curbing my visits. The situation was all rather tense. In my early years in the apartheid environment, when a head teacher asked for permission for me to visit his school, an anonymous authority in Pretoria decreed that I should not be allowed to enter the building whilst the pupils were in attendance! What did they know or what did they think they knew? That has been the only school, of the hundreds in the world in which I have worked, where I have been refused entry!

Lesotho was, literally, surrounded by those 'Riding out the Darkness'[22] and although the country was comparatively calm, it was important for me to be aware of the situation into which I was proposing to lead other people, for it was not completely immune from the carnage of apartheid as demonstrated by the South African raid in Maseru on Thursday, 9th December 1982. This incursion, resulting in the death of twelve Basotho, took place within a stone's throw of the Anglican cathedral and even closer to the bishop's house.

No one could get to Lesotho without travelling through, or over, apartheid repression and this was the surrounding environment within which the church in Lesotho was enclosed. Experience of working and living in these African countries gave me a solid grounding into the life of the Church, as in each country I made contact with the Church and my licence to officiate in my parish as an Anglican Reader took on a wider international dimension. Retaining some geographical balance I undertook a series of assignments in another oppressed area of our troubled world working in Israel, the West Bank and the Gaza Strip. I would not be accused of being 'hooked on Africa'.

Even though my professional work took me to other 'hot spots' in the world, by now I was in southern Africa some four or five times a year. My research and lecturing took a lot of time and energy: in one exceptional month in South Africa I did not sleep in the same bed for more than two consecutive nights. Nevertheless, I had the opportunity to pursue an answer to David Jenkins' enquiry, the prospect of which was just one of many absorbing activities that spurred me through the horrors of apartheid. Whenever I was in Maseru I attended the Anglican Cathedral Church of St. Mary and St. James but, as so often happens, it was my first visit that I recall most vividly.

David Buchan and I had risen early one Sunday morning to go to the 8.00 a.m. celebration of holy communion. As we left our comfortable hotel, unfortified by breakfast, the cold, midwinter breeze from the mountains sliced through our very beings, showing no respect for the cathedral by carrying the dust of Lesotho into every crevice; it was so very cold and no warmer inside the cathedral. There was no one there when we arrived well before the time advertised, but that was wrong: it should have read 8.30 a.m. for 8.00 a.m! Fortunately the church was open so we waited on a backless wooden bench, huddled close together, on the left-hand side of the nave, looking towards the altar standing in a small apse. It was a long, cold wait for the start of the service little of which we would understand except by cerebral, liturgical and ritual reference to its English counterpart. Gradually scores of substantial Basotho ladies, 'traditionally built', surrounded us with colourful blankets concealing the blue-and-navy uniforms of the Mothers' Union or rather more everyday simple clothing.

Why David and I, thus surrounded, were completely shunned by other men we couldn't, in a whispered conversation, decide. As the small cathedral church filled to capacity it became all too obvious. In our ignorance of local custom we had sat on the wrong, that is the female, side of the central aisle and now there was no escape! Male tradition demanded in that day and age that we should sit on the right-hand side of the nave and we began to feel more than a trifle uncomfortable. We hadn't exactly entered the ladies' toilets but we felt as if we had done the next worse thing!

Once the service had gained momentum the leader, Suffragan Bishop Fortesque ('Forty') Makhetha, spotted these two white men and, in his impeccable English, he welcomed us most warmly. During his greeting he asked us to stand, making us feel, unintentionally I'm sure, downright conspicuous which of course we would have been in our whiteness even if we had been on the correct side for men. None of that lessened the vigour of our reception as there was much cheering, hand-clapping and female ululation. The reception was rapturous, the noise deafening and our embarrassment, although it never completely dispersed, was at least diminishing! After the service we met people on both sides of the ecclesiastical divide, lay and clerical, joining with them at the adjacent Anglican Training Centre, where we enjoyed the Basotho pastime of talking whilst they dispensed their generous hospitality. Not, I remember thinking, unlike the north-east of England. Was it, I wondered, a behavioural consequence arising from the toughness of a life dependent upon mining, the one for coal, the other for gold?

That cathedral visit, some twelve years before David Jenkins' request, introduced me to many long-lasting friendships. Over the intervening years the number of my Basotho colleagues and contacts increased spectacularly, making me well placed to float the idea of some sort of association between the two regions, Durham and Lesotho. During these years I had also benefited from some extensive travelling throughout the country; there were not many regions in which I had not worked. The exploration of lowlands, foothills and mountains had brought me into contact with all types of Basotho society, the complete range of occupations and various degrees of wealth and poverty. As a Reader in the Church I was, by now, particularly well placed to straddle the ecclesiastical divide of lay and ordained people, a divide that was more entrenched in Lesotho than in Durham. My official lay ministry also helped me to counter one other critical feature, namely the suspicion that some secular officials held about the Church, its work and its motivation for engaging in activities that are not immediately recognisable as 'religious'. That was to become, albeit slowly, a very crucial quality for me to bring into future negotiations. So with my ecclesiastical foot firmly on the ground, so to speak, I had long talks with the diocesan bishop, Philip Mokuku, who warmed to the idea and spent many hours speculating about how it might be established and developed. I was careful not to raise hopes and deliberately dampened the exuberant enthusiasm of some, as I was anxious to clarify in my own mind what sort of association it might be wise to pursue across 6,000 miles (9,656 kms) of the world's surface.

Back in Durham, where Pam was surviving as wife, mother, teacher and chauffeur to and from the airport, there were two very different, and very special, places to which I used to retreat. They each offered me their own special milieux into which I could withdraw to think and pray, to reflect and refresh. They were as different as a yacht is to a retreat house, for that is what they were. Most of the serious thinking and talking about the nascent proposal took place whilst on retreat with the Community of the Resurrection at their retreat house, Emmaus, in Sunderland. One of the resident priests there was Aelred Stubbs,[23] who knew Lesotho and the

Basotho intimately having lived there for four years following his expulsion from apartheid South Africa. During that time he occupied a small rondavel, one that I was to inhabit frequently in the years to come, situated in the grounds of the Convent of the Society of the Precious Blood at Masite.

How fortunate I was! I enjoyed his company and he enjoyed talking about southern Africa, so we spent many happy hours talking over the possibilities, difficulties and, indeed, the dangers of my work not only in Lesotho, but also in the despicable apartheid environment. His perceptive intellect strongly modified my own, sometimes impetuous, actions symptomatic of my more famous biblical namesake. I used to leave Emmaus spiritually uplifted, physically restored and intellectually invigorated, arriving home to share with Pam what I imagined 'the other project' could be. After others had knocked the ideas about, I would then go over to Auckland Castle where, so to speak, the drawbridge was always down and the portcullis always up for me to analyse the ideas with David Jenkins. After an hour or so in his study we repaired once again to North Broadgate, to enter into the ancient presence of Queen Elizabeth I[24] to discuss an activity that would be honoured by Queen Elizabeth II eight years later.[25] Over lunch we vigorously argued our ideas and discussed the hopes of the Basotho that I had brought back with me and together we planned the way forward. At the concept stage this was all very necessary work so as not to relax into thinking the first ideas were all-embracing or sufficient to be carried forward by initial enthusiasm that would be unlikely to continue unabated.

What was also very necessary was for us to relax together as a family and we did that in many ways but especially on our boat *Tanna,* so-called because as a young boy I saved sixpence[26] each week from my rather meagre pocket money so I could buy myself a boat. On Wednesday, 5th April 1978, there was a quiet launching of *Tanna* from the boatyard of John Dandridge in Newhaven. With my Yachtmaster Certificate[27] carefully tucked away in my waterproofs and a collection of North Sea charts spread out on the navigation table, I started many thousands of nautical miles[28] cruising the east coast of England and the north coast of Holland. This really was, unashamedly, escapism, but the challenges of the North Sea helped to invigorate and return us with new, realistic enthusiasm to tackle 'the other project'.

When ashore it was important to remember that we were not exactly cultivating virgin soil; there was a historical perspective to consider. The only published history of the Anglican Church in Lesotho[29] records that one of the first people to establish contact between the two regions was the Rev'd Philip de Lande Falkner who was ordained in Durham cathedral and served as curate at St. John's Church, Hebburn, before going to the

Diocese of Bloemfontein in 1905. From 1927 to 1929 he was Director of Quthing Mission, in the south of Lesotho, before returning to Bloemfontein, South Africa. This itinerant priest, who had no less than thirteen appointments during his long ministry in southern Africa, returned to Lesotho in 1935 staying for the next thirteen years in Hlotse and, finally, in nearby Tsikoane. When he arrived at St. Paul's Church, Tsikoane, Philip Falkner was about to forge another tenuous link with Durham. He was completely unaware that a baby girl he baptised there was, in due time, to give birth in 1977 to a son, Obed Sebapalo. Obed, who is a Government Registrar in Thaba-Tseka, was awarded the LINK's 2010–11 Alphonce Mohapi scholarship to help him with his studies to become a self-supporting priest. Philip Falkner left Tsikoane (where one of the LINK's feeding projects was located some 50 years later) for Bloemfontein in 1948 then moved to Johannesburg where he died in 1965. Moving in the opposite direction, as it were, the Anglican religious order the Society of the Sacred Mission, which began its work in Lesotho by establishing St. Agnes' Mission at Teyateyaneng in 1904[30] travelled northwards eighty years later in 1984 and opened a priory in the old vicarage of St. Nicholas Church, Durham, just a couple of hundred yards (180 metres) from our own 1720s house where a different form of mission was beginning to take shape albeit rather slowly. When Lesotho gained its independence in October 1966, people in the Jarrow area of County Durham raised money to help build the Church of St. Bartholomew at Sekameng in the lowlands of Lesotho,[31] an area where the future Durham-Lesotho LINK was to work twenty years later on a more environmentally focused activity. Using the resources of other sympathetic agencies numerous informal visits between the people of the two regions were arranged and these served to keep alive the personal contacts between Lesotho and Durham.

Perhaps more importantly these specialised contacts served also to provide a strong basis for the future development that, by this time, had become firmly implanted in my mind, just waiting for the right time to be implemented. The wait was longer than I had anticipated, as I was still working in many African countries on educational assignments and literacy projects. One Mosotho to keep alive the connections already established was Ignatius Malebo. In 1980, thanks to the financial support of the Society for the Propagation of the Gospel, he travelled from the parish of Peka, a small village some 35 miles (56 kms) north-east of Maseru, to spend a year working in the diocese of Durham. He became a familiar figure in many parishes as he travelled around the region, to be joined later by his wife, Adolphine Regina. My wife and I were delighted that Ignatius was in the diocese when we celebrated our silver wedding anniversary, enabling him to take part in a service of celebration in

Durham City Hall, where all the services were held during the refurbishment of St. Nicholas Church.

It was during the visit to Durham of Ignatius that the area secretary of the Leprosy Mission lent me a film to show to a group of Chinese students about a place that had been deeply etched upon my memory: Bọtšabelo. It was four years earlier that I made the first of many visits to this Leprosy Hospital; although that word 'hospital' does not convey the repulsive conditions I found there on Tuesday, 24th August 1976. I don't think I shall ever forget that visit: my journal records that 'it was one of my most disturbing experiences'.[32] I vividly remember being shown around the appallingly squalid environment by a diminutive Roman Catholic priest, Fr. la Brecque, and wondering what on earth could be done to improve the disgraceful living conditions. When I arrived back in Durham I gave a graphic account of my visit to George Marchant (who was then the vicar of St. Nicholas Church) and so it was that, a year later when Walter Maasch the General Secretary of the South African Leprosy Mission came to see me, I was able to present him with a substantial cheque representing the generosity of the congregation. However welcome that was, and it was very welcome, it was, nevertheless, a short-term measure that, hopefully, might bring some temporary relief. Other people were doing other, more substantial things to improve matters.

In 1977 the Leprosy Mission sent Margaret Phillips, with her extensive experience of leprosy in Uganda, to Botšabelo. Her strikingly detailed account[33] of what she found there and what she and others were able to achieve is an astonishing story of patient, persistent and prayerful endeavour. Both in Durham and in my mind, these spasmodic activities kept alive the notion that perhaps an active Durham-Lesotho connection might be practicable and I worked to encourage and increase these informal contacts. I saw them as a strong foundation for the future; the more I could bring people together, I argued to myself, the more firmly and securely would they would eventually unite.

Ignatius was based at Holy Trinity Church, Hartlepool, where he worked closely with the parish priest, Matthew Joy, who two years later, with his wife, Alsie, and their two young daughters, Clare and Sarah, left the winter of Hartlepool for the summer of Lesotho. In January 1982 they flew to southern Africa to spend six months in Lesotho, Matthew working in the Anglican diocese and Alsie in the primary school of the National University of Lesotho, where one of my former Basotho students was head teacher. It must have been an enjoyable experience for their young daughters as eleven years later, in 1993, Clare was to return to Lesotho to work at St. Catherine's High School, Maseru. Perhaps all this was a manifestation of inherited factors, because Alsie was a former student of my college in Durham and had lived during her student days, with ten other students, in the house that was now formally described as my official residence; or, less pretentiously, as my tied cottage. A young member of Holy Trinity, Hartlepool, Debbie Steel, responded to a request, three months after her parish priest had left for Lesotho, for help with the administrative work at St. Catherine's High School, Maseru, an Anglican-founded residential school for girls, where she worked for six months as an assistant bursar. A few days in Maseru in April enabled me to see them all happily settled in what to them was their strange new environment as they came to grips with the pattern of a different culture.

By now three substantial elements in my thinking were coming together. First, there was the expensive refurbishment of my parish church and the lack of interest in 'the other project'; secondly, there was the need for some sort of association with an overseas diocese that would help Durham overcome its institutional lethargy for missionary activity. To these two a third could now be added. During my talks with the Bishop of Lesotho, Philip Mokuku, he had expressed the wish of the diocese of Lesotho to establish a Department of Development, which, if it were to be effective, would be a mammoth undertaking for a church that even then was struggling to make financial ends meet. I suspected that this aspiration was prompted by the impressive development projects in Lesotho directed by Urbain Mailhot of the Roman Catholic Order of Mary Immaculate but, whatever the motive that spurred Philip's comment, it fitted well into my embryonic concept. Urbain and I were to work closely together in the years that lay ahead, during which time he would be a wise counsellor, a cautious optimist and a realistic adviser on matters as diverse as the size of breeze blocks and sensitive personalities.

Leaving the searing heat of summer in the lowlands of Lesotho, Philip Mokuku arrived in a cold England on New Year's Day 1983 to stay with my wife and me and then to move on to St. John's College, ostensibly for a term of theological study. I went in the opposite direction to work in Zimbabwe and then Lesotho for most of February, briefly returning home before making my first visit to troubled Zaire[34] for much of March. We had to take every short opportunity to meet to share our thoughts on any possible future association between the two dioceses and regions. It also gave others the chance to meet and our house sometimes felt that Lesotho and southern Africa were flowing through it at a rate of knots, leaving in our visitors' book some notable names: Michael Lapsley, Matthew Joy, Dale Barton, Aelred Stubbs and Cos Desmond.

After Philip had left Durham my part in all of this activity was to keep interest alive and as part of that task I visited Barbara Stephenson, the headmistress of Durham High School, to talk about a visit I had made to

St. Catherine's High School, Maseru. I drew the parallels of both being church foundations and girls' schools. Early in July 1983, after the pressure of examinations had diminished, I visited the school again to speak to fifth- and sixth-formers about Lesotho. These early contacts were strengthened when, as part of its centenary celebrations in 1984, Durham High School helped with the refurbishment of the library and the chapel at St. Catherine's. Subsequently, this work was extended through the development of an audio-visual teaching centre and further cooperation continues some twenty-eight years later. These young people were the modern pioneers of the strengthening connection between Lesotho and Durham. There was no supporting structure other than my connecting voice and that, I knew, was a weakness. My year ended working in Israel and Jordan, to which was added later the Gaza Strip. Working with Christians and Muslims in that region was to command much of my time and energy as the demand for educational innovation strengthened. Nevertheless, Durham and Lesotho were never overwhelmed in my thinking.

What now needed to be addressed was what sort of association, relationship, alliance, organisation, partnership would be the most appropriate. Travelling for thousands of miles in the discomfort of aeroplanes trying to accommodate my 6 feet 2 inches (1.88 m) into a space not quite that size gave me the chance to think rather more divergently than I revealed at the time. If I were to start some sort of relationship between the two regions I was determined that it should not be a static, comfortable alliance articulating pleasant platitudes but producing little of lasting value. I wanted to bring the gospel of Christ into the sort of action of which He would approve and also perhaps, for some theologians, to gain the support of His brother.[35] There had to be a common bond and, of course, we had that in our loyalty to Christ, but what then would we do to express that devotion? Psychologically, I knew that the best way was to give the people of both places a common task, if possible, against a common enemy (widely interpreted). From my analysis of the informal contacts that had taken place over the previous years I also strongly believed that the association, or whatever it would be called eventually, had to have a strong foundation in those who make up the two areas: the people. I did not underestimate the importance of hierarchies in all societies and organisations (indeed, I had my place in more than one), but I did have a clear understanding that the strength of the sole pinnacle relied on the foundation masses, so important to my thinking was the bringing together of all the people of both dioceses.

During our many discussions Philip Mokuku frequently reverted to the need for the Anglican Church in Lesotho to have a Department of Development, but when I began to think realistically about this I came up against a serious barrier. What I had in mind would be expensive. From where was the money coming? The diocese of Lesotho had virtually none and the diocese of Durham had little. The people who had the money were the secular organisations; they had the money and we had the people who had the purpose and the projects. Perhaps we should both be learning to work more closely together. As money came into my thinking I had to ask myself where the funding was coming from both for the organisation and running of any alliance, to say nothing of the cost of any activities in which it might engage.

After working in Lesotho for some twelve years I had colleagues not only within the Anglican Church, but also within the Roman Catholic Church and the Lesotho Evangelical Church. In the secular sector I had worked with and knew many government officials and ministers most of whom were connected in some way with education. Since 1973 I had been working in Lesotho with Charles Bohloko, who went on to be the Permanent Secretary at the Ministry of Education. So with my other foot, the secular one, firmly on the ground I welcomed the warm relationship I had with successive British High Commissioners and their staff, to which was soon added delegates of the European Union. Should we invite all these people to the ball? All these questions made boring flights, plastic food and uncomfortable airports almost bearable; things were coming together.

In 1985, David Jenkins invited me to make an illustrated presentation to the Durham Diocesan Synod on Saturday, 2nd November. It was almost a disaster but one that became hilarious. In a university lecture hall, the place of scholarly talks and erudite debates, at the crucial moment Ian Calvert, who had worked tirelessly for the proposal to establish a relationship with an overseas diocese, slipped up, literally. He dropped the box of slides! As the pictures were haphazardly projected some rapid adaptation of what I had proposed to say was needed and the usual sombre mood of synod became uproarious. When calm was restored before the vote Alan Piper, the chairman of the Diocesan Mission Committee and the small support group that I had formed, warned members of synod that they were about to make a decision that would 'marry the Diocese of Durham to the Diocese of Lesotho: it's a lifetime commitment'.[36] I remember hoping that it would be a synodical decision that would commit future generations beyond my lifetime, as I knew there were problems in Lesotho that would take much longer to resolve. Despite Alan's forewarning members were enthusiastic and because of it seriously dedicated. Apart from the abstention of one clergyman, who later became a strong, vigorous supporter and the secretary of one of the many working parties, the vote was unanimously in favour of establishing a connection with Lesotho. But what did that mean?

If a year can be described as pivotal then 1986 was certainly one for Pam and me, our two children and 'the other project'. It was one of those cyclonic points around which life sometimes seems to revolve with increasing speed rather like a rotating storm of wind moving progressively over land or sea. For the first time we were experiencing a prolonged period of life without our children at home as our son, Edmund, was studying at Cambridge University and flight BA263 took our daughter, Rachel, to Jamaica for a year to work in the Wortley Children's Home in Kingston, before going to Southampton University. Except for special occasions our family would never again be together in one place at one time for one purpose. So it was that Pam and I had our first day alone together for the past eighteen years on Sunday, 12th January 1986, but we were not to be allowed to twiddle our proverbial thumbs as there was a further request in the offing.

I had received a letter from Lesotho three days earlier! That in itself was a very rare event because, at this time in their oral society, the Basotho would travel many tough miles simply to talk, rather than write, to someone about a relatively minor matter. After all, the two types of telephone that then existed, functional and decorative, were not particularly helpful. When you did find a working model it was often extremely difficult to get to the person you wanted at the other end. Neither was it easy to write a letter, for there was the very real effort required bringing together paper, envelope, pen, ink, blotting paper, stamp and time even before finding somewhere to post it on its slow journey by truck, donkey and foot. Then follows an impatient wait for the answer whilst the person to whom the letter was addressed goes through the same time-consuming process. Far easier to talk in person and get the answer quickly. So, to receive a letter was unusual, but it did serve to remind me of the effort that had been put into an action to which most Europeans gave little thought. Communication has, not surprisingly, changed over the years, but that adjustment has been slow as face-to-face meetings have been gradually replaced by a technology not impervious to the dust of Africa.

The letter I received was from Philip Mokuku, inviting me to undertake a preaching tour in the diocese of Lesotho; why it took me eighteen days to reply I do not record in my journal, but perhaps I was more than conscious that, if I accepted, Pam would now be left alone. Then, as if to accentuate that reservation and to make the year more notable, one day later she came home from hospital with a Robert Jones[37] following an operation on her right knee after a fall that kept her away from her twenty-one 5-year-olds for seven weeks; at least this was some relief from a barrage of 'misses' all day long! However, despite some hesitation we decided that I should accept Philip's unprecedented invitation, for it would not only be a wonderful experience, but it would also provide a splendid opportunity to launch, if Lesotho agreed, what by now had come to be called the Durham-Lesotho LINK. It was now thirteen years since I first went to Lesotho; some six years since George Carey and I had our divergence of opinion; three years since I seriously considered founding an active relationship between Durham and Lesotho and just two months since the positive support of the Durham Diocesan Synod. This invitation seemed to be the confirmation that something could and should be done and a strong indication that I was the person to do it.

In the afternoon of Monday, 10th February 1986, I drove over to Auckland Castle to spend a pleasant hour with David Jenkins, who backed his enthusiastic reception of the preaching tour by generously offering to pay for the air fare. Drawing on some twelve years' experience of worshipping and working with the Basotho in the Anglican Church in Lesotho, and some not inconsiderable time working with the English in the Anglican Church of England, I was able to say to this modern-day turbulent priest, with some diffidence, that if Lesotho accepted our proposal I was ready to establish a structure that would enable the relationship between the two dioceses to be more constructively active. The tuning was finished; the overture was giving way to *accelerando.*

Based on the experience of the previous few years there was, in our judgement, a widespread wish for something more prescribed and structured. Not least my own professional work had changed dramatically and my wife and I were willing for me to spend the next few years (then we had no idea how long that 'few years' would be) using my time founding and voluntarily leading whatever arrangement I might start between Durham and Lesotho. The time and effort of those engaged in the early interminable discussions and debates had not been overlooked or wasted as they raised people's expectations, interest and enthusiasm, but David Jenkins and I wanted to see some action and, with his support, I was proposing to take it. It was now time to bring everything together into an arrangement showing what Christians working together could do and could, with great faith, achieve.

Thursday, 10th April 1986 was a very busy day. I had just been elected Chairman of Traidcraft and started the day exercising some of the less attractive responsibilities of correcting the critical financial situation that the company was facing and which I had been charged to reverse within the next three years. After lunch I drove home using the time to switch from commercial to ecclesiastical mode as I was to meet with David Jenkins, who came to see me to talk through the details of my forthcoming visit to Lesotho.

In characteristic pastoral concern he asked how Pam would cope during the nine weeks I was away. By now she had considerable experience, although there was the added complication of a leg that was slow to heal. Nevertheless, with her strong encouragement and the overwhelming support of Durham Diocesan Synod behind me, I felt relaxed as I attended the remaining four meetings of an extraordinary day. I was confident that the plan I was to set before the Lesotho Diocesan Council would find favour amongst the Basotho and to that end David recorded a message to the members of the council that was to meet to consider, amongst other things, the proposal that had been so long in its formulation. So, with that message on a reel-to-reel tape tucked away in my luggage, I set off again for Lesotho where, on Friday, 16th May 1986, Bishop Philip Mokuku reported to the Lesotho Diocesan Council on our earlier expedition that we had just completed in the Bokong and Ha 'Mikia regions in the Malibamatšo Valley. I then spoke about the proposed link between the two dioceses and played David's message in which, distinctively, he said:

> Bishop Philip and friends, this is Bishop David from Durham speaking. I wanted to take this opportunity of Peter Green's visit to send you my greetings and the greetings of all of us from the diocese. There is no need to tell you that we all live in very difficult times at the moment and things are sometimes very uncertain, but what we are quite sure about is the gospel and the power of the risen Christ and our fellowship in the Holy Spirit. It is a great privilege to share this with you now and I want to wish you well and to say that I hope Peter's visit is the beginning of our working out how we can help and support one another and what we can do together and how we can pray together. I greatly look forward to hearing from Peter when he comes back, the contacts he has been able to make and the suggestions you are making to us through him. Clearly it will take time to work things out and we must go slowly and faithfully and hopefully and with great friendship while we find out where we can go together, what we can do together and how we can support one another in the Lord's business. God bless you all.

The message was enthusiastically received and Philip Mokuku gave generous, wholehearted support to the proposal and the motion to form the LINK was passed. We were in business, but serious work would only commence after a period of faithful uncertainty had directed much of our thinking as we struggled to determine what exactly was 'the Lord's business'[38] for the new association. For now, Philip and I concentrated on the nine-week tour of the diocese that his invitation had instigated. I had always been conscious of the need to engage the people of both dioceses in this new venture and that presented problems of communication of a different type in both dioceses. For now it was Lesotho, a small country of long distances as one travelled over mountains and many miles up and down valleys to reach a spot that had perhaps been visible all day, but only accessible after hours of a rough, tough journey. We walked, flew in small aircraft, drove four-wheel-drive vehicles and rode horses over hundreds of miles taking the message that Lesotho was to join forces with Durham in spreading the good news of the gospel through participating in positive Christian action. The journeys that we made into the remote regions of the country meeting hundreds of Basotho also provided us with the chance to assess how that might best be achieved.

So, what did I find? Had the Basotho changed since I first met them in 1973 and, if so, how? What was the country like in 1986? What was the Durham-Lesotho LINK actually going to do?

It was time to saddle up!

---

1. Carey, George, *The Church in the Market Place* (Eastbourne: Kingsway Publications Ltd., 1984).
2. White, Peter A., *Portrait of County Durham* (London: Robert Hale, 1967) p. 155.
3. Mark 16:15 (NIV): (Jesus) said to them, 'Go into all the world and preach the good news to all creation.'
4. Cross, F. L. and Livingstone, E. A. (eds.), *The Oxford Dictionary of the Christian Church* (Oxford: Oxford University Press, 1988) p. 970.
5. Joel 2:28 (NIV): I will pour out my Spirit on all people. Your sons and daughters will prophesy, your old men will dream dreams, your young men will see visions.
6. Thomson, J. D. et al., *The New Bible Dictionary*, Douglas, J. D. (ed.) (Leicester: The Inter-Varsity Fellowship, 1963) p. 1312
7. Green, Peter, *Faith and Work* <http://www.christianacademicnetwork.net> [accessed 2007].
8. Mark 16:15 (NIV): Ibid.
9. Russell, Bertrand, *The Problems of Philosophy* (Oxford: Oxford University Press, 1959).
10. Joel 1:4 (NIV): What the locust swarm has left the great locusts have eaten; what the great locusts have left the young locusts have eaten; what the young locusts have left other locusts have eaten.
11. Thatcher, Margaret, *The Downing Street Years 1979–1990* (New York: Harper Perennial, 1995) pp. 597–580.

12. Joel 2:29 (NIV): Even on my servants, both men and women, I will pour out my Spirit in those days.
13. Thatcher, Margaret, *The Path to Power* (New York: HarperCollins, 1995).
14. Thatcher, Margaret, *Education: A Framework for Expansion* (London: HMSO, 1972).
15. James of Rusholme, Lord (Chairman): *Teacher Education and Training* (London: HMSO, 1972).
16. Green, Peter A., *Attitudes of Teachers of West Indian Immigrant Children* (Nottingham: M.Phil. 1972).
17. Sharpe, M. R. L., *Everyday Sesotho Grammar* (Morija: Sesuto Book Depot, 1970).
18. Partners in Mission report. Despite extensive research in Durham no copy of this report seems to have survived. The minutes of the Bishop's Council and Standing Committee meeting of Saturday, 3rd May 1980 record some discontent. Minute 18/80 reads: 'The Questionnaire on Partners in Mission which had been circulated by the Secretary of the PIM Preparatory Group was completed after discussion with members. It was felt that, both in terms of clarity in spelling out the issues and as an instrument of measuring response, this document fell some way short of the ideal.' Clearly the enquiry got off to a bad start.
19. Compiled by the Durham Federation of Women's Institutes: *The Durham Village Book* (Published jointly by Countryside Books, Newbury and the DFWI Durham, 1992) p. 53.
20. Sisulu, Elinor, *Walter and Albertina Sisulu: In our Lifetime* (Great Britain: Abacus, 2003) p. 383.
21. Raath, Jan, (Harare) 'Priest Hurt in Explosion' *The Times*, No. 63,693. p.11 'Overseas News' Monday, 30th April 1990. *The Times* report gives the date of this atrocious attack as Saturday, 28th April 1990 but in a personal message Michael records the date as Friday, 27th April 1990.
22. Sisulu, Elinor, Ibid. pp. 345–533.
23. Aelred Stubbs died at Mirfield, West Yorkshire, on Sunday, 17th October 2004 aged 81 years. An obituary appeared in *The Daily Telegraph* on Monday, 13th December 2004. His funeral was held at the Community of the Resurrection, Mirfield, on Saturday, 23rd October 2004.
24. On the front wall of the Queen's Head Hotel in Bishop Auckland there is a plaque depicting the head of Queen Elizabeth I (1558–1603).
25. On 31st December 1994, Her Majesty Queen Elizabeth II honoured the author with Membership of the Order of the British Empire, which she conferred at Buckingham Palace on Tuesday, 7th March 1995, 'in recognition of outstanding services to Anglo-Basotho relations'.
26. Before decimal coinage was introduced into British currency the slang expression for six pennies, or sixpence, was 'tanner'.
27. The Yachtmaster (offshore) Certificate (number 2498) is a maritime competence qualification.
28. The nautical mile is used by all seafarers of whatever nationality. It is 1.1508 land miles or 1.852 kms.
29. Dove, R., *Anglican Pioneers in Lesotho*: p.120 (No publisher given). Circa 1975.

30. Houghton, Michael, *S.S.M at T.Y. (1904–1975)* (Morija Printing Works, 1976).

31. On Wednesday, 26th September 1991, the author spoke about the LINK to Jarrow Deanery when Tom Rigg told him of their fund-raising in 1966 to build a church in Sekameng, Lesotho.

32. Green, Peter, 'Personal Daily Journal' (Tuesday, 24th August 1976).

33. Phillips, Margaret, *Do Not Unsaddle Your Horse: A Story of Leprosy Work in Africa* (West Malling, Mathabo Press, 2002).

34. Since 17th May 1997, Zaire has been known as The Democratic Republic of the Congo.

35. See the book of James (GNB). As three men with the name James are mentioned in the Bible there is some uncertainty about the claim of certain Biblical scholars that the writer of the Book of James was, in fact, Christ's brother.

36. Minutes of Durham Diocesan Synod, Saturday, 2nd November 1985.

37. Robert Jones is the name of a bulky pressure bandage and plaster used to immobilise the leg.

38. Quoted from David Jenkins' recorded message.

Chapter Two

'Saddle Up!'

Jesus said to them again,
'Peace be with you.
As the Father has sent me so I send you.'[1]

The southern hemisphere was the place to be on the evening of Saturday, 19th April 1986. I found the sight of Halley's Comet quite awesome, perhaps more so because of the transparent clarity of the Lesotho evening sky with its negligible light pollution. After supper Philip Mokuku, the suffragan bishop Donald Nestor and I stood in the vegetable garden of the bishop's house looking upward, overwhelmed at a wonder of creation that would not return in this manner for the next seventy-five or seventy-six years. We knew that none of us would ever have another chance; we had to take our opportunity now and we did! Having arrived that morning at the new Moshoeshoe I International Airport this was my first evening back in Lesotho in order to undertake a commission during which I was to launch what I had been painstakingly constructing on the slipway for the past three years.

I was determined that we should follow David Jenkins' guidance to 'go slowly and faithfully and hopefully and with great friendship while we find out where we can go together, what we can do together and how we can support one another in the Lord's business'.[2] There were many ways in which those qualities might be sought, but there were no established ways that would achieve them and the other features of the LINK that so very many people had already acclaimed. A period of five years as a member of General Synod had given me regular opportunities to have extensive conversations with senior diocesan Church of England representatives, both lay and clerical, who had made me very aware that many of the diocesan partners-in-mission associations had produced little more than disillusionment amongst foundation Christians. I was determined that the Durham-Lesotho enterprise would not follow that path so the thought, as it was light-heartedly put to me, that Halley's Comet might be 'heaven's welcome' was uncannily daunting.

Before flight QL333, quite literally, bumped into Lesotho that morning I had spent a week in Johannesburg tilling the provincial soil. It was during that time that I met the Bishop of Johannesburg, Desmond Tutu, soon to become Archbishop and, the following year, a Freeman of the City of Durham. He reminded me much to his amusement when we met subsequently that this allowed him to graze his cows on a field near to my house and 'no'! I quickly assured him, I was not looking for a job as a herdboy. Much else was to happen before he had any authority to exercise that doubtful privilege. Once I had found Desmond's hideaway in the aged, rundown St. Alban's Church at the corner of Ridout and Anderson Street in the concrete jungle of Johannesburg we had a useful hour together.

This was our first meeting together, so the first thing we did was to pray together and that formed a firm basis for our discussing and planning. Mindful of the fact that Lesotho already had a faltering association with Johannesburg, I cautiously outlined what I had in mind for the Durham-Lesotho LINK and he enthusiastically welcomed the stress on the notion of being One Body in Christ. Additionally, to my relief and delight, he keenly supported the vision of drawing people together through common practical activity designed to serve the community whether the people who would benefit were Christian or not. As a former Bishop of Lesotho[3] he knew the country well and gave freely of his advice, warmly and enthusiastically supporting the proposal for the LINK. As I had also worked extensively in other parts of the province not all of our time was taken with Lesotho. We discussed Namibia, Swaziland and Botswana as well as South Africa and, of course, apartheid, finding that we were closely aligned over many of the problems that then existed, particularly in the field of education.

I left with a long list of contacts he asked me to pursue, buoyed, encouraged and stimulated by the vigorous discussion in which we had engaged for such a seemingly short time. He then asked the Rev'd Mashikane Montjane to take me back to St. Peter's Priory, Rosettenville, which he did, physically, but as we drove through apartheid Johannesburg, it was to Soweto that he took me mentally and emotionally, with his vivid description of what life was like there. Disguised in my cassock and with Kingston Erson as my mentor, I first went into Kliptown, Nancefield and Orlando, illegally but quite unashamedly, in August 1973.

Having avoided arrest in Soweto and other human dumping grounds[4] for thirteen years, I was now being asked to engage in the much more public exploit of worshipping and preaching at the church where Mashikane was priest-in-charge, St. Andrew's, Pimville, Soweto. What a wonderful opportunity to demonstrate support at a time when tension was at its highest and another state of emergency just days away. How could I resist? Yes, I would join with them on Sunday, 8th June 1986, but only after I had been to Baragwanath Hospital[5] to speak at the holy communion service there on my return from Lesotho; however, for now it was the Basotho on whom I had to concentrate.

Back in Durham it was comparatively easy spreading news of the proposed LINK. The diocese had an efficient communication network so, as the ideas drew closer to being realised, they were widely discussed. Not so in the oral society of Lesotho, with its unreliable telephones and a population density of about a quarter of that in Durham restricting the exchange of ideas. People didn't meet so often. Church services became important gatherings at which people would talk about the suggestion. Radio Lesotho transmitted emergency messages but the effectiveness of that facility relied, of course, on the availability of radios and, more critically, on batteries to power them and in the foothills and mountains these were neither widely accessible nor affordable. In the 1980s the most dependable method of communication was a single sideband transmission system operated by the Roman Catholics to connect all their mission stations. Although I was to be grateful in the years to come for their willingness to let me use it, this was an individual-to-individual system unsuitable for our present purpose of spreading news of the LINK to a large number of people with whom we wanted to discuss its formation, operation and potential.

So, on Tuesday, 22nd April 1986, leaving Maseru only twenty minutes late, I began a twentieth-century trek with Suzuki, Philip and Vincent Makosholo that would, in due time, revert to an earlier horseback era bringing me face-to-face with those people the LINK was to serve in lowlands, foothills and mountains. Now I was to drive to Mantšonyane, a spectacular journey that I had done many times over the past thirteen years but one that never ceased to amaze me at its grandeur and magnificence. We were still in the lowlands not far into our journey when, having the benefit over the other two of being awake and of the driving mirrors, I was conscious that a vehicle behind us was flashing its lights. It was the suffragan bishop taking care of his diocesan bishop and his guest! Shortly after we had set out Donald Nestor had discovered that we had forgotten to pack an essential element of our equipment that no trek in Lesotho can be successfully completed without: blankets!

Fully equipped, or so we ignorantly but happily thought, Donald returned to urban Maseru and we pressed onwards and upward, spiralling towards rural Mantšonyane through some romantically named passes: Bushmen's Pass at 7,441 feet (2,268 m); Molimo-Nthuse or God Help Me Pass at 7,605 feet (2,318 m) where the tarred surface stopped and the bone-shaking began; Blue Mountain Pass at 8,642 feet (2,634 m). Four-wheel-drive, sloping, hairpin bends leading into reverse-camber blind corners did nothing to detract from the quiet solitude and silent magnificence of the mountains on which the old season's grass was beginning to succumb to overgrazing and that which had just managed to survive was beginning to wilt in nature's erosive harshness. Each hill and valley, however small, concealed rondavels and kraals huddled together in small villages located near an essential water supply usually provided by a mountain stream. The surrounding area was often flamboyantly decorated by the daily washing spread across nearby rocks that had heated in the morning sunshine to form effective drying stones.

Reaching Mantšonyane we took on petrol at the store from a 'proper' pump where, to get any fuel at all, it was necessary to move the handle backwards and forwards rather like the action required to work a manual bilge pump on a boat. This is the only place in the world that I have ever come across a visual justification for the name petrol 'pump'. It warranted a photograph as episcopal energy produced the spirit (petroleum) for the next stage of the journey, but Philip's pumping was too slow for the lady in charge, who emerged from her small hut and, with quiet determination, took over the exacting task of operating the Shell lever-pump. Her thick woollen cardigan, red woolly hat and a traditional Basotho blanket, symmetrically decorated in black, grey and white, folded double and draped from the waist downwards, gave her generous form generous protection against the mountain wind and she was not now going to miss the chance of some warmth-generating action for which she had waited all day in this remotely elevated filling station.

Still climbing slowly at 8,832 feet (2,692 m), Philip drove us through the Pass of Jackals, not that we actually saw any jackals although they can still be found in Lesotho both in fact and, more often, in fiction. When, late at night, grandmother gathers her extended family round the last embers of the cooking fire and the story she's telling needs a crafty character, that is often represented by the jackal as in *Wolf and Jackal and the Beautiful Girl* or, if grandmother wants to emphasize good and evil, she may turn to *Jackal and Hen* or *The Dove, the Heron, and Jackal.*[6] Jackals can be found lurking with evil intent in more than one volume[7] but around the fire, with its soothing warmth, hypnotic smell and crackling symphony they seem closer and even personal to the tired young mind about to fall asleep. There was, however, nothing soothing or hypnotic about the road we were now travelling. The occasional levelling of the earthen surface by huge graders was soon washed into regular corrugations by a deluge of rain and now we had to suffer the consequences as, in the failing light, we drove onwards and upwards to Mokhoabong Pass at 9,449 feet (2,880 m). In the evening we reached the mountain with the white mark, Thaba-Tseka, after a drive of 112 miles (180 kms), arriving just as the setting sun created mountain shadows that starkly emphasized the horizon silhouette of the mountain itself.

As we approached the small town the sun stabbed through a col between mountain peaks, flooding the valley with inflamed russet, gold and yellow streaks, showing a momentary beauty before darkening to an unsympathetic reality that seemed to envelop us as we looked for the house where we were to lodge that night. Although deeply tanned by the sun passing through the thin mountain air David Khan,[8] a member of that exclusive guild of white Basotho, greeted us warmly. We stayed for one night in his rough stone-built rectangular house with a roof of reddish-coloured corrugated iron surrounded by guttering draining rainwater into a large storage tank. Wearily we climbed the steps into the house, where we were pleased to feed in traditional Basotho manner with the men eating first at the table and the women in the kitchen around the cooking fire. We ate rice, mutton (*nama*) and a green vegetable not unlike spinach (*moroho*) and drank weak, sweet tea. After the evening meal Vincent Makosholo (who was chaplain to hospitals and prisons) led us, and the family, in evening prayers.

I slept like a proverbial log after we had recognised that necessity had to overcome the inconvenience of the outside latrine (which in Durham would be called the 'nettie'), leaning at a rakish angle under a group of three trees at an uncomfortable and dangerously long distance from the house. We soon overcame any self-consciousness we may have had, agreeing on where the 'night pot' was to be situated, and woe betide any user who did not replace it in exactly the agreed place so it could be found in the dark of night! Contented we went to sleep. Early morning ablutions finished, we had a substantial breakfast of *lehala*, a sorghum porridge mixed with milk, after which the work began.

We walked the short distance to Holy Cross Church, a small rectangular building about 45 feet (14 m) long built in natural uncut stone with no outward sign that it was a church. The only door was at the end of the building directly opposite the altar that, at the other end, was raised on a solid platform and covered with a cloth embroidered with a geometrical design in blue and red. On the wall above there was a rough wooden cross beneath which stood a tarnished candelabrum supporting three partly used candles. The interior was clean and tidy and was lit by two small, glazed, metal-framed windows on each side, unusually all intact. Wooden benches of doubtful stability enabled the congregation to sit underneath the exposed struts and rafters supporting the inevitable corrugated-iron roof.

On this St. George's Day the nearly all female congregation was surprisingly small; being a Wednesday was probably the reason. At the holy communion service, conducted with great dignity and sensitivity, I preached on what it means to be 'One Body in Christ' and the sharing that entails. Before the service Philip had baptised two baby girls, Ntebaleng Mathandela who was dressed in a child-sized traditional Basotho blanket and Kananelo Ngwenya dressed, untraditionally, in white dress, white stockings, white hat and white shoes all contrasting quite dramatically with her black skin. Sharing the joy of their mothers I took photographs, later sending them copies from Durham after which I received a generous thank-you letter that, in itself, was a joy to me in its unusualness. That was in 1986 – where are they now, I wonder, twenty-five years later? After the service I spoke to the people about the LINK and, as the chairman of the Durham mission committee did in the Diocesan Synod the previous November, the bishop, unknowingly, used the analogy of 'marriage'. It was incredible that our first task after the service was to visit the local government office to obtain a stamp for a marriage licence!

David Khan had been a generous host but now, on 23rd April 1986, we had to press on into the rugged interior and soon became fully occupied with survival as we faced another extremely difficult journey in a four-wheel-drive, this time over unmade, waterlogged tracks. It was such an advantage for me to have been in Lesotho on and off for thirteen years as these conditions were no longer unusual. Even so, familiarity did not make them pleasant. We left Thaba-Tseka at 13:30 hours and driving as hard and fast as conditions would safely allow for the next four hours we covered just over 31 miles (50 kms) at an average speed of almost 8 miles per hour (13 kms/hr). As we went over boulders and into gullies, sliding and crashing along, it was a constant battle to keep the little Suzuki vehicle upright.

To get some relief from the battering we were suffering we stopped at St. Paul's School in the little village of Ha Soai, which sits within a tight bend on the track and perches precariously on an east-facing escarpment overlooking the river valley and the confluence of the rivers Malimabatšo and Matsoku. By Lesotho educational norms this was a small school of just ninety-two pupils, two teachers, six classes and four desks. When the senior teacher was introducing us and told the children, 'This is Doctor Green,' a group of younger children immediately burst into tears! It was disconcerting but they thought I had arrived to give them injections which is the only time they had ever seen a white 'doctor-man'! After calm had been restored I spoke to them about Durham and we moved on.

At least we intended to move on but that was not so easy in the Lesotho of those days; the Highland Water Scheme has since tarred the road. A few yards (m) down the steep hillside track we found it blocked by a large, heavily laden lorry with something broken that prevented it from moving. I engaged four-wheel drive, Vincent engaged two-legged mobility and navigated a hillside path while Philip engaged the Holy Spirit and prayed. It was more touch than go and slowly but with sufficient momentum to prevent the Suzuki from wallowing in not so glorious mud, we moved forward. Was this *really* what David Jenkins meant when he said we must 'go slowly and faithfully and hopefully and with great friendship while we find out where we can go together, what we can do together and how we can support one another'? Well, the four of us must have done our very different tasks effectively, because thirty minutes later we were on our way to Ha Sekhohola, battling with loose soil and rocks to get to St. Agnes' Church before darkness fell. On the way we passed two ladies walking with enormous bundles of wood on their heads and a small dog yapping at their ankles. This reminded me of an illustration I had once seen on a banner that was being paraded in the annual Durham Miners' Gala and which I now tucked away in the depths of my consciousness for later use.

We reached the small church just before nightfall. The shadows were long and dense and equivocally disguised our surroundings, making us unsure of both ourselves and the environment; it was a strange experience. Very unusually, when we arrived there was no one to meet or greet us; this was very untypical and slightly bewildering. Were we expected or even welcome? After the rough, tough and noisy drive we had experienced there was an unnerving quietness that bordered on the unrealistic. St. Agnes is a simple rectangular hall some 50 feet (16 m) long and 25 feet (8 m) wide with the usual corrugated-iron pitched roof held on by wires fixed to the walls and, as at Thaba-Tseka, no external indication that it was a church. The building was open but there was nothing strange about that as few of them can be closed in any case. Set on the side of a big hill it is surrounded by large but gently sloping mountains that in the gloom of dusk I found heavily oppressive, perhaps because I am an East Anglican by birth and early upbringing, much preferring wide, open, uncluttered spaces. Philip went off in search of someone, or indeed anyone, returning a few minutes later with a group of chattering women bearing thin flock mattresses for us to sleep on in the church. There was also a large supply of thin blankets all smelling strongly of smoke; it wasn't long before I smelt likewise so quite soon I didn't notice anything strange at all.

The three of us gathered round the solid stone altar. Obeying the rubric of 1662 I took the north end;[9] Vincent, who rarely obeyed anything, took the south end and Philip, being used to 'serving from behind the counter' took the position between us. Outside, and also to some considerable extent inside, a strong, cold wind was blowing so we spent a lot of time blocking the numerous broken windows in an attempt to keep out the bitter wind howling round the 9,000 foot (2,745 m) mountain; we were only partially successful.

With camp established it was now time for some much-needed food and drink. Two men brought in a small wooden table that was covered by a gaudily coloured plastic cloth on which a single candle stub in a bottle lit the proceedings whilst creating a ghostly atmosphere. A small paraffin stove had also been brought in on which a lady heated, but not boiled, some water into which tea leaves were then tipped, followed by milk and copious amounts of sugar. Whilst all this was going on the food arrived in the form of undercooked steamed bread and sour porridge. Now, I like most European food (except mayonnaise and vinegar on hot fish), but undercooked steamed bread and sour porridge are my Lesotho dislikes. Nevertheless, this was surely a Lesotho version of the 'Widow's Mite'.[10] They had probably given all that they had but I must confess, hungry though I was, I found it difficult to swallow the gooey hunks of soggy, steamed bread washed down with warm, weak, excessively sweet tea especially as I do not normally take sugar! Incongruously we had cups and saucers with spoons, but we ate dinner dressed not in bib and tucker but in anoraks and blankets. Later, how much later I do not remember, the mattress did little to soften the floor, but I quickly fell asleep intoxicated by smoke-laden blankets and inebriated by an ultra-heavy, stodgy meal.

I slept well in the church but public ablutions outside took a little longer to get used to, especially as dozens of people decided to arrive at that particular time. Stripped off to the waist (that is top down!) and using the Suzuki wing mirror as a substitute for a shaving mirror prompted the comment from two watchful young boys (I knew just enough Sesotho), 'Cor! he's white all over!' Still smelling highly of smoke I didn't exactly *feel* white all over but I was rapidly beginning to cope with the very public nature of one's toilet; it was rather like washing and shaving on Durham Market Square. I wonder if that is why George Carey entitled his book *The Church in the Market Place.*

Dozens soon became scores with babies galore for baptism and innumerable young people for confirmation. There were masses of people everywhere laughing, talking, socialising, shouting; it was just like a market place and there was I in the midst of them still partially stripped off and getting very cold in the process. In this parish the children arrived in their generally poor, tatty, old clothes, also to be stripped off outside (I know how they felt) and then changed into their clean 'church best'. Finally everyone trooped inside, by which time I had dressed in my 'church best' – a dusty, crumbled cassock and surplice. Then I remembered, I don't know why, that we'd had no breakfast but then probably no one else had, either. The service started at no particular time, just when everyone seemed ready. There was no hurry. Everyone took their time except, perhaps, for the one Englishman who was getting anxious over some small detail; all of which reminded me of one of Philip's pertinent observations: 'You English have the watches, but we Basotho, we have the time'!

One consequence of that relaxed societal attitude was the arrival of people throughout the service right up to the last hymn, by which time I had preached on the theme of 'trust'. Philip's talk about the proposed LINK, during which he used photographs from the Durham Book I'd given him, was greeted with much cheering, clapping and ululation. In his introduction he had the mostly female congregation repeating the names of our family 'Peter', 'Pam', 'Edmund', 'Rachel'; it was all good fun with plenty of 'audience participation'! The code of dress here was almost entirely that of traditional Basotho blankets and colourful woollen hats with many of the children without shoes. Despite the poverty my notes, written immediately after the service, state that 'they seem a happy congregation'.

It was then on to lunch in a small local rondavel where Philip and I were treated to a typically Sotho celebration meal. Huge quantities of well-cooked mutton from a sheep especially slaughtered for us was served along with potatoes that I suspect were prepared for me in case I did not eat the *papa* (*mealie pap*): I ate both. There was a mass of steamed bread, this time well cooked, and a large bowl of *lesheleshele* (a porridge made from mealies and water) with hot tea to drink (still spliced with excessive quantities of sugar); but we *had* missed breakfast. Following Basotho custom, still common in the mountains, the lady who had been responsible for cooking the meal said grace[11] and then left the men eating at the table to join her companions around the fire in the cooking rondavel (*mokhoro*).

The greeting when we arrived at St. Agnes' Church, Ha Sekhohola, yesterday evening may have been muted but now our departure was anything but quiet as we left with the gift of an uncooked leg of a sheep; how *do* you pack a leg of mutton, dripping blood, in limited stowage space? This was accompanied by much cheering and shouting, to which the Suzuki, with episcopal encouragement, added its contribution as Philip laid his hands on its hooter. With little complaint it took us safely northward, west and then south into a hairpin bend so sharp that we came out just avoiding a full circle. We then headed north again, then east and finally west, during another terribly rough journey that not only boxed the compass but went up and down in the process! Although not quite so wet it was all rather like tacking at sea in *Tanna* during a force-six blow which was about the force of the mountain wind as it hurtled round Kolberg, the 9,219 foot (2,810 m) peak of the white mountain.

Our drive of some 48 miles (77 kms) had taken us exactly three hours at an average speed of 16 miles an hour (26 kms/h) to bring us to Bokong. Because there was not much else there we soon found the implausibly named White City Café, where we were welcomed not with the refreshing drink that at least one of us had hoped for, but by a group of Basotho riders. All were dressed in their traditional colourful blankets and their unconventional woolly hats (just like many Durham men) carrying short sticks to encourage their troop of eleven horses. There was a cold, late-afternoon chill and so the greetings were unusually short but nonetheless warm, almost to the point of affectionate. As we exchanged four wheels for four legs there was some anxiety about the white man's ability to cope with what lay ahead but with the benefit of ignorance, I attempted to look confident; little did I know what was to come. I was allocated a large black horse elegantly dressed with a black-and-white crocheted blanket beneath the saddle. I think the logic of the conclusion was that the tallest man, me, took the tallest horse, Kidboy. 6 feet 2 inches (1.88 m) on an unknown number of 4-inch (10 centimetre) hands! We saddled up, loaded the packhorses, dressed in whatever warm clothes we could lay our hands on and mounted our horses, to venture into an interior of incredible beauty that concealed a vicious harshness ignored by the neophyte at considerable cost.

As we aimed for Ha Kosetabole I relaxed in the long experience I had of Lesotho grateful that I was not a novice in this harsh environement. After leaving White City Café the first few minutes riding, were fairly easy. Kidboy, was going well and I had time to adjust to his rhythm before the difficult section of our ride. The village where we were to stay that night was, for a bird, less than 4 miles (6 kms) flying distance to the north of Bokong but now between us and our beds was the fast flowing Bokong River winding its way through a deep valley that took many hours of rough, dangerous riding to negotiate. As the darkness of the night stealthly embraced us we were all relieved to reach the north-facing slope of the Bokong Valley, which was so steep that on my left the incline seemed to stretch interminably upwards whereas on my right there seemed to be nothing but fresh air. The precariously narrow track that had been cut into the side of this slope was less than a foot wide (30 cm) in places so we all, experienced and novice alike, dismounted and led our horses down. It was so narrow that when riding, the foot in the nearside stirrup hit protruding rocks. As the track sometimes disappeared completely we were grateful to the Basotho guides who had met us with the horses and it was they who now took us safely into the deep valley where we again mounted to ford the Bokong River. With water at stirrup-level the going was not too difficult with only one or two slips as the horses lost their footing on submerged rocks and once across the fast-flowing current, we climbed again to the accompaniment of the '*mokorotlo*' response singing of the Basotho men plus others we seemed to collect on the trek. It was eerily dark by now but that wasn't too much of a problem provided the horse immediately in front could be seen and followed.

We arrived at Ha Kosetabole to an exuberant *molilietsane*[12] welcome. We were now at 7,380 feet (2,260 m). I was tired, sweaty, dirty and sore after many hours in the saddle admiring the stamina of the more experienced, much younger, Basotho horsemen. They were still singing as they dismounted and continued their celebrations uninterrupted, adding a vigorous dance routine to the song and kicking up as much dust as the horses that now stood around sweating profusely, drinking and eating. Someone put some extra wood on the open fire making the moving shadows more intense and distorted as they fell on obstructions, adding yet another ghostly dimension to the lithe, supple movements of the agile, singing dancers. In the gloom of late evening it was all rather weird, but it was not long before the singing and dancing came to an end, whereupon we offloaded the packhorses and established ourselves in the rondavel that had been allocated to Philip and me. By now I had forgotten about food and drink, but fortunately the ladies of the village had not and we were fed with a substantial meal of stewed goat meat, *papa* and rice with the inevitable weak, sweet tea all served round the fire under the crystal-clear African sky with its millions of brilliant twinkling stars. It was a tranquil setting; there was little noise other than the breeze wafting round the hills which was so cold that we all huddled into our blankets while some fifteen people gathered in our rondavel for evening prayers.

As I was preparing for bed after everyone had gone I was troubled by masses of flies. Perhaps they found me attractive because there were no late-night washing facilities to remove the residual mixture of human and horse sweat. They seemed to get everywhere so I spent much of the night, as far as I was aware, curled up under a mass of blankets. I think that any bed would have felt comfortable, this one certainly did, but apart from the physical discomfort of the flies, there was another disturbing element to the stay in this rondavel. Just before getting into bed I noticed that the mattress on the old iron-framed bedstead was unusually high from the ground. Tall as I am, when sitting on the mattress on the bed, my feet didn't touch the mud-and-dung floor. On investigation I discovered that each leg of the bed was standing on a used food tin filled with stones and soil, thus raising its height by some 4 inches (10 centimetres). Philip explained that the reason behind this was to give the evil spirits, the *thokolosi,* more room to escape during the night.

This was only one of the many indications of superstitious beliefs, with porcupine quills and dead twigs with a variety of sticks and feathers stuck into the roof thatching inside the hut, in addition to two black crosses burned onto the rafters opposite the doorway entrance by, so I was told, the local witch doctor; all this was alarming in a so-called Christian community. It prompted Philip and me to talk into the night about superstitious practices and I was surprised to learn that many priests are superstitious, one even refusing to take food from any member of his many congregations for fear of being poisoned. Apparently this is much more prevalent in rural than urban areas, as is the strong fear of lightning[13] since many Basotho are killed in thunderstorms particularly in the Leribe District that we were approaching. Later I was to experience something of this deep fear when Philip and I were with a church congregation in the rural lowlands and a young woman in her early twenties had a paroxysmal spasm when talking to us about her experiences in a thunderstorm.

Sleep came easily that night in the mountains and I cannot remember, and neither did I record, the end of the conversation. While early morning toilet in a 'dry stream' was no less public here than it was at Ha Sekhohola, here there was one major difference: because the dry stream at Ha Kosetabole was deep in a *donga* (a deep gully caused by water erosion) the spectators, mostly young boys, had a better grandstand view standing around the elevated edge! However, I was now more practised and less self-conscious, so I was able to conduct myself with a degree of dignity that comes from experience and arrived for breakfast round the fire without undue embarrassment. My severely chipped enamel bowl, that was to appear later on a wooden bench as a baptismal font, was filled almost to overflowing with *lesheleshele,* after which we ate 'fat cakes' (rather like doughnuts) and steamed bread flavoured with vanilla. It was all rather 'heavy' but it filled empty stomachs quite effectively.

After breakfast I was able to look around the village for the first time. It was difficult to judge its size as there were few boundary marks. There were no fences, only a small group of five stunted trees. Indeed, there was nothing to show any demarcation, not even the lines of boulders that are evident in some villages as a reminder of the biblical command, 'Never move an old boundary-mark that your ancestors established'.[14] Where we were staying there was a group of ten rondavels situated close together, but whether that was just one family or many I never did discover. In this village the rondavels were all built of large stones bound together with a plaster of cow dung and mud and thatched with grass over a natural wooden frame making a gently pitched roof. A short walk enabled me to try talking with some of the local Basotho, albeit not very successfully.

Defeated by the local dialect I repaired with Philip to St. Michael's Church, a small rectangular building built many years ago. There we conducted baptisms, confirmations and holy communion for some 120 people. With Philip translating I preached briefly on the strength of Christian love, how it bound people together and how, because we became one in Christ, we became stronger. A large crowd of men and women with scores of children sat on wooden benches or the floor or leant against the walls inseparable from their blankets. I knew that the Basotho like stories, especially ones that were demonstrated in some way, so I used the illustration of the bundle of sticks being bound with string being much stronger than the individual sticks that go into the bundle. Most of those present could identify with the image because this is what women do before carrying large bundles of sticks great distances on their heads for firewood. I gave six children one stick each, which each one of them broke quite easily. The same children were then given six more sticks which we bound together with love represented by a piece of string and not one child could break the bundle.

Even in this well-known analogy there was a connection with Durham. Years earlier I had seen the story illustrated during the annual Miners' Gala in Durham city. The banner of a miners' lodge depicted the weakness of separate, isolated individuals becoming strong when they are bound together as one in union with each other. I had seen a practical expression of this earlier in our journey. Outside after the service, as the odd free-range chicken that had avoided capture clucked around and a few dogs scrabbled for titbits to eat, all of that seemed a long distance away. For now it simply served as an appropriate introduction to Philip's talk about the Durham-Lesotho LINK when he picked up on this theme of being bound together as one in the love of Christ, making us all stronger. With the help of some enlarged photographs we spoke about the proposed LINK and it was there that I first began to realise the magnitude of the task ahead if the LINK was going to make any realistic impact on the widespread poverty that was all around me in this village. For now, however, I had to concentrate on making the proposal known and listen to the ideas and needs of the Basotho. This engaged us until early afternoon, when we had to break away from the crowd and move on to Ha 'Mikia, whilst praying that after we had departed the parish priest would continue the work that we had initiated.

In brilliant sunshine that seemed to burn through the thin mountain air as it was being cooled by a strong breeze, we left St. Michael's Church, Ha Kosetabole, returning to the village for lunch. Our meal had been prepared for us in a three-legged cooking pot over an open fire that seemed intent on disproving the saying that where there is smoke there is fire. A lady was attending to the cooking whilst two others leant against the wall of the rondavel under the overhanging thatch silently watching. The result was a thin stew that Philip and I ate using an ancient, bent spoon sitting on a couple of rocks within the cooking area before loading the packhorses and saddling up for the next sector of our venture into the interior of this rugged, captivating country. The horses were well rested, fed and watered, our Basotho guides were ready to go and then the noise began. For me, as a 56-year-old academic, it was all rather surreal as I settled into my saddle and tried to get comfortable for the next four hours. Nonetheless, I enjoyed what I knew few other people in the world would ever be privileged to experience.

For me, this was like taking a step backward into an earlier era. What better place to break through the time barrier than in the homeland of the dinosaur and brontosaurus? Whilst physically I was, in a sense, going backwards, mentally I cast my thoughts years ahead. In years to come the Bokong Valley, through which I was now riding on horseback, would be totally inaccessible as it was to be flooded by the Lesotho Highlands Water Project. I was entering a time capsule or, perhaps, I was the time capsule, for I had to return to Durham taking with me this forward and backward time-bound experience. Guided now by a mounted troop of Basotho men for whom this was an everyday way of life we rode, as the Royal Navy would put it, 'in line astern', slowly descending into the valley whilst carefully guiding the horses as they tentatively picked their way along the narrow rock-strewn track.

Just before we reached the Malibamatšo River at a particularly difficult section a packhorse slipped as it was being led around some fallen boulders. It was a nerve-racking moment as it was immediately in front of Kidboy, but fortunately it was also being led by a Mosotho on foot and somehow I stayed on its back, trusting its four experienced hooves rather than my two novice feet. As the horse in front fell so the weight of its load dragged it down until a strategically placed rock stopped it with a terrifying jolt that ejected most of its load, including three parts of the bishop's collapsible crosier. Order was restored remarkably quickly; the horse recovered quicker than I did and after everything that had been scattered across the mountainside had been rescued and repacked, we continued the hazardous journey, slipping and sliding our way down the precipitous slope. It was so steep that at some points we were forced to lean back in the saddle until we were almost lying on the back of the horse with our feet in the stirrups almost up to its shoulders. Whenever I hear the command of Jesus to his disciples to take the gospel into all the world,[15] I do wonder if he had anything like this in mind!

One advantage of being line astern was that I could watch what the Basotho were doing and imitate their actions; it was not for the faint-hearted. I was greatly relieved to hear the sound of the Malibamatšo River as it flowed gently through the valley on its long, downhill journey westward across the breadth of Africa. The word *Malibamatšo* in Sesotho means 'Blackpool' in English but any relationship between the two places escapes me: this was indeed another world at another time and I was being submerged. The horses drank copious amount of the river and thus refreshed gained renewed vigour for a brisk gallop along the strand to an indeterminate point where the Basotho guides just turned right and went uphill! I could see no track but through the thick, heavy dust I could just see the rear of the horse immediately in front of Kidboy.

Then came my worst heart-stopping, almost, incident in this dramatic trek! As Kidboy and I left the strand I almost left Kidboy! The base of the hillside was much higher than the strand and as he leapt at the track, he slipped at its crumbling edge and I almost went over his head. I was just inches (cm) away from disaster but somehow, still unknown to me, I regained the saddle and my equilibrium. It was not pleasant! Kidboy took a little while to settle down: I took a long while to settle down.

It was now becoming increasingly dark, cold and windy; my cold sweat seemed to take hours to warm to body heat. The shadows lengthened, the mountains changed colours and contours and, to my inexperienced eye, there were no distinctive landmarks. It was some relief to me that the troop reduced speed in order to pass a lone horseman approaching us on the narrow track. As we squeezed past we all had to stop, greet him with a handshake and the words '*Khotso, ntate*' (Peace, father). I was about sixth or seventh in the line of horsemen and, in the obscurity of dusk, fairly well disguised in a Basotho blanket and woollen hat; he excitedly expressed his surprise at meeting an Englishman in the remote interior of Lesotho on horseback! I must confess that I was also rather surprised that I was still on horseback in the remote interior of Lesotho!

After three and a quarter hours of hard riding our arrival at Ha 'Mikia was joyfully boisterous. People there rarely saw their bishop and even less often did they see a visitor from overseas so the local folk were going to make the most of it. A double event required a double celebration acknowledged with double the noise. As we dismounted in the gloom of the evening our horses were taken away for refreshment and rest but not so for their riders! Tired though we were we had to go through the welcoming procedure of shaking everyone's hand by the most appropriate of the many ways that may be found in Lesotho. So what was 'appropriate'? Well, there are several: there is the common gripping of right hands followed by two or three shakes; then there is the more familiar clasping of both hands with two or three shakes; thirdly, the junior of the two persons (by age or social status) may hold their forearm, allowing the hand of that arm to droop loosely for the senior of the two to shake the offered hand; the most complicated is to shake the right hand, slide the hand upwards to grip the thumbs only to slide it back again to shake the hand once more; the custom when one person has a dirty right hand is for that person to offer the right wrist with the hand drooping for the other person to grasp and shake the wrist.

On that particular night in Ha 'Mikia, no one was too worried about what was and what was not 'appropriate'; joyful fascination overcame diffidence or timidity. In the excitement I could not understand any of the rapid Sesotho. I was completely reliant upon Philip's translation and was very grateful when, after about thirty minutes, the welcome drew to an end and he told me it was time to go to our rondavel. After more than three hours in the saddle, interrupted by a momentary aberration, I was pleased to stretch my legs with a short walk to a rondavel built of rough stones and roofed by weathered grass thatching, some of which had blown away leaving ominous-looking gaps. At the top of three stone steps there was an ill-fitting wooden door on each side of which was a small window that was unusually fully glazed. Ha 'Mikia can be subjected to some vicious weather, lying at about 8,000 feet (2,438 m) on the side of a small tributary of the Malibamatšo River but now, in the twenty-first century, twenty-five years later, it is just one of many small rivers feeding the huge Katse Dam, the product of the biggest engineering project in the southern hemisphere of the world. Time capsule?

Inside were two small iron bedsteads, each covered with four or five blankets but, unlike Ha Kosetabole, neither was raised to permit the evil spirits to escape more easily, which didn't give me any cause for concern. There was also a small wooden table of dubious strength with two upright wooden chairs and nothing else other than an empty wine bottle that supported the stub of candle whose flickering flame threatened to plunge us into darkness each time the creaky door was opened. The sole decoration was a dust-covered coloured picture rescued, I suspect, from a travel magazine and now attached with three oversized nails, at a rakish angle, to the mud-and-dung wall. A culture that develops close to nature pays little attention to straight lines, vertical precision or horizontal exactness for there is nothing to copy. This simple decoration was no exception. The three nails that were available were used to fix the left-hand edge of the picture and its lower edge at a slanting angle, thus encouraging the top right-hand corner to curl over, obscuring most of the picture. All rather strange to my European eyes.

A lady of ample proportions, protected from the increasingly strong mountain breeze by her Basotho blanket worn as a long skirt, brought us a welcome meal of chicken and rice with the usual weak, sweet tea; it tasted wonderful. The atmosphere of our dinner was now enlivened by music of hymns and songs from my small tape recorder, bringing the voice of a friend of mine from Durham to Ha 'Mikia. It was totally out of place but Philip enjoyed the songs from *Mission England Praise*[16] as did those numerous inhabitants of Ha 'Mikia of all ages who, attracted by the music, had gathered round the door and windows! Fortunately the tape came to an end before the candle so we finished eating, prayed together and then tumbled into bed, a bed that was very definitely damp, horribly damp. I gradually became more and more clammy but weariness overcame even that discomfort and I slept soundly even if unhealthily.

The next morning was a Saturday, when the traditional slaughter of a sheep for visitors took place, as is the custom, right outside our hut. Its liver was cooked over the open fire and served for our breakfast after we had consumed large quantities of *lesheleshele* and, a welcome change in our diet, *rooibos* (red bush) tea. Over breakfast Philip explained that when a sheep is slaughtered for a visitor the lungs are given to the man who killed the animal and the intestines are given to the men who have helped. The women cook these delicacies in a separate pot reserved for that purpose. I was pleased that we had been served liver for breakfast!

Philip had many people to see; he was in great demand. Having found a comfortable stance on the limited furniture in the hut I eventually settled to write my journal. Remarkably I didn't feel stiff after the ride, but I had a sore backside where I hadn't quite matched the contours of the saddle which must have been broken in by someone with a rear end of a rather different shape to mine. Now, as the sun was peeping round one of the many surrounding mountain peaks, I was using a quiet moment to record events and whilst I was writing inside the hut I heard from outside the Sesotho shout equivalent to the Durham knock on the door, '*Koko koko*!' The bishop was not there – who would want me? '*Kena!*' At my invitation to enter the ill-fitting door was forced open and in walked the Mosotho horseman who, yesterday, had so carefully led us through two rivers and across two mountain ranges into another way of life and, as I was to discover later in the day, of death.

With his colourful blanket wrapped around his slight body he nervously began, in hesitant English, to enquire if I'd slept well and if I was comfortable. Coupling a diplomatic half-truth with an invitation to sit down on my chair whilst I moved to the bed, we managed to talk and laugh with each other in his uncertain, wavering English and my fault-infested Sesotho. Continuing our introductory enquiries we asked after each other's health, families, cattle (a topic to which I had little to contribute) and how we had rested and eaten. Reassured that we were both fit and well and wrapping his blanket around himself in a nervous introduction, he (I'm sorry, I never did record his name) came to the point of his visit which was to tell me that he thought my riding of Kidboy was very good! As he was an expert horseman I was ridiculously pleased that he had taken the trouble to come and offer his congratulations that, on reflection, took some effort. As we parted his praise made me wonder if I had inherited that particular skill from my father who was in the cavalry during the 1914–1918 war. Like so many things in Lesotho, our conversation had taken a long time and as the sun had warmed the air I went outside to sit on a large boulder near my hut; perhaps I was also glowing in the praise of a Mosotho horseman!

Throughout the dry, bright morning people continued to arrive in the village from distant communities, mostly women on foot carrying large loads on their heads with a baby on their backs and some with older, shoeless children following on behind; for how many miles I didn't dare to ask or hazard to estimate. Some of the men were on horseback, others were walking, but nearly all of them, like me, were wrapped in thick, heavy blankets and most came over to speak with me. That gave me the chance to talk about the LINK we hoped to establish and to listen to their concerns and needs. It was almost a 'wild west' scene with the clamour of Basotho voices and the frequent boisterous Sesotho greetings of people who had not seen each other for a long time, mixed with the noise and pungent smell of animals and humans all of whom were covered by smoke from fires cooking lunch. In addition to all the many horses there were sheep (with tails hanging down), mohair goats (with tails standing up), a few dogs chasing the occasional cat, chickens with chicks and, in this region, many other varieties of bird. All were feeding on the pickings of sorghum spilt from bags brought from afar to share or to sell and all was seasoned by the dust raised, and then sprinkled, by the playful running of countless children. My concept of the church in the market place assumed a completely new dimension!

The overcast afternoon was emotionally poignant. After lunch Philip walked a long way to a distant hut across the deep valley around which Ha 'Mikia is clustered. Just before we arrived a 2-year-old boy had died of pneumonia and Philip was to lead the family funeral procession to All Saints' Church. Pneumonia is a virulent killer, especially of young children in the mountains, and in the early years of the twenty-first century was (leaving aside the devastation of HIV/AIDS) second only to tuberculosis as the major cause of mortality[17] in the Mantšonyane region, where the LINK was eventually to make a major contribution to health care. For now, however, our attention was on yet another sad death just as that of any child would be but here, in the small, close-knit community of Ha 'Mikia, where the boy was known by everyone, the grief was felt perhaps more deeply amongst everyone of whatever age.

As Philip led the extended family round the head of the sunbathed valley to All Saints' Church Vincent was quietly leading introductory prayers. The walk took a long time and prayers were followed by solemn singing, mournful as only the unaccompanied harmony of the Basotho can be in times of sadness; singing was the bond of their grief as the large, sombre congregation waited for the procession to arrive. Vincent and I met the cortège at the door where the reverent silence was broken only by occasional, controlled sobbing. Four men, each one holding the corner of an old hessian sack on which rested the small 'coffin', carried the body into the church. The 'coffin' was made from two cardboard boxes held together with string containing the body that, itself, was wrapped in a spotlessly clean white cloth. A fifth man carried a chipped enamel mug of water from which Philip, using a twig plucked from a bush, anointed the body, coffin and mourners.

We offered prayers, took a collection from the 300 or so people inside and outside the church and sang a couple of hymns, after which Philip spoke briefly before we all walked behind the cardboard coffin to the pathetically tiny grave. As we arrived a man jumped in and received the coffin, covering it with more sacking before the three of us, and the widowed mother, sprinkled it with earth. Each of the male mourners took his turn to shovel in a token of earth, filling the grave, before a large stone was placed at its head and another at its foot; they were pitifully close to each other. It was then that the collection was given to the grieving mother: it amounted to five maloti.[18] In 1986, the year of the London Stock Exchange 'Big Bang',[19] five maloti was worth approximately £1.70 sterling and, in Durham, would have bought two pints (just over one litre) of Newcastle Brown, the local beer. The funeral money in Ha 'Mikia was donated as an expression of care but, for me, it became a measure of poverty.

After returning with the mourners to their hut Philip rejoined us in All Saints' Church, where he conducted twelve infant and adult baptisms. Everyone remotely eligible wanted to make full use of this occasional episcopal visit. With the sad events of the day still very much alive in my mind I wondered how many of the babies would survive the scourge of pneumonia to reach the age of two. When we reached the adult baptisms I was reminded of my own initiation at the age of twenty-three.

It took place during Morning Prayer at St. Helen's Church, Ipswich, Suffolk. After the order of service had been announced by an elderly verger, and the congregation had turned in their 1662 *Book of Common*

Prayer to the Service for the Baptism of Infants, the verger turned towards me, gave me a long, rather penetrating, stare and said in his monotone voice, 'Oh, no! We want the service for those in Riper Years, page 127.' At twenty-three I didn't exactly feel 'in riper years', but that was the service that took me into the formal structure of this very same church that my voluntary work had now brought me 6,000 miles (9,656 kms) distant and 33 years later: such is the 'Global Odyssey'[20] of the Anglican Church.

Now in Ha 'Mikia, before everyone dispersed, Philip and I spoke to the people outside in the cool breeze about the proposed LINK between Durham and Lesotho. Philip and Vincent stayed to hear confessions in the church whilst outside I continued talking to individuals about the LINK and listened to their needs and aspirations before returning to the rondavel where I had intended to spend time writing. That was wishful thinking. When I reached the hut I was extremely uncomfortable around the ankles and the lower parts of my legs and had to spend the next hour divesting myself of Black jack, which my botanist colleagues would know as *Bidens pilosa* (the South American bur-marigold). Much to my discomfort my lower clothing was saturated with the hooked seed of this plant. One by tedious one I spent the next hour plucking this vicious barbed seed from my socks and trousers.

By the time I had finished and written my notes of an eventful day Philip and I were ready for the evening meal that the lady who had cooked it brought to our rondavel; well, perhaps not quite ready! It was the male speciality, the sheep's intestines! They were not to my liking although the taste was not unpleasant providing you didn't give it too much thought. It was the texture I did not like. It was very much like eating elastic bands; not that I have ever eaten elastic bands but at least what I imagine they would be like: rubbery and indigestible. Whatever it was, I told myself, it was a thoughtful gesture of friendship.

Over this chewy, gristly meal Philip told me that this morning I had made an error of judgement; not as grave as some later ones in another place. This one was nothing more than making my own bed. I had earlier noticed that he'd left his unmade but thought nothing of it other than did episcopal privilege really go this far! Now my cultural education was expanded as I was told that making beds was the work of women that I should not take away from them. In some ways this is a tough life (I don't think I would want it any tougher) but in other ways the strict division of labour clarifies and restricts responsibilities classified by gender. Some things, however, were not as clearly categorised as a young Mosotho boy discovered when he called at our hut to engage my meagre technical knowledge, asking me to set his digital watch, insisting it should operate as a 24-hour clock. The watch was small; my hands were cold; the candle was flickering towards extinction; I had negligible knowledge of digital watches (despite the expectation carried by my skin colour); I was a great disappointment. He left; the candle went out; Philip and I went to bed. It was eight o'clock in the evening or, as my recent visitor would say, 'twenty-hundred hours'.

Another day without travelling helped the recovery of my posterior but the loud crying of a baby in a nearby hut had disturbed the night so we woke unrefreshed even though the damp bed was drying out. I was learning to appreciate much that Christians in Durham take for granted: a toilet or even a hole in the ground with a seat; toilet paper (not that Lesotho has any available but the leaves of a banana plant are almost adequate as I was to discover in a venture the LINK was to make into Uganda in June, 1993);[21] a mirror; knives and forks; fruit, of which there was practically none here at this time of year. I felt low in spirit: I must have got out of bed the wrong side that morning but it was Sunday, 27th April 1986 and there was much to do.

Philip, who had somehow managed to sleep through the disturbances, and I walked slowly to All Saint's Church up a moderately sloping track that had me puffing; I blamed the altitude of somewhere around 8,200 feet (2,500 m) but that didn't help to lessen the discomfort. Once we were in the church and everyone was ready Vincent started the eucharist that embodied many other services. There were dozens of confirmations; communion for 320; an admission service for members of the Mothers' Union all smartly turned out in their blue-and-navy uniforms; a service of thanksgiving for something that I never did quite comprehend.

Having seemingly exhausted the scope of services we turned to the laying on of hands for healing, firstly of a man with diabetes who, I was told, was losing the use of his legs. Lastly, although there were no visible signs of injury, a young girl came forward who it was said, had been struck by lightning and was still fearful of it. Such a reaction was understandable as we were to experience a few hours later in a storm of incredible ferocity but now, after such a succession of varied services, the message of the Durham-Lesotho LINK almost paled into insignificance. Nevertheless, we had a constructive meeting outside when Philip spoke to the people about the idea, what might be achieved and how they could take part. Illustrating his talk with numerous large pictures I wondered how they were perceived. How do we understand a dual carriageway when we have never seen a single road? How are washing machines, televisions, microwave ovens and tumble dryers perceived by the Basotho or, for that matter, how does the person in Durham understand the need to carry water for many miles, to travel by horse over mountain tracks, to bury their dead in cardboard boxes? Nevertheless, we showed pictures and the crowd listened politely, afterwards engaging in animated conversation about the LINK. Listening to Philip I realised how useful it had been for him to visit Durham and to live for a short time with my family before the formal launch of the LINK.

Our talking was dramatically curtailed by a late-afternoon storm that was as violent as it was colourful. Everyone found shelter somewhere as few had any form of protection against the torrential rain that could be seen eroding Lesotho as part of its land mass was subtly captured to be taken on a long, sad journey and finally drowned in the southern Atlantic hundreds of exhausting miles (kms) to the west. The thunder exploded with a vengeance so forceful that we became irrationally fearful of the consequences. It seemed determined to destroy something and such was our vulnerability we didn't know quite what. The lightning stabbed the sky, piercing its dullness to illuminate it for a split second, presenting us with theatrically sharp silhouettes of mountains, rondavels or a solitary tree on a rugged horizon, beyond which only the imagination could penetrate. The rain was ferocious but the sun was victorious, generating a magnificently brilliant rainbow that seemed to say that good had triumphed and glory had come out of horror.

We spent a pleasant evening sitting on logs and rocks round the wood fire that generated just enough heat to encourage people to stay and talk. With hands wrapped round large tin mugs, they spoke of their ambitions and hopes for the proposal that Philip had presented so clearly to them. I listened carefully and wrote my journal with some difficulty as the sun had set behind the mountains dominating the quiet village leaving only the firelight, diminished by wood smoke, to illuminate the pages. Vincent was getting anxious about our journey tomorrow: he wanted to leave very early to enable us to get to Thaba-Tseka that same evening and the rain would have swollen the rivers and made the tracks more difficult to negotiate.

After supper of more mutton, cabbage and carrots with the added luxury of potatoes Philip engaged me in a long talk about the socio-political problems of Lesotho but I didn't contribute or learn very much. Tiredness from the continuous activity of the day, warmth from the fire, comfort from my Basotho blanket, physically replete after the wholesome meal; not a combination that encourages mental activity at 8,000 feet (2,450 m) late in the evening. Leaving the tuneful fire to crackle away by itself we sloshed our way through the mud to our rondavel trying to ignore Vincent's threats to waken us early the next morning: he did, before sunrise, at 6.15 a.m.

The breakfast menu was conditioned by the hour. *Lesheleshele* without milk: the cows had not been milked! Boiled eggs without bread: the ladies had not steamed any by that hour! To Vincent's relief, we loaded the packhorses and saddled up and after many farewells and much handshaking and cheering rode into the rough country along no discernible track: was this really the way we came three days ago? I now had to justify the equestrian accolade that a couple of days previously our Mosotho guide had bestowed on me but now, in daylight, we rode much more briskly to cross the Malibamatšo engorged by the recent rains. Kidboy went well; he was a powerful horse and, unlike his rider, was completely rested. We were beginning to understand each other and I was enjoying myself. There were ten riders plus two packhorses and we stopped at the river and scanned the water upstream for any evidence of flash flooding which could have been extremely dangerous. There were no signs to demand any extra caution so we crossed with no one avoiding wet feet; although mine were perhaps wetter than others as Kidboy stopped to drink the cool, refreshing water. He was preparing for the fast, hard ride to Ha Kosetabole that, although rough, was well within our mutual competence.

With increasing confidence I was much more relaxed on this return ride and not too concerned about following the horse in front or keeping pace with the troop. I was keenly observing the Basotho, trying to replicate their riding with both reins in one hand and stick (*molamu*) in the other with as much as possible concealed under one's blanket, which was closely wrapped round the body with woolly hat pulled well down, singing, antiphonally, a two-part Sesotho song. I like to think it was only my colour that gave me away!

After three and a half hours of fast riding we reached Ha Kosetabole, where we rested our horses and ourselves for an all-too-brief thirty minutes whilst they drank water and ate what grass they could find and we drank weak tea and ate what fat cakes were given us. We left with the gift of a goat that fortunately had been slaughtered, cleaned and, providentially, fitted across the neck and in front of the saddle, not of Kidboy but another horse in the troop. Mounting again at 12.30 p.m. we left Ha Kosetabole for the roughest part of the ride as we descended into the Bokong Valley to ford the Bokong River, dismounting only once, when we led the horses down a particularly difficult section that was breathtakingly steep with part of the track washed away in the recent rains.

Once we were safely across the river we then had a long, slippery climb to the village café, White City, that was not made any easier by heavy rain from louring clouds that darkened the sky, limiting visibility and making everything dark, gloomy and threatening almost to the point of being sinister. It was very uncomfortable; my blanket was soaked, the saddle was wet, I was cold as the rain brought with it a sudden drop in temperature and, as a consequence of all this, a drop in spirits. No one was singing. The heavy breathing of the horses and the pungent smell of their sweat made us realise that in these conditions concentration was not only more important than ever but also evermore difficult.

We made the café without any further incident and relaxed in this remarkably stocked mountain oasis that contained everything necessary not only for survival but also for comfort. Although the owner was away (and, surprisingly, was not English), he had left instructions for us to have 'a cup of tea' that, with considerable generosity, had been translated by the ladies of the village into a magnificent late lunch. There was a table full of salads, beetroot, sweet potatoes, boiled potatoes, cabbage, a dish of eighteen hard-boiled eggs (which, since we did not eat them, we were given with cans of drink when we left), meat, a huge dish of boiled rice, carrots, peaches, cold jelly and hot custard! It was of banquet proportions and all sixteen of us ate sumptuously, and also enjoyed 'a cup of tea'!

Tired and wet but well fed, the time had come to move into the next and final phase of our journey to Thaba-Tseka, so it was 'goodbye' to Kidboy who had served me well, to our Basotho guides who had cared for us safely and to 'Mamonate (the wife of the owner of the White City Café) who had fed us abundantly, and out into the heavy rain that had not eased during lunch. Seeking the protection of the Suzuki we immediately engaged four-wheel drive to get us through the most appalling conditions with the 'road' barely discernible. Mud, rocks, water all conspired to slow our journey southward to the small village of Khohlo-Ntšo, the black valley.

There, wet and bedraggled, we visited an old lady who had been sick for many days and had asked, how I just do not know, that we stop so Bishop Philip could give her communion. Her old rectangular stone-built 'house' was a single room divided by a net curtain into a sleeping area at one end and a living area with the minimum of furniture. A simple administration, grateful thanks, a brief chat; this was the Church going out to the sick.

We left in failing light, undeterred by the constant rain, only to be stopped almost immediately by a broken-down vintage van blocking the track. A lorry that had come to rescue it was itself stuck in a field of mud. Philip and Vincent left me in the Suzuki and, remarkably, gathered sufficient manpower to bodily lift the van to one side sufficiently for me to squeeze past on the side of the hill so that if I had slipped I would get some protection from the van. Once past Ha Sekhohola our next stop was the village of Ha Soai, where we left a cheque with a man who just seemed to appear out of the gloom the moment we arrived: how did he know and what did they do with a cheque in this remote wilderness? I discovered it was the teachers' salary but what I never did discover is why we did not leave it when we called at St. Paul's School five days previously! Here were two more Basotho mysteries to add to others that were gradually beginning to accumulate.

Pushing on with the intention of passing Ha Leoka by mid-afternoon, the figurative description soon became literal as Philip and Vincent wallowed ankle-deep in mud and slime to do just that! We slid off the track getting bogged down and they pushed whilst I tried to ease the Suzuki to firmer ground of which we could find none. Recalling the edict of the old sea dog who taught me marine navigation that 'the best way out of danger is the reverse of how you got in: the 180-degree solution', I was, with the aid of more pushing, able to reverse out of the mud. Once we were moving south again we passed Ha Khoanyane and Maboloka, arriving at Thaba-Tseka at 10.00 p.m. after driving just over 47 miles (76 kms) in 7 hours, an average of just 6.75 miles (11 kms) an hour.

Back at the home of David Khan we were given a wholesome meal after which, not surprisingly, I slept like the proverbial log. The next morning the three of us bade him '*sala hantle*' (stay well) as he sent us on our way with the Sotho farewell '*tsamaea hantle*' (go well). Little did any of us realise the finality of what had just passed between us: David died shortly after we had left him apparently fit and well. On Thursday, 15th May 1986, Philip and I were to take his funeral in the lowlands at Masite. Of that we knew nothing as Philip now drove down the Mountain Road to Maseru.

We made only one stop. To take pictures of women threshing wheat by hand, keeping the straw for roof thatching and winnowing in the light breeze. I was invited to 'try my hand' but I made an insignificant contribution to their collective effort! Threshing by banging the ears of the sorghum on the ground was hard work but nothing compared to winnowing. This involved using both hands to hold a large, shallow bowl of grain and chaff above the head, slowly letting it slide out so the breeze blew out the chaff into one pile and allowing the heavier sorghum to fall into another pile. The experienced ended with two neat piles perfectly winnowed. It was a task that looked easy but wasn't: I finished with aching arms and with seed and chaff scattered all over the place.

Back in Maseru after our six-day trek into one of the remotest mountain regions of Lesotho the task of sorting, the joy of bathing, the delight of clean clothes, the necessity of writing and the agony of aches and pains kept me occupied until early evening. The bishop's wife, 'Matšepo (the mother of Tšepo),[22] welcomed us home with a substantial meal but even then there was no rest. We were joined by two enthusiastic American Peace Corps workers who wanted to discuss their agricultural project that was going to change the world and to find out if the LINK would cooperate with them in its development. I was grateful that I was able to point out that we were not yet in existence and went to bed!

The next six days were to be full of groundwork meetings. I wanted to gain wide support from a diverse range of people and organisations, which I needed if only a few of the ideas I had gathered and formulated were to be acceptable and feasible. One of the principles I wanted to stress, both within the LINK and elsewhere, was the ability of the Church to work with secular authority for the good of all people. That the Church could, and if it was to exercise its Christian influence should, work in harmony with others would be essential if the LINK was to achieve its potential but it was not going to be easy. Both in Lesotho and Durham, for totally different reasons, there are widespread misgivings about Church activities (based, sometimes, on historically rooted jealousy and emotionally powered enmity) especially if those activities are perceived as more rightly the prerogative of secular agencies. The immense wealth, in the middle-ages and even beyond, of the diocese of Durham, coupled with its wide temporal power, bestowed upon the holder of the See the majestic title of Prince Bishop.[23]

Although the present-day bishop no longer enjoys, or bears the burden of, that title, or the full grandeur of Auckland Castle, he does have an address decorated by multimillion-pound art treasures. He also has the convenience of a chauffeur-driven luxury car, the pomp and ceremony surrounding the office and membership of the House of Lords, all of which encourage a perceived image by the generally 'down-to-earth', north-east population that the office is still closely related to that of a modern-day secular prince. In Durham past aristocratic priorities tend to determine present plebeian perceptions.[24] I was under no illusion. Any attempt to straddle the religious–secular divide was not going to be easy so, I argued to myself, we should work from accurate knowledge of each other's countries, conditions and cultures. Whether we stand in Lesotho or Durham we should seek to know who 'they' are; them and us.

---

1. John 20:21 (GNB).
2. David Jenkins' recorded talk played to the Lesotho Diocesan Council meeting on Friday, 16th May 1986 (see Chapter One).
3. Desmond Tutu, the second Diocesan Bishop of Lesotho, was enthroned on Sunday, 1st August 1976 during a five-hour service attended by myself. He remained in the diocese until 1978 when he became the first black general secretary of the South African Council of Churches based in Johannesburg. On 13th November 1984, he was elected Bishop of Johannesburg. Some Basotho were critical at his short period of office in the Diocese of Lesotho and felt let down when he left. He said he would like to retire there but has not done so.

4. Desmond, Cosmos, *The Discarded People* (Penguin Books, 1971). Despite his banning order Cos and I used to meet at his house each time I was in Johannesburg. It was there that his wife, Snoeks, first introduced me to Winnie Mandela and where I met many others involved in the struggle against apartheid. Anselm Prior, a Roman Catholic Franciscan priest, first took me (suitably disguised) into some of the appalling 'dumping grounds' that Cos first revealed in his book.
5. Baragwanath Hospital, now known as Chris Hani Baragwanath Hospital, is situated in Soweto and is the largest hospital in the world with approximately 3,200 beds and about 6,760 staff working in an estate covering 173 acres (70 hectares). It was opened in 1941.
6. Postma, Minnie, *Tales from the Basotho* (Austin: American Folklore Society, University of Texas, 1974). Original translated by Susie McDermid (Johannesburg: Afrikaanse Pers-Boekhandel, 1964).
7. Brownlee, F., *Lion and Jackal: with other nature folk tales from South Africa* (London: George Allen and Unwin, 1938).
8. Among the Basotho there is some dispute as to whether this name should have a final 'g' (Khang) or not.
9. In the 1662 version of *The Book of Common Prayer*, one of the introductory rubrics for the Holy Communion service states, 'And the Priest standing at the north side of the Table ...'
10. Mark 12:41b–44 (GNB): Many rich men dropped in a lot of money; then a poor widow came along and dropped in two little copper coins, worth about a penny. He called his disciples together and said to them, 'I tell you that this poor widow put more in the offering box than all the others. For the others put in what they had to spare of their riches; but she, poor as she is, put in all she had – she gave all she had to live on'.
11. A Sesotho grace often said by the woman who has cooked the meal:

    Morena, hlohonolofatsa limpho tsena,
    matsoho a li entseng
    le 'mele e tla li amohela. Amen.

    Lord, bless these gifts,
    the hands that prepared them
    and the bodies which now receive them. Amen.
12. The shriek of applause used as a welcome by a crowd of men and women that is rather louder and more varied than the usual female ululation.
13. Sechefo, Justinus, *Customs and Superstitions in Lesotho* (the title page uses 'Basutoland') (The Social Centre, Anthropological Studies, Roma: undated) (almost certainly pre-1966) p. 28.
14. Proverbs 22:28 (NIV): Do not move an ancient boundary stone set up by your forefathers. One of the Thirty Wise Sayings.
15. Mark 16:15 (NIV): (Jesus) said to them, 'Go into all the world and preach the good news to all creation'.
16. *Mission England Praise* (Marshall Pickering, an imprint of HarperCollinsReligious, London, 1984).

17. Annual Report of St James' Mission Hospital: 2001–2002 (p. 11).

18. The monetary unit of Lesotho currency is the Loti (plural maloti) and sente (plural lisente) and is equal in exchange value to the South African Rand. In 1986 the exchange rate was around £1.00 = M3.00 and in early 2010 the rate was £1.00 = M12.00.

19. The deregulation of the London Stock Exchange that allowed computer share dealing.

20. Johnson, Howard A., *Global Odyssey: Visiting The Anglican Churches* (London, Geoffrey Bles, 1963) p. 78. Canon Johnson, whilst recognising the strategic importance of Lesotho (Basutoland), did not visit the Anglican Church there.

21. In June 1993, the Durham-Lesotho LINK investigated ways in which it might cooperate with a charity in Uganda with the object of developing a tripartite organisation so that African charities could work together. The problems were too extensive and the idea was reluctantly abandoned.

22. When a Mosotho woman marries she adopts the name the couple have agreed to call their first son and becomes, in this example, the mother of Tšepo.

23. Whellan, Francis, *The History, Topography, and Directory of the County Palatine of Durham: 1984* (n.p.).

24. Page, William, Volumes I – II – III and Cookson, Gillian, Volume IV; *The Victoria History of the Counties of England – Durham 1907.* Four volumes 2005. (Institute of Historical Research, University of London, since 1933).

Chapter Three

Them and Us

First of all, then, I (Paul) urge that petitions, prayers, requests and thanksgivings be offered to God for all people. [1]

Christian faith is essentially about people so, if we were to take seriously the main tenet of the Durham-Lesotho LINK that we were to strive to be One Body in Christ, then the crucial focus of the LINK had to be on people, both the serving and those they were attempting to serve. In short we had to get to know each other. I'd had the benefit of doing that over the past thirteen years but what now? In my thinking during some long airport lingering it followed that I had to distinguish, both for myself and for others in Lesotho and Durham, the differences and similarities between the two groups, where and how they live, who they are, what they do and, perhaps even, why. Solitary individual brainstorming whiled away many a monotonous hour waiting in airport lounges and my notebook gradually filled.

Whichever way you look at it, northward or southward, any understanding of 'them and us' or 'us and them' depends, of course, on who you are, Dunelmian or Mosotho, and where you are, Lesotho or Durham. So that each could get to know the other it became essential to reflect on differences and similarities from both perspectives. If we really were to stand any chance of becoming One Body in Christ the question I had to address was how I was going to bring these two diverse groups of people together. How could each learn from the other? What were the most distinctively significant features that needed to occupy our thinking?

Apart, perhaps, from the Basotho, who came into direct contact with their colonial 'protectors' before independence in 1966, few people in either place, despite previous tenuous contacts, had even heard of each other before the Durham-Lesotho LINK was founded and those who had certainly found it difficult to pronounce the names correctly. Familiar as they were with Durban just a short distance to the east on the coast of South Africa, the Basotho transposed the long 'u' of Durban to this new word, with only two different letters, they were gradually learning: 'Durham'. On one notable occasion they even had postal workers in Durban looking for my Durham address and had me wondering why I had not received a batch of papers I had been promised. Whilst all this was happening with typical Basotho good humour, in the northern part of the LINK the people of Durham were coming to terms, very slowly and rather more sombrely, with a completely new way of pronouncing 'th', learning to say '*Le-sooh-too*' for Lesotho, '*Moo-sooh-too*' for Mosotho, '*Ba-sooh-too*' for Basotho and '*Se-sooh-too*' for Sesotho. We were miles apart, metaphorically as well as geographically, but not only in our language and speech.

In 1986 the first question asked by most people, black or white, was 'Where is it?' Unlike life in 2010, when a couple of clicks would answer that question, there was no widespread access to the Internet and certainly none in Lesotho. Timothy Berners-Lee, the British physicist who rejected his Anglican upbringing, ironically just after his confirmation, had still to invent the World Wide Web[2] that now, twenty-five years later at <http://www.durham-lesotholink.org.uk>, will give the answer and provide the publicity we urgently needed. However, we could not turn the clock forward and we needed an answer in 1986.

So that year, applying the Arno Peters' projection of the world map,[3] in preference to the more commonly used Mercator projection, Paul Judson, a former graphic artist training for the Anglican ordained ministry, took my rough sketch and designed a simple bookmark showing Durham in the north and Lesotho in the south joined together by a striking symbolic cross. On the back of the bookmark was my first attempt at a logo and a short list of facts about each region. It was a simple introductory message, cheap to reproduce, constantly in sight and an easily distributed idea. The sceptics were critical of the 40,000 that were printed but they were free, personal and readily available in churches and public libraries in both Durham and Lesotho. The cynics were wrong; such was the demand we could have used many thousands more but in the early years money was tight and we printed all we could afford at the time. The design was used for many years and was reproduced on tens of thousands of leaflets publicising our larger projects in forestry and feeding.

There were also more mobile and wider applications and it was not long before the LINK became known beyond the borders of Durham, at which point we received enquiries and offers of help from other countries, counties and dioceses. As news of its work began to spread around the UK a van bringing a collection of tools from Rusthall Parish

Church in Kent prominently displayed on its side a much-enlarged version of the design; few who met it on its 650 mile (1,046 kms) journey to Durham and back could have missed seeing it. It was a happy coincidence that when the van-load of tools arrived at my house a Mosotho lawyer, Winston Churchill Maqutu, then Registrar of the Diocese of Lesotho, was staying with my wife and me. He used his quiet, eloquent command of English to receive the hundreds of tools that would eventually find their way from Kent via Durham into active service in Lesotho. About the same time a somewhat more permanent use was made of the design when Paul Judson used it as the centrepiece for the banner Martha Bissett, a highly skilled needlewoman from St. Paul's Church, Ryhope, made for the cathedral in Maseru, Lesotho.

Martha's dexterous fingers, that had taken her to Buckingham Palace to have tea with Queen Elizabeth, spent many hours working on a banner that covers an area of 6 by 4.5 feet (1.8 by 1.4 m).[4] It was completed two years after she had begun feverishly working on the banner (perhaps she was well named[5]), when it was displayed for a short time in Durham Cathedral before being carefully packed into my suitcase with bookmarks, photographs and books plus one spare set of clothes; there was rarely room for more. It arrived in Maseru during the heat of summer in January 1990 but, because I had to go to Namibia for two weeks, I was not able to present it to the diocese until Sunday, 11th February. That morning I preached at the second and third services of the day and at the third service Philip Mokuku presided at the eucharist. The enlarged and reordered cathedral was full to overflowing and the banner had been carefully, perhaps even lovingly, smoothed by a lady who had spent many hours ironing it, not with a modern electric iron such as my wife uses but with two flat irons that were heated alternately on a fire just as my mother used to do! To watch her was a vivid reminder that scores of people, over many years, have worked in Lesotho and Durham for the LINK almost unknown and even unnamed and now, amidst much ululation, cheering and clapping, the banner was hoisted into the rafters of the cathedral above the bishop's chair, where it proved to be an excellent visual aid.

The design of the banner, an enhanced and emboldened version of the bookmark, showed quite clearly some essential features of the LINK that I wanted to project in both communities. In Lesotho, on that glorious summer February morning, the significance of each part was explained and produced its own ecstatic welcome from an excited and vocal cathedral congregation:

- firstly, the banner showed where Durham was, way 'up there' in the north;

- secondly, that Lesotho was in the southern hemisphere, way 'down there';
- thirdly, confirming what most people suspected, that they were a long distance apart;
- fourthly, that even so they could be joined by the Cross of Christ as the Holy Spirit knows no boundaries of country, class, colour or circumstance;
- a fifth characteristic of the LINK was the proclamation that through the Cross 'we are One Body in Christ' – '*re 'mele o le mong ho Kreste*';
- sixth, that the black and white of the lettering together gives a clearer message than when they are separate and apart;
- seventh, the encircling of the world by God's love, that encompasses us all, also involves us all;
- eighth, that the blue uniform colour of the Mothers' Union was chosen as the background in recognition of the contribution that it makes to the life of the Church.

I think Martha Bissett would have been pleased: I hoped so as I received the Basotho acclamation on her behalf. The bishop anointed the banner with water and incensed it and it now hangs in the apse at the east end of the Cathedral Church of St. Mary and St. James, Maseru, to remind everyone not only of where the two places are but also that they are linked by the Cross of Christ. If we managed to convey those critical facts in the early years, and there was a lot of evidence at the time that many people had begun to focus their interest on both places, that was an excellent start but it was only a start and had its limitations.

Successful though all this was I felt a much more direct contact with members of the Church in Durham was required to maintain the early dynamic interest and provide up-to-date information about the LINK. My regular visits to Lesotho, now four or five times a year working on professional assignments as well as for the LINK, were a constant reminder there of the vibrant presence of the LINK. There was, as yet, no equivalent Basotho presence in Durham and in spite of the scores of talks and sermons I gave around the county and diocese, it wasn't quite the same as I lived there, I was white (or nearly so) and people expected to see me there! That is except for the occasion when, unexpectedly, I met a friend in Durham city to be greeted by his comment 'Oh! I see you're commuting to Durham these days!'

To overcome this weakness of communication, after some careful negotiating the LINK was granted a bimonthly page in the diocesan pamphlet 'The Durham Lamp', thus enabling current news of the LINK to be published every couple of months to a wide audience. This form of contact also had three other considerable benefits. It enabled the Basotho to feel an active part of the LINK as they were making a key contribution through the publication of brief articles written in Lesotho by Basotho. Additionally, the use of 'The Durham Lamp' as a means of communicating also provided a physical connection with Lesotho, as I took multiple copies in my suitcase which still only had space for one set of my clothes! As the work of the LINK outgrew the capacity of this very useful little publication it provided the impetus for the start of '*MOHO – Together*, a twice-yearly, two-colour newsletter that we started in November 1990.

None of this effort actually gave any information about where each country was to be found. For those wanting to discover more about these two weird and wonderful places with peculiar names that were currently establishing an out-of-the-ordinary association more information was required. Those who had access to an atlas, albeit probably an old, tattered, school Philips' publication,[6] and were able to follow the coordinates of 30° south and 28° east could not possibly miss the grandeur and magnificence of Lesotho. If their global-positioning system were accurate, they would be in the beautiful Maletsunyane Valley in the Mohale's Hoek district of southern Lesotho. Looking up the valley to the north would be Semonkong and westward the Thaba-Putsoa (Blue Mountain) Range. But they should not linger long on their atlas journey. Now that Lesotho has been found Durham beckons. Travelling northward from 30° south, across the equator, to 54° north is roughly 6,000 miles (9,655 kms) and, if we go a little further to 54° 45' north and coordinate that with 2° west we shall have reached another valley, that of the River Wear (Basotho beware! This is pronounced as weir, to rhyme with 'fear', so quite different from the clothes you wear).

If our navigation has been accurate we shall be standing in the north-west of County Durham overlooking the small town of Stanhope. As we look up this narrow river valley to the west, much less dramatic though no less beautiful than the Maletsunyane Valley, the Pennine range of hills rise with the highest, Cross Fell, stretching upwards to a mere 2,930 feet (893 m). This is no challenge to the imposing mountains of Lesotho, with its loftiest almost four times higher and even its lowest being 1,600 feet (488 m) above Durham's highest spot! So the entire land mass of Lesotho is higher than that of Durham. Lesotho rises dramatically from its low point of 4,593 feet (1,400 m) near the confluence of the mighty Orange (otherwise Senqu) River with the smaller Makhaleng River to the majestic, imposing 11,424 feet (3,482 m) of Thabana Ntlenyana.

High altitudes in Lesotho and Durham present both 'them' and 'us' with difficulties of understanding and pronunciation when speaking with and about each other. The 'fell' of Durham ('fell' rhymes with 'bell', 'hell', 'sell', 'tell', 'well') that comes from Old Norse and Old Saxon is used mainly in northern England and Scotland for a large hill and so is frequently heard in Durham to describe the hills in the west of the county, where energetic people pass their leisure time walking and enjoying the rugged beauty of the countryside. As the people of northern England get pleasure from walking in the fells so the Basotho, more academically, get pleasure from their mountain, '*thaba*'.[7] Using that word as a verb its meaning becomes 'to be glad and to rejoice'. Expressing their joy, thankful parents derive from *thaba* the Basotho girl's name Thabelo.[8]

Our atlas adventurer was left in western Durham gazing out across the Wear valley towards the small town of Stanhope where, in this northern section of the LINK, it is much more crowded with people than it is in Lesotho. The size of County Durham, with which the Anglican Diocese of Durham was almost coterminous until the county boundary was redrawn in 1974, is about 551,470 acres (223,180 hectares) into which 492,300 people[9] are crowded. That gives each Dunelmian just over an acre in which to live, which is considerably less than the 4 acres available, statistically, to each Mosotho, as she or he lives in a country more than thirteen times larger than Durham. In contrast there are about four times as many Basotho living in Lesotho; with which the Anglican Diocese of Lesotho is conterminous. Although the data are inconsistent there were approximately 1,865,000 Basotho living in the 7,501,440 acres (3,035,833 hectares) of Lesotho in 2004, thus giving each Mosotho four times as much space as their Durham counterpart. In the league table of the land size of nations, Lesotho ranks 140th, just slightly smaller than Belgium. Unlike Durham it is completely landlocked, being surrounded by the Republic of South Africa.[10] No such restriction confines the northern part of the LINK, where a coastline of some 11 miles (18 kms) provides access to the North Sea and beyond, with land borders on to the counties of North Yorkshire, Cumbria and Northumberland. Unlike Lesotho there is no siege; escape is convenient and easy; physical freedom is absolute.

What are those acres like? Durham's pastureland, criss-crossed by low drystone walls, grazes large flocks of sheep whereas Lesotho's unfenced lowlands nurture thousands of mohair goats and cattle that are cared for during daylight by young boys who herd them into village kraals at night. Much of Durham's undulating countryside has small farms dotted over lush grassland that is rarely denied the sufficient rain that Lesotho's subsistence farming sometimes needs so desperately at specific times of the year. During the northern winter months the lowlands of Lesotho are growing peaches, apricots and apples with cereal crops of maize and sorghum whereas arable crops in Durham are limited to its coastal plain, so inland there is space for sheep grazing. Intensive farming in Durham ensures that almost all the land is farmed, whereas it is calculated that in Lesotho only about 7.0 per cent is cultivated, the remainder being bare rock or land that is impossible to plant.

Not unusually, altitude conditions rural life in both places, especially so in Lesotho although there are some similarities here and there. In whichever place you are you would find that winter snow in the upper regions attracts visiting skiers and climbers. Bare rock is a feature at the higher levels but especially in Lesotho where enormous gullies, known locally as *dongas*, carve their relentless wounds through the mountains, carrying away life-giving rain water and fertile soil in a blood-orange discharge emptying into the mighty Senqu alias Orange River. The momentum of the Senqu takes it across the continent releasing it into the freedom of the Atlantic Ocean where as the soil sinks to a new resting place the rain survives, in a more saline existence, safe in the knowledge that water never dies.

However dramatic these differences there are similarities. As the LINK's woodland and forestry projects revealed, one of those similarities is the lack of trees in both places. Whilst trees, woodlands and forests do exist, many more than twenty-five years ago, they are still in lesser numbers than advocated by environmentalists. The present lack of trees in Durham partially accounts for the enormous wealth that lay concealed beneath its surface. Precious stones may not suggest any immediately obvious connection between Lesotho and Durham but local colloquial speech, and much hard labour underground, has produced many black diamonds[11] in the northern region. More black diamonds have come to the surface in Durham than the precious brilliant white ones that may still be awaiting discovery in the north of Lesotho. So, it may just be worthwhile searching around the Pass of Guns at 10,630 feet (3,240 m) on the boundary between the districts of Mokhotlong and Butha-Buthe where, unlike Durham, mining is again active. It certainly rewarded 'Mè (Mrs) Ernestine Ramaboa who, in 1967, discovered the large diamond subsequently named the Lesotho Brown, just one of four diamonds found in Lesotho that are in the top-twenty largest diamonds ever to be found in the world.[12]

Letšeng-la-Terae is a mine that, until a short while ago, was designated as 'disused' but has now uncovered, as well as the Lesotho Brown (601 carat), the Star of Lesotho (123 carat), the Lesotho Promise (603 carat), the Letšeng Legacy (493 carat) and, most recently, Leseli Letšeng (Light of Letšeng, 478 carat) that was sold in 2008 in Amsterdam for 18.4 million US dollars. Whereas the British government returned the black diamonds of Durham into private ownership, the Lesotho government retain a 30 per cent share in the genuine white diamonds of Butha-Buthe, but whether black or white has, over the years, been the most economically valuable is almost impossible to compute. Both have had a significant financial and social impact on the two regions that constitute the Durham-Lesotho LINK. Until the early 1990s mining was a major economic contributor to both societies but ten years later relatively few miners are employed in the Letšeng mine. The decline goes beyond the borders of Lesotho. In excess of 8,000 Basotho men used to work in the gold mines of South Africa, gaining a reputation as first-class ore hewers. Somewhat ironically, until the end of apartheid black miners were reliant upon the proceeds of gold nuggets and white diamonds whilst white miners in Durham relied heavily on black nuggets until the foreclosure of coal mining. At least the diamond mine continues productively.

In Durham one of the many demands on the hard, dangerously earned, miner's money was for housing. This contrasts with his Mosotho counterpart who, if he lived in a rural area, would, with his family, build his own at minimal expense. Taking what was usually a substantial loan, which he would spend much of his lifetime repaying, the Durham miner would buy a rectangular-shaped brick or stone-built, tiled or slate-roofed, small house of some five or six rooms on two levels. Behind this there would be a small garden where he might grow vegetables, with leeks taking pride of place because of local competitions to see who could grow the largest specimen. For those miners who could not afford to finance a loan there was the option of renting a house and probably finishing his working life in an Aged Miners' Home, the rented accommodation provided by the mine owners.

Unlike the Durham coal miner, the Mosotho gold miner would spend long periods away from home living in bad communal conditions that I was able to see for myself in 1974 after going underground at the South African Geduld Gold Mine in Welkom.[13] There he would live in a room about 8 feet square (2.5 m), six men to a room sleeping in three double-tiered bunks. The house that he would return to, about once a month if he were fortunate, would have been built by members of his family with rocks and stones bound together with a mortar made from animal dung and mud. Those built entirely of mud on a rough wooden frame are not uncommon but whichever material is used, it would most likely be circular in shape with a conical roof thatched with reeds or grass. Inside there would be negligible light filtering through dust-covered, ill-fitting windows with an equally ill-fitting door attempting to exclude wind and animals. Each hut, about 10 to 15 feet (3 to 4.5 m) in diameter, would have one use. With more land space than his opposite number in the north, the Mosotho would have a single-level hut for sleeping and perhaps another for cooking in bad weather with a further hut as storage space. If the gold miner were returning to a town or large settlement his house might be rectangular and might have a corrugated-iron roof wired down to the walls to prevent its disappearance in ferocious gale-force winds that can sweep off the mountains. As a further insurance against disaster a flat, or nearly so, roof would be strewn with large rocks to weigh it down.

So, home-sweet-home for the diamond hunter in Lesotho or the gold miner in South Africa, compared with the coal hewer in Durham, is substantially different. Both would be centrally heated with Durham many years behind Lesotho with its open wood fire on the floor in the centre of the living hut radiating its heat with the smoke drifting away into the rafters and out through the thatch. One of the first of my many mistakes in Lesotho was to think that the hut I was passing with smoke pouring out of its roof was on fire! Very many years later, after the disappearance of the coal miners' cheap, subsidised coal that had burnt inefficiently in an open fire or stove, Durham would have gas or oil-fired boilers to heat water that was then pumped round the house to keep it and its occupants warm.

Domestic provision between north and south was, and still is, hugely different with perhaps the greatest differences being between the residences of the two diocesan bishops. In the first twenty-five years of the LINK there have been three Durham Diocesan bishops, David Jenkins, Michael Turnbull and Tom Wright, and four in the diocese of Lesotho, Philip Mokuku, Andrew Duma, Joseph Tsubella and Adam Taaso. None of these seven bishops has had to take 'a substantial loan' to provide housing for their families as their respective dioceses provided living accommodation of hugely different proportions to each other and to those occupied by Christians in Durham and Lesotho dioceses.

In Maseru the bishop's house, nestling behind a huge mulberry tree, with the consequent mess of fallen fruit in late summer, is but a stone's throw from the cathedral and is of adequate space with sufficient domestic and working rooms. It is built of cut stone under a pitched corrugated-iron roof but is constantly in need of refurbishment. There is also a little chapel set amidst the vegetable garden and small grounds on the edge of the land occupied by the Anglican Training Centre, the cathedral and modest church housing stretching along Pulane Street. Moving northwards we find the Bishop of Durham accommodated in the ancient palatial stronghold of Auckland Castle, of more than adequate space set within 800 acres (324 hectares) of Auckland Park,[14] with its ninety rooms providing a four-bedroom apartment[15] for the bishop and his family; more than sufficient domestic and working rooms; a conference centre; the diocesan offices and, in addition, a large chapel. Like Lesotho, the Durham residence is also constantly in need of refurbishment but unlike Lesotho, where the bishop's house is only 100 yards (90 m) from the cathedral, Auckland Castle is situated some 7 miles (11 kms) from the cathedral.

Whatever these enormous differences, of rather more significance for most people than the size of episcopal residences would be the style of worship within the different churches. Not surprisingly there are considerable variations within each diocese, but worship in both tends to be more towards the sacramental and ritualistic mode, a manner even more pronounced in Lesotho than in Durham. The question we had to consider in the LINK was how much would the other feel at ease with the way in which worship was conducted? Would many feel, as one Mosotho lady did at a holy communion service in a church where the ministers did not wear robes, that she could not receive the communion elements from someone who was 'not a proper priest'? Could, indeed should, the LINK influence such thinking, especially when it is genuinely and sincerely held? Between our two dioceses there are some striking and unusual similarities but there are also some massive differences. Nature, history, culture, environment, location and tradition have all, at some time or another, been influential. I prayed that energetic cooperation in a common task would draw people together. Those common tasks had still to be identified.

When distinguishing differences and similarities it is all too easy to identify skin colour as a major difference; that was until I met a few white people who had been born and bred in Lesotho and who proudly told me they were Basotho, whatever their skin colour. Their national allegiance and personal loyalty was strongly focused on Lesotho which, they asserted, was their 'one and only home'. This limited, multicoloured state of affairs in the southern hemisphere of the LINK is little different in its northern counterpart where, in County Durham, the multiracial society of the United Kingdom has not become so widely established as in many other areas of the country (98.6 per cent of the population of County Durham is white Anglo-Saxon).[16] When mass immigration to Britain took place in the 1960s and 1970s, employment in coal mining and shipbuilding, on which the north-eastern economy relied, was not an attractive option to people from overseas. As a consequence, compared to many other places in the United Kingdom, only a few black faces are genuinely local Dunelmian.

We are left with the observation that most of the two million people in Lesotho are a shade of black and most of the half-million people in Durham are a shade of white. To the acutely observant there is a point at which the dark-skinned person from Durham (of which I am one) is not unlike the light-skinned person from Lesotho and, much to the good-humoured teasing of many Basotho, after two weeks of their sun I was nearly their colour. One other feature of colour: hair! Unlike me Philip

Mokuku was overjoyed when I began to show the first grey streaks in my otherwise dark hair. Pointing to the ageing process around my temples, he eloquently made the point that Basotho (as with some other Africans) revered the man with greying hair, paying great respect to the wisdom it was said to depict. Time would tell if he were accurate in his assessment but noticeably he failed to mention my steel-blue eyes being so starkly different from the prominent dark brown of the Basotho!

A connection between colour and language is not immediately obvious but there is a tenuous, fascinating association linking the speech of the Basotho with the colour 'brown'. The general description, Sotho, given to the language of the people of Lesotho and some southern African groups, has been credited to a subgroup of the Nguni tribe found in Swaziland, the Mbo. There the word *sotho* (very occasionally spelt 'sootho' but always pronounced as such) was used as an adjective for the colour 'dark brown', although there is some uncertainty as to the context in which it was used.[17] Nonetheless, evidence exists that the word *sotho* was used in its written form in the early nineteenth century.[18] The prefix 'Se' denotes the southern form of the Sotho language and Sesotho is widely spoken by individual Mosotho who make up the Basotho people of Lesotho; which all goes to show the importance of knowing the root of the noun and how difficult it is for the linguistic beginner to use a Sesotho dictionary without that knowledge! Even though Sesotho is the national language of Lesotho, one consequence of its colonial days is that English remains, with Sesotho, one of the two official languages. Even so, other languages are also used and particularly in the south-western regions, where Xhosa and Sephuthi are frequently heard and where strong demands are still being made for children to be taught in their own regional languages.[19] Nevertheless, English is widely spoken by those Basotho who are formally educated and is often the preferred mode of communication particularly in urban lowland areas, gaining support because of the lack of Sesotho vocabulary for modern technological and social concepts.

In the northern hemisphere, some fifty years behind Sesotho, the Geordie dialect was making its tentative entry into the public arena. There is evidence that Sotho was being written around 1824, but Geordie was not being used widely until about 1875. Sesotho may be difficult for the English ear and tongue but what would Basotho ears hear in the north-east of England of which Durham is a part? Certainly not the English of their former Lesotho classrooms. The hundreds of Basotho that the LINK has enabled to visit Durham in the past twenty-five years would not be long in the area before some local person would greet him or her with 'Areet, pet?' Overcoming their silent amazement, to translate the word 'pet' into 'domestic animal' would hardly convey the endearment intended by the greeting any more than 'Areet' would be translated as 'all right'. On a railway station, in an English society dominated by the immediate seconds rather than the protracted hours of life in Lesotho, 'Haway' would not express the sense of urgency needed if the train was about to depart! Language was something to which we would have to pay careful and prayerful attention as did the crowd at the first Pentecost.[20] Perhaps we could join them 'in amazement and wonder', filled with the Holy Spirit, speculating how it is 'that all of us hear them speaking in our own native language'. Now that really would make us One Body!

The painstaking work of one of the early volunteers to go to Lesotho helped the LINK in this process. Because of Sister Magdalena's early advice and insistence and my wife's patience I was able to follow the services in Sesotho with a fair degree of understanding. However, I recognised that with the increasing popularity of our adult exchange programmes, with more and more people travelling in both directions, there would be many who were likely to be at a complete loss during services. In the 1970s I had sat through what seemed like interminable debates in the English General Synod about the liturgy for the eucharist and now, in the late 1980s, here I was discussing how to make it more accessible in Lesotho. In 1975 the Province of Southern Africa had published 'pew book(s)' in both Sesotho[21] and English[22] but in two distinctly separate books! For our purposes these two languages needed to be brought together in a related way so that the eucharist service could be followed with easy reference to the other language.

In 1988 a Durham student who had just finished his degree had been to see me in Durham and offered his services for a year as a volunteer in Lesotho. At the time I had no idea how I would use his kind offer but I nevertheless accepted with delight that here was another pair of hands that could share the weight of what needed to be done and quickly if I was to retain the initial enthusiastic momentum for the LINK. I explained what I wanted and he set about arranging the already published material in two parallel pages, Sesotho on the left-hand page and English on the right-hand page, with each section and rubric on both pages consecutively numbered so it was easy to cross reference at any point in the service. Later we added, on the inside of the back cover, the words and music of the LINK song *We are One Body in Christ.*[23] I have no record of how many we printed but I do remember that it was insufficient as demand came not only from Durham visitors, but also from the Basotho themselves.

During twenty-five years of the LINK the difference in languages has not been a serious stumbling block with either 'them' or 'us', whoever we are. What has been more of an obstacle is the conceptual confusion arising from the widely different experiences of each group. For example, the experience of a cathedral that a person from Durham has, and they may have seen many, is vastly different from the understanding of a cathedral that a person from Lesotho has. They, most probably, would have seen only the Roman Catholic, Anglican and Lesotho Evangelical Church cathedrals in Maseru. In Lesotho the mental image for an Anglican stimulated by the word 'cathedral' is that of a modest stone building with a corrugated-iron roof built in 1905,[24] subsequently extended and now able to accommodate some 400 people. In Durham the mental picture changes greatly. For a local Anglican the word 'cathedral' rouses in the mind a picture of a huge, mainly Norman structure built over many years between 1093 and 1133, now the biggest building in the region, standing on a hill dominating the city and capable of holding some 3,000 people. Indeed, this was so when the second Diocesan Bishop of Lesotho, Desmond Tutu, spoke there after receiving the Honorary Freedom of the City of Durham on Tuesday, 10th March 1987.

The cognitive problem is in the contrasting differences of the mental images that the one word 'cathedral' encourages in two people who have had widely different experiences of the actual buildings. When first-hand experiences are not available it is wise to avoid oral descriptions, particularly those that have to take place in a foreign language. Cognitive images are most easily and accurately generated by pictorial acuity but I was not able to project images from my collection of slides in a country where, at that time, electricity was not available outside some of the larger towns. I had to find another answer to the problem and that I did with the eager help of Durham Photographic Society, who helped us through this difficulty.

Its members were very enthusiastic and armed with a list of suggestions to convey a visual projection of the culture of Durham, they clicked away with their cameras. We were learning how to utilise other people's skills and enthusiasm on behalf of the LINK and when we had the splendid photographs enlarged, encapsulating two pictures back-to-back and adding captions in English and Sesotho, we had a first-class visual aid that could be used anywhere in Lesotho. All we needed were two trees (often difficult to find), two nails in opposite walls (frequently available) or, if the worst came to the worst, two willing men with strong arms (but had to be persuaded). With holes punched in each of the top corners of the pictures, they could be strung up like a line of washing so large congregations could gather around them.

One set was given to each parish priest for him to use as he travelled around his enormous parish with its, often, fifteen or sixteen churches. They were easily packed for transport on horseback, withstood the severe weather conditions, were pictorially attractive and hugely successful so we had to fend off numerous requests to buy them to decorate huts and churches. Even today, twenty-five years later, examples can still be found embellishing family rondavels dotted around Lesotho.

At the northern end, as there was no PowerPoint available then, Durham had to make do with my amateur colour slides, the product of an ancient, well-travelled Agfa camera, but the hundreds of slides that are in the Lesotho picture library gave the flexibility to compose suitable displays on specialist topics to specialist groups. New concepts were being established; conventional ideas were being broadened and questioned, traditional perceptions were being refined; black and white people were beginning to think about each other in an informed, up-to-date way. So were the rich and poor!

However uncomfortable for Christians, that thinking should never overlook the fact that there are huge disparities in the financial wealth and poverty of individuals living in Lesotho and those living in Durham. When I first went to Lesotho in 1973 the distinction was greater than when I started the LINK thirteen years later in 1986, but even then the disparity was massive and has remained so over the past twenty-five years. There are slight differences between whichever scales are consulted, Gross Domestic Product (GDP), Gross National Income (GNI) or the Gini coefficient as a measure of inequality of income distribution but, setting aside spurious objectivity, the same simple general conclusion can be drawn: most people in Lesotho are, financially and materially, considerably poorer than those in Durham. To convey something of the disparity that exists between the two regions we should note that, of those countries listed by the International Monetary Fund (IMF) and ranked by nominal GDP, the UK is the fifth richest country with Lesotho ranked 153 of 179 countries of the world. The range of that inequality is also reflected in the 2007 World Bank rankings of 180 countries with the United Kingdom occupying the same ranking as the fifth richest and Lesotho creeping up two places to position 151.[25]

However, Durham is only part of the UK and has never been one of its wealthiest regions, and in the early years of the new millennium the gap in economic performance between the county and other British economies was widening. In 2008 the value of goods and services produced in Durham (Gross Value Added per capita) was amongst the lowest in the UK. Even if Durham's uncertain economic future[26] is taken into account we are still left with the indisputable fact that it has considerably more wealth than Lesotho. Perhaps the present poor economic performance of Durham will draw its people even closer to those of Lesotho, but with the GDP of the UK roughly 1,750 times greater than that of Lesotho there is a long way to go. Whether you look at it as one of 'us' or one of 'them', the financial gap is enormous and its effect on the work of the LINK could not be ignored.

Although it is important for our thinking to encompass the differences that exist between people getting to know each other it can be all too easy to lapse into ignoring those things we share in common. The Durham-Lesotho LINK is committed to serve and work amongst all people and not just Christians or, indeed, just those in any particular denomination. The LINK is there to provide opportunities for Christians in Lesotho and Durham to live their faith in an active, practical manner and to that end we needed also to know what was common within the two groups. Of course, the first common feature of those actively engaged in the LINK was their allegiance to Christ. We share a common belief but, importantly, we have constantly to remind ourselves that we are serving those who had little or no Christian commitment. Given that basis, what is the same about us?

Since 1986 much has changed. We now all live under a constitutional monarch, in Lesotho His Majesty King Letsie III[27] and in Durham Her Majesty Queen Elizabeth II,[28] within the British Commonwealth of Nations. Ever since Moshoeshoe,[29] the founder of the Basotho nation, asked Queen Victoria[30] in 1860 for the protection of British troops the two countries have been closely related. In 1947, shortly after the end of the Second World War in which Basotho troops served with great distinction and considerable loss, King George VI visited Lesotho, when the main road through the capital city was given a tarred surface and from that time has been known as Kingsway. It was a great sorrow to many of us in the Durham-Lesotho LINK when the British Labour Government closed the British Council offices in Maseru in June 2001 and withdrew the British High Commission from Lesotho at the end of 2005. The high commission had been there almost forty years since Lesotho achieved independence from Britain in October 1966.

As will become evident throughout this record of its work, both missions have been exceptionally helpful to the LINK. This was particularly so during the first eight-year phase of its life. Now to leave a loyal nation that had served the Commonwealth with honour without a diplomatic mission, and to place diplomatic services in Pretoria with all its accompanying emotional tensions, seems indefensible and unwarranted.[31] Perhaps the result of that unpalatable action makes the continuing presence in Lesotho of the LINK even more important and noteworthy than it might have otherwise been.

May 1986 was an eventful month. Not only was it then that the LINK officially started, but it was also when Philip Mokuku asked me to accompany him to Bethlehem with the leader of the Lesotho Evangelical Church, Koatanye Mahase, and the Roman Catholic bishop, Paul Khoarai. Just to avoid any further confusion this was not a re-enactment of three wise men following a star to visit the scene of the Nativity in the

Holy Land. It was a journey of four men (wise? only time would tell) following the R26 road through apartheid South Africa to Bethlehem to visit a Mosotho politician living in exile in South Africa.

I still vividly recall the day in all its detail; Saturday, 31st May 1986, when I drove a small, rather fragile car the 100 miles (161 kms) from Maseru to Bethlehem via Ficksburg, where we collected Paul Khoarai from the not unusual dense congestion at the border crossing. We were on our way to talk to former school teacher Ntsu Mokhehle who, in 1952, founded the Basutoland (as Lesotho was then named and spelt) African Congress political party. Despite two earlier civilian incumbents,[32] seven years after our visit he was to become Lesotho's first undisputed (by most), democratically elected prime minister. It was a long, tense but eventually productive day and the 100 miles (161 kms) back to Lesotho seemed to go on interminably as did the talking and the planning. At the border post the South African Defence Force projected an aura of suspicion as they kept us waiting with transit papers and passports clasped in tired, sticky hands before we drove the last few yards across the Maseru Bridge. These events have been fully chronicled elsewhere by Monyane Moleleki,[33] but three LINK 'them and us' stories emerge from this Bethlehem venture, all of which demonstrate how useful to the LINK these early personal contacts were becoming.

A lot happened during the next seven years following the trip to Bethlehem and it wasn't until April 1993 that a connection with the LINK came into prominence. That month I attended a lecture in Maseru given by Monyane Moleleki, who was at the start of a distinguished career in Lesotho politics and was then Minister for Water; later to be expanded to Minister for Natural Resources. He was also gathering material for a book he was writing about the leader of his political party, Ntsu Mokhehle. Mention during his lecture of the Maqalika Dam on the outskirts of Maseru gave me an idea that, unknown to me at the time, would have some far-reaching effects on the work of the LINK. After his lecture we arranged to meet in his office the following week when I was able to help him in a small way with his book and when he helped me enormously with the LINK. My journal records that, 'He was excited by the work of the LINK and was very supportive of the proposed youth activities project (and) is going to recommend that we are given permission to use Maqalika Dam for water sports'.[34] That was a huge breakthrough and one that had massive implications for the future development of the LINK itself.

Shortly after the trip to Bethlehem I met with Ntsu's brother, Thaele, and that meeting was to result in his arrival in Durham in May 1993, a visit that gave him many first-hand experiences of the differences and similarities between Durham and Lesotho. A short time before, he had been appointed sub-dean of the cathedral in Maseru having been priest of a large parish in the Hlotse region of Lesotho and so, for a short time, he was pleased to leave his horse in the Leribe District and fly to the United Kingdom to accept an invitation from the Dean of Durham Cathedral to exercise his ministry at Durham Cathedral before spending a month in each of three Durham deaneries: Stockton, Barnard Castle and Jarrow. Paul Baker, Vicar of Jarrow Team Ministry, writing in '*MOHO – Together,*[35] provides an insight into the practical value of such visits. He wrote:

> We tried to give Thaele a taste of life on Tyneside and in the churches of the Jarrow Deanery. This included joining the worship of half a dozen churches, preaching and taking part in a dialogue about his experience of living and ministering in Lesotho. Other diverse events and contacts were schools, the Industrial Mission, the Metro Centre, Holy Island, Hexham and the Wall, a concert, a fraternal and parish hospitality and with it the discovery of cider.

Thinking about 'them and us', Paul goes on to make a perceptive observation:

> We also learnt a lot about our own country with the benefit of Thaele's different perspective: he helped us to see ourselves. I'm glad to say that this involved a good deal of laughter about our respective situations. The most profound discovery for me during Thaele's stay, one that had never come home to me before, was that there is a real unity between our very different churches, far greater than all the contrasts: God drawing us together in Christ; we can face the future together in new heart.

The third Bethlehem story takes us to Easter 1994. Easter is a wonderful event for Christians and this year it was especially so for twelve people from Durham, when the celebrations assumed an additional dimension because they were able to worship, rejoice and celebrate with their fellow Christians in Lesotho. The two-week exchange visit brought Christians from both dioceses face-to-face for a second time in an active programme of events that included amongst its many highlights a meeting on Easter Day, Sunday, 3rd April, with the Prime Minister, none other than Ntsu Mokhehle. I introduced the Durham Dozen in pairs, after which he spent two hours with the group talking about Lesotho, the LINK and its work which he said he hoped would continue, 'as so many come and go'! One other person there was Monyane Moleleki, who explained to the prime minister the agreement he and I had reached about using the Maqalika Dam. Referring to the Lesotho Highland Water Project that the visitors had explored the previous week Ntsu responded by emphasising that 'there will be many more lakes in the future'. Concerned at the sudden introduction to vast stretches of open water many Basotho were to experience, the prime minister remarked how important it was for people to develop 'water awareness'[36] to which the LINK would make a significant contribution some years hence.

Not many visitors to a foreign country get to meet its king and his father, its prime minister and a minister of state and to lunch with their own country's High Commissioner all within a couple of weeks but the Durham Dozen accomplished all of that whilst living closely with their fellow Christians.[37] Perhaps we were, slowly, becoming 'One Body in Christ'; 'them' and 'us' were, gradually, becoming 'we'.

Amazing what results from a visit to Bethlehem!

Strange as it may seem to 'us' and 'them' we are, at the beginning of the twenty-first century, politically quite similar. That has not always been the case for when the LINK started in May 1986, Margaret Thatcher had been democratically elected seven years previously and was firmly established in 10 Downing Street. By then Lesotho had been through twenty-one years of political upheaval under the short civilian leadership of the first prime minister, Sekhonyana Maseribane, followed by Leabua Jonathan who suspended the constitution. Even so Lesotho was effectively being governed by a Military Council under the chairmanship of General Justin Lekhanya. However, all that changed in April 1993, by which time Ntsu Mokhehle had returned from Bethlehem to lead the Basotho Congress Party to victory in a general election. Democracy now superseded dictatorship and except for a period of four weeks in 1994, Ntsu Mokhehle held the post of prime minister until May 1998, when a general election returned the newly formed Lesotho Congress for Democracy under the leadership of Pakalitha Mosisili, who became prime minister.

Using a mixture of 'first past the post' and proportional representation his party was re-elected in February 2007 for a further five years and so Gordon Brown in the north had to seek re-election before his opposite number in the south. In both parliaments in which they serve, with Lesotho roughly one-third the size of Westminster, there is a lower and upper house with Lesotho closely following the Westminster model; although debates in local ward meetings in Lesotho (known as *lipitso*)[38] tend to be less confrontational and more consensual than similar discussions in local council meetings in Durham. With equally turbulent histories behind both 'them' and 'us' both groups now live within democracies under constitutional monarchs.

Within both democracies the provision of an effective educational system has always been of fundamental importance. Unlike Durham, in the twenty-first century it is the churches in Lesotho that still provide the majority of school buildings and have done so since the arrival of the first missionaries from France in 1833. Some forty years after that event the Church in Durham was gradually being displaced as the State took over responsibility for public education in 1870, leaving the Anglican Church in Durham accountable, in 2009, for just 61 schools, of which 56 are primary and 5 secondary.[39] This is a small contribution compared to that of the Anglican Diocese of Lesotho with its responsibility for 173 primary and 37 post-primary schools.[40] The large-scale investment in education by all the Lesotho churches, for whatever reason, can best be assessed by the total of 1,295 primary schools in the country that cater for some 433,000 children who attend these schools, of which only 59 are provided by the State. Education in Lesotho is a large, if not the largest, cooperative endeavour between Church and State with 'the education budget remain(ing) the highest of all ministries and is set to grow over the next three years'.[41]

In the northern part of the LINK education vies with defence and health for this pinnacle position whilst much further south the increasing emphasis on the State's contribution to education in Lesotho follows, albeit involuntarily, the evolutionary pattern of the English education system of the late 1800s. The State is now paying teaching staff salaries, covering the cost of school textbooks and financing school meals for those pupils in classes that qualify under the yearly introduction of so-called free primary education. Nevertheless, there are serious educational and social problems.

Because young boys were often engaged in looking after cattle it was girls that benefited mostly from primary education in Lesotho whereas in Durham there is no such distinction. When boys are released from their herding duties by younger siblings it is not unusual to have teenage boys in infant school classes, especially in rural mountainous areas. As a result the learning and social problems accompanying this pattern of working were considerable and would be completely alien to Durham. The new millennium, with the introduction of non-contributory education and a free midday meal, has brought an improvement in the provision, if not the quality, of education in Lesotho.

It usually comes as a huge surprise to most people, certainly to the Basotho, that there is no compulsion in England, and therefore in Durham, for a child to go to school. Whereas education is compulsory in

England, sending a child to school to be educated is not, if the child's parents or guardians can demonstrate to the local education authority that adequate education is being provided. Not so in Lesotho, where it is compulsory to send a child to school; although there is little capability to enforce it as the enrolment rate of 61 per cent in 1999 showed.

All teachers in Durham's schools hold fully qualified status and most are assisted in their classrooms by teaching auxiliaries, but the professional environment in Lesotho is very different. Recent research indicates that class sizes there are large, with little or no improvement having taken place over the past thirty or forty years. In the first class that I attempted to teach in Lesotho in 1973 there were 75 children seated on the floor and in subsequent years I was to teach even larger numbers in one class. The pupil–teacher ratio in some classes, particularly those for younger children can, even now, be as high as 100:1, improving to 40:1 in later school years, whereas in Durham it is illegal to exceed 30:1 in infant schools and is rarely higher in classes for older children. Although the Church has, over many years, provided school buildings, what goes on inside them in both regions is the responsibility of the State. At that point there are also some stark differences. [42]

Unqualified teachers in Lesotho, and even some qualified ones, confronted with large numbers of children in one class with few, if any, teaching materials and aids, do whatever they can to maintain law and order in a heroic attempt to preserve a calm learning environment. In whatever country of the world this scenario occurs (and it is, regrettably, the majority of countries) it inevitably leads to a didactic form of teaching and an emphasis on rote repetition to the detriment of understanding, conceptual formation and creative thinking. Unfortunately, this mode of teaching does sometimes occur in Durham schools, where qualified teachers do not have to contend with the overwhelmingly poor conditions that exist in schools in Lesotho. It is not surprising that those candidates for places in either of the two universities in Durham, or the two universities in Lesotho, who have received this type of teaching find they are in serious difficulties in their first year of higher education. So, whilst 'them' and 'us' approve of education the differences between south and north are considerable, as are those in the provision of health care.

In recognising the importance of a nation's health, democratic societies tend to give high priority to the provision of health care but for a poor country like Lesotho, this precedence can impose a huge financial and medical burden that is considerably easier for Durham to bear. For Christians, tending those who are ill is an essential element of their life, as on many occasions they are invoked to care for and heal the sick.[43] To obey that command in the hostile medical environment of Lesotho is far more demanding than in the relative tranquillity of health provision in the United Kingdom; and, therefore, in Durham. Measuring the provision and quality of overall health care the World Health Organisation ranks the UK eighteenth compared to Lesotho's position at 183 out of the 190 countries listed. Whilst exercising caution about applying too much credibility to what might be, to some extent, deceptive data they are sufficiently reliable for our purposes, given the huge disparity they show, to justify the observation that the health care in Durham is vastly superior to that in Lesotho. During the first six years of the new millennium the total expenditure on health care as a percentage of GDP has shown, in the UK, a gradual increase from 7.2 per cent to 8.2 per cent, whereas that for Lesotho has declined from 6.2 per cent to 5.6 per cent[44] at a time when demand is rapidly increasing amongst the population.

Given these data it is not surprising to discover that the life expectancy of a baby boy born in Durham at the beginning of the new millennium was 69.7 years but, were he to be born in Lesotho, it is most likely that he would live for only 36.6 years. For his sister the comparative age span, according to the World Health Organisation, would be 73.7 years in Durham and 37.2 years in Lesotho.[45] Once again it is wise not to give too much credence to the actual figures but simply to recognise the wide disparity they demonstrate. Furthermore, in a population of about 2,000,000 Basotho, some 270,000 (13.5 per cent)[46] of people are infected with HIV/AIDS compared to only 77,400 (0.2 per cent)[47] of the adult population in the UK and, by extrapolation, also in Durham. Therefore, a woman born in Durham can expect to live over thirty-six years longer than her counterpart in Lesotho whereas the life of a man born in Lesotho is likely to be about thirty-three years less than his opposite number in Durham. This almost certainly understates the actual inequality of existing age disparities between Lesotho and Durham, where Highly Active Antiretroviral Therapy is available. In a society where the old are almost totally dependent upon the young during their advancing years premature death, with its consequent reduction in lifespan, is particularly challenging in Lesotho. Whichever 'health' scales we study the same picture emerges each time and the conclusion cannot be avoided that the differences between 'them' and 'us' in the provision of health care is enormous.

The disparities are destined to become larger as Durham sees new hospitals springing up all over the county and diocese whereas Lesotho, after years of waiting, is only now planning to replace its major hospital in Maseru. Furthermore, Lesotho finds acute difficulty in funding the recurrent expenditure necessary to run those hospitals and clinics that are already established. The hub of all medical care in Lesotho, the Queen Elizabeth II Hospital in Maseru known informally, perhaps even affectionately, as Queen Two, is to be replaced with a new national 390-bed hospital that should open its doors in 2011 on the site of the old Botšabelo Leprosy Hospital. However, we must not linger, so without ignoring the huge problems of health care that exist in our respective regions, we must now leave Queen Two, turn left to walk half a mile or so (1.5 kms) along Kingsway towards the Maseru Bridge Border Post and there study an interesting connection between Lesotho and Durham.

The 15 miles (25 kms) of single track railway line branching off from the main line at Marseilles, South Africa, wends its way, with only one sharp bend, fairly directly towards the border post to cross the Caledon, Mohokare or Phuthi River (when will it decide what its name should be?)[48] by the Maseru Bridge. Here, it enters Lesotho for a further 2 miles (3 kms) or so before stopping in the Maseru West Industrial Estate at Lesotho's only railway station. From there it connects to nowhere except historically, by passing through the inventive mind of George Stephenson, to Durham where the first steam locomotive, *The Rocket*, that he is accredited with inventing, took its first cargo from the Durham town of Darlington all of 11 miles (18 kms) to Stockton on Tuesday, 27th September 1825. Missing the anniversary by only two days, the first steam locomotive entered Lesotho eighty years later on Monday, 25th September 1905.

This was a memorable year of double significance as it also witnessed the arrival in the Diocese of Bloemfontein (of which Lesotho was then part) of the Rev'd Philip de Lande Falkner. Two years earlier Philip Falkner had been ordained priest in Durham Cathedral after serving a year as curate in St. John's Church, Hebburn, County Durham. He went on to serve in seven churches in the dioceses of Bloemfontein and Johannesburg before going to Quthing, Lesotho, in 1927. He stayed there for only two years before returning to Bloemfontein where he worked for the next six years but the attractions of Lesotho were strong and he went back in 1935 to work in Leribe and Tsikoane which he left in 1948 as his ministry drew to a close. This was, perhaps, the first substantial contribution Durham made to Lesotho.[49]

There is no evidence Philip Falkner was on that first train that, having reached Maseru, found the only place to which it could now go was back to Marseilles; there was no other track then as there is no other track now over 100 years later. Meanwhile, as people in Durham benefited from its strategic location on the direct main line route that had been laid from London to Scotland, the Basotho were travelling in their mountain kingdom, even in the flat lowlands, on foot or horseback until, and even after, the arrival of the internal combustion engine some time, by deduction, between 1905 and 1912.[50] Traffic congestion is now a serious problem in Maseru as it can be in Durham city.

It has taken a long time since then for an adequate road system to be developed in Lesotho and there was no large-scale improvement until the Lesotho Highlands Water Project required high-quality roads in order to transport heavy engineering equipment to the Katse Dam site. Even so travel across the whole country demonstrates the large disparity existing between the two regions in the provision of surfaced roads particularly as Durham, thanks to its generous support by successive Labour Party governments, has benefited from one of the most advanced road networks in the United Kingdom. This superior provision of roads has led to much safer road travel in Durham than Lesotho, which has to contend with the severe difficulties the rugged mountain terrain imposes upon transport development. Nevertheless, for those that can afford to fly, Lesotho has compensating travel advantages with its network of local airstrips of varying degrees of smoothness that connect many of the major towns with the capital and its airport, Moshoeshoe II. From there it is just one hour's flying time to Johannesburg to connect with international flights around the world. Unlike Lesotho, Durham has no airport or public airstrips of its own; although there are two major airports within easy reach and by lending its name to one of them, Durham seems to claim a right to its services. In whichever way the transport of the two regions is analysed the principal method of travel is muscular in Lesotho and mechanical in Durham.

Since the beginning of time snow and rain falling in the mountains of Lesotho have been running off into the Senqu, Senqunyane, Malibamatšo and Matsoku rivers to flow out of the country, taking with it precious fertile topsoil, crossing the continent to go straight out into the Atlantic Ocean. The Basotho were letting their one recurring natural resource drain through the fingers of their country to escape capture when it could have provided an essential reserve of life-giving water. In 1986 (it really was a momentous year), all that came to an end with the signing of a treaty with the Republic of South Africa. After a three-year feasibility study undertaken in the mid-1980s the time had come to make the first scar in the soil of Lesotho to start the Lesotho Highlands Water Project, which was to make a dramatic change to the landscape of Lesotho and promote, unconsciously, an affinity with the northern part of the LINK. The first reservoirs of this enormous project, the Katse and Mohale dams, were not the first to be built in Lesotho but they were the first of any substantial size and also the first to incorporate the generation of hydroelectric power. Stark difference was turning into welcomed similarity: both 'them' and 'us' were conserving water. In the north, Durham had twelve large reservoirs developed in the fells between the years 1894 and 1967, not only providing essential storage for large quantities of water, but also making available welcome space for the leisure activities of many people and natural habitats for wildlife conservation.

On a bright, chilly morning during Durham's visit to Lesotho, twelve people (who had come to be known as the Durham Dozen) stood rather self-consciously in unfamiliar protective headgear at the base of the 607 foot (185 m) Katse Dam, gazing up in amazement at the semicircular concrete wall almost three times the height of Durham Cathedral's 217 foot (66 m) central tower! That was to be just one of many visits people associated with the LINK were to make to Katse. The first was when I accepted an invitation from the minister for the Lesotho Highlands Water Project, Mohomane Lebotsa, finding myself once again at Makhoabeng, this time for the official opening of the Katse Bridge on Friday, 9th December 1988. As a different sort of minister, Mohomane was a self-supporting priest of the Anglican Church so the LINK had an early personal contact with this international development. Some years later the LINK provided training in water skills for those who lived around the site of the dam.[51]

But now, on Tuesday, 29th March 1994, the Durham Dozen had their concept of 'reservoir' and 'dam' enlarged as they tried to imagine the beautiful Malibamatso Valley, along which I had ridden on horseback in April 1986 to spread the news of the LINK. Now it was being flooded, much to the anguish of those whose homes would be lost. Even more distressing to the Basotho was the submerging of their ancestors' graves.[52] The sheer scale of the physical development, the largest engineering project in the southern hemisphere of the world, was of little consequence compared to the scale of the accompanying torment and emotional misery. If we were to be One Body in Christ, even out here in the most remote and isolated regions of Lesotho, we all had to share in the misery as well as the joy. What we have in common is not only reservoirs, water and waterfalls, but also joy and misery. At High Force in Durham, the largest waterfall in England plunges 69 feet (21 m), but that is a mere trickle compared to the highest waterfall in southern Africa at Semonkong, Lesotho. This spectacular cascade is sometimes named after a French missionary, as Le Bihan Falls. It drops vertically almost ten times further than High Force, plunging 643 feet (196 m) into the Maletsunyane River.

How 'us' and 'them' were to be made into 'we' was a subject of much informal discussion between both us and them, both here and there. I had often wondered how these two diverse groups of people could be brought together but, of course, it was not a question of bringing two groups together or, for that matter, who was to do it. They were not to be just 'one body' but they were to be One Body in Christ. Christ was to be the unifying power. The common bond of being in, with and for Christ would make these diverse people 'one' and I now saw my role as providing the joint activities that would assist them to become one. We, 'them' and 'us', used the same handbook albeit in different languages, Bible or Bibele, but containing the same message by using the same concepts. As the hyphen in the Durham-Lesotho LINK, it was my responsibility to translate the message contained in the handbook into practices that would enable them, however dissimilar they were, to become one. The weft and warp by lying in different directions give an underlying, disguised strength to the beautiful tapestries made by Helang Basali, the women's cooperative in Teyateyaneng, so that the variety of other qualities can display the creative beauty of the coloured mohair and demonstrate the skills and dedication of the weavers. Lesotho and Durham were the weft and warp of the LINK. Woven together they could display a strong Christian witness.

To enable all that to happen I knew I had to bring both peoples together physically in a common activity. Words of good intent from their ecclesiastical representatives could not do that but people meeting and living with each other could. Having successfully used the idea of youth exchange visits there was little reason why something similar should not be equally successful with adults.[53] So, after much preparation, Durham welcomed twelve Basotho in August 1993 for a two-week visit that was described by one Mosotho:

> ... it took less than ten minutes from arrival in Durham to meet our hosts ... On the two Sundays (we) were given the chance to talk about the Church and life in Lesotho ... We were struck by the cleanliness of all public places ... and the abundant farmland ... church bell-ringers had prepared a welcome peel (*sic*) for us ... The climax of the visit was when the Basotho presented the banner from Lesotho to Durham Cathedral and the LINK's song, *We are One Body in Christ, One in Word and Work,* was sung jointly ... We invite those who hosted Basotho ... to come during Easter 1994. Our reason is that the people of Lesotho loved the people of Durham because of the great things they have done ... Now they love them more because they saw the words of the song are true when they shared in the One Body and Blood of Christ during the Holy Communion.[54]

So it was that seven months later, twelve Dunelmians journeyed to Lesotho to become the guests of those Basotho they had welcomed into their homes the previous year. One comment summed up this remarkable coming together: 'The abiding impression is the love that has been extended to us unstintingly by our brothers and sisters in Christ here in Lesotho'.[55] That sentiment was also expressed by another member of the Durham Dozen when describing their visit:

> The Basotho are generous in material things but also in their spiritual awareness. Links and friendships were made that will not be forgotten because we met real people who are living out their faith on a daily basis in a very natural and committed way ... It's not an idyllic place and many live at the raw edge of life, yet they have this enormous capacity to recognise their place in creation and constantly praise God for everything, taking nothing for granted ... Lesotho is part of us now ... our visit ... affected us enormously.[56]

The LINK was slowly changing 'us' and 'them' and, to the Devil's consternation, 'we' were gradually becoming just that, as One Body in Christ'. 'Us' and 'them', with all our individual differences, were brought together in exchange visits that showed more clearly than any other element that the LINK was a living organism within the jungle of life's conflicting demands.

It is now time for us to explore that jungle.

---

1 Timothy 2:1(GNB).

2. Berners-Lee, Timothy and Fischetti, Mark, *Weaving the Web: The Past, Present and Future* (UK: Orion Business, 1999).

3. Dr Arno Peters of the University of Bremen, 1973. Sometimes referred to as the Gall-Peters projection. It is claimed this projection gives a more accurate rendition proportional to the land surfaces of countries of the world (1973).

4. Astley, Jeff and Green, Peter, *One in Word and Work* (The Durham-Lesotho LINK, 1992) p. 13.

5. The story of Mary and Martha in Luke 10;38–42 (NIV).

6. *Philips' Modern School Atlas* that can be found in many African schools (London: George Philip & Son Ltd., 1950) edition 41.

7. Thaba in Sesotho is mountain in English (pronounced: tar-ba).

8. Thabelo in Sesotho is a girl's name (pronounced: tar – bay – lo).

9. A report by the Chief Executive, Durham County Council, The Future Population of County Durham (2005).

10. *Whitaker's Almanack* (London: A & C Black, 2006) p. 905.

11. 'Black diamonds' describes the coal that was extensively mined in Durham until the 1970s.

12. After Chapter Three was written Reuters News Agency announced on Tuesday, 2nd November 2010 that two more large diamonds had been discovered at the Letšeng mine. In August of that year a diamond weighing 196 carats was found and two months later one of 185 carats was discovered. They were sold in Antwerp by tender for a total of US$22.7 million (approximately 15 million Great Britain Pounds) to the South African Diamond Corporation. See <www.reuters.com>.
13. I was invited to visit the Geduld Gold Mine, Welkom, where, on Thursday, 15th August 1974, I went below ground with a mining team to the 4,200 foot (1,280 m) level on my way back to Durham from Lesotho.
14. See website <www.auckland-castle.co.uk/park.asp>.
15. Bates, Stephen, *The Guardian*, Monday, 27th May 2002.
16. Census in England and Wales, 29th April 2001. Office of National Statistics, 2001.
17. Mabille, A. and Dieterlen, H., *Southern Sotho-English Dictionary* (Lesotho: Morija Sesuto Book Depot, 1974) p. 366.
18. Haliburton, Gordon, *Historical Dictionary of Lesotho*, African Historical Dictionaries No. 10 (Metuchen, USA: The Scarecrow Press, Inc. 1977) p. 164.
19. Ambrose, David, *Summary of Events in Lesotho* Vol. 15, No. 3. Third Quarter (2008) p. 14.
20. Acts 2:7–8: Utterly amazed, they asked, 'Are not all these men who are speaking Galileans? Then how is it that each of us hears them in his own native language?'
21. *Missa Litšebeletso tsa Hoseng le Mantsiboea* (E.L.D. Trust, 1975) Sesotho edition. Reprinted 1977.
22. *The Holy Eucharist Morning & Evening Prayer* (Church of the Province of South Africa, 1975) (English edn. Third impression 1975).
23. See Chapter Seven: Sing a New Song (p. 187).
24. Dove, Reginald, *Anglican Pioneers in Lesotho* (n.p., c.1975).
25. Gross Domestic Product. (World Bank, 2007).
26. *County Durham Economic Strategy 2008–2013* (County Durham Economic Partnership, 2008).
27. King Letsie III from 7th February 1996 to present date (previously, King Moshoeshoe II from 12th November 1990 to 25th January 1995).
28. Queen Elizabeth II from 6th February 1952 to present date.
29. Moshoeshoe I (pronounced, Mo – swaysh – way).
30. Becker, Peter, *Hill of Destiny: the life and times of Moshesh, founder of the Basotho* (London: Longman Group, 1969) p. 275.
31. On Tuesday, 1st March 2011 the British Coalition government took another unpalatable decision when it announced that by 2016 Britain would stop providing bilateral aid to Lesotho although it would continue its aid support of South Africa!
32. Lesotho's first prime minister, for two months, was Sekhonyana 'Maseribane, who was followed by Leabua Jonathan who held office for nearly twenty-one years from Wednesday, 7th July 1965 to Monday, 20th January 1986.
33. Moleleki, Monyane, *Pale ea Bophelo ba NTSU* (Lesotho, Morija Printing Works, 1994) p. xxiv.

34. Green, Peter, 'Personal Daily Journal' (Monday, 26th April 1993).
35. Baker, Paul, *Fr. Thaele Mokhehle in Jarrow 'MOHO – Together*, No. 7 (November 1993) p. 6.
36. Green, Peter, Ibid. (Sunday, 3rd April 1994).
37. Durham Dozen's Visit, Easter 1994. An anonymous review of this visit can be found in *'MOHO – Together*, No. 8 (May 1994) p. 3.
38. In the plural (dee – *peet* – so) and in the singular (*peet* – so). A meeting of all residents in a village, called by the Chief, to discuss important matters affecting members of the community and at which the aim is to reach consensus.
39. Information from Durham Diocesan Schools Officer, Kate Martin, February 2009.
40. Information from Diocese of Lesotho Education Office, 15th April 2009.
41. Kingdom of Lesotho Government, *Poverty Reduction Strategy 2004–2005 to 2006–2007*, Chapter 9: Improve Quality & Access to Education (p. 76). Full text can be found on website http://www.lesotho.gov.ls.
42. For additional examples of the differences between educational provision see Chapter Nine: Ha Mohatlane (p. 239).
43. Matthew 10:8 (NIV): Heal the sick, raise the dead, cleanse those who have leprosy, drive out demons. Freely you have received, freely give.
44. World Health Organisation: Statistical Information System 2000 to 2005.
45. World Health Organisation: Disability-adjusted life expectancy at birth, 1999.
46. Joint United Nations Programme on HIV/AIDS 2008.
47. UNAIDS – UK. United Nations (2006) p.476.
48. Ambrose, David, *Summary of Events in Lesotho*, Vol. 15, No. 3: (Third Quarter, 2008) p. 5, provides a detailed account of the historical background to these three names.
49. *Crockford's Clerical Directory 1963–64*, p.390. I acknowledge with thanks the assistance of Liz Moody, Archive Assistant at the Lambeth Palace Library, for her valuable help in researching this information.
50. In personal correspondence dated 10th April 2010, Professor David Ambrose relates an oral tradition that a car was imported over the railway bridge (therefore after 1905) by trader George Hobson (after whom Hobson Square is named). There is some evidence that paramount Chief Griffith (c.1871–1939) had a car in 1912 so the first one seems to have arrived in Lesotho some time during those two dates.
51. See Chapter Eleven: Yap! Yap! Yap! (p. 317).
52. Matli, Moeketsi Boniface, *The Social Impacts of a Large Development Project – Lesotho Highlands Water Project*, M.Sc. thesis, University of Free State, 2005.
53. Chapter Eleven: Yap! Yap! Yap! (p. 317).
54. Tseko, Florence, *Adult Exchange '93 – A Great Success 'MOHO – Together, No. 7* (November 1993) p. 2.
55. Durham Dozen's Visit, Easter 1994. An anonymous review of this visit can be found in *'MOHO – Together*, No. 8 (May 1994) p. 3.
56. Francis, Pat, *Durham Dozen get to Work 'MOHO – Together, No. 9* (November 1994) p. 4.

Chapter Four

In the Jungle

In the desert prepare
the way for the LORD,
make straight in the wilderness
a highway for our God.[1]

The wilderness of any jungle is dangerous: this one especially so. You enter at your peril. The interior is murky, the shadows are dense, the way ahead is gloomy and the path, if there is one, is unclear. There are many sidetracks leading nowhere. Camouflaged dangers hide in the undergrowth waiting to pounce, bite or constrict and the tenderfoot explorer may be innocently walking into their clutch. Unseen hazards threaten those pioneers who recklessly ignore their invisible presence as the intrepid peer intensely through, round and over dense foliage lit only by the occasional shaft of sunlight piercing the forest treetops. The humid jungle atmosphere reduces the adventurer into insignificance as small, concealed dangers, either imagined or real, exert their quiet influence and take their toll with bite after infectious bite. Much safer to relax with a good book under the cooling shade of a wide-topped tree whilst I write this for the record rather than for the reading: 'Well, yes: come if you must, but stay close; it is all too easy to get lost in the mist, and the mysteries, of the jungle into which we now must venture'.

Jungles contain many species of flora and fauna, each contributing to what appears, at first sight, to be an organic mess. It was this almost impenetrable confusion that the LINK ventured into; it could not be avoided as the jungle is, after all, part of God's living world not to be ignored by Christians. We could not stand on the outside looking in: to be effective we had to get inside. The separate elements of the jungle are all parts of the living whole, reacting, rejuvenating, renewing and reviving, constantly changing and dramatically illustrative of a social organism. If the LINK were to be an efficient agent of change and an integral part of that process in Lesotho and Durham then it, too, had to be a lively organism able to adapt within a constantly changing environment. However unadventurous and tedious, compared to exploring the mountains of Lesotho on horseback and the fells of Durham on foot, careful thought had to be given to the coordination of the various parts of the LINK. How did they all fit together within, and between, the two regions? As we struggle through the jungle how fortunate we are that 'God did not give us a spirit of timidity, but a spirit of power, of love and of self-discipline',[2] for we shall certainly need all three.

Organisation and administration, depending upon its nature, can have one of two contrary effects. On the one hand there is the system that can encourage freedom within which to be creative by allowing autonomy to generate new ideas, release energetic activity and build collective confidence. Conversely, a different form of organisation and its administration can impose a restrictive style that inhibits, regulates and controls, producing uncertain, qualified, moribund reactions lacking creative thinking or imaginative action. Even though the organisational structure of the LINK evolved from the harsh realities of necessity it proved, as we had hoped, to be a system that promoted active participation by scores of people. The diocese of Durham needed to respond urgently to critical appraisal of its missionary apathy and the diocese of Lesotho wanted the Church to engage energetically in local development activities.

When I started the LINK I had the benefit of many years of extensive exploration in both dioceses but I had no preconceived notion of what the organisation could, or should, be. I had to cultivate, out of a virgin jungle of personalities, talents, characteristics, motives, abilities and desires, not just an organisation but, more importantly, a vigorous activity that, at its beginning, had no common structure. Even though others had tried to penetrate the tangled vegetation of the jungle none had ventured very deeply; the soil was untrodden; where were the bogs, where were the cliffs, where were the swamps? If I were to survive within the dense, tangled morass of two Anglican dioceses it would be wise, before I started exploring, so I argued with myself, to follow Hadfield's[3] dictum 'to know myself, to accept myself and to be myself'! Working in an unpaid, voluntary capacity and providing all the equipment necessary for jungle exploration following Hadfield's advice was comparatively easy, especially as those who were supporting me knew my strengths and weaknesses.

In various roles I had often spoken about three generally accepted broad concepts of leadership style, to which I now had to add a fourth. As

I was by this time deep in the jungle morass I had to move rapidly from the theoretical to the explicitly practical. To guide others through one organisational and administrative jungle was an intimidating prospect but to take them through two jungles lying 6,000 miles (9,655 kms) apart was daunting. I thought I knew myself, I attempted to be myself and tried, not always successfully, to accept myself but when on those occasions I wavered from those standards my wife, family and friends told me so. The question I had to address early in the life of the LINK was what form of leadership would sustain others in, and take them safely through, the jungle? I knew that for the LINK, and for me, a laissez-faire type of leadership was a non-starter so that left authoritarian, democratic and, because of Basotho cultural pressures, consensus techniques. Years had already been spent within the diocese of Durham democratically considering what to do, whether to do it, when to do it, where to do it and how to do it, that to engage in further time-consuming, fully democratic leadership would, I thought, be unacceptable and devilishly tempt those elements that were waiting to destroy intruders.

That was at one end of the leadership continuum. At the other end was the consensus style that took perhaps longer than any other form to make its decisions, resulting in a slowness that would allow jungle predators to swoop, leap or, even, land silently for the kill before an escape route or adequate protection had been established. Its intrinsic weakness is that within a hierarchical structure, such as the Anglican Church, it disguises a rigid authoritarian stance exercised by the most dominantly powerful voices.

A licensed Reader, more appropriately and unmistakably described as a lay minister, is in a fortunate position as he or she moves around a diocese taking services, preaching and listening. Within any jungle listening is particularly important and where there is a cavernous gap between the laity and the clerical the Reader, being a bit of each, can often bridge the ravine. It is an advantage to be able to talk and listen to people in a diocese and I sensed from many conversations, in both Lesotho and Durham, that there was an eagerness amongst people for positive leadership that would organise and cultivate the jungle, perhaps even prune and pollard it, in preparation for productive mission. So it was that for the first couple of years the LINK flourished under a mildly authoritarian mode of leadership but, conscious of dangers lurking in the undergrowth when leading in that manner, it was a style modified by regular discussions with Philip Mokuku and other advisers in Lesotho.[4]

In Durham I frequently sat in the heat and humidity of the jungle with the four clergymen[5] who had first considered the mission needs of Durham diocese. They, with three laypeople,[6] acted as my 'support group', to which I could refer and to which I could look for guidance, prayer and gentle criticism. They formed a strong and reliable base camp within which challenges could be explored and addressed. But as we progressed deeper into the bewildering complexity of the jungle, it became obvious that I needed someone in Durham to assist me in carrying the burden of administration. During the first couple of years my wife, Pam, had given many hours of family time to the LINK but with ever-increasing demands on her time and energies that could not continue, so when Richard Briggs, who had been closely involved with the community woodland project, volunteered to assist me I welcomed his generous offer with open arms. Response times were becoming shorter, new initiatives developing and demands on me increasing and it was Richard's back-room work that made it possible to react positively. Thereafter, with a 'right-hand man' in Durham, administration and organisation became much more manageable and efficient.

Having decided on the objective (to be One Body in Christ), directed the aim (Lesotho and Durham) and progressed the activity (One in Word and Work), we now had to decide on an organisational structure within which the mass of volunteers we had attracted could best undertake the tasks that would achieve the objective. For this purpose I thought in terms of a series of working parties, each with its own chairperson, secretary and treasurer and each group sufficiently flexible to be expanded or contracted, or even closed, when its specific task changed or was completed. Although numbers varied according to the demands of the work programme there were, by the end of the fourth year of the LINK, eleven working parties in Durham (plus the support group) involving over seventy people. There were working parties for banners, books, containers, development (dealing with large projects), education, hospitality, medical, publicity, teachers, tools and woodlands.

Membership was, to some extent, self-selecting according to people's interests. The response to our prayers, appeals and personal approaches was almost overwhelming: we had an embarrassment of riches from people wanting to make their own contribution to this new missionary activity. People were beginning to feel involved not just through the use of their cheque books but also through their work and that drew them into a jungle of activity. It proved to be a very effective system with which people could quickly and conveniently identify according to their particular interests and, perhaps even more importantly, an arrangement within which they could genuinely avoid other activities in which they were not particularly interested.

The undoubted success of the organisation in Durham enticed us to try to graft this structure into the jungle of Lesotho but that was too simplistic. Although there was a succession of support groups in Lesotho none, in the early years, was particularly effective. Why should the tough life of most Basotho be made even tougher by trying to support an activity that was taking place hundreds of miles away, round three or four mountain ranges and in a subculture, determined largely by altitude, about which they knew little and perhaps even disapproved? At that time, but less so in later years, there seemed to be a tacit acceptance in Basotho society of the authoritarian personality that was probably a cultural inheritance embodied in the power and position of the regional chief.

Another influential factor in Lesotho, that generally worked in favour of the LINK and made the structure adopted in Durham inappropriate, was the minimal reliance they placed on formal groupings. As we were to experience in later years scores of Basotho would come together to engage in a specific task, demonstrating that in Lesotho there was a much closer relationship between those working for a project. The project would, unlike the Durham scene, become a major factor in their lives. Decisions were often made at meals and at the village *pitso* (a meeting under the chairmanship of the Chief); there was less reliance upon formal groups than in Durham. Whatever the reason, the organisational structure established in Durham was clearly unsuitable for Lesotho and whilst no separate working parties were formed, local specialist groups, according to the needs of the project, were established. If you were a member of a local project group you didn't have to travel far to meetings, you knew the location and the people intimately and, more importantly, you could talk to the Chief about the project. The Chief's close knowledge of the area and its needs was particularly helpful in our detailed exploration of his region. We lost few men or women in the jungle as once they became enthusiastic, they tended to stay with the groundbreaking pioneers. This system operated well but it needed close contact with the Lesotho base camp so I was pleased to be co-opted on to the Lesotho Diocesan Council as that gave the LINK an important point of reference within the country. Two widely spaced arenas; two widely different organisations; one target.

Back in Durham, for the first couple of years of the LINK's existence it operated as a 'freelance' group of people of many different religious denominations.[7] Both Anglican bishops received short annual written reports but the organisation was not part of the official diocesan structure, in either Lesotho or Durham. Working as an unpaid volunteer gave me a degree of autonomy modified by a freely accepted responsibility to my family, my bishops and myself. Although that degree of independence was useful, indeed perhaps even essential as we entered the tangle of the jungle, it became a difficulty when negotiations with official bodies such as the European Union and British government development agencies came on to our agenda. We could see reasonably clearly through the jungle in which we were now operating but, understandably, those agencies wanted to distinguish the snags and dangers that might be lurking deep in the dense flora of our semi-structured existence. In 1988, when I was under considerable, and unexpected, pressure from the European Union delegate[8] in Maseru to establish a school feeding project, it was necessary to provide the authorities in Brussels with a registered charity number that we did not then have.

In Durham I saw what I thought would be a short-term emergency solution to this problem. By providing the European Union with the registered charity number of the Durham Diocesan Board of Finance, any money that might be granted by Europe could be sent to us through them. Oh dear! How naïve I was! It took hours of telephoning, talking, discussing and negotiating before I was allowed to see, let alone use, the all-important charity number and only then after episcopal intervention! Knowing that the rolling five-year programme we had drafted would require the raising of hundreds of thousands of pounds from the European Union and what was then the Overseas Development Administration of the British Government (ODA), it was obvious that this piece of Durham jungle had to be cleared of the deadly species *diocesus magnus dilatorius.* Immediately after this experience (that almost lost us £100,000 and nearly deprived hundreds of children of hundreds of meals) we set into motion steps to become a separate legally registered charity.

In a remarkably short space of time for this exercise the LINK was registered as an independent, self-regulating, autonomous charity with its own board of trustees.[9] Our legal status was now quite clear: we were responsible solely to the Charity Commissioners of England and Wales. The LINK is not, as some assume, an integral part of either the diocese of Lesotho or of Durham but is a registered charity working for both dioceses under its own legal constitution. Clearing away that much of the jungle scrub made it considerably easier to negotiate with other bodies; it also gave us more freedom but with that freedom came more responsibility.

That patch of jungle in which we operated in the north-east of England is lit by many shafts of brilliant sunlight piercing through the dense forest and illuminating many a small mission enterprise supported by parish churches. From the very outset of the LINK's operations it was made crystal clear that this new development should in no way inhibit any established mission support of parish churches. Of course, there was no way in which we could control the support that was forthcoming and, over the past twenty-five years, we have been very grateful for the wonderfully generous giving that we have received but, as David Jenkins once said, 'people will give to whatever they are attracted and want to give'. The Durham-Lesotho LINK was there for any one congregation, or any one person, to support if they so wished. We hoped that it might be of use to small church congregations who wanted a close personal contact with missionary work but had no such contacts. Inevitably the success of the LINK prompted its critics to ambush and bite us as they emerged from concealment in the undergrowth.

A representative of one long-established missionary society expressed grave concern that money was being redirected to the LINK and asked us to accept only 'new money' but failed to advise us on how we were to distinguish what was 'new money'. Some months later when in Lesotho I asked a representative of the same society what was the purpose of his ten-day presence in the country, to be told that he was 'just visiting'. At the time I did wonder how well 'old money' was being used! Perhaps the LINK was attracting new money for new initiatives that prompted the established societies to look to their laurels and, although for the old change is difficult, adopt new approaches to mission. There was little doubt that some people were, in the mid-1980s, disillusioned with the conventional practices of the established societies and it is interesting to observe how those societies have since changed their mission strategies.[10] Perhaps the LINK was a wake-up call to them.

By the time the Durham-Lesotho LINK ventured into the jungle other charities had already braved the climate and others were soon to follow.[11] Although not a registered charity at the time one group working solely in the UK, but specifically on behalf of the Anglican Church in Lesotho, was the Lesotho Diocesan Association which was started by the first Bishop of Lesotho, John Maund,[12] during a visit he made to the United Kingdom in 1953. The Anglican Diocese of Lesotho had been formed in July 1950 out of the huge Diocese of Bloemfontein in the Orange Free State of South Africa. However, it had been started with virtually no money in the treasury so John Maund turned to his home country for the financial support required by a new diocese with an indeterminate number of denominational adherents,[13] a nascent administration and few trained local clergy. Ever since its inception the Association has provided a financial lifeline for a diocese serving a country that has variably occupied the sixth or seventh position in the world Poverty League,[14] so it was important for the LINK to acknowledge that contribution by not competing for resources that upheld its work.

Some years before the Durham-Lesotho LINK started I had accepted an invitation to join what was then the Exccutive Committee (later to be the Charity Board of Trustees) of the Association so I was acutely aware of the possible conflict of interests that could arise between the two groups. The Rev'd Canon Cyprian Thorpe,[15] who was then Chairman of the Association, and I agreed that the Association would continue to concentrate on the direct funding of church activities and that the LINK would not encroach upon that sphere but would concentrate on development projects and programmes as originally requested by, and agreed with, Philip Mokuku. This division has worked well and where, exceptionally, there has been some deviation from the adopted position that has only been by mutual agreement between the Association and the LINK: there is no tangle in that part of the jungle. Any digression has happened in any major way only twice, both in commemoration of enthusiasts of the Association and the LINK.

In a terrible car accident on Thursday, 27th May 1999,[16] three Durham clergy were killed, one of whom, Catherine Hooper, was an active supporter of the LINK helping especially with liturgical advice and activities. Catherine's two visits to Lesotho had impressed upon her the bad housing in which some parish priests lived and her parents asked that the memorial fund established in her memory should be used to build new rectories. This was a welcome addition to the Association's programme of rebuilding rectories in which the LINK was pleased to be involved. In the other instance the Association commemorated the life of Donald Nestor[17] when it donated its substantial memorial fund to the LINK so it could expand its centre of operations on the shore of the Maqalika Dam by building an additional meeting room named the Nestor Room. Donald, who was born in Calcutta, India, went to Lesotho in 1972, served as Chaplain to the National University of Lesotho and then taught at Lelapa La Jesu, the Anglican seminary on the university campus. He was a suffragan bishop of Lesotho for twelve years and made frequent visits to Durham to promote the work of the LINK. Durham was a county in which he spent some of his childhood and to which he returned in his retirement to live with the Society of the Sacred Mission in St. Antony's Priory, the former vicarage of St. Nicholas Church and just five minutes' walk from my house.

In a video film produced for the LINK by Northumberland University that was shown to the Durham Diocesan Synod he spoke of his hopes for the development of the LINK; he preached in Durham Cathedral on the spiritual influence of the LINK and talked, with much enthusiasm around the diocese about its development work. In Lesotho he gave practical support to our work, spending many days with me trekking in the remote mountain regions using his excellent command of the language to translate for the Basotho and to interpret for me when I was stuck in a linguistic torrent of Sesotho: noise in the jungle can be deafening. The two organisations, Association and LINK, have happily walked with each other through the jungle over the past twenty-five years to the benefit of the Christian Church.

One other English-based Christian charity that was already in the jungle and with which we had discussions about the LINK's future activities was the The Basotho Educational Trust, which was founded in 1982 after a visit to Lesotho by a group of students from Imperial College, London. Distressed by the poverty they saw, they argued that education in practical skills could be a way to break the cycle of no education, no skills, no employment, no money, no education, leading into continuing poverty. This small charity raises money to fund the fees of about seventy young men and women in seven different secondary and tertiary educational establishments at a cost of approximately £15,000 each year. This enables the students to take training courses in skills such as bricklaying, catering, carpentry, computing, electronics, motor mechanics and tailoring. As this was an area of jungle the LINK did not wish to explore there has been no clash of activities.

So, we had agreed with others what patch of the jungle the LINK would survey and occupy; we had what promised to be an efficient organisational structure; we had large numbers of enthusiastic people and we knew what the task was to be but how were we going to pay for it all? In the first ten years of the LINK there were two distinctly different categories of financing: voluntary and statutory. The voluntary giving came largely from the generosity of the people of the north-east of England. We were never concerned about the funding of our large projects but we were always amazed at the unstintingly liberal giving, not just from the churches, but also from people of all ages and denominations and, indeed, none.

Despite the munificence of our hundreds of supporters we were cautious never to take the funding of projects for granted. We planned carefully, advertised widely, prayed earnestly and worked hard. We made sure people knew what their money was needed for; we asked God to guide and bless our efforts; we found a use for whatever enthusiasts had to offer so that everyone felt involved. With the exception of our biggest development, for all our other large projects (distinguished with a budget over £100,000) the working party involved had to raise 15 per cent of the total budget: no small challenge that each working party met by its target date.

The second source of financing, statutory funding from the European Union and the British government, was also extremely hard and arduous work. We knew we were in a highly competitive market that necessitated employing the same elements that we exercised for the voluntary giving: planning, publicising, praying and persevering. However, the scale was larger, the emphasis stronger, the arena totally different. The jungle was the same but the climate had changed with the season!

How did we travel from hope to reality? What was the journey like and who came with me? In most cases it was a long, arduous trek that could last for five or six years from abstract thought to physical realisation. Before setting off careful preparation was crucial. Long-term thinking and planning was essential but extremely difficult in a culture where a top-ranking official once remarked to me in the humid heat of the jungle, 'Peter, I can't possibly consider next year; it's difficult enough, when survival is at stake, to think about tomorrow!' Perhaps part of my immediate personal contribution was to undertake that type of thinking for the Basotho with whom I worked and in due time to encourage, and to show the benefit of forward-thinking and planning.

The first stage of the trek was often across some rough terrain as the idea was vigorously discussed and then carried forward to become, in the course of time, a firm suggestion. Having received a suggestion in Lesotho I would take my Sesotho voice, Steven Molokeng, with me to meet the Chief of the area where the project would be located and he would call a *pitso* so I could talk to the people and leaders within the community. Concurrently I would talk to the bishop and other diocesan workers who might be involved, such as the parish priest and congregation, and listen to advice from a large circle of people involved in development, after which the next stop was the Lesotho Diocesan Council. Once I had cleared away any undergrowth of doubt to reveal what looked like a clear path ahead we would send out a scout to test our perception of the track ahead and produce a feasibility study based on objective evidence to support enthusiasts' more subjective feelings. If the scout's report indicated that the proposal was reasonable and practicable I would talk to the British High Commissioner and his staff and also to the European delegation in Maseru.

When I reached the Durham jungle discussions would usually start with the chairperson of the working party that would be most closely involved and, for the larger project proposals, with the development group. By this time roughly calculated budgets would be available and if I felt there was sufficient support from all the separate strands I would write a first draft of the proposal. My assistant, Richard Briggs, would then take this draft and produce a second. After assessment this would become a third, a fourth and so on until we were both satisfied we had presented a clear, accurate proposal. The proposal for the Ha Mohatlane Community Education Centre went to six drafts, but we consoled ourselves by recognising that we were asking for a considerable amount of taxpayers' money and we wanted to build up a reputation for outstandingly well-presented submissions. With the final draft, or what we thought of as the final draft, safely stowed in my baggage between my spare set of underclothes and those items people had asked me to take to Lesotho, further discussions in Lesotho followed.

I met with Basotho architects, quantity surveyors and structural engineers, and discussed mountain logistics and labour availability in remote regions. All this inevitably resulted in many pencilled margin notes, deletions and insertions with revision of budgets as I tried, no more accurately than most bankers, to estimate inflation and exchange rates over the next four or five years. *The Financial Times* became 'required reading' before some last frenetic fine-tuning took place ahead of a quick dash to the telephone and fax machine (no emails in those early days) so Richard could meet a rapidly approaching deadline for applications to London and Brussels. There followed an audible sigh of relief that spanned 6,000 miles (9,656 kms); we made it! We never once missed the eight deadlines for our submissions but sometimes it was a close thing.

Within the LINK organisation in Durham the development working party sought partial external funding from statutory bodies to support the local fund-raising of the working party leading the project. For example, the medical group mounted the local fund-raising for the Ha Popa Rural Health Centre and, later, the education group raised funds for the Ha Mohatlane Community Education Centre, both working parties raising 15 per cent of the total estimated cost of their respective projects. The development group raised the balance, attracting 50 per cent from the European Union (EU) and 35 per cent from the British government. Any expenditure in excess of budget had to be covered by the LINK so careful supervision of projects was essential, particularly in the harsh environment of mountainous Lesotho where time was made for man and not man for time!

To sustain our presence in the jungle we had to have access to finance. None of us had any love for money[18] and neither did we have any desire to wander from the pathway to plunge into an unseen abyss, but we did recognise it was money that oiled the progress of our exploring. After the Durham and Lesotho support groups had agreed to go ahead with a proposal, large projects and programmes were submitted to the EU and the British ODA. Those that were subsequently approved, after negotiations in East Kilbride,[19] London and Brussels, were financed in this way:

For example:

Agreed budget	100%	£100,000
Co-funding contribution from the EU	50% of budget	50,000
Co-funding contribution from the ODA	35% of budget	35,000
LINK funding/voluntary funding	15% of budget	15,000

LINK voluntary funding benefited from covenants and, later, Gift Aid tax rebates of 33 per cent reducing in later years to 28 per cent of each qualifying pound, so to the project it became worth approximately £1.28. Not all donations qualified for rebates. In the example given above the LINK would have to raise £11,719 gift-aided money (which would then attract a tax rebate of £3,281) to mount a project with an approved budget of £100,000. Thus, in the above example every pound donated under the Gift Aid scheme 'released' about £8.54 for approved projects.[20]

Not all funding was as precise as our analysis might imply. Smaller project funding was financed by the appropriate working party generally in one of two ways. Some small projects were either partially or fully financed (or assisted 'in kind') by other agencies, churches or by individuals, with the LINK providing the organisation and supplementary funding to put an accepted proposal into action. This type of cooperative, multi-funding activity:

- financed the original community woodland project mounted in cooperation with Durham County Council;
- assisted approved visits by young people to the other region;
- arranged study placements in higher education;
- provided scholarships for university degrees;
- aided volunteer workers;
- promoted exchange programmes;
- provided hospitality in both regions;
- assisted the dispatch of containers;
- supported publicity.

For the second type of small project funding the working parties would be directly responsible for raising all the money required for the project. To demonstrate this we need to turn no further than to the second phase of the community woodland project; the Herculean effort of the tools working party when it supplied thousands of tools to poor artisans who possessed the skills of their trade but not the equipment to enable the exercise of them; some of the smaller medical projects, all of which were fully financed by the appropriate working party. The responsibility of funding a project rested with each working party and to coordinate the work I attended, when I was in Durham, meetings of all working parties and the leader of each working party, when involved with large-scale fund-raising, attended meetings of the support group. It all worked relatively smoothly and there was rarely a time when we were anxious over the lack of money.

This was partly because of the excellent financial management of successive treasurers but also, importantly, to the responsible attitudes that the organisational structure of the LINK encouraged. There was a high degree of personal involvement and, therefore, responsibility to the corporate effort that gave pioneers in the jungle a strong sense of security. Collectively we were financially well advised and despite some jungle gravel occasionally getting into our boots to irritate progress, the substantial reserve fund we established provided us with the knowledge that a soft landing would result should we ever trip up in this tangle of jungle undergrowth. The reserve was essential to finance our cash flow which was so often disrupted by delays in receiving promised funds from other sources.

If we were to be One Body in Christ we were in the jungle together and although raising finance for the LINK's work involved the investment of many hours' labour in Durham, just as much strenuous effort was also invested in Lesotho. Raising money in pounds, dollars, rand, maloti and euros is only five steps into a financial quagmire. My subsequent hesitant steps were to take me deeper into the interior of international finance and were tentative and even, at times, faltering.

It was exactly on the LINK's third birthday, Tuesday, 16th May 1989, that I ventured into one small part of the concrete edifice that I came to know quite well as the Central Bank of Lesotho. It stood in all its glory at the junction of two pathways where I had seen it rising over a couple of years or so, admiring its vigorous, luxuriant growth and wondering when it was all going to stop. At the red robot (traffic lights) that occasionally controlled the traffic at that junction I waited, sometimes in vain, often to be overtaken, wondering what it was like inside; now I was to find out. There it stood growing out of a hillock resplendent in its grandeur, high and mighty lord over all it surveyed, resplendent in grey stone, plate glass leaves with chromium stems and not a few cubic yards (m) of marble. Apart from the new royal palace only a stone's throw away it was, in 1989, the most imposing building in Lesotho.

My borrowed, rather battered and just-about-alive bakkie (pick-up truck) looked somewhat out of place parked in front of the enormous bank alongside the latest model of a shining Mercedes. Rather self-consciously I walked across the forecourt to the grand entrance where I was met, I suspect rather suspiciously, by a huge, heavily armed security guard who became even more doubtful of my legitimacy when I said I had come to see the governor, Dr Anthony Maruping; although there was a noticeable relaxation when he checked my name with reception. As I waited (a Mosotho once remarked to me 'waiting in Lesotho, Peter, is an occupation', a slight twist on 'he serves who only stands and waits'), I found it rather disconcerting to be greeted very politely by a well-spoken receptionist in a smart navy suit, coiffure neatly arranged, with a revolver tucked into his belt! As I stood admiring the verdant living plants displayed inside an air-conditioned interior, so unlike their natural habitat, my attention was directed to a nearby office with a small opening rather like that found in a wayside kiosk. Above it was displayed a notice, written only in English: ALL FIREARMS MUST BE DEPOSITED. Had someone concluded that only English-speaking people carried guns? I, for one, would prove them wrong; my word was accepted without further investigation.

Knowing how important face-to-face meetings are in Basotho society the purpose of this visit, in May 1989, was to reconnect with Ntate L. F. Leuta, whom I had met some years previously but had lost contact with during a period in which he had risen in the banking world to become responsible for Financial Exchange Control. By now I knew that the financing of our poultry unit project was going to exceed £100,000 and with other proposals in multiples of that amount, I concluded that if the financing of our major projects was to be efficient I had to come to terms with the fine distinctions of foreign monetary exchange. Some project money would, hopefully, come in the form of European euros, some in Great Britain pounds, some in American dollars, some in South African rand (of which, in those days, there were two types: financial and commercial) and some in Lesotho maloti (which is at parity with the rand), all with their different rates of exchange. There was some dense, dark undergrowth to battle my way through in this part of the jungle, hiding some nasty dangers that I needed to be guarded against and guided through to enable the money raised in Durham to be translated into the best possible use in Lesotho, whilst losing as little as possible in charges, commissions and spurious exchange rates. I needed guidance through the financial jungle.

As the lift whisked me high above the foliage and I went deeper into the banking jungle, I turned over in my mind the arguments that were the product of a lot of time already spent preparing for this meeting when I wanted to focus on the exchange of other currencies into South African rand. We had a very friendly meeting, during which officials sketched out a route map for me to follow through the almost impenetrable vegetation in which the law of the jungle evidently held sway. The controls, regulations, laws, policies and conventions were mind-boggling and all required careful interpretation when making an application for exchanging other currencies through the financial rand. I began to wonder, why bother?

The answer was all contained within the figures! On the day we met, the international money market rate for the financial rand against the US dollar was 4.13118, whereas the commercial rand was changing at 2.66153 against the US dollar. So, if I could pull it off we would gain somewhere in the region of an extra 55 per cent, a huge supplementation on some of the LINK's funds! I had done my homework in detail and we had a well-informed discussion about the topics that would be influential on a final decision: capital assets (few); inflation (12 per cent); recurrent expenditure (covered); cash flow (financed); income generation (none); employment provision (some); export potential (none). It all sounded rather bleak.

'My ears were getting tired',[21] but knowing how important it was, particularly in Lesotho, never to leave a meeting without deciding on the date of the next one, we agreed to meet again in January of the next year; would it really take that long? The prospects were not very encouraging and the lift quickly took me down to earth with a jolt. There, I assured the security guard that, no, I did not have a gun to collect, and left wondering whether I would ever find my way through the undergrowth! I slumped, rather dejected, into the driving-seat of the bakkie feeling as if the jungle were going to devour me as an innocent amateur; but I wasn't quite ready to give in. Was this what putting the gospel into action was all about?

The next stop in the financial jungle was the squat stone-built Standard Bank in Kingsway, the main road through Maseru, thus named to commemorate the visit in 1947 of King George VI.[22] The bank was now almost hidden behind cars, trucks and lorries that were massed along its front like shrubbery in the forest and where, fifteen years earlier, I would have tied up my horse. Now that society had rapidly advanced and become more civilised, heavily armed guards patrolled both outside and inside the bank! Perhaps it is unwise to go into the jungle without a gun? Wondering what humanity had achieved, I eventually reached the front door of the Standard Bank. Because of its long queues and lingering waiting times, the Basotho called this bank the 'Standing Bank'! It was a place of social gathering where finance took second place whilst you ate your sandwiches, met your friends and read your book or the newspapers. As I was fully 'occupied' waiting for twenty minutes I had time to reflect on what might have happened to the £15,000 that our Durham treasurer had sent, via the bank's international branch in Johannesburg, South Africa, to our account held by the Standard Bank in Lesotho. I was trying to track its whereabouts, but when I did eventually see the bank manager he was equivocally evasive, finding that the convenient camouflage of the jungle concealed many a hiding place. Nevertheless, during the meeting I did pick up the scent: £15,000 can be quite pungent! It was to stay with me for many months.

It was almost the end of January 1991 before I was able to make a return visit to the Central Bank of Lesotho, by which time I was much more confident that we would be granted permission to exchange some of our funds at the hugely beneficial financial exchange rate. Much work had taken place across the airways between my house in Durham, Maseru and Johannesburg and now more lengthy, face-to-face negotiations brought a vivid shaft of light through the dark jungle of regulations. I left the bank wondering how efficient the process would be as on this day, 28th January, the calendar hanging at a wonky angle on the wall of the room in which we were talking was still showing December of the previous year! As I thought I was nearing success I tried to be more charitable wondering, in the heat of Lesotho's mid-summer, if the calendar was being kept for the beauty of the snow-covered hills it showed. I did not leave with completely empty hands: I had the date of the next meeting!

But, there was still the matter of the lost £15,000! Thinking how grateful I should be that our funds were banked with the 'standing bank' rather than the 'losing bank' (as English-speaking Basotho called the Lesotho Bank), I picked up the spoor again in Johannesburg on Monday, 26th August 1991. What a day that was! Pam and I had just spent a restful, fascinating five days living in the natural jungle of the Kruger Park with its noisy, nosy inhabitants just outside the front door of the ranger's house where we had been grateful guests. Now it was back to the concrete and financial jungle of Johannesburg. Our host dropped us at the Standard Bank in Simmonds Street, where the manager denied any knowledge of our long-lost fortune but did suggest that we might pick up the scent just round the corner in Fox Street, where another office of the Standard Bank might be able to help. It wasn't! The scent seemed to be cooling but I left with a comprehensive list of the bank's branches. We began to tick them off one by one.

We reached the branch in nearby Commissioner Street, where I spoke to a helpful lady clerk who did not deny the presence of our money but required the 'outward SWIFT number' from our bank in Durham! Nothing very swift about this process. It was not until Tuesday, 10th September 1991 that I received a telephone call in Durham to say that the £15,000 had been found in an interest-bearing holding account and was being exchanged at the financial rate and sent to our account in Lesotho! We had found our money, £15,000 that had increased its value to almost £23,500, but what we had not done was to attract an explanation! We were content to let that remain one of the mysteries concealed by the jungle mist that percolates every obscure crevice of international finance. There were other matters that we needed to address if we were to survive.

With organisation, administration and finance moving along steadily and smoothly we needed to pay attention to our publicity. Jesus describes his disciples who had gathered round him to listen to the Beatitudes as 'the salt of the earth' and then immediately went on to warn them not to lose their saltiness, because if they did then they would be of no use to anyone![23] Having planted that thought firmly in their minds, Jesus cautioned against the temptation of hiding their faith, as no one would light a lamp and then put it under a bowl. What was the message this teaching was making for the LINK? Within the support group it seemed that we needed to let our faith shine out as a beacon from a lamp stand so everyone could benefit from its light. We were aware, despite many long, sweltering hours in the jungle, that there were still many people in Lesotho and Durham who knew little, if anything, about the expedition. How was the LINK to manifest the teaching of Jesus in the jungle of modern living? We were making progress in the jungle of organisational structures and finance, we were working happily with secular authorities, but now its initial efforts at promoting its work needed reinforcing. We needed to project our presence and message in a more permanent style than that provided by its 3,500 prayer leaflets, 40,000 bookmarks, innumerable slide shows and, later, PowerPoint presentations, video films and countless talks and sermons. Although they were useful, and are still effectively employed, their effect could be short-lived, so what were we to do?

The publicity track wound its way quietly through the densest part of the jungle as we looked for other ways that were consistent with those already established in which to keep the LINK and its Christian message before the public. The track often divided and we did, sometimes, go down side paths that took us to nowhere in particular but one, which led to the cathedral in Durham, gave us an annual exposure to many hundreds of people, for which we have always been grateful. The suggestion that the Durham-Lesotho LINK should provide the reader for the seventh lesson[24] in the immensely popular Festival of Nine Lessons and Carols was enthusiastically received, especially as a Mosotho was often available and generally delighted to be invited to read. The first reader was Ntate Paul Mohobela from the small town of Peka situated on the northern road some 33 miles (53 kms) from Maseru. He was studying civil engineering at Teesside University and on Christmas Eve 1989, his cheerful black face was sandwiched between the white representatives of Durham city and the local churches. One other major benefit of this mutual contribution by the LINK and the cathedral was, as Paul Mohobela expressed it, that 'the experience gave of a sense of belonging'.

One other way we overcame the need to keep people in Durham informed about what we were doing in the jungle and why we were there anyway was by exhibiting a professionally produced static display in publicly frequented places, such as the hugely popular Gateshead Flower Festival that, in 1990, was a densely populated jungle of plants and people, many hundreds of whom had time to pause to study our display. It attracted a lot of attention but in some way we needed to project our presence and message in a more permanent manner and there, in Durham, was a massive doorstep over which lay the answer. With a cautiously estimated quarter of a million people crossing that threshold each year to admire the magnificent interior of Durham Cathedral, we concluded that a display of the LINK's work, even if it were looked at by only a fraction of those visitors, would convey something of our work to a large number of people from around the world. Talks with the dean and chapter were friendly and productive, resulting in a small photographic display frequently improved and enhanced over the years as the LINK's work changed, developed and progressed. People of many different nationalities sent letters of interest and support with not a few of them containing financial contributions. It might, so the publicity working party believed, also attract active interest in our work. It did, as one person born in Lesotho records:

> … I came across an exhibition displaying the work of the Lesotho and Durham Diocesan LINK. The photographic display of BaSotho (sic), dressed in their colourful blankets in the Maluti Mountains, where we had been only a few months before, ended with an invitation to support the work of the LINK. Whether or not it was a coincidence or a strange providence that had brought us to Durham, I left the cathedral with a lightness in my step. Here was a place to be. Here was work to do.[25]

Many others have joined this enthusiast. There was certainly plenty of work to do and we had many willing hands to do it, but we needed to strengthen our presence in the surrounding jungle of competing claims. A further opportunity arose in 1993. Some years after we first set up the display, Durham Cathedral celebrated the nine hundredth anniversary of the arrival of the itinerant Lindisfarne monks via the Farne Islands and Chester-le-Street. Jesus, in his sermon on the mount, said to his disciples, 'A city on a hill cannot be hidden'[26]; neither, we might add, can a cathedral of the magnitude of Durham. In 1093 the monks who carried the relics of St. Cuthbert from Lindisfarne started to build a new shrine on a peninsula of the River Wear that protects one of Durham's many hills. So what contribution might the LINK make to this historic commemoration? The suggestion made in 1986 that there might be a television link between the two cathedrals proved to be unrealistic seven years later; the BBC was short of money! We had to explore some other paths that might connect Lesotho to Durham Cathedral and to the occasion. Strange as it may seem the answer lay in St. Agnes' Mission, Lesotho, established at Teyateyaneng in 1904 by the Society of the Sacred Mission,[27] a branch of which is now established in the former St. Nicholas Vicarage, Durham.

St. Agnes' Mission lies to the south-west of the two-way tarred road as it enters Teyateyaneng, before going through the town on its way to Peka and northwards to Hlotse and Butha-Buthe, beyond which lies Sefako (the place of hailstorms) where two LINK woodland sites are situated. A short dirt track leads westwards from the tar, passing St. Agnes' High School on the left of the track where the LINK built one of its poultry units. Just behind the large, rectangular stone-built church and its rectory is a small weaving enterprise started on a shoe string in 1985 by Christabel Jackson from New Zealand and South African John Brown. Its name, Helang Basali, has become associated with high-quality handmade tapestries woven in a mohair and wool mixture to original designs. In Sesotho '*helang*' is a shout of astonishment and '*basali*' means 'women' and it is with much surprise that one finds a small group of women designing, processing and weaving exquisitely beautiful tapestries in such an out-of-the-way place.

Over the years I visited TY (much easier to say than Teyateyaneng!) many times so I was able to make frequent visits to Helang Basali and often talked to Christabel, John and the ladies about their work. Now the topic of conversation was the design and weaving of a long, narrow tapestry that would grace a corner of the north transept of what is one of the most famous cathedrals in the world. There, lit by a spotlight above the static exhibition already in place, it would be a visible presentation of the link between Lesotho and Durham and a demonstration of the creativity and skill of the Basotho weavers. What is not obvious to the casual visitor is the LINK's continuing cooperation with secular authority, shown here by its close association in this enterprise with Durham City Council, who contributed towards the cost of the tapestry. Unfortunately the plaque displayed below the tapestry is not well written, completely accurate or fully explicit:

This banner was woven in Lesotho.
It celebrates the link between the diocese of Durham and Lesotho.
A gift of the diocese of Lesotho and the city of Durham,
it marks the 900th Anniversary of the Foundation of Durham Cathedral.

However expensive, money was only a small part of the whole exercise; however inexplicit, the work of the LINK is still demonstrated. None of my luggage during 1992 was checked in without containing at least one full-scale drawing of the proposed design for the tapestry and subsequently I spent many hours with Stephen Pedley, the chairman of the support group, discussing, changing and arguing about the patterns that had been submitted by Helang Basali designers. By this time Stephen was a residential canon at the cathedral and that helped the process through its many stages until we all agreed on a design that depicts a journey through the country and mountains of Lesotho, reaching up to heaven. The weaving results in a gentleness of line with each element blending into the sequence of images to create an inspiring presentation of life in the rugged environment of Lesotho.

The tapestry started its life in Teyateyaneng mid-February 1993 and continues to be admired by many people as it hangs with a dignified appearance amongst the grandeur of Durham Cathedral. It serves its purpose well as its admirers stand in the north transept of the ancient cathedral in Durham to be translated, by the photographic display, to modern-day life in distant Lesotho. It has been there since Sunday, 5th September 1993, a day of celebration when the Mayor and Mayoress of Durham, with some 300 of its citizens, gathered for evensong. This was followed by an informal dedication, during which the dean of the cathedral in Maseru, Edwin Chaka (who was the first leader of the LINK in Lesotho), made a short speech of presentation. During this speech he offered congratulations to Durham Cathedral on its nine hundredth birthday from a cathedral that was a mere forty-three years old! Nine Basotho from the adult exchange group who were present sang and danced their way to the Prior's Hall for the conclusion of a memorable day.

The priors of former years might well have been pleased with the way the overseas mission was progressing, given the difficulties any group would encounter in a jungle as dense and confusing as the one we were exploring and with a large number of tenderfoot pioneers. Organisation was in place; administration was operating smoothly; financial support was generous; cooperation with other agencies, both religious and secular, was firmly established. What else shows on the dusty jungle map that might influence the LINK's work and effectiveness in achieving its objectives?

Peering at and through the conflicting signs and symbols, colours and contours, it is noticeable from the sketch map that the tracks of the pioneers radiate from, and return to, one particular spot: the base camp. In any complex activity involving scores of people it is advisable, perhaps even necessary, to have a focus of activity from which information, knowledge and encouragement is drawn and to which ideas, concerns, contributions, hopes and tensions are taken; a hub which is the centre of coordination, a field headquarters. There has to be a clearing in the jungle somewhere and the diocese of Lesotho provided one for the southern region in the Anglican Training Centre.

Early during the first phase of our work in Lesotho (1986 to 1994) a small room, with no telephone and little furniture, was provided rent-free. It was right in the centre of the jungle, convenient, easily accessible to visitors of which there were plenty as our operations expanded and, most importantly, it was a very positive contribution to the LINK by the diocese of Lesotho, which was now being closely identified with the LINK's work; One in Word and Work was moving through the jungle along some rough tracks from slogan to reality. It was there that our first computer, our first salaried Lesotho executive officer, Steven Molokeng, and our first paid part-time assistant, Jeanette O'Neill, started their work for the LINK. This was our Lesotho base camp, situated in the shadows of the cathedral, from which all work radiated into the country during the first eight-year phase of the LINK, a period that saw its most vigorous growth, the setting of the high standards of work and the extensive mission activity for which it came to be recognised.[28]

Any jungle changes, but none more so than the social jungle. Inhabitants die and are born; others come into the jungle from outside, bringing with them new skills and ambitions; some things develop more rapidly than others; some begin to dominate; some collapse; the explorers themselves change, becoming older and more experienced; new dangers emerge. The jungle is never the same as it was yesterday, let alone the year before.

One of the biggest dangers in the jungle is one that explorers carry in with them: a lack of knowledge. What is poisonous, toxic, venomous, deadly? Worse for the pioneers than not knowing, is not knowing that they don't know.[29] This can lead to the dangerous pretence that they think they do know and this can be deadly in the jungle we are exploring. This was manifested early during the second phase of the LINK. During their trek through dense jungle in 1996, the trustees carried a heavy burden. They were challenged by a suggestion that some recent legislation regulating charities[30] demanded that the activities of the separate working parties, that had functioned so keenly and efficiently, were no longer permissible and, with their finances, should be centralised and moved to the trustees' direct control.

To grasp the erroneous nature of this analysis of the rules of engagement, the trustees had to look no further than the organisation of the Church itself. If it were an accurate interpretation of new regulations, then all finance and activities of parish churches that were not separate registered charities would have to be subsumed to the diocese and that really would be the final nail in the parish coffin! The trustees did not know they had taken a wrong path and they did not know that they did not know that danger loomed. One of the most useful and strongest elements of the LINK's organisation was virtually destroyed by a fallacy and working parties became advisory groups. To the Devil's amusement, a silent boa constrictor had slunk from the undergrowth and almost squeezed the life out of the body of its victim.

That was the first stage of their demise. Members of the new 'advisory' groups simply did not have sufficient experience of working with the Basotho on which to base sound advice. Whom were they to advise anyway? Who would now do the work? Individuals joined working parties to work; they did not join advisory groups to 'advise' and their wishes and attributes did not change by altering the description of their group. The second stage of their demise was the withdrawal of their close involvement with the mission of the LINK. In the first phase of the LINK there were, in Durham, over seventy people expressing their personal contribution through their work. They were responsible, trusted by the leadership, individually committed and strongly influential; they felt they were an integral part of the LINK's mission and that through them it was taking the mission into the community of the north-east of England. The third stage of their demise can be found in the jungle fog surrounding the structure at the time. Peering through the murky way ahead there seems to have been a lack of clear understanding that the LINK was started for the benefit of Durham as much as for the benefit of Lesotho. The benefits that were accruing to Durham by having large numbers of people directly involved in the mission were, on this evidence, being overlooked.

Nevertheless the LINK kept tramping through the jungle, but the track soon became a steep, downward slope on which it was deceptively easier to walk. However, that was to turn, imperceptibly, into a slippery slope as members of the former working parties became disillusioned and found other outlets for their energies. They had been told they were 'without delegated powers'[31] so, inevitably, by the end of 2004, as the victims of a centralised internal takeover, they disappeared from the LINK's annual report of that year. That group of seventy-plus people with their skills and enthusiasm was a great loss to both Durham and to Lesotho, but there was no turning back and many are thankful that the LINK is still alive and plodding ahead through the tangled mass. It was all rather untimely, as the LINK was working through its second phase under new leadership: a new executive officer in Durham, a new executive officer in Lesotho, a new bishop in Durham and also a new bishop in Lesotho.

Those exploring the southern jungle during the second phase (1994–2002) found an empty house complete with a working telephone and so the LINK vacated its original home to move into more spacious rooms in Pulane Street. The Youth Activities Project was still using the Maqalika Dam and part of its shoreline for its water activities. That had been negotiated with the then minister of natural resources, Monyane Moleleki, in 1993–1994 and now, in 2002, with a foothold firmly established, ownership was formalised and the LINK began building an attractive centre of operations. Established there it began its third phase (2002–2011), taking it into its quarter-century under the joint leadership of Rob and Margaret Bianchi in Durham and Likome Mabula in Lesotho.

It had always been the intention, right from the first years of the LINK's existence, to bring Lesotho closer into the centre of operations. We never wanted Durham to dominate the LINK's work although we recognised that in the early years it would be the source of most of its money and also, given the origin of its founding, its leadership. As we progressed through the uncomfortable environment of the jungle we had to exercise a collective quality. Paraphrasing words of John the Baptist,[32] as Lesotho became greater so Durham must become less, to which we should add 'until balance is achieved in oneness'. This development helped to bring the Lesotho element of the LINK one step closer to where we had always hoped it would eventually be; together with Durham in the jungle tramping towards a common objective.

When the buildings were opened on Friday, 24th September 2004 by His Majesty King Letsie III it was not his first contact with the LINK. As Prince Mohato, he and I had lunched together on Sunday, 4th February 1990 with the British High Commissioner, the European delegate and the director of the British Council[33] in Lesotho. Only a few days beforehand, the prince had returned to Lesotho after studying at the University of Bristol, where he had completed a diploma in English legal studies. It should, therefore, have come as no surprise to those of us gathered round his lunch table when he floated the idea of the LINK establishing a series of Citizens' Advice Bureaux around Lesotho. He was keen that the Basotho should have easier access to national law, intricate and complex though it is.[34-35] We talked at some length about how his hopes might be realised and I left with some determination to see what might be done, believing these bureaux could also provide an excellent channel for the gospel message. After much hard work and frustration the idea was abandoned as I just could not find the finance to establish such a scheme and, more importantly, to sustain it. The LINK was very young and inexperienced and the jungle was dense and dangerous and I was keen that anything we planted should be nurtured to maturity.

The King's second contact with the LINK was during the morning of Tuesday, 5th April 1994 in the royal village of Matsieng where his father, King Moshoeshoe II, introduced him to the Durham Dozen visitors, whom he met again at the royal palace in the afternoon of the same day. I was grateful that he did not remember (or, at least, gave no indication that he remembered) his suggestion that the LINK should start a string of Community Advice Bureaux! Two kings in one day in one country?[36]

A base camp had been established in Lesotho and its potential realised. But what of the clearings in the northern jungle? In Durham I ran the LINK from my study in our family house near to St. Nicholas

Church and within a few minutes' walk, along a reasonable track, of the Society of the Sacred Mission's St. Antony's Priory. My study was where the LINK's pulse could be found throughout the first eight years of its life, before Paul Jefferson (the first Durham executive officer) led the work from his home into its second phase. Responsibility was then passed in 2002 to joint leaders Rob and Margaret Bianchi. Throughout its twenty-five years mission contribution to the dioceses of Durham and Lesotho the LINK has benefited substantially by the unseen contributions of its leaders in their provision of physical space, thus avoiding costly office overheads. The value of this contribution has never been quantified but it can be judged roughly by the very low administration costs incurred by the LINK, particularly in its early jungle ventures. Examples from the LINK's annual report and accounts show that administration costs in 1992 were 4.4 per cent of total expenditure; in 1993 they were just 2.6 per cent. Over that two-year period expedition costs averaged, incredibly, at just 3.5 per cent of total expenditure. It was, however, unrealistic to expect that exceptionally low level to continue into the second and third phases of the LINK's life. As salaries in Durham became part of the equation in the final quarter of 1994, the administration costs rose to 7.9 per cent of total expenditure. It may have been hot and sticky in the jungle but it was still not costing an arm and a leg.[37]

I had, by now, been in the jungle for a long time, working for Lesotho for over twenty years, the last eight of which I had been leading the Durham-Lesotho LINK along some fairly rough tracks through dense undergrowth. Now, in 1993, I was facing strong demands for my services in other jungles. These, with one or two notable exceptions, I had strongly resisted as I believed it important to dedicate myself to one region, thus enabling its people to recognise my commitment and to feel a compassionate, loving and knowledgeable relationship. Nevertheless, the changes to which the jungle is naturally subject were inexorably taking place and I was increasingly being challenged, both externally and internally, to make myself available in a bigger jungle. I had invested heavily in Lesotho and now to consider withdrawing was difficult, but one day during 1993 a telephone call made me think seriously that I ought to explore other regions. The conversation went like this:

'Good morning; Peter Green.'

To be answered by a lady's voice, 'Are you the Lesotho man?!'

Rather taken-aback I said, 'Well, yes, I suppose you might describe me as such but ...'

I didn't have time to complete what I might have said before the lady launched into her request for a talk about, of course, Lesotho! Now I'd heard of 'typecasting' but this was serious; was I really 'the Lesotho man'?

The organisation and administration had served the LINK well and would continue to do so for nine or ten years, but change was inevitable and, I thought, desirable, so I told the trustees that I would be withdrawing from my responsibilities to the Durham-Lesotho LINK as from Wednesday, 31st August 1994, whereupon they started to hunt in the jungle for Durham's first executive officer. After a wide advertising campaign, attracting thirty-six applicants from men and women all over the country, that post was eventually filled by a Durham farm manager, Paul Jefferson, from Thursday, 1st September 1994 to the end of June 2002. Paul was a member of the woodland working party so he knew how the LINK worked, the people involved, where its weaknesses were and its major objective. In turn he was followed by married 'clerical couple' Rob and Margaret Bianchi, who already had close connections with the LINK as leaders of the Youth Activities Project. During its twenty-five years the Durham-Lesotho LINK has been through three distinct phases: 1986 to 1994, 1994 to 2003 and 2003 to the present date, 2011. Having brought the LINK to life and sustained it through the jungle I was about to expand my work into thirty-two countries[38] of the world, located in each of the seven commonly recognised continents except Antarctica. Well, there has to be something to look forward to and anticipate!

'Hello, you're still with me, then! Well, yes, that was pretty tough going, but apart from one serious accident, we didn't slip up very often and I did warn you when we started exploring that organisation, administration, finance and publicity are not the most attractive parts of the jungle they occupy. Anyway, they are now well rooted in place and under control and we can see how necessary they are to the general well-being of the expedition. So, now they are all growing and operating efficiently, let's make our way together to the edge of the jungle whilst we still have time and go into the field of operations and there engage in something a little more, what shall I say ... well, down to earth!'

---

1. Isaiah 40:3 (NIV).
2. 2 Timothy 1:7 (NIV).
3. Hadfield, J. A., *Psychology and Morals* (London: Methuen, 1923).
4. Those to whom I turned for advice most frequently were: Steven Molokeng; Donald Nestor; David Wells; John and Judy Gay; John Edwards, the British High Commissioner and his

successors; Achim Kratz, the European delegate and those who followed him; Urbain Mailhot. OMI.

5. Stephen Pedley; Ian Calvert; Nick Beddow; Philip Thomas, joined later by Tom Thubron.
6. Alan Piper (chairman); Marjorie Skelton; Geoffrey Mansfield (secretary).
7. Inevitably most were from the Anglican Church, but also represented were Roman Catholics, Quakers, Methodists and Baptists.
8. Achim Kratz was the European Delegate; a post equivalent to an ambassador.
9. The LINK became a charitable trust on 26th March 1990 (registered number 702809).
10. It took a long time for some to wake up to the reality of the newly evolving situation. It was not until 2005 that the newly named Church Mission Society stirred sufficiently for the general secretary to write: 'We are moving out of the partnership phase. Not denying what has gone before, "partnership" no longer serves us well because the Northern Church came to think of itself as the centre of mission. In this new phase the peoples of the world are being thrown together to live side by side in unprecedented ways'. Dakin, Tim, YES (magazine of the Church Mission Society) p. 5. May–August 2005.
11. Most notably Dolen Cymru, the Wales Lesotho Link which was founded in March 1985. Its story can be found in Williams, Paul, *Wales' African Twin* (Pwllheli: Cyhoeddiadau'r Gair, June 2008). Sentebele was founded in April 2006 by British Prince Harry and Lesotho's Prince Seeiso 'to help the forgotten victims of poverty'.
12. John Arthur Arrowsmith Maund was consecrated in Cape Town in 1950 and enthroned in Maseru on Sunday, 14th January 1951. After the Second World War he was awarded the Military Cross for bravery under fire. In retirement he served as an assistant bishop in the Diocese of St. Edmundsbury and Ipswich; the diocese in which I was licensed as a Reader on Saturday, 13th June 1964. John died in Malvern at the age of 88 years on Thursday, 9th July 1998.
13. Haliburton, Gordon, *Historical Dictionary of LESOTHO* (Metuchen, N.J., The Scarecrow Press, 1977) p. 8. Estimated in 1950 to be 'in the region of 70,000'.
14. See Chapter Three: Them and Us (p. 53).
15. Thorpe, Cyprian, *Look Back in Joy* (London: New Millennium, 1996).
16. The car in which they were travelling was stationary at lights controlling traffic at roadworks on the A1 Felton bypass in Northumberland when it was crushed between two heavy lorries. The other two priests were William Taylor of Heworth and Michael Hough of Low Fell, both serving in adjacent parishes to Catherine Hooper of Windy Nook and all in Gateshead. Catherine's funeral was in St Alban's Church, Windy Nook, on Saturday, 5th June 1999.
17. Donald Nestor died Friday, 10th January 2003 aged 64 years. An obituary appeared in *The Daily Telegraph* on Tuesday, 21st January 2003.
18. 1Timothy 6:10 (NIV): For the love of money is a root of all kinds of evil. Some people, eager for money, have wandered from the faith and pierced themselves with many griefs.
19. The office of the ODA's joint funding scheme was in East Kilbride and there we negotiated with Anna Turner and Robin Russell.

20. This example assumes that the Gift Aid tax rebate was 28 per cent but this was lowered in later years in line with a reduction in income tax. It should also be noted that co-funding by the EU and the ODA was based on agreed budget figures and the understanding that the LINK would raise 15 per cent of the total budget which was then seen as a 'release' mechanism for the co-funding. Occasionally there were some elements that the LINK wanted to include in a project but were unable to convince those responsible for co-funding. Nevertheless, relationships with both agencies were very professional and agreeable. If those elements were eventually included the LINK covered the full cost.

21. A Basotho proverb.

22. King George VI visited Lesotho for two days on Tuesday, 11th and Wednesday, 12th March 1947 to acknowledge the sacrificial contribution the Basotho had made to the UK during the Second World War. Kingsway was Lesotho's first stretch of tarred road, around which much of the capital city has since been developed.

23. Matthew 5:13–16 (NIV): You are the salt of the earth. But if the salt loses its saltiness, how can it be made salty again? It is no longer good for anything, except to be thrown out and trampled by men. You are the light of the world. A city on a hill cannot be hidden. Neither do people light a lamp and put it under a bowl. Instead they put it on its stand, and it gives light to everyone in the house. In the same way, let your light shine before men, that they may see your good deeds and praise your Father in heaven.

24. Matthew 2:1–11 (NIV): Wise men from the east worship the Christ child.

25. Yeats, Charles, *Prisoner of Conscience* (London: Rider, 2005) p. 157.

26. Matthew 5:14 (NIV): You are the light of the world. A city on a hill cannot be hidden.

27. Houghton, Michael, *SSM at TY* (Morija Printing Works,1976).

28. Luckman, Kenneth, *Place of Compassion* (Hertford: Authors OnLine, 2001) p. 110.

29. Laing, R. D., *Knots* (London: Penguin Books, 1976) p. 55.

30. The Charities Act 1993. (The Stationery Office Limited, 1993).

31. Durham-Lesotho LINK, 'Annual Report and Accounts' section 7.2 (e) (1996) p. 6.

32. John 3:30: He must become greater; I must become less.

33. In February 1990 these were: British High Commissioner, John Edwards; EU Delegate, Achim Kratz; British Council representative, David Bates.

34. Poulter, Sebastian, *Family Law and Litigation in Basotho Society* (Oxford: Clarendon Press, 1976). This text provides a useful review of Basotho family law based on research in the postcolonial period.

35. Maqutu, Winston C. M., *Contemporary Family Law of Lesotho* (Roma: National University of Lesotho, 1992). This text gives a clear introduction to the indigenous family law of Lesotho, confusing though it is, as Basotho culture emerges into the twenty-first century. It is a useful accompaniment to Poulter, above. 'Churchill', as he is known to his friends, has now resigned from the Lesotho judiciary.

36. Prince Mohato was sworn in as King Letsie III on Monday, 12th November 1990 after his father had been forced into exile to the UK where he remained for two years. On Wednesday,

25th January 1995, Letsie abdicated and King Moshoeshoe II was reinstated. A year later on Monday, 15th January 1996, his father was killed in a road accident, on the Maseru–Mantšonyane mountain road, after which Letsie was then reinstalled as King Letsie III on Wednesday, 7th February 1996. Amidst all this constitutional turmoil how King Moshoeshoe II ever managed to meet the Durham Dozen on the morning of Tuesday, 5th April 1994 and get King Letsie III to grant them an audience that same afternoon is one of the mysteries of the jungle, but my journal records the events which are pictorially substantiated by photographs. Since they both demonstrated a keen sense of humour perhaps one can say, without any disrespect, this really was a matter of backing both horses in the race!

37. An idiom that refers to hugely expensive costs. It entered English from America after World War Two and seems to originate from the enormous cost of losing an arm and a leg in battle.
38. The countries are: Belgium, Bolivia, Botswana, Burundi, Canada, Cyprus, France, Gaza Strip, Ghana, Honduras, India, Iran, Israel, Jamaica, Kenya, Lesotho, Namibia, Nicaragua, Palestine, Papua New Guinea, Poland, Romania, Russia, Seychelles, South Africa (including the former Bophuthatswana, Ciskei, KwaZulu, and Transkei), Swaziland, Uganda, Ukraine, USA, the former Zaire, Zambia and Zimbabwe.

Chapter Five

Trees of the Field

You will go out in joy
and be led forth in peace;
the mountains and hills will burst into song before you,
and all the trees of the field will clap their hands.[1]

Shortly after Paul had established the Church in Corinth he was deluged with problems. The multi-ethnic, transient people passing through this centre of trade and commerce were depraved and corrupt but despite the magnitude of the moral difficulties that confronted Paul, in his first letter to them he stressed the responsibility of Christians to look after God's world. Using the words of the Psalmist[2] he reminded the people in an all-embracing phrase that 'The earth is the Lord's and everything in it'[3] when he may also have had in mind the words of Moses to the king of Egypt, '... the earth is the Lord's'.[4] Scriptural support is overwhelming for the notion that we are tenants, just for a short time, of God's earth and so, if Christians in Durham and Lesotho really were to be One Body in Christ, what I saw when I first flew into Lesotho on Monday, 16th July 1973 was now our joint responsibility. There was God's earth, some 8,000 feet (2,440 m) below, devastated by erosion on a scale I had not previously seen nor, for that matter, have I seen since. My bird's eye view of the damage showed enormous areas ravaged by heavy rain and powerful winds. Attacking together, they had torn into, across and through over-cultivated and deforested land, leaving gaping wounds from where Lesotho's ochre-coloured soil has slid away to swell the Orange River as it flows westward across the continent into the Atlantic Ocean, leaving Lesotho's rocks stark bare like the carcass of some mammoth skeleton with its skin torn back from the lifeless corpse.

Erosion was even more widespread thirteen years later when the LINK was getting into gear and discussing project ideas with the Basotho. As the talking went on and on and on, in what seemed an interminable debate, the earlier disturbing experience sparked an idea for the first large project of the Durham-Lesotho LINK. As an initial large venture the community woodland project had many advantages for a fledging organisation, not least because I knew that here was a recognisably similar problem: the lack of trees in Durham and Lesotho. Because the Basotho found it difficult to imagine that Durham, resplendent in a continent of plenty, needed something as commonplace as trees, it was not easy to convince them that trees could give the people of both regions a common identity. As Christians we had that in our allegiance to Christ, but we now had to express that commitment in a common task and planting trees could provide the focus.

As Christians we had a mutual responsibility to look after the world that we inhabited for a few years. Lesotho had been deforested over very many years; people needed wood for their fires to keep warm and to cook their food, especially in the cold of the mountains where it was most difficult to grow trees. The 'treeline' took on a new meaning: it was a lifeline that was quickly becoming more difficult to find in Lesotho. History tells us that there was a time when the whole of this part of Africa had big cats wandering through dense forests, but both cats and trees have now disappeared, to be replaced by disfiguring *dongas* cutting through and washing away the soil, to an extent that only about 10 per cent of the country is now suitable for cultivation. The complex root systems of trees can bind soil, helping to stem its loss; their leaves provide necessary humus; small branches contribute fuel; trunks supply timber and their daily shade from the blistering summer sun is welcomed by both animals and people.

There was certainly nothing new about the need for tree-planting in Lesotho. One of the first French missionaries, Eugène Casalis, who arrived at Thaba-Bosiu in June 1833, quickly introduced tree-planting,[5] with another attempt being made by the British administration following almost a hundred years later.[6] Now, in 1986, I wanted to introduce four additional dimensions that would, I hoped, strengthen the notion that we were One in Word and Work. How could tree-planting strengthen the bond between the people of Durham and Lesotho? Could we somehow bring together the Christian faith of Dunelmians and Basotho and use it as a motivation to grow woodlands throughout two communities and two cultures? Might it also be possible to use a community woodlands project to encourage the young to care for their physical environment? Above all else could the LINK show that tree-planting and nurture were activities in which Christians would be carrying out scriptural teaching? 'In the beginning was the word',[7] but it was only the beginning; we now needed to advance our faith and this might be a way to do just that. After all, if we were to be bound together by Christian love, 'our love should not be just words and talk; it must be true love, which shows itself in action.'[8]

A scarcity of trees in Durham is not as immediately obvious as it is in Lesotho. Flying over Durham, unlike the reaction to flying over Lesotho, there is no instant feeling that here is a place denuded of trees. Woodlands and forests can be seen dotted around the countryside without too much searching through the clouds. Despite that, in the mid-1980s Durham had fewer trees than most other European countries, with only about 5.8 per cent of the county covered by trees compared to Germany that had 30 per cent and, even with the scarcity of precious land, much of it laboriously reclaimed from the sea, Holland was 10-per-cent protected by trees. To make matters worse, in Durham it was estimated that at that time many trees were disappearing because of disease, age and commercial development such as opencast mining.[9] So, with the need for tree-planting in both regions visibly obvious, what I now had to do was to raise the awareness of the mutual problem. Identifying any problem is, of course, the first stage in finding its solution; concealed problems remain unsolved until, like the deforestation of Lesotho, they reach an almost overpowering scale. Once identified, finding a solution to the problem relies on asking the right questions; wrong questions produce wrong answers. So, what were the questions I needed to ask both of others and of myself?

Connecting arboriculture to the faith of Christians, I thought, should not be too difficult given that the notion of looking after God's world was a paramount biblical message. However, I knew that I could not rely on collective passive knowledge being translated into individual action. I could preach about the problem; I could relate it to the Christian faith; but if Durham and Lesotho were to show any tangible evidence of being One in Word and Work, then their hands, black and white, had to be provided with the means of engaging in the same work. For my part I had to bring the word and the work into one and make that blend pertinent to those doing the work. There was, I thought, an essential need to keep the task small so it did not overwhelm the thinking of the people whom I was targeting, so that they felt it was manageable and that they were in control. It followed that the woodland should be local so the community respected it and could grasp the benefit it would be to them. Basotho men would stop seeing their crops and the soil in which they grow, and sometimes even their animals, sliding into *dongas*; the women would not have to trek miles to find, gather and then carry wood back to their village, supporting its weight on their heads whilst carrying their baby on their backs. A continuing supply of wood close at hand was going to be a boon to many women.

As trees began to cover the eyesore of mining slag heaps in Durham and deep *dongas* in Lesotho, the people would see an improvement in their landscape and they would be alerted to the need to care for their environment. Furthermore, if individuals in both places invested in the trees, then they would be more likely to look after them, nurturing them to maturity; so initially they must possess and plant the saplings. In my mind all this translated into a Durham-Lesotho LINK community woodland project on small sites dotted around Lesotho and Durham with the LINK providing the sites, the fencing, the saplings; the people providing the labour to prepare, to plant and to protect. If we were faithful in doing all of this then surely God would provide the means of growth, but who would provide the money? How was I to make it happen? There seemed to be no end to the questions, which was quite acceptable to me providing there was no end to the answers. What I had to learn was the wisdom of waiting, even if irksome, for the answers whilst recognising that if others provided them, they would thereby have a measure of responsibility, whereas if I answered them, even if I could, I would be solely accountable.

Given my background in the world of professional education I very much wanted to introduce an educational element into what I was now thinking of as the Durham-Lesotho community woodlands project. To find how this aspiration might be achieved I had to be patient for just over another year while I pushed ahead with the organisation that would allow the launch of the project. When I did find an answer it was close at hand but there was much to do before I could take advantage of that convenience. I had to get my ideas accepted in Lesotho and Durham and then find land, fencing, saplings, labour and money. How was all that to be achieved?

In Maseru my ideas for the LINK's first major project received qualified, and rather hesitant, approval by the Lesotho-Durham support group[10], at which the most powerful voices expressed their concern that the proposal should not increase the workload of 'personnel already heavily committed'.[11] This was not encouraging given the amount of hard work that had already been invested and it certainly did not convey an illustration of an active, vibrant mission church! With the 1988 planting season only four months away, I was worried that dawdling Anglicanism would delay the start by a year and that I could not accept as, apart from the need to pull many separate strands together and to keep current enthusiasm alive, I had also to consider the Durham timetable. Clearly I had to stay at least one step ahead of the constraining elements who had already discussed the proposal at two meetings, so I did not take too seriously the decision to pass the matter to the Lesotho Diocesan planning committee. That committee then requested another report from me about a still-to-be-arranged meeting I hoped to have with Ministry of Agriculture officials. It would then make a formal proposal to a fifth meeting, the diocesan council, just one month before the planting of the first saplings! I just could not wait: having put my hand to the plough I was determined not to look back.[12]

Despairing at the Church's lifeless, lukewarm response I went off next day to see what Peter Rosling, the British High Commissioner, had to say about my ideas. According to my notes, written at the time, he 'received the proposals very enthusiastically and offered his support wherever possible'[13] and he even went one step further by offering £500 for fencing. He certainly put British taxpayers' money where his mouth was. Now what I had to do was to put it to good use! He sensed my frustration with the response of the Church and before I left his office he had taken another positive step, arranging for me to meet the next day with four officials from the Ministry of Agriculture. This was much more productive. Our discussion about the future of the Durham-Lesotho LINK was the first of many that I would enjoy having with him and his successors, all of whom I found to be ready to listen, positively critical and practically supportive. But as I climbed the slope from the High Commission building with conflicting emotions, it seemed that I had a steeper hill to climb. I felt an uncomfortable drag between the encouragement of secular support and the sadness of pious lethargy; I was in the middle and had to unite them. Could they be pulled into one?

The meeting at the Ministry of Agriculture, arranged by Peter Rosling with such speed and efficiency, lasted for just on three hours. With three professional foresters and a researcher[14] we went through a long agenda that I'd previously prepared, starting with an outline of my vision for the woodland project and its place within the LINK. It was all very timely. The Ministry had just made a policy decision to involve non-governmental organisations, but they had not anticipated such a rapid initiative as the one I was presenting. In fact, their decision had not yet been made public so I went to the meeting with no idea about how my plans would be received and was mildly surprised at the welcome given to the possibility of the Ministry working with the LINK. Their professional assessment was encouraging. Innocently straying outside his professional vocation, one forester actually wondered if the LINK could be used to 'help bring the churches together'! That was an ironical suggestion I had not foreseen; my thinking had not been that adventurous.

In this present context I was limited to thinking about the success of the woodland project but I did wonder why such a thought had not crossed the minds of the Church group on the previous day. Perhaps secular thinking, on some occasions, is more creative than ecclesiastical pondering. The chief forestry officer, Tšepo Senekane, summed up our discussion, welcoming the Durham-Lesotho initiative. There was strong approval for the community-based approach; the forestry division of the Ministry of Agriculture would provide technical support; the forestry officer would accompany me when I visited any sites to assess their suitability for woodland plantations; his professional advice would always be available; school tree nurseries should be incorporated into the project where viable. Then the parting gift: the government tree nurseries would supply saplings without charge. Arrangements for our first large-scale project were looking up!

On the Basotho timescale it was not a long wait before I asked for professional advice. Twenty-six days after first meeting the forestry officer, Dutchman Gart van Leersum, we were working together in the field. During those twenty-six days Edwin Chaka who, in addition to his duties as dean of the cathedral, was leading the LINK in Lesotho with great skill borne of his detailed cultural knowledge, broadcast the crucial need for land in which to plant the first major Durham-Lesotho LINK project. Edwin and I concocted a plan in which he informally suggested to influential people in the right quarters that the parish in which he had formerly served as rector should make available some of the land attached to the Rectory of St. Matthew's Parish, Malealea. There was one other considerable, but not immediately obvious, advantage of a site in Malealea; the Chief of the region was an Anglican! Edwin, together with Matthias Lebona, the parish priest, pulled it off and the LINK was granted the use of some two hectares of deep, fertile land adjacent to the rectory for its first woodland site. We had taken a useful first step but it was only a first step; we now had to get the Chief's support; the parish council's agreement; the headmaster's cooperation. Would I ever get one tree planted, let alone the hoped-for thousands?

So it was that during the very early, very hot, morning of Monday, 16th November 1987, I waited some three hours for the use of the diocese's little four-wheel-drive Suzuki to make my first journey to Malealea in the Mafeteng district. Since arriving in Lesotho fourteen years previously I had been trying to learn that the time for an appointment is often thought of as the time you depart for the engagement not the time to arrive, but, as an ex-Royal Navy man, that has not been easy. However, this delay was slightly easier to accept when, during the wait, I received a visit from the editor of *SEEK*, the provincial newspaper of the Anglican Church of Southern Africa. He used the time to quiz me about the LINK and I used it to elicit a few column inches (cm) for an article about the LINK. We arranged to meet again in Johannesburg to continue our discussions, none of which might have taken place if other arrangements had been on time. Even if we did depart at 11.00 a.m. for an 8.00 a.m. start there was a certain satisfaction in successfully getting four people and a vehicle in the same place at the same time, albeit late, for the same purpose. All we needed now was spirit: petroleum, personal and holy.

Eventually, heading south on a tarred, potholed main road, Edwin zigzagged the 28 miles (45 kms) to Motsekuoa where we turned from tar to dirt as we drove into the powerfully glaring sun. Avoiding some of the potholes and hitting others, I reflected that my first journey along this southern road was fourteen years earlier on my way to the Roman Catholic Mission at Bethel. Then the surface of this road was severely corrugated, compacted earth that shook every bone of the body for about five hours. Getting there involved going through the 'place of the wind', Moyeni (otherwise known as Quthing), turning north-eastwards, on the way stopping to view the dinosaur footprints preserved in the rocks and pausing to speculate what the countryside was like when they were around. Reaching Mount Moorosi we turned left, at what seemed like no particular point, to find the ford across the massive Orange River to get to Bethel on the other side. One advantage of my long initiation into Lesotho was the memory of what things used to be like and how, in some places, conditions for the traveller had improved. I concluded that one of the advances was that John McAdam[15] had greatly benefited the travelling public here and that view was quickly confirmed now that we had turned left and hit the dirt road, causing much of the surface to fly as dust through the air.

Precariously we drove along the track, the true nature of which, in recent years, a bureaucratic mind has tried to disguise by naming it on road maps as the B25. Once you are driving through the dust of other vehicles, over narrow bridges sometimes nothing more substantial than two strips of concrete just wide enough to allow a couple of inches (cm) error, around *dongas*, avoiding donkeys, horses, sheep and goats, there was no disguising the difficulty of using a twentieth-century invention in an eighteenth-century environment. Here there were no fences: what was I going to do with the £500 the British High Commissioner had promised me for fencing? I was soon to discover that in Lesotho there was only a vague notion of demarcation, certainly nothing like enclosure in England since the 1100s[16] which was, perhaps, why an educated young Basotho man once asked me how we dealt with the problem of cows on the streets of London. In the remote areas of the foothills and mountains the Mosaic directive still held sway: 'Do not move your neighbour's boundary stone ...'[17] or 'landmark'.[18] Unfortunately Moses didn't seem to appreciate that animals could not imagine a line existing between two stones, to say nothing of it being a boundary at which it should stop, never to eat beyond!

It was a rough, tough and sometimes painful ride made bearable by Edwin's cheerful commentary on the places we went through. As we gradually climbed in height our heading turned from south-east to due south passing on the left the Emmaus Roman Catholic Mission at Makhakhe (now on the B251), but since there were no service stations we stopped, for our convenience, at a *donga,* literally making a pit-stop! Whilst we took a break to stretch our legs I took careful note of the landmarks (that is, those that could not be moved) because I was beginning to suspect that I would be travelling this track many times over the next few years. After a few more vibrating miles we came to Matelile where there was much cheering, waving and ululation. The people had recognised Edwin who, much to my consternation, enthusiastically returned their greetings by waving with both hands as we jolted and weaved along at increasing speed. Escaping from the large crowds of people of all ages who were drawn from their huts by the noise, we took the next track on the left (the cartographers haven't yet given it a number), climbing eastward to 6,572 feet (2,003 m), where we obeyed the decree of an early trader in Malealea, Mervyn Smith, whose words are moulded into a metal plaque set incongruously in the rocks at the narrow stony pass into the Malealea Valley:

Wayfarer! Pause, and look upon a Gateway of Paradise[19]

And what a sight it was; the pain of the journey was washed away as I gazed down across the fertile valley that was proudly displaying its ability to grow trees, not many, but just enough to say 'come and join us'.

Perhaps Virgil had guided us through the agony of the journey to get to this gateway of paradise, but now I felt that I was infringing the tangible beauty that surrounded me even in the uncompromising light brown rocks. I was content just to be there soaking up the silence, the remoteness, the wonder and the magnificence. Now I needed someone to take me through the gateway; someone like Dante's Beatrice to guide me through paradise! The backdrop to the beautiful valley was the Thaba-Putsoa (Blue Mountain) range in which, although I didn't know it then, I was to work during the next six years, for many a long day, and sometimes many a long night. From Bethel I had already explored the southern ranges around Nohana and Ketane some twelve years previously with my friend, French-Canadian Roman Catholic missionary priest Michel Bissonnette. Even though I never did have the need to withdraw a molar (at least I haven't thus far), Michel taught me so much else about survival in the mountains, about Lesotho and the Basotho that became increasingly useful through the years. In the year before I arrived in Malealea I had saddled up and ridden through the Bokong Valley to the north-east.[20] Today the mountains, in their early-afternoon cold blue dress, looked harsh, unyielding almost to a point of dominance, standing there superior, brutal and all-powerful. I felt small: I was small.

Refreshed in body, mind and spirit I turned away from this awesome spectacle to return to the dust-covered Suzuki; it was then that I saw two women whom our work might help. They were about 5 feet 6 inches (1.7 m) tall, sturdy and well built, which they needed to be to support the enormous loads they were carrying on their heads. They shuffled their way along the stony track that, only a short time before, had us grumbling inside the truck. The rolled-up circle of cloth on their heads could not have provided much protection from the huge bundle of sticks and twigs, some sprouting leaves, bound together by grass twisted into a rope. The faggots were larger than either of the women who must have walked miles across hill and valley to find and collect their burdens. This side of paradise there were no trees, at least none in sight. As we all shared the traditional Sesotho greeting '*khotso*' (peace) I was strangely aware that their dress was out of harmony with the harshness of their surroundings. It was almost absurd to see them dressed in smart, brightly coloured skirts, one brilliant red and the other an equally brilliant yellow. Was this, as they carried home their burdens on that swelteringly hot afternoon, a visual rebelliousness of the bright against the drab, the clean against the dusty, the stylish against the mundane?

Leaving these two overladen women with their piles of firewood, the four men returned to their little vehicle to drive into the valley where they were to report to the Chief of Malealea with Qaba. Edwin had briefed me well; we must get the Chief on our side if we were to stand any hope of success. We parked the Suzuki near a low, dreary, dilapidated building that I was astonished to learn was St. Matthew's Rectory,[21] the home of Matthias Lebona who took us to the Chief's hut. On the way we passed the little church and the primary school and saw the rather better building of the secondary school some distance away. The sun had no mercy; it burned relentlessly. Some compassion, spurious though it was, came from the cooling air wafting from the distant mountains as I struggled along the rough pathway to the Chief's house. The gently embracing wind disguised my scorching as the sweat cooled and lowered my skin temperature but not my burning. How fortunate I was to be dark-skinned.

Edwin Chaka, his spirits running heartily at greeting so many people he knew, looked after me carefully as he led the way along the narrow track to a rectangular stone-built hut with its rusting corrugated-iron roof held in place by large rocks that had been placed on top so as to retain some semblance of dignity among the more traditional conical grass thatching. It was about 15 feet by 10 (4.6 m by 3) with two small windows, one each side of its ill-fitting wooden door from where Chief Setlakotlako[22] welcomed us. He was a short, small, thin, dark-skinned man whose age I would not care to guess as his moustache and deep furrows, gouged by the harsh climate, disguised his facial expressions. There were flecks of grey in his short, cropped black hair that, as I had already learned from Philip Mokuku, invests, in the brown eyes of the Basotho, a superior status. Nevertheless he was lithe, leaping to greet me with a crushing handshake and a flood of Sesotho that I could neither keep pace with nor understand. Sister Magdalena would *not* have been pleased! The overwhelming joy of our meeting went on for a long time as the Chief and Edwin reviewed, in some amazing detail, the years since they had last met. This gave me time to look around. Inside there was a bare minimum of furniture, the three of us occupying all the ancient upright, squeaky wooden chairs that were available on the uneven floor. The interior was plastered with what was, I learned very early on in my Lesotho experience, a mixture of mud and cow dung. At one side there was an old, rather battered rectangular wooden table around which six people could have sat; in its centre a paraffin lamp had pride of place even though the glass was heavily smoked. The only concession to decoration was three coloured pictures irregularly torn from old magazines and now attached at drunken angles to two of the walls by rust-covered nails.

The warm greetings continued in a flood of Sesotho whilst I listened in awe, wondering whether I would ever reach that speed! Apart from being a linguistic necessity it was certainly a diplomatic advantage to have Edwin with me as he had been the very popular parish priest of Malealea some years earlier. Chief Setlakotlako was so delighted to see him again I began to wonder if we would ever get round to talking about the real purpose of our visit. My concept of patience was being instilled with a new dimension; I kept telling myself I had to be patient, extremely patient, perhaps even long suffering. Under a corrugated-iron roof the scorching heat of a Lesotho summer did little to improve my endurance; it must have been well into the upper thirties. Then it was my turn! My wife (one), my children (two), my work, my house, my home, my country, my car, my cows (none), my distant relatives, my dog (nil), my food, my village, my land, my father, my mother, my brothers (providentially, in this context at least, I have none) and sisters (fortunately I have only one), my horse (I don't have one); they were all subjected to minute questioning that was even more prolonged because, I'm sorry, Sister, we had to talk through Edwin's interpretation.

Fearing that any silence on my part might be interpreted as disdainful, I quickly realised that I should break the pregnant pause of my mental exhaustion by showing the same interest in the Chief's wife, children, work, house, home, country, car, cows (countless), distant relatives (innumerable), dog, food, village, land, father, mother, brothers (unfortunately he had six), sisters (unluckily he had three), horses (many); to do otherwise might have been considered as aloofness. After another couple of hot hours, during which I hoped I hadn't tactlessly missed any essential person, the cultural ritual drew slowly to a close. The Chief had, to his satisfaction, established my standing in British society, accepted me into the Basotho community and now, with establishment complete, Edwin thought it wise, before the sun completed its day's work and went to sleep behind Thaba-Putsoa, to raise the subject of our visit! Not that we had eaten any dinner but even so all of us were, by now, post-prandially tired, especially the Chief; Edwin had timed his presentation of our request with great skill.

Yes, the Chief assured us, he would like us to plant trees as they would help the people of the village and he would give instructions for the herdboys to keep their sheep and goats out of the plantation. As, at the time, there was some political tension between chiefs and government, when Edwin and I had gone to meet with the Chief Matthias, exercising some subtle diplomacy, had taken the Ministry of Agriculture forester, Gart van Leersum, to meet the village headman and the chairman of the village development committee. Now, amicably, the seven of us inspected land allocated years ago to the Anglican Church but with which nothing had been done since. It was flat with a good depth of soil and water was available just a short distance away. It also had the beginnings of a *donga* so that our hope to provide a means of soil conservation could be incorporated in this site. Also, importantly, the rectory overlooked it and therefore some measure of supervision could be given and it was the nearest to the church. The second site was on the side of a steep hill, rocky and with very little depth of soil. It sloped down into a glorious valley at the bottom of which was a large *donga*. Planting there would have been dangerous. The third site further up the valley was very similar. Turning back towards the school the fourth site was a large tract of land, with adequate soil depth and water nearby but with outcrops of rock. For our pilot project Gart recommended the church land and the Chief also agreed to reserve the fourth site for us that would be used mainly by the school children. Agreement all round was sealed by more sweaty handshaking as the sun went to bed.

Consensus leadership certainly takes time, effort and patience, but the knowledge that there is unanimity can be reassuring, even if one is left with the suspicion that perhaps not everybody agreed with the final decision. So was it a final decision? As we mapped out the boundary of the first of our woodland sites the chairman of the village development committee set about arranging a meeting of his committee for the following month and Edwin agreed to return in January to explain the project to the villagers and what was required of them. Final decision or not, we all shook hands again for Gart to take photographs. I thought it was time to leave but far from it: I never made the Suzuki. The Chief said I couldn't go without seeing the school; the village headman said I couldn't go without seeing the development of a *donga* by Ntate Musi; Matthias said I couldn't go without seeing the church.

The school, alongside the site, was a sad reflection on poor educational provision. By this time 'school was out', although crowds of children were still playing around and seven of their teachers, all ladies, were waiting to greet me. One wore old-style traditional garb complete with *kòtò* (knobkerrie) and *thupa* (stick), seen nowadays only on ceremonial occasions: I was greatly honoured. The others were dressed in smart European-style dresses, skirts and blouses. They told me that they taught all the classes, usually six or seven, in the one old church building with no separate classrooms and few desks or forms. Most of the children had to sit on the earth floor whilst writing, if they had paper and pencil, on their knees or the floor. Nailed to the wall at the end opposite the original apse was a broken blackboard with notes from a former lesson still displayed. Few of the windows had any complete panes of glass; some had none at all. Visual aids for mathematics, old enough to have collected considerable layers of dust, were attached to a string nailed to the wall and discarded garments were littering the interior, with some thrown across the roof trusses. It was all rather depressing. The old church building was much larger than the present one, so I asked myself the obvious question: is this a sign of declining numbers of people attending church services? I spent a few minutes, perhaps rather longer, laughing and joking with the huge crowd of children who had gathered to enjoy themselves thoroughly at my poor Sesotho, and I at their poor English, as they walked with me past, I noted, a water standpipe convenient for the woodland site.

I was intrigued by the second request, to visit a *donga* developed by Ntate Musi into an agriculture project situated on the edge of the village. My interest was stirred because I remembered a man of that name attending my college in the mid-1970s as part of the educational project that had now closed. I also wanted to see what I could learn from this development that might be useful in the future for the LINK. We trekked a long way but it was worth all the effort. Ntate Musi, the younger brother of the man I knew, was to become headmaster of the Malealea Secondary School. That was to prove to be a very useful connection when it came to introducing the tree nursery as part of the educational element. Now I was shown a remarkable agricultural development that was the result of many hours of hard work. The south-facing *donga* was comparatively shallow to most of them so, to limit further soil erosion, Ntate Musi had built a succession of drystone dam walls through which the water percolated, leaving behind barriers of alluvium soil in which he was growing an impressive array of vegetables. The sides of the *donga* had been planted with pecan trees that not only produced high-quality and high-value nuts, but also provided shade for the crops in the *donga* beneath. A further feature was the construction of a small reservoir from which he drew water for, among other things, a shower he had made at the side of the *donga*. He worked hard, washed off the sweat and went home clean. It was a remarkable reclamation, the result of dedicated work but now, tucking it away at the back of my mind, we went on to visit the church.

St. Matthew's Church was a small rectangular building about 45 feet long and 20 feet wide (14 m by 6 m), built of cut stone with a single-span corrugated-iron roof with interior exposed roof struts. Down each side of the nave were three pairs of long, narrow windows each fully glazed; unusually the interior was pleasantly light. The 24 backless wooden forms arranged on the earthen floor, providing a central and two side aisles, could accommodate about 120 people. The altar, draped with a clean white cloth, was on a small dais in the chancel set in an apse. There was no sign of any service books. It was all fresh and tidy giving the impression of care and attention even if, outside, the wonky cross at the apex of the roof looked as though it were about to crash to the ground. I noted that it was within convenient walking distance of our selected woodland site; that was very expedient. Standing in the lengthening shadows by the main door we all agreed that planting the site would be preceded by a service of dedication, emphasising the Christian obligation to care for God's world. Saplings would be handed to the congregation as they left the church and, at the woodland site, Matthias would pray for God's blessing on the project. However, there was much to do before we sought divine approval.

It was time for me to find the Suzuki which, this time, I did without distraction. Although there were prolonged farewells to Chief Setlakotlako; the parish priest Matthias Lebona; the village headman; the chairman of the village development committee; plus others who had joined us by this time, we did manage to withdraw with some dignity. Feeling that a useful start had been made we bumped our way back to the B25, turned northwards to reach the relatively smooth A2 and then on to Maseru, leaving paradise to its inhabitants with the promise to help them plant 4,000 trees in 5 acres (2 hectares).

Back in Maseru and supper! The first food since an early breakfast was welcome, as was a bath and bed after a sixteen-hour day that saw the LINK take its first tentative steps towards what was to become a highly significant contribution to environmental protection that was years ahead of other ecological enterprises in the field! We were in business; hopefully the Lord's business!

With only three days to go before I left Lesotho for South Africa, Zimbabwe[23] and Zambia[24] (where I was to switch into educational mode) there was much to be arranged. Edwin, who was enjoying his additional new responsibilities, came to discuss arrangements for the next few weeks. We agreed that he would return to Malealea next month to keep up the momentum by meeting with the village development committee, the Church council and the headmaster of the secondary school, when he would explain the details of the project. In January, with all the local leaders, Edwin would speak at a village *pitso*. This public assembly is a grand reunion where everyone sits around on the ground wrapped in their colourful blankets and has the right to be heard, to ask questions, make comments and, hopefully, begin to feel involved in the project. The Chief is normally the last person to speak at a *pitso*, when he attempts to bring together the views expressed by the people, ending with the national motto '*Khotso – Pula – Nala*' (Peace – Rain – Prosperity). It is, inevitably, a long, drawn-out means of consensus politics that is gradually fading into the history of Lesotho but which is, as we were to experience in 1988, a useful bonding tradition.

Providing all went well at the *pitso* Edwin would arrange for the site to be ploughed and fenced ready for the great planting day on Tuesday, 15th March 1988 and the following month the tree nursery at the secondary school would be started. If it all worked out the timing was just what I had hoped for, with the local people making the decisions that most closely affected them whilst I was out of sight thousands of miles away in Durham. It would then begin to become our project with a common purpose, located in their parish, guided by their leaders, for the benefit of everyone. It was to be some years later that my style of operating in Lesotho was recognised by a British High Commissioner who said to me, 'I think one of the great strengths of the Durham LINK, Peter, is that you go away!' I knew what he meant (at least, I like to think I did!).

That perceptive observation was easier to put into words than into practice. As my departure date became general knowledge going away became increasingly difficult as appointments became compacted. When I was to meet with the Minister of Health about the LINK's medical contribution, the staff timed our discussion to take place half an hour after I had taken off from Moshoeshoe Airport! Now it was 17th November 1987, St. Hild's Day, so it was appropriate that I spent most of this day working in the educational field as I had been vice-principal of a college dedicated to St. Hild. She had been recalled from my home region of East Anglia to lead a religious house in County Durham (where I now lived) before she founded a monastery for both men and women. Here in Lesotho it had been arranged for me to visit Hoohlo Primary School in Maseru, where I met with the three lady teachers who were struggling with overcrowding, poor facilities, inadequate resources and squalid buildings. These visible and obvious handicaps were accentuated by less noticeable difficulties such as poor wages, their own meagre professional education, and limited guidance and advice available to them. Predictably the teachers were both psychologically distraught and professionally frustrated. Nevertheless, they displayed an admirable cheerfulness that filtered through to their pupils and after an enjoyable morning in the school with some enthusiastic children I went to lunch thinking about how the LINK might contribute to education. Providentially I was dining with one of the best head teachers and one of the most effective classroom teachers I ever worked with in Lesotho, Steven Molokeng and Alina Pholosi from St. Agnes' Primary School, Teyateyaneng. I shared my ideas with them and listened carefully to their suggestions and advice to take back to Durham, where in due time they would both work for the LINK.

Having started the day with the most junior members of the educational establishment and fortified by a Chinese lunch, I now moved to the pinnacle (as he would have been in most societies), the Minister of Education himself, Mr Tiheli, supported by his Minister of State.[25] In his small, cramped office there was a potentially dangerous feature that can be found in many offices and rooms in Lesotho. To create some humidity in an otherwise very dry atmosphere a small tin of water is precariously balanced on the top of an electric fire, so I had to be very careful not to disturb its balance as I talked about the LINK's Christian basis, our start on the community woodland project and its educational contribution to the curriculum by the development of tree nurseries in schools. It was not long before we moved into a general discussion of education and that dialogue soon narrowed to the serious difficulties being faced in teacher education, at which point I felt we were moving out of the LINK's orbit into my professional arena. However, that formed a useful basis from which to launch some ideas that would be more manageable by the LINK such as a school building programme, the establishment of libraries, environmental education (thinking of the tree nurseries) and a programme of scholarships, all of which received valuable ministerial support.

However important and useful that ministerial support was I had to recognise that over and above that level was the powerful military regime that in 1987 controlled the government of Lesotho. So it was I found myself, once again, going through all the points I had discussed earlier with the minister but this time with his military overseer, the colonel in charge of education for the Military Council, Colonel Sekhobe Letsie. He was polite and courteous but I did find it inhibiting discussing education literally looking down the barrel of a gun.

Escaping without damage I went on to see the Permanent (soon, in the uncertain temporary world of political appointments, to be renamed Principal) Secretary of Education with whom I had worked since 1973, Charles Bohloko. He immediately spoke about the problems of the National Teacher Training College (as it was then described) particularly those related to the practical teaching element but, as my time was rapidly slipping away, I quickly moved the conversation on to the work of the LINK. As we drew towards the end of our time together his kind offer to drive me to the airport when I left Lesotho made me feel uncomfortable that I had not pursued what was obviously a major talking point in the Ministry of Education. Back at the Anglican Centre I hoped that by supper I would be free of educational problems but no, the retired suffragan bishop who had welcomed my friend and me on my first visit to the cathedral fourteen years earlier arrived to talk about his hope that his granddaughter would read medicine in a British university! I went to bed realising that I had to balance my time carefully between work for the LINK and other demands whilst remaining conscious also that my long association with Lesotho was opening many doors for the LINK that would otherwise be difficult to enter. It wasn't only trees that we were planting.

One door that was wide open during all my efforts to get the LINK established was that of the British High Commission. The morning of the last full day of my seven-week visit brought a telephone call from the Second Secretary, Dennis Quinn, with the welcome news that we could now spend up to 2,500 maloti (which was, at the then current exchange rate, £850 of British taxpayers' money) on fencing the Malealea community woodlands site. Grateful though I was I could see difficulties looming. It is very unusual in Lesotho to find any form of fencing in rural districts, so fencing was a potentially contentious issue that I was content to leave to the negotiating skills of Edwin Chaka in the knowledge that we had the money if local people decided to protect the saplings from the large number of goats that fed in the area. In Lesotho professional foresters considered a plantation to have been successful if just half the planted saplings survived to maturity: I wanted the LINK to do better. We were planning for today and planting for tomorrow. Planting had to be followed by nurture; feeding goats on tree saplings could be expensive.

All of this progress I was able to report to a meeting of the forestry division at the Ministry of Agriculture that we just managed to get into the timetable before I left. There we agreed that the site should be ploughed immediately and that Edwin Chaka should suggest to the people when he addressed the *pitso* that we plant a mixed woodland of pine, fir, willow, poplar and eucalyptus. In January 1988, when he returned from the *pitso* he brought back a suggestion that those people who planted the community woodland should be given fruit trees for their personal use and this idea was eventually included in the project.

Even if the trees were not yet clapping their hands I hoped at least Thaba- Putsoa would be encouraged to 'burst into song'[26] at the progress we were making. I felt we had made a good start to a major project that was being built on a unit structure that ensured that if one community woodland failed it would not bring down the whole project. As we were beginning to talk about expansion into other regions the strength of the unit structure became more important as each unit could be adapted to suit local conditions and we would learn from our experience without committing large sums of money at any one time. Furthermore, I was very pleased at the progress we had made towards the principle of working with a secular organisation especially as, in this case, it was also a government body.

The local people encouraged me by the manner in which they had shown an active interest in surrounding the project with their faith. They wanted to sing hymns as they carried their saplings to the site and Matthias, who knew his flock well, also expected that when the time came, they would dance their way to the site. Back in Maseru Philip Mokuku was supportive, but I was disappointed that other Church leaders did not seem to be more enthusiastic about linking activity with faith though perhaps, I told myself, I had wrongly interpreted the apparent lethargy. Conceivably I should have given more attention to explaining this principle, but since the overall message of the biblical book of James was the importance of blending faith and action I suppose I assumed the example would have been widely accepted and understood. Perhaps I had been too naïve, but I wasn't too troubled since Edwin and Matthias were keen enough and experienced Basotho. I did wonder, however, what would happen after I had gone.

But go I must! It was the end of a seven-week visit that had spanned agriculture, medicine, education and theology and provided me with a wealth of ideas. I now had to present those ideas to Durham supporters of the LINK which was just eighteen months old. Now, at Moshoeshoe Airport, the 15:20 flight was bang on Basotho time, leaving promptly at 16:00 hours. What would Moshoeshoe have said? Before I could give that question any attention I found it a little disconcerting to watch a man, who I assumed was an aircraft mechanic, run across the runway with a small screwdriver, lift a flap on the engine cowling and delve into the interior, presumably to make some essential last-minute adjustment. We reached Johannesburg safely.

With Lesotho, South Africa, Zimbabwe and Zambia more than 6,000 miles (9,656 kms) behind me and carrying a clutch of ideas that I hoped would hatch into viable initiatives, I arrived back in Gatwick Airport in the early morning of Thursday, 3rd December 1987. Leaving my friend and protagonist George Carey to his episcopal consecration across the city in Southwark Cathedral I struggled by train back to Durham where, arriving in broad daylight, I quickly realised the necessity of changing my cultural behaviour. As I was to discover over the years, and what became evident when expanding the woodland project into Ha Ralehlatsa, the Basotho can be a superstitious people and although rarely practised these days there was a time when a traveller, on his return home, would avoid the eyes of anyone falling upon him before entering his home lest evil befall him. Here was I arriving home at midday! The next morning the first duty of a Mosotho was to report to the Chief, another cultural lesson that, as I was to learn to my embarrassment when I failed to report to a bishop before talking with his suffragan, is now obscurely construed yet, in some places, still observed.

As an experienced sailor I certainly knew that time and tide waited for no man but now I had to learn the rather more difficult lesson that the planting season in Lesotho was also time-bound. It was a more difficult lesson because the boundary within which the time limit existed was so much longer and not so precisely defined. Time and tides are contained, in most places, within twenty-four hours – a planting season, vaguely, within about two months. This phenomenon created an impression that there would always be sufficient time available for planting. So, back in Durham there was work to do and not much time in which to do it, but my first couple of days back home required, in addition to cultural changes, as always, quite a lot of personal adjustment. Although we had kept in frequent contact Pam had much to share with me and I with her. There was a mass of paper to wade through; few wide-open spaces to alleviate the hemmed-in, claustrophobic feeling; a different mode of communicating and, a diocesan appetite for information to quench.

Whilst David Jenkins was wondering if the Church of England would ever see the wood from the trees, one of the LINK's many working parties (so-called to evade the negative connotations provoked by the concept of 'committee'), the woodland working party, was wondering how we were going to raise the money that was required to plant the trees. Given that I had negotiated in Lesotho for the government tree nurseries to provide the LINK with 4,000 saplings free of charge, the British High Commission had agreed to pay for fencing and the people were providing the labour, little further finance was required for this first site. Thanks to various small fund-raising events and some generous gifts from Durham parishes there was sufficient money available to finance the Malealea planting and the group agreed to support the venture. Now we had to think about all the other nine potential sites that had been identified in Lesotho, for which we could not expect the same generous giving either of labour, money or trees. There was no doubt in our collective thinking that if we really were conducting the Lord's business, He would provide[27] the means, but we had to mobilise the resources and release the money. As we were working with strong secular support in Lesotho I thought it appropriate at this point to talk again to the chairman of Durham County Council (was this the Durham equivalent of reporting to the Chief?) who, when I had earlier described the work of the LINK and its potential, was extremely helpful and supportive.

Now that I had something definite to present to him the chairman, Bob Pendleberry, was extremely enthusiastic. We met in his large, palatial office in County Hall during the latter part of the morning of Wednesday, 23rd March 1988 and were later joined by a high-powered group of staff:[28] the chief executive, the county council treasurer, the county council secretary and solicitor, and a representative of the council's Environment Department. This really was the Church going out into 'all the world'[29] (even though it was on our doorstep).

To those who had just joined us I briefly explained the Christian ethos of the LINK and how this related to our obligation to care for the environment. Describing the problem of serious soil erosion in Lesotho, the resulting *dongas* and the need for fuel and shade, I illustrated how trees might help to alleviate some of these difficulties. I touched, I hope lightly but firmly, on the small number of trees in County Durham and how Lesotho and Durham might, together, identify a similar problem and seek a common solution. Equipped with large copies of pictures to illustrate the points I was making, interest was high. It was all very positive but the question I concluded with was, 'How could it all fit together?'

After a few minutes of intensive brainstorming the County Hall group came up with the idea that we should mount a Durham-Lesotho tree week, for which they would provide all the necessary resources for its advertisement and implementation if the LINK would provide illustrative material and information relating to Lesotho. This encouraging advance stimulated by the LINK's initiative was all very timely, as the lack of trees in Durham had been recognised early enough for the Environment Department of the county council to take action with assistance from the government-sponsored countryside commission. Here was a splendid opportunity for Church and State to cooperate in a way that I had hoped and prayed for when I started the LINK. We all lunched together in a mood of optimism. It was not until years later, when global warming became a fashionable topic, that we realised that the LINK, in 1987, had been many years in advance of most others in promoting the essential work of conservation.

The hard work that followed in the offices of the county council was matched by a strenuous effort in the Durham woodlands working party: it was justifying its description. Leaflets were printed in their thousands and distributed through scores of outlets in both the diocese and the county. To make this a really combined effort some leaflets included this personal prayer:

> Heavenly Father,
>
> I pray that the tree(s) I have bought will flourish and grow not only to beautify Your world, but also to conserve its soil and to provide fuel for warmth and timber for building. Bless Your people in Lesotho who care for the tree(s); give to each of them the skill required to nurture the woodlands so that they may grow into maturity to show the full glory of Your creation. I pray that Christians in both Durham and Lesotho may be bound together in this common task through Jesus Christ, Lord of us all.
>
> Amen.

So in Durham, Sunday, 27th November 1988 was designated Plant-a-Tree Day; church services focused on the work of the LINK; six sites in the county of Durham had been selected; people were asked to pay one pound for a tree to plant in Durham, the money going to the LINK's woodland working party for trees in Lesotho. Although by this time the first site at Malealea had been planted and was growing strongly, the Durham contribution financed the planting of the second site at Malealea, started a tree nursery in the school there and provided an essential basis for the planting of nine other sites in Lesotho. The message 'Plant a tree in Co. Durham – buy a tree for Lesotho' was projected very clearly, helped by widely used envelope stickers showing the outline of a tree around a Christian cross. With two messages in one vehicle, together with an easy-to-grasp description of Lesotho, it was an attractive and heartening start not only to involvement in the woodland project, but also to the notion of secular-spiritual collaboration. More vividly the Basotho would say, 'Father, you have placed the bean in its right pod!'[30] Time would tell its version.

Lunching in Durham with a sailing friend, my birthday, on the Ides of March[31] 1988, was pleasant and in the evening at home a small party with church friends concluded an enjoyable day, but in Lesotho it was wonderful! There, the Basotho presented me with one of the best presents I could have wished for. Wrapped in their blankets as protection from the early morning chill, even in this summer month, they streamed into the Malealea Valley from the surrounding hills packing themselves, as only Basotho can, into the small St. Matthew's Church. There, Matthias Lebona presided at the eucharist and Edwin Chaka, whose address at the January *pitso* had obviously been well received, spoke about the duty of Christians to look after God's world and how important trees were in that process. As everyone left the church they continued to sing songs of praise as they were given saplings to plant and yes, Matthias had been right, many of the women did dance their way to the site, which had been well prepared in time for this great event. How I wish I were there: how good it was I was not!

Planting trees is only the beginning and takes little time. Caring for them is a much longer process that, in Lesotho, needs strong support from the Chief and his people. Fortunately we had both on our side, upheld by the authority of the Church and biblical teaching that reminded us all that 'The one who sows and the one who waters really do not matter. It is God who matters, because he makes the plant grow'.[32] To help that growth we had agreed with the local people to fence the site so the saplings were adequately protected from marauding herds of goats, or so we thought. However, this may have been an unforeseen weakness that was difficult to resolve. Droppers, veld netting and stretchers, all new to me, that exclude animals from the planted area help the grass within the site to grow to an attractive density so herdboys are tempted to break down fences to let in their herds to eat the lush grass. Given that luxuriant grazing might be many miles distant that is understandable, but goats can be destructive to newly planted saplings and fortunately that was appreciated by Chief Setlakotlako, who issued dire warnings to any who offended. Few did but those who succumbed to the temptation were quickly spotted from St. Matthew's Rectory. The site had been well chosen. Watching over his flock brought a new dimension to Matthias Lebona's ministry! Despite some serious periods of drought it also produced the outstandingly vigorous growth that I saw when I visited the site nine years after the first planting.

The LINK's executive officer, with a forester from the Ministry of Agriculture, frequently checked the site during the next six years when fences were repaired and dead trees replaced. The school tree nursery started and the other sites were planted. It became quite a showpiece in the LINK's achievements, especially as chiefs of other areas were taken there to show them what could be achieved. Malealea became influential in the establishment of nine other community woodland sites.[33] They were not all so successful but this first one, for which we all knew success was so important, became the model on which all others were planted. There were local differences that had to be accommodated. Church land was not always available so some plantations were developed on land belonging to church schools such as that of Sekameng High School where the head teacher, Joshua Hlakoane,[34] was instrumental in establishing a thriving plantation of 400 oaks, pines and eucalyptus, to be expanded by a mass of peach trees.[35] Although we had our failures they were few and the unit structure of the project limited any serious damage or loss that was caused.

Ralehlatsa Primary School in the lowlands just south of Peka on the main north road was, after an initial problem, a success beyond our expectations. In addition to the sometimes fear-provoking, off-road-and-track, four-wheel driving to get there, when we did we met with a different, though not isolated, fear-provoking social problem. The land we were allocated within the school boundary was on the perimeter of the extensive site. Nearby was a small collection of huts occupied by local people who were superstitious Basotho who believed that evil spirits lived in forests and woods.[36] They did not want trees planted near their huts! By the time we were seeking to develop this site Steven Molokeng had been appointed the first full-time executive officer of the LINK in Lesotho and he spent many hours talking to the local residents in his skilful, sensitive way, eventually persuading them to become involved by helping with the planting. He did his work well, for this became one of the most successful of our woodland sites helping, much to the pleasure of those who had earlier resisted the planting, to stabilise an extremely sandy and dusty area. The people also went one important step further, assisting with the educational element by helping to start a tree nursery and planting the saplings with the children.

Whilst working at Ralehlatsa we had bestowed upon us an embarrassment of riches! If they can avoid the ravages of frost and drought, trees grow very quickly in the lowlands of Lesotho and one day, about four years after the planting at the primary school when strong, vigorous growth was clearly evident, the Chief of the area came to see what progress the plantation was making. Morena Katiso Ramaisa greeted Steven and me very warmly before spending a long time going through the cultural preliminaries. I was used to this by now but I sensed there was something more to his manner than was usually evident. He was delighted with the woodland and standing in the waist-high trees he looked across the Ralehlatsa Valley and promptly allocated to the LINK a huge swathe of land just beyond where most of the people lived. As we stood there his heavily gnarled hand gently took my less laboured one and we stood there holding hands (as men in Lesotho tend to do) whilst he pointed with his other hand to a small *donga* on the distant south-facing slope. Once I'd spotted the *donga* and we had agreed we were looking at the same one, he gave a broad sweep of his free arm, almost losing his blanket in the excited process, indicating a vast area he was willing to provide for tree-planting, stopping at the next *donga* only after his dramatic gesture had covered hundreds of acres (hectares).

I was speechless; not because I could not fully express myself in Sesotho but because I was overwhelmed! Steven thanked him profusely and I undertook to speak to my colleagues about his kind offer, but I could give him no immediate assurance about our ability to use his generous allocation. Obviously despite the superstitious feelings of some of his people our success at Ralehlatsa had stimulated a strong desire in the Chief to participate in the achievement. On the way back to Teyateyaneng Steven assured a rather sceptical Englishman that it was a genuine offer that I should take seriously. This abundance of land embodied a huge cultural divide. Standing there looking at the huge area I ruefully reflected that the only land I owned in England was a small back garden about the size of a tennis court! I felt drawn into the Chief's enthusiasm but, conversely, I knew that I needed to maintain a balance in our work. I was about to discover that our success might make that exceedingly difficult.

From tiny, mountainous Lesotho my next stop was the massive, low-lying Namibia, one of the least densely populated countries of the world where in 2009, an imperial statistician would have found hidden away just 6.7 people in every square mile; whereas the metric explorer would find 2.6 people concealed in every square kilometre. In Owamboland, in northern Namibia, where a single strand wire fence marked the southern border of Angola, I was based at St. Mary's Mission, Odibo. I was assisting with a large, European-funded water project designed to alleviate a serious shortage of potable water. The Anglican Church in Namibia, in partnership with a small British charity, Cooperation for Development, was sinking groundwater wells in some of the most remote arid areas of Owamboland. When I was not learning what life was like for a mole by frequent descents into the bowels of the earth, learning about no-fines concrete[37] and how to get back to base following the spoor we had made earlier in the day, I was hearing from the director of CD, as the charity was conveniently called, about a forestry project proposal he had submitted to Brussels for funding from the commission's tropical rainforest budget. Terry Lacey knew of the LINK's community woodlands in Lesotho and, as our spoor led us to supper, we discussed the strategies and techniques the LINK had successfully employed and if they might be expanded and used in his proposal.

He was keen to harness the LINK's experience and we felt some obligation to assist as CD, for its part, had been generous in its financial support of our work, contributing liberally from its European Commission block grant.[38] Around the change in decade from the 1980s to the 1990s work in Namibia, Botswana and Kenya occupied much of my time so it was some months later that we met in Lesotho, where CD's director and its treasurer[39] accompanied me to four of our woodland sites before meeting with Philip Mokuku and Steven Molokeng. Terry Lacey outlined what CD had in mind: a million trees to be planted in five years fully funded by the EU's tropical rainforest budget. It all sounded very attractive but by no stretch of anyone's imagination (except perhaps Terry's) could Lesotho ever sprout a tropical rainforest! During the discussion I sensed there was some caution and hesitancy amongst the Basotho, so as Terry left the airport that evening I cautioned against over-optimism. I was wrong; at least, I was wrong for the present. The proposal was further discussed amongst nine senior diocesan officials[40] on Monday, 18th June 1990 when, much to my surprise, they enthusiastically set up an executive committee to continue investigating the consequences if the LINK undertook the community forestry project in conjunction with CD. I wondered if they had grasped its implications and, mystified, I flew off to Kenya.

A cooperative forestry project that had started with a discussion in Namibia and progressed in Lesotho was now about to be drafted in Kenya and taken back to the UK for further discussion both there and in Brussels. The LINK was certainly crossing international boundaries. It was in the guest house of the Church of the Province of Kenya in Nairobi that I wrote the first of many drafts and where I began to realise that cooperation with another charity, with different objectives, working methods, structures and budgeting practices was going to be very difficult. Nevertheless, when I returned to Durham the woodland working party saw this as a natural development of its much smaller community woodlands and was keen to seize the opportunity to make a further substantial contribution to the LINK's mission. Independently assessing the new project the development group also gave its support to the proposal and as Steven Molokeng, the LINK's Lesotho executive officer, was in Durham at this time making a series of school visits, we also had the benefit of his advice. This, together with the discussions that had already taken place in Maseru, maintained the principle of close engagement with the Basotho when new projects were being considered.

With that strong support I went to Brussels for a couple of days in October 1990[41] where I hoped to achieve, with CD, some clarity on the commission's notion of 'tropical'. In the course of conversation with Marcus Roberts I sensed there was some latitude within which to manoeuvre, but whether that would go sufficiently far south to incorporate Lesotho remained unclear. If we kept to specific guidelines showing how the proposed project would fit into the government's overall plan, Marcus was confident that any submission would be well received. He recommended that our background reading should include the Tropical Forest Action Plan of the United Nation's Food and Agricultural Organisation in Rome. There was obviously still a lot of homework to be done. We concluded by reviewing the LINK's community woodland project in the course of which, when talking about the role of the Church in Lesotho, he said he was involved with the English Church in Brussels and commented on the 'absurdity' of it being part of the diocese of Gibraltar.

Unprepared for this, and with more than enough to cope with, I withdrew with some inept remark about the organisation of the Anglican Church and found my way, by means of the disorientating half-flights of stairs for which the building is well known, to the office of Carola Köster, with whom I had been negotiating for our co-funded projects. The head of the NGO section, M. Reithinger, was also present when we reviewed the LINK's work and progress, producing a favourable report on our work that had been submitted by the European Union delegate in Maseru. Even if we were critical (as I was) of our work and progress our standing amongst the commission's staff was high to the point of dangerous; there was a long way to fall! Avoiding a suggestion that the LINK might become involved in a Jamaican banana 941-project (everything seemed to be distinguished by numbers), I left DG VIII (numbers that confusingly fluctuated between Rome and Arabia) to board Flight SN595 to Newcastle. As I dozed some 12,000 feet (3,660 m) above the North Sea I reflected that I had come away not exactly successful in determining what bureaucrats in Brussels think a tropical rainforest really is, admiring the semantics but still concerned about the concept's flexibility and its ability to assimilate Lesotho.

There was little opportunity in what was left of 1990 to do much about what we were now calling the Community Forestry Project. I had to return to Namibia for most of November and the LINK's many micro-projects were taking a lot of time, effort and long-distance telephoning. Behind the Durham scene Richard Briggs was writing up the next draft based on my notes and the information, suggestions and warnings that had been gleaned from Brussels. Early in December the architect's first plans for Ha Popa Rural Health Centre landed on my Durham desk and needed immediate attention so we could go out to tender. I was preparing to launch the Ha Mohatlane Community Education Centre feasibility study and the booklet on the first five years of the LINK's work had been drafted. There was so much going on that the five years expanded to six. There was a benefit though: the delay enabled the inclusion of the first public mention of the forestry proposal! Before returning to South Africa and Lesotho in January 1991, Pam and I had a wonderful Christmas with three visiting Basotho who were studying in three different UK universities, two of whom were on courses arranged by the LINK.[42]

Events in Lesotho had been happening at a rather more leisurely pace but no less importantly. By the time I returned in mid-January, having survived the flight from Johannesburg to Maseru on one engine, it was obvious much thinking and talking about the proposed forestry project had taken place. In between the arrival of a group of Durham youth, scholarship interviews, meetings with architects about the design of Ha Popa, the drafting of advertisements for a Literary Fellowship at Durham Cathedral and the checking of the accounts of the poultry unit project, time was found for Philip and me to talk about forestry. He quizzed me extensively about CD and its possible relationship with the diocese of Lesotho. This worried him and I was unable to allay his fears. We met with the original group he had set up to consider the proposal which, after a lot of agonising, resulted in a request that the forestry proposal be implemented only under the auspices of the LINK. This put me in a difficult position but when I met, in Chesham on Thursday, 30th May 1991, with representatives of Cooperation for Development, the decision of the Basotho was taken calmly and with quiet composure. As CD had serious problems with some of its projects there was, I think, relief at the decision and Terry Lacey suggested that I should go to Brussels in September to discuss the possible handover.

I didn't think that a face-to-face meeting in Brussels was necessary at this stage and replaced that idea with a long telephone conversation with Marcus Robbins. When we spoke during the morning of Wednesday, 11th September 1991 he 'was very positive about the possibility of replacing the Lesotho Forestry Project submitted by CD with a modified version from the Durham-Lesotho LINK'.[43] He gave me a number of comprehensive guidelines based on the European Commission's ecology budget, a copy of which he sent me later. I noted the nuances he used during our talk: 'taking over' was changed to 'the possibility of replacing' and 'the proposal' was replaced with 'a modified version'. We were at the beginning of a lot of work and I now needed to know if there was sufficient support in Durham to justify the effort that would be required to get saplings into the ground.

The next evening Richard Briggs and Paul Jefferson, the chairman of the woodland working party, discussed with me the prospect of starting what would, in financial terms, be our largest project. After we had prayed and talked through the principles, objectives and practicalities we drank copious amounts of coffee and tea and Paul agreed to recommend to his working party on Monday, 7th October 1991 that we go ahead with the preliminary work. Little did Paul (or, for that matter, any of us) realise at the time he would be responsible three years later, in his new role as executive officer of the LINK, for the project he was now agreeing to launch! Now, late in the evening, we were deciding to go ahead not with the project as such, that was still years away, but with all the preliminary work that it entailed in the hope that it would result in large numbers of trees growing in Lesotho and a large number of people developing a real understanding of looking after God's world and forming a new, more meaningful relationship with Him.

The well-rehearsed submission process began almost immediately, but we had to be cautious as we were in new territory and on a different budget line to that with which we were familiar. I was grateful that the nuances I had picked up in my conversation with Marcus Robbins allowed us to 'replace' the original CD proposal with a 'modified' version, which was less ambitious but still sufficiently enterprising to be appealing to the European Commission to attract a 100 per cent grant. That was obviously a strong attraction but, less obviously, a grave weakness that this project never fully overcame. Unlike all our previous projects this was not co-funded or joint-funded but a project fully funded by the European Commission that the LINK agreed to implement. It made no financial demands upon the LINK and its working parties: that much we had taken over from CD. Consequently we had a minimum of direct influence on the manner of operating, and the purpose and target of the project. The LINK was not in the business of just planting trees but in the much more complex activity of 'the Lord's business'[44] because 'Jesus is for everyone'.[45] The 'word' had to accompany the 'work'. Now, with all the finance being given by an outside agent much of the work had already been done; results became all important with negligible attention being given to the means of attaining them. Instead of being an active partner with the Commission, the Overseas Development Administration (as it then was) and its other donors, the LINK became more an agent of the Commission reducing the status of the woodland working party to that of an advisory group, limiting its involvement and, importantly, its responsibility, with an accompanying decline in interest. Perhaps this was a foreboding of sad things to come but that was a long way ahead.

For the present we were to discover a grain of truth in the Basotho proverb 'everything has its own time', but it didn't make the delay any easier to bear. After submitting our modified replacement proposal we waited, and waited, and waited. I spoke to Marcus Robbins again on Monday, 16th December 1991 when I emphasised that the planting season in Lesotho was short and almost upon us. He promised to try to bring forward a decision on the project so we could get started but to no effect. The slow progress of the Commission was still in bottom gear and it was March before we received the promise of a decision by the end of April when the planting period for 1992 would be drawing to an end. A decision was not forthcoming. It was replaced by a series of questions about the inflation rate, the speed of planting and the availability of land and another suggestion of further talks at the beginning of July that resulted in the promise of a decision in August. I needed to know, either 'for' or 'against', so other activities of the LINK could be planned, knowing what demands would be made upon our meagre resources, both human and financial. At least I did know that our modified submission had not been lost and was being taken seriously, but now that we had been working on this proposal for over two years I felt it appropriate to engage the help of the Durham Member of the European Parliament, Stephen Hughes, to bring the matter to a conclusion. Equipped with my briefing papers he asked the right questions of the right people in the right places. Meanwhile in Maseru during October,[46] the Forestry Department staff were also getting impatient as they saw the 1993 planting slipping away.

Slip away it did. Comfortable, air-conditioned rooms in the European concrete-and-chrome jungle are not conducive to planting trees in the soil of Lesotho, but there was some stirring after Stephen Hughes began his probing questions. Pressure in Lesotho, from my regular meetings with the new European delegate, Joachim Zuidberg, brought support in February, doubt in May and approval in September.[47] We had been granted 85 per cent of our budget. This was confirmed on Monday, 15th November 1993, in a telephone conversation I had with the Commission's head of the Environmental Department, Tim Clark, when he quantified it as £577,494 over three years but (there always is a qualification) we would have to find a huge capital deposit and fund the first three months from our own financial resources. Would all the trees in the fields of Lesotho ever 'clap their hands'?

Having reached this stage of the saga I felt under attack but I very much wanted to 'finish the race and complete the task the Lord Jesus (had) given me; the task of testifying to the gospel'. As the Lesotho Diocesan Synod was voting on the other side of the world in favour of the ordination of women I was raising, with the help of Mark Hayes of the Shared Interest Society[48] based in Newcastle, plus the generous assistance of the Lesotho Diocesan Association, a capital deposit of £57,500 for a bank guarantee of the European loan. Surely this was the final lap! Having lost half of the 1993–1994 planting season, could we now go into action?

Richard Briggs and I were on our way to Lesotho and relaxing in Brussels Airport on Wednesday, 19th January 1994, when I picked up a discarded copy of *The Guardian* newspaper, hoping to enjoy a quiet moment before a long flight, only to read a disturbing headline: 'Lesotho Rebels Exchange Fire in a short gun battle in Maseru.' It was a fight between loyal and rebel troops with the mutineers demanding a 100 per cent pay rise and seemingly intent on overthrowing the government elected just a few months previously. I showed the article to Richard who, with a stiff, British upper lip, agreed that we should continue with our planned journey. What we did not know was that our respective wives had received worrying telephone calls telling them that the 'British High Commissioner was not allowing British subjects to enter Lesotho'.

The next day we had a similar call waiting for us in Jan Smuts Airport in Johannesburg but, knowing that the High Commissioner had no authority to determine who enters another country, we made enquiries about the safest way to travel into Lesotho. From numerous phone calls I discovered that the southern road from the airport to the capital passed through an area that was under fire from the military uprising, so we changed our direct flight to Maseru to another that would take us to Bloemfontein. There the LINK's administrator, Jeanette O'Neill, collected us so that we might safely pass through the Maseru Bridge Border Post, where we hit another unexpected snag. I was normally allowed to stay in Lesotho for ninety days but today, as we were to discover, was anything but normal and Richard and I were only welcome to stay for three days! That would give us just enough time to apply for an extension that was eventually granted five days later after hours of queuing at the immigration office; such is bureaucracy in times of tension.

Richard went off to stay at the O'Neills' house and I settled into 'my' room at John and Judy Gay's home within the Anglican complex just a couple of minutes from the cathedral and the royal palace. I woke the next morning, Sunday, to the sound of heavy shelling interspersed with light-arms fire, so it was no surprise to receive a phone call from Richard saying that as he was in the line of fire from a nearby hill across to the Maseru army barracks he thought it wise to stay where he was. I agreed and went off to the cathedral to lead the intercessions for peace at the eucharist against a noisy background of heavy firing, when our prayers assumed a new urgency and poignancy. After the service some twenty people gathered at the Gays' home for refreshment and advice on how to avoid what the BBC World Service called 'heavy fighting'.

By now the Foreign and Commonwealth Office was advising British subjects not to travel to Lesotho, but fortunately that warning was issued after we had left. When soldiers on the ground took a postprandial nap everyone dispersed in comparative safety until shelling restarted at four o'clock for another three hours and came uncomfortably close to the royal palace. Unusually for this time of year torrential rain dampened further enthusiasm for fighting. Having worked out our escape route to the north should the need arise we spent a quiet night.

The purpose of Richard's visit to Lesotho was to start the community forestry project with Steven Molokeng, so it was a relief that the following day was quiet, allowing prearranged meetings to take place. This included one with the chief forestry officer, Mr Senekane, who had been so helpful in getting our smaller community woodlands established around the country. As on previous occasions we didn't leave this meeting empty-handed: he gave us 100,000 saplings free of charge. We could draw them from government tree nurseries during the present year. Now all Richard and Steven had to do was to get them planted! Before then. however, they had many other things to do: advertise, interview eager applicants, appoint staff, meet chiefs and obtain land for planting, explain the project to people and buy vehicles. Before the winter frosts arrived in mid-April they had made a start with 10,000 trees planted in the southern part of the country.[49] The LINK appointed Nathaniel Chaphi as Project Manager assisted by two young foresters, Sentle Rabale and Aaron Mothokho, and Richard returned to Durham to report a sound start, despite the hold-up caused by the delayed approval by the European Commission. It had been over four years to get to this stage reminding me that 'everything has its own time'.

The Basotho proverb, whilst not an exact reflection of the message in Ecclesiastes, is a reminder that there is 'a time for everything' and in the LINK we had now reached our 'time to weep and to mourn'.[50] In the early afternoon of Monday, 20th June 1994 I received a telephone call from a Lt Colonel Nalete stationed at the Mohale's Hoek Police Station in the south of the country. After identifying who I was he told me that our vehicle with the registration AE336 driven by Nathaniel Chaphi had overturned the previous day. No other vehicle or person was involved. The driver was admitted into hospital where he died in the early hours of that morning. The remains of the vehicle, which was one of the brand-new bakkies bought just a few months previously for the forestry project, was in the police compound at Mohale's Hoek. I was to learn later that the police believed the cause to be excessive speed.

Now there was much to do so I called Steven Molokeng from a meeting, Jeanette O'Niell from home and Beatrice Ngozwana, the Mothers' Union worker, from her office to advise us on the best way to handle this situation whilst respecting cultural norms. Taking Steven with me I went in search of the widow who lived in Qoaling near Lithoteng, a distant suburb of Maseru. The tracks, all without visible road names, wound in between mostly rectangular concrete-block houses without numbers or names, so we had a difficult search but eventually found Mrs Chaphi. She invited us into her modest home of one living room which was sparsely furnished with a threadbare upholstered settee on which she sat whilst Steven and I occupied the remaining two wooden chairs. There were some soft furnishings, cushions, blankets, curtains and a rug scattered around the room. Speaking in Sesotho, Steven gently broke the news to her and translated my condolences, all of which she took remarkably calmly. She told us that she knew we had brought her bad news because last night she had had a premonition that something dreadful had happened that evening; it was a most extraordinary reaction. We prayed with her and made arrangements for Steven to call on her again. I assured her the LINK would support her over the next few weeks and that I would be available to the relatives if they wished to see me at any time. She was extremely courageous and I left admiring her resilience in adversity.

The next day, still reeling from the events of yesterday, Mrs Chaphi's eldest son, Daniel, came to see me with another male relative, Pitso. Daniel gave me the names of all the family members for whom he was now responsible. In addition to his own nuclear family he was now, in Basotho culture, responsible for eight other people. The sudden, unexpected burden was lying heavily upon him so I felt I had to give all the time he wanted and we talked, leisurely and calmly, about his father's salary, insurance, how the body of his father would be collected from Mohale's Hoek and financing the funeral. Whilst staying within the boundaries of responsibility to its donors the LINK went beyond its legal obligations in its support. The contingency budget line assumed a new dimension. On a cold but sunny Saturday, 2nd July 1994, a large crowd gathered on the family land situated on the way to Ha Khotso not far from Nazareth, on the mountain road, to listen to many long speeches before the burial. It was all appropriately solemn and very dignified.

The LINK entered its second phase in the later part of 1994 under new leadership. Paul Jefferson had been appointed as its first salaried executive officer and in Lesotho, Rosalia Ramoholi was appointed to succeed Steven Molokeng. With the tragic death of the community forest project officer his two assistants, Sentle and Aaron, carried a heavy burden of responsibility. Not suspecting that they were about to experience the worst winter in Lesotho for twenty-one years, these two young men continued an intensive programme organising the planting of 200,000 pine, cypress and eucalyptus trees. In order to limit travelling expenses, and to be close to government tree nurseries, the work was concentrated in the Quthing district in the very south of the country which was, therefore, height for height, its coldest region. This is also an area known, for very good reasons, as 'The Place of the Wind'.

Back in Durham the diocese was going through its own turbulent time as Michael Turnbull, encumbered by a serious personal problem, was enthroned the seventieth Bishop of Durham.[51] The going was rough and tough, but it was going to become rougher and tougher.

Steven Molokeng's earlier work resulted in chiefs allocating land for nine communities, which was then divided into family plots in which the people planted saplings given to them by the project. Each plot was used by the family for growing trees for timber or fuel as they wished. Despite the untimely encroachment into the planting season by Brussels bureaucracy some 10,000 trees were planted in the first three months of 1994, but then winter attacked and killed them. That bad winter was followed by a long drought so, by the end of the year, the project was a year behind its planned schedule. During the first three months of 1995 some rain fell but only 2,000 saplings were planted. Surveying and training continued. Not surprisingly despondency set in. Nevertheless the good reputation the LINK had developed encouraged the European Commission to extend the project into a fourth year within the original budget and so the understandable gloom was short-lived. A new lease of life brought a new project manager, Richard Ramoeletsi, and two additional forestry assistants, Limpho Kutoane and Khoajane Moseme. It was not long before 1,000 plots had been allocated to villagers and by the end of 1995 *'MOHO – Together* was reporting that another 50,000 trees had been planted and encouraging photographs began appearing in this biannual publication.

The project's five foresters worked tirelessly and were heartened by some good rains during 1996 and also by an upsurge in the initiative of villagers who were beginning to realise what an enormous benefit might be forthcoming from this project. With the one-year extension came another change that was also a type of extension. The failure to meet planting targets caused a reassessment of that element of the original project with a recognition that insufficient care had been given to early consultations within communities. Clearly the advice of Edwin Chaka and the experience gained at Malealea had not been fully translated to the Quthing district. These shortcomings were now recognised before irreparable damage was caused and were addressed by placing 'a greater emphasis on consultation, advice and education'.[52] Village tree groups, the planting of fruit trees, the development of local tree nurseries and the building of dams all began to be regularly reported together with the work of surveying and mapping the project sites recognising the contribution of volunteer Tim Holmes and of Skill Share Africa.

By the end of 1996 the LINK had to endure two more serious blows to this heavily attacked Community Forestry Project: two more of its foresters were to die. Moseme Khoajane was killed in August in a road accident when a drunken lorry driver failed to negotiate a sharp bend and, in June shortly after his marriage, Aaron Mothokho, who had been with the project from its start, died from a perforated stomach ulcer. In the face of these tragedies the LINK demonstrated a strong resilience and the project continued to progress well. To add to these unavoidable staff upheavals the project manager moved, in October, from the south of the country to work on another European-funded project in the north. It is to the credit of those remaining and to the third manager to be appointed, Mophethe Sekamane, that during 1997 and early 1998 it is recorded that 41,000 more pine, acacia and willow trees were planted. Helped by the mild winter months of June, July and August, followed by good rains during the next summer, growth was vigorous with a remarkably high 95 per cent survival rate.

Amid all this timber and fuel production the value of fruit crops was not ignored and the project provided farmers with 1,660 apple, pear, peach, apricot and plum trees. Educational work in schools continued, combined with starting two nurseries supplemented by a holding nursery that helped to reduce transport costs. With the project about to close it continued to expand its influence in Phamong camp in the Mohale's Hoek district, situated to the north of the original Quthing district where, looking to the future, it planted 160,000 seedlings ready for the next, and for this project the last, planting season. A comprehensive account of the result of the Community Forestry Project states that:

> Up to the end of 1998 the project has planted over a quarter of a million trees with an estimated survival rate of 80 per cent. Over one hundred villages, thirteen schools, and numerous individuals have planted trees. Four tree nurseries have been established and literally hundreds of people, over fifty per cent being women, now officially own their own trees. Trees that were in the initial plantings of 1993 (sic: this should be 1994) are now over twelve feet high and are sufficiently well developed to allow limited grazing around them. They have also had their lower branches trimmed thereby providing fuel wood, for which some were originally planted. Villagers are already coming back to plant more land and looking for alternative uses for the valuable assets they now have.[53]

When the LINK started in 1986 we exercised our responsibility to care for God's world by planting thousands of trees. The Christian faith of many people was actively demonstrated in practical action and has since continued to occupy an important place in the LINK's mission. Recognising the new threat to the world from carbon emissions from air travel, in 2007 the LINK launched a new tree project, Trees4Lesotho.[54] It is still in its early years so the saplings are still in the nursery.

It was in Namibia that I first discussed the possibility of the LINK assuming responsibility for the Community Forestry Project. There followed almost eight years of careful planning by many people to bring it to a successful conclusion in Lesotho where, with God's blessing, 'all the trees of the field will clap their hands'. Others will then be able to 'go out with joy' from their rondavels to listen as 'the mountains and hills burst into song before (them)'.

The LINK planned for the present and planted for the future.

---

1. Isaiah 55:12 (NIV): ... all the trees of the field will clap their hands.
2. Psalms 24:1 (NIV): The earth is the Lord's, and everything in it, the world, and all who live in it.
3. 1 Corinthians 10:26 (NIV): The earth is the Lord's, and everything in it.
4. Exodus 9:29 (NIV): ... the earth is the Lord's.
5. Gill, Stephen J., *A Short History of Lesotho* (Lesotho: Morija Museum and Archives, 1993) p. 80.
6. Ibid. p. 179.
7. John 1:1 (NIV): In the beginning was the Word, and the Word was with God, and the Word was God.
8. 1 John 3:18 (GNB): My children, our love should not be just words and talk; it must be true love, which shows itself in action.
9. Information leaflet published by the Environment Department Durham County Council, 1988.
10. The membership of the Lesotho support group at this time was Bishop Philip Mokuku; Suffragan Bishop Donald Nestor; Dean Israel Qwelane; Rev'd David Wells SSM; Rev'd Martin Mkwibiso; Mrs Dorothy Haines (Diocesan Secretary). Meetings at which the woodland project was discussed were held on Tuesday, 13th October 1987 and a week later on Tuesday, 20th October 1987.
11. Green, Peter, 'Report on a visit to the Diocese of Lesotho 1st October 1987' section 12, appendix 1.
12. Luke 9:62 (NIV): No one who puts his hand to the plough and looks back is fit for service in the kingdom of God.
13. Green, Peter, 'Personal Daily Journal' (Tuesday, 20th October 1987).
14. Those present at the meeting on Wednesday, 21st October 1987 were Chief Forestry Officer Tšepo Senekane; British Technical Adviser David May; Community Forestry Officer Gart van Leersum; Research Officer Thuso Green.
15. A reference to John Louden McAdam (1756–1836) who surfaced roads with a mixture of tar and stones.
16. Enclosure of land began in England in the 1100s with statutes in 1235 and 1285 followed by the General Enclosures Act of 1810 and the Enclosure Act of 1845.

17. Deuteronomy 19:14a (NIV): Do not move your neighbour's boundary stone.

18. Deuteronomy 19:14a (RSV): ... you shall not remove your neighbour's landmark ...

19. Ambrose, David, *The Guide to Lesotho* (Lesotho: Winchester Press, 1974). Slightly misquoted on p. 157.

20. See Chapter Two: Saddle Up (p. 25)

21. This was one of two rectories replaced by the LINK twelve years later in memory of the Rev'd Catherine Hooper. The other was at Ha 'Mikia. See Chapter Four: In the Jungle (p. 106, endnote 16).

22. Pronounced *See-clar-ko-clar-ko.*

23. To work at College Press on my Sesotho and Setswana children's books: *Monate wa Setswana 1 and 2* (Macmillan Boleswa, Manzini, 1986). Translated into Venda as *Polelo ke Lehumo* (Macmillan Boleswa, Manzini, 1991).

24. Collingwood, Jeremy, *As A Witness to the Light* (Terra Nova Publications International, Bradford on Avon, Wiltshire, UK. 2006). This work provides an account of the author's contribution, from 1987 to 2005, to the establishment of Chengelo School, Mkushi, Zambia, and his chairmanship of the supporting UK charity he founded in 1992, the Chengelo Educational Trust (UK), from which he retired in April 2010.

25. In 1987 the Lesotho Minister of State for Education was Ntate Mabathoana.

26. Isaiah 55:12b (NIV): The mountains and hills will burst into song before you, and all the trees of the field will clap their hands.

27. Isaiah 61:2b–3 (GNB): He has sent me to comfort all who mourn, To give to those who mourn in Zion joy and gladness instead of grief, a song of praise instead of sorrow. They will be like trees that the Lord himself has planted. They will all do what is right, and God will be praised for what he has done.

28. The chief executive was Mr Peter Dawson; the county council treasurer Mr Kingsley-Smith; the county council secretary and solicitor Mr Roger Humphries, and Mr Richard Briggs (environment department).

29. Mark 16:15 (NIV): (Jesus) said to them, 'Go into all the world and preach the good news to all creation'.

30. A Basotho proverb quoted by Lanham, Peter and Mopeli-Paulus, A. S., *Blanket Boy's Moon* (London: Collins, 1953) p. 46.

31. Shakespeare, William, *Julius Caesar,* I, ii,18.

32. 1 Corinthians 3:7 (GNB): The one who sows and the one who waters really do not matter. It is God who matters, because he makes the plant grow.

33. The sites that we were negotiating at this time were, from north to south, at: Sefako; Mots'oane; Ralehlatsa; Majoe-a-litšoene; Rankhelepe; Sekameng; Qhalasi; Quthing, and Mokhotlong (in the north-east).

34. Joshua Hlakoane was killed in a car accident. He was a remarkably dedicated head teacher who supervised the building and development of an excellent church high school. His death was a severe loss to both Lesotho and the LINK.

35. *Molepe*, 'Story of a School' vol. 13, no. 14 (Lesotho Airways In-flight magazine, 1989): pp. 9–11.

36. Appleyard, Simon and Green, Christine, *This England*, 'A Heritage of Trees' vol. 15, no. 3 (Autumn, 1982) pp. 18–20. This article explains that amongst primitive European people tree worship was the basis of the Celtic religion with trees harbouring dangerous gods and demons. The Basotho are not the only people fearful of evil spirits in the trees. Was the superstition carried by former missionaries?

37. A porous cement mixture used in the manufacture of some lower concrete rings used to line a hand-dug well through which water can percolate. Local men dug wells up to a depth of 50 feet (15 m).

38. During the first phase of the LINK (1986 to 1994) the charity Cooperation for Development allocated £23,000 from its European block grant to the poultry unit project, the community woodlands, Ha Popa Rural Health Centre and the Ha Mohatlane Community Education Centre. A 'Donor's View' assessing progress on these projects (except Ha Popa) can be found in *'MOHO – Together*, No. 8 (May 1994) p. 4.

39. Dr Terry Lacey and the Rev'd Guy Wilkinson were Director and Treasurer respectively of Cooperation for Development.

40. They were Philip Mokuku; Lebohang Kheekhe; Joseph Leodi; Justin Rafutho; Mohomane Lebotsa; Philip Posholi; Florina Mokhethi; Beatrice Ngozwana; Mrs Talker with Steven Molokeng, and myself.

41. The meetings in the European Commission were held on Wednesday, 17th and Thursday, 18th October 1990. Some of them were also attended by representatives of Cooperation for Development including its Chairman of Trustees, Anthony Simpson.

42. Lebohang Kheekhe at Edinburgh; Ntebo Ngozwana at Sunderland; Paul Mohobela at Teesside.

43. Green, Peter, 'Personal Daily Journal' (Wednesday, 11th September 1991).

44. Jenkins, David, *Message to Lesotho.* See Chapter One: 'In the Beginning was the Word' (p. 1).

45. Green, Peter, sermon preached in Maseru Cathedral: *'Jesus is for Everyone'*: Sunday 1st June 1986.

46. Those who met on Wednesday, 14th October 1992 were: Elliot Sehekane; David May; Thulo Qhotsokoane; Steven Molokeng, and Peter Green.

47. Friday, 17th September 1993.

48. Shared Interest Society is a Newcastle-based charity that was founded by Mark Hayes and aims to provide credit to help disadvantaged communities work themselves out of poverty.

49. See *'MOHO – Together* No. 10 (May 1995) p. 2.

50. Ecclesiastes 3:4 (NIV): '... a time to weep and a time to laugh, a time to mourn and a time to dance.'

51. *The Independent* newspaper dated Sunday, 25th September 1994 further publicised what *The News of the World* revealed on the same day – namely that twenty-six years earlier the new bishop, Michael Turnbull, had been charged with a 'gross indecency' offence. This threw people in the Diocese of Durham into temporary confusion whilst coming to terms with the revelation, but it was of minimal impact in the Diocese of Lesotho.

52. I acknowledge that much of this information comes from reports in *'MOHO – Together* and the LINK annual reports. This quote comes from *'MOHO – Together*, No. 12 (May 1996) p. 3.
53. Durham-Lesotho Diocesan LINK, 'Annual Report and Accounts' section 5.2 (1998) p. 5.
54. *Durham Newslink*, the newspaper of the Diocese of Durham (September–October 2007) p. 9; (November–December 2007) p. 7; (January–February 2008) pp. 3, 9.

Chapter Six

Ha Popa

When Jesus had called the Twelve together,
he gave them power and authority
to drive out all demons and to cure diseases,
and he sent them out to preach
the kingdom of God and to heal the sick.[1]

Chief Petrose Lekolomi of Ha Chooko as well as being a patient man was also a caring person. He was a minor chief wielding major influence in his small mountain village lying in the remote central Maluti region. He was feeling isolated and was very concerned about the ill and frail who, if their condition were serious and needed urgent medical attention, had to travel across the mountains by horse or by foot, or even be carried by friends on a makeshift stretcher, to seek professional care in the lowlands. In his day there was no mountain road such as Philip Mokuku and I travelled on in 1986 on the first leg of our preaching trip across the Bokong Valley to Ha 'Mikia. It was then that we also spoke to people about the soon-to-be-established Durham-Lesotho LINK and there was certainly no improved surfaced mountain road as we know it in the twenty-first century. In the early 1950s it was little more than a track for much of the 80 miles (130 kms) to Maseru and the journey, with its twists and turns, ups and downs, was no mean feat for the fit and healthy, but for the sick and suffering it was a hazardous and tortuous undertaking that did nothing to improve the poor health for which they sought diagnosis, treatment and healing.

Petrose Lekolomi was also well aware that when any of his superstitious people were inflicted by illness it was all too easy for them, with nothing else available, to turn to the iniquitous medicine men and witch doctors, especially if the alternative was a long and dangerous mountain trek. He wanted to protect vulnerable sick and old people from impostors which may, possibly, have been a desire accentuated by his own 71 years.[2] His concern was finding expression in 1951, the same year that John Maund was enthroned[3] as the first Anglican Bishop of Basutoland (as Lesotho was then called). The new bishop had lost no time in exploring his new diocese. Later that same year he rode his horse into the small village of Ha Chooko, nestling at 7,382 feet (2,250 m) between the rivers Mantšonyane and Tenane. There he met with Chief Lekolomi who himself lost no time as he stressed the urgency for the Anglican Church not only to send a priest to his village to start a mission, but also to find a medical doctor to start a hospital that would serve the community. Not surprisingly John Maund was quicker in achieving the start of a mission station than he was in satisfying the request for a hospital. The first took one year; the second ten!

When confronted with the immediate prospect of carrying your relative with a broken femur up mountain track, into river basin, across *donga* gorge, on the way relying on other people for rest and refreshment, struggling perhaps four or five days to get to Queen Elizabeth II Hospital in Maseru where the fracture could be set, ten years is a long time. Those conditions had never been experienced by people in London. They were taking their time in considering the building of a hospital where even the concept of 'hospital' was confusingly different to that held by a Mosotho. But ten years it took before the support that John Maund sought from the Society for the Propagation of the Gospel[4] was turned into action when in 1961 the missionary society sent three men to Lesotho to carry out the pioneering work required to establish a hospital for the Basotho of the Maluti mountain region. A builder, Gerald Garroway, a medical doctor, Ken Luckman, and a nurse, Arnold Skelton, went to Lesotho arriving eventually in Ha Chooko on Thursday, 1st June 1961 to start building a structure and a service from which many thousands have subsequently benefited. The old name for the site on which the hospital was built in nearby Mantšonyane was, most appropriately, in Sesotho *khauhelo,* translated into English as 'place of compassion'.

It is a fascinating story of the practice of faith by three disciplined men who, incredibly, after just two years work, were to run St. James' Mission Hospital.[5] The exercise of their hard work, strong faith and professional skills resulted in a hospital of about seventy beds that, remarkably, admitted its first patient just two years after they had started building but twelve years after the Chief of Chooko had made his initial request; he must have been a tolerant and a patient man. At long last the Maluti region had the hospital that Chief Lekolomi so wanted for the people of Ha Chooko. As people moved between their rondavels, cooked their meals and ploughed their fields they could see the low, squat building across the Mantšonyane River and how wonderfully accessible it was to all the people in the village who needed its services. Not unusually (the LINK is a case in point), a few months after the hospital had begun to function the official opening was held on Saturday, 7th September 1963 in the presence of about 1,000 joyful Basotho. One small retrospective twist of circumstance connects that ceremony with the present-day Durham-Lesotho LINK; the Chairman of the hospital's governing body at that time was Mr Neil Yeats, an uncle of Charles Yeats who was so strongly influenced by the LINK's exhibition in Durham Cathedral[6] twenty-nine years later.

In England, exactly ten years before St. James' Hospital opened in Lesotho, I was in serious need of specialist medical attention that would, eventually and undeniably, be influential in the provision of medical services in the Maluti Mountains. For three long months at the end of 1953 death beckoned me before slowly, oh, so slowly, its sting was drawn and I gradually moved away from its grasping clutches to lie in my bed for another nine months. During this time the *pleuritic tubercular bacillus* gradually succumbed to the skill, dedication, devotion, commitment, love and prayers of medics, parents, priest and girlfriend, to say little of those in the background who had discovered, developed and supplied medication; then there were also the two guinea-pigs who died that I might live. It was all rather traumatic. Little did I realise then that the experience would provide a solid foundation on which to build some future work in one of the remotest and poorest parts of a country that I had only a cursory knowledge of thanks to an unexpected encounter three years earlier on Pneumonia Bridge.[7] In the late 1980s that was all of thirty plus years away but there was more to come!

Just after my girlfriend became my wife, I had another year-long fight with the dreaded tubercular foe that had changed its point of attack but was no less vicious in keeping me and everyone else fully occupied. The battlefield was constantly changing from home to hospital, to clinic, to sanatorium. But in the conflict I was never alone, unlike many of those for whom I was to work in the future. I was supported by people, surrounded by facilities, saturated with love and sustained by prayer. We came through it together and the present, unknown to me at the time, was to provide a contrasting scenario against which to assess the future. Suffering, often painfully, I did not have to crawl across mountains in the vague hope that I could find medical treatment; medical treatment came to me. When it came I did not have to worry about paying for it as my community had already done so. I was not reliant upon friends to carry me to hospital on a makeshift stretcher; a comfortable ambulance took me over smooth roads. There was no anxiety about collecting clean water to drink; it came out of a nearby convenient tap ready to drink. I benefited from other people's vision and society's provision without which my life, if I was to have one, might have been dramatically different. I think I can claim to know quite a lot about being ill.

Nevertheless, all that had now sunk below the horizon but was still, undoubtedly, part of my psychological cargo. I travelled with its consequences and thirty years later, when I found myself in hospital once again, I had no resistance against a desire to assist the Basotho to improve their medical facilities. I took with me the poignant clutter of thoughts amassed during years of resistance against an illness that had effectively prevented me from doing much of what I had wanted to achieve in my twenties. For me they really were the tubercular twenties but now, in 1986, I was walking into hospital fit and well thanks to the provision of the community of which I was part. There is little doubt in my mind that I was strongly influenced by my zymotic experiences when I spoke to the hospital chaplain about changing vision into provision in Lesotho. How could we help the Basotho improve their meagre medical facilities and how could we encourage others to assist us in providing facilities similar to those that had helped to preserve my life?

Frank White and I had known each other for many years since he was curate at St. Nicholas Church in the centre of Durham city, and I was confident that if I could encourage him to extend his ministry into the southern hemisphere positive action would result. It did! Shortly after the formal start of the LINK in 1986 Frank and I had discussions with three eminent virologists,[8] all of whom had wide interests in the health of people in the so-called 'developing world'. Our Durham world was also developing quite rapidly! The ideas, suggestions and proposals we presented were critically analysed and each of these high-powered medical experts gave us strong encouragement to continue the informal work that was gradually developing in response to numerous requests that were being received from Lesotho. Although in the LINK we were determined never to impose (in any sector in which we worked), only to respond, we realised that if we were to work as One Body we had to share ideas, resources and knowledge. To enable the Basotho to gain the maximum benefit from the LINK's contribution we had to make known to them what might be possible. Equipped with Frank's briefing, and my long-distance gazing at funding possibilities, I carefully explained at numerous meetings in Lesotho with medical personnel, including successive ministers of health, what I thought might be possible. I left those ideas to germinate in the minds of many, but in the meantime the work progressed in Durham under Frank's careful attention.

At this time, 1988, and for many years to come, the medical group was a very active segment of the Durham-Lesotho LINK with their work becoming widely known throughout the north-east of England. In addition to financial donations from individuals the group attracted generous gifts of medical equipment and supplies from hospitals,[9] general medical practioners, social services departments and pharmaceutical companies.[10] In January 1988, twelve large cartons containing small items of medical equipment, surgeons' operating gowns (the style had recently changed in England!) and 800 blankets were shipped to Lesotho. One box of surgical equipment went to a doctor working in Maseru for the Ministry of Health and the other eleven found a warm reception at St. James' Mission Hospital, in the mountains at Mantšonyane. This was our first experience of transporting large quantities of goods to Lesotho and we were grateful for the help and advice we received. We listened carefully. We sent nothing to Lesotho that had not been rigorously checked before dispatch and in this, often tedious, process we were fortunate in having the practical help of medical volunteers[11] and a qualified pharmacist,[12] so we were confident that everything that was sent was 'in-date', of good quality and of realistic use.

The mid-to-late-1980s saw the big British night-time switch from blankets to duvets, so it wasn't too surprising that we had a deluge of blankets from every corner of Durham and beyond. Not only were we practically submerged but it was all rather ironical that in our second consignment we found ourselves sending vast numbers of blankets to the very country where blankets are traditionally worn as outer garments! We were more sensitive about the irony than the Basotho; they didn't mind. They were very pleased to be benefiting from the British switch. There was also a by-product for members of the medical group, who were amazed to learn how small a space is occupied by 800 blankets when they are compressed by a special machine lent by a commercial firm![13] No formal appeal for gifts was made but nonetheless they poured in, creating a massive storage problem that Durham Health Authority solved for us by providing temporary storage space. I did half wonder, not very seriously, if a large collection of medical books and journals for the specialist library at St. James' Hospital would cause a 'demarcation dispute' between the medical and book working parties: it didn't. We had an embarrassment of riches but that gave us a headache. Although we had, by now, some experience of packing blankets, a further 1,000 stretched our packing resources in Durham and our distribution arrangements in Lesotho. The real challenge came with the generous gift of post-operative beds and with help, we did manage to get them from the lowlands of Durham to the mountains of Lesotho, but it was a struggle.

Inevitably this work prompted the question of whether or not it was financially viable to send all this equipment over 6,000 miles (9,656 kms) rather than just collecting the money in Durham to purchase the same equipment in Lesotho. We were helped with sending our first assignment by the charity Action Aid, who generously gave us free space in a shipping container it was sending to South Africa, but the question still merited discussion to determine our future action. Most of our talking in the affected working groups highlighted seven significant points.

The question assumes that money would be forthcoming instead of donations of equipment and there was no guarantee that would happen. There is also the assumption that similar medical supplies would be available locally, but there was no assurance that would be so. If we did not accept the gifts, what impression would that give to potential donors in Durham? What would become of the surplus equipment in Durham; would it simply be dumped? Should the LINK not, working in and for a poor country, try to prevent waste in a rich country? The question also overlooked the benefit of corporate involvement in the LINK; the county council was helping the woodland and education groups so why not connect the medical sector by involving Durham hospitals and medics? Perhaps the most pertinent aspect was one that was difficult to grasp. Was there not an advantage to the Church in Durham to be seen not asking for money, as was usually the case, but working with the community to solve a common problem? We continued to transport large quantities of equipment and a couple of years later the LINK, operating on a much bigger scale, had started a container group. This group worked in conjunction with Safmarine Shipping Company[14] providing transport for equipment collected not only by the medical group, but also by the tools and education groups.

So, the answer to the original question about the viability of sending equipment to Lesotho was an unqualified 'yes', but the answer to some questions frequently, and generally reluctantly, had to be 'no'. Throughout the life of the Durham-Lesotho LINK difficult decisions have had to be made, especially in the early years when resources were severely restricted. One of the first of these uncomfortable decisions involved the medical group. The interdenominational Christian Council of Lesotho asked for our support for their alcohol and drug abuse programme but at the time the LINK did not have contact with those skilled in this area, so after some heart-searching it made one of its first difficult decisions not to become involved. We had to focus our medical activities and it soon became apparent, both in Lesotho and in Durham, that our principal relationship in these early days should be with St. James' Mission Hospital, Mantšonyane, and its eight health centres and clinics[15] dotted around the Maluti Mountains. To work in that environment was not, in itself, an easy option, but the Basotho felt it was an area in which the LINK could make a significant contribution: time would tell.

Much of this activity preceded the first formal meeting of the medical group, which took place on Monday, 18th January 1988 in the postgraduate medical centre in what was then known as Dryburn Hospital, Durham.[16] Medical supplies continued to flow as containers left for Lesotho, but then in the early summer of 1988 there was a serious crisis in the St. James' Hospital funding. Mission hospitals throughout Lesotho attempt to keep their staff salaries in line with those paid in the state sector, but when the government of Lesotho suddenly implemented a huge salary increase the bill for the staff at St. James' rose by a massive 60 per cent, rocketing almost out of sight. On the twenty-fifth anniversary of the opening of the hospital it was threatened with closure unless £25,000 could be raised within the six months[17] that were covered by its financial reserves. The medical superintendent at the time, Dutchman Jan Voskens, writing in June 1988, said, '… we feel defeated and only hope for a miracle.'

The LINK had never set out to be a funding agency but here was a crisis its medical group could not ignore and it didn't. It set about tackling the emergency calling on the generosity of British charities[18] and, thanks to them and 'some equally generous gifts from individuals' (including an anonymous gift of £5,000), more than the required £25,000 was mobilised by the LINK in just a few weeks and, just in time, we were able to send £26,350 to the hospital to save it from closure.[19] On the same morning that the chairman of the medical group telephoned Lesotho to say that the money had been raised, the hospital treasurer had just returned from the bank having withdrawn the last remaining funds. Had the Dutch hope been fulfilled?

I was soon to learn that another Dutch hope was lying dormant just waiting to become active. Ha Popa first came onto my agenda during the evening of Monday, 28th November 1988. It had been a long, exceptionally hot and tiring drive from Maseru over the Mountain Road to Mantšonyane where, at St. James' Mission Hospital, an energetic young Netherlander, Paul Borgdorff, met me. Paul had just taken over from his fellow countryman, Jan Voskens, as medical superintendent and we quickly settled into his small, sparsely equipped office to review the work of the LINK's medical group and to discuss a long list of topics before either of us became horizontal for the night. The earlier contributions of the LINK to the hospital had already been described to Paul so he was no stranger to what collaboration might be possible. We worked through the list talking about the provision of additional hospital equipment; supplementing medical staff; further contributions to a medical library; a water project; and then, for the first time, the rural health centre at Ha

Popa. I listened carefully and made copious notes as Paul described problems, limits the present building imposed upon medical treatment and what might be achieved given more adequate buildings. We agreed to an early start the next morning. The time for Compline was long past: it was now time for Prone.

I was up at five o'clock for a substantial breakfast; none of us had any idea when we would be eating again. We[20] left in a Toyota Land Cruiser amidst a swirl of dust just as the sun was making its presence felt, seductively peeping over the mountains; on this November summer day it would become searingly hot. This was to be another 'first' for me but, suspecting it would not be another 'last', I settled down to relax and enjoy the beauty of the mountains just coming to life as the sun warmed us on our way. What I should have been doing was noting the directions, but as there were few that wasn't particularly difficult or demanding. Coming out of the hospital grounds leave the airstrip on your left, crash through half a dozen potholes (there are probably more now), wave to the man ploughing his field with two oxen and go on to the T-junction. At this point pause to decide whether to go left or right. Left would take you through the Roman Catholic mission at Auray and right through nothing much at all: we turned right. Just beyond Auray there is a very steep gravel slope with numerous hairpin bends that is best avoided in wet weather as even a four-wheel-drive vehicle can find it difficult. On future trips if I were on horseback I tended to go through Auray to avoid a section of the mountain road beyond Mantšonyane that could have slow traffic going down to the lowlands. In dry weather it doesn't much matter which you choose, as they both lead to the same road that eventually takes you to Ha Popa; well, at least, the Ha Popa we wanted. In Lesotho there are two other Popas both of them in the Roma Valley, which is a long way from our planned destination today.

This morning, for no particular reason, we turned right and went round Mantšonyane settlement, where we turned left at the Indian store (where you can buy almost anything) and drove on to Cheche's Pass at 8,350 feet (2,545 m). Turning left again we joined a track where someone had helpfully nailed together two old bits of wood into a 'T' shape and painted HA POPA on the horizontal arm, but had failed to indicate which of the two directions we should take! Fortunately this was not the first time Paul Borgdorff had used this route and the telecommunications mast that is soon visible after turning off the mountain road came into view, to be passed on its eastern side; so where the sun was rising.

We were now driving along a narrow dirt track that followed the mountain ridge high above the Senqunyane River on our right side and the Mantšonyane River on our left, zigzagging our way southward through small settlements of cheering and waving Basotho who recognised the hospital Land Cruiser. After almost 18 miles (29 kms) of twists and turns, ups and downs, slips and slides, bumps and bangs, Paul delicately persuaded the Land Cruiser, pointing nose downward, to take a sharp right-hand bend where, on its outward side, the track had been built up with rocks to make a more or less level (not to be confused with smooth) surface from one edge to the other. It then continued steeply downwards into the valley where forty or fifty sheep, driven by one small boy who was probably about 10 years old, blocked our journey. As we waited for a gap to appear in the flock we were able to view the scene at the centre of which was a rough stone-built rectangular hut about 20 feet (6 m) by 10 feet (3 m) with a single-pitch, rusting corrugated-iron roof of two different heights sloping in the same direction. There were two wooden doors and two small glazed windows all painted pale blue. It was, we were soon to discover when the sheep allowed, two semi-detached rooms that were announcing themselves in large whitewashed rocks set in the hillside as POPA CLINIC. The sheep, unused to the sound of a Japanese vehicle driven by a Dutchman taking an Englishman to a Lesotho clinic, moved with considerable four-footed agility from the track up, and down, the adjoining hillside much to the consternation of the small herdboy. He followed them with blanket billowing and stick waving as he tried, not very successfully, to regain some sort of control. A pair of over-large cut-down wellington boots, whose origin was undoubtedly a South African gold mine, conspicuously hindered his two-footed agility. It was one of those rare occasions when I was glad I had a limited Sesotho vocabulary!

As the sheep dispersed the international conglomerate drove on, reaching Popa Clinic which displayed an ominously large vertical crack down one corner. Leaving that to one side I entered through the left-hand pale blue door and found myself in a small room equipped with an examination couch; vertical weighing scales with a height measure attached; an iron-framed table with a blue plastic surface; a small set of wall cupboards with, of course, blue doors. A dim light was creeping in from a small window that was shielded by a small dark blue curtain suspended from a sagging, vaguely horizontal, wire fixed to the wall by two nails, the left-hand one, for some mysterious reason, higher than the other. Breaking, with a silent violence, the colour coordination, one red plastic chair completed the furnishings.

From the examination-cum-treatment room I went outside and moved into the more sparsely furnished, slightly smaller, room equipped with a second red plastic chair, a long wooden form that, not surprisingly, was painted blue and a double-tiered wooden bunk bed with foam rubber mattresses. I paused to wonder. If I were ill, would I prefer to be on the lower or the upper bunk? A question I never did answer as I then spotted in one corner a stack, not of essential medical equipment, but of essential travelling equipment, a saddle, two saddlebags and a horse blanket. This was Ha Popa Rural Health Centre in 1988.

The clinic at Ha Popa seems to have begun life some eight years previously in 1980[21] as a village health post where health workers would hold sessions, more or less spasmodically, when required. Such irregular, unsystematic records as there are suggest that three years later staffing was still rather haphazard, being reliant upon primary health care staff using horses to travel, with their medical equipment, the 18 miles (29 kms) from their base in Mantšonyane. The type of clinic provision is also unclear as, by 1983, words such as 'semi-permanent' and 'mobile' began to creep into use. Care also has to be exercised when reading and interpreting the hospital annual reports. One 'annual' report does, in fact, cover the two years of 1993 and 1994 and because, understandably, the more important medical work had to take precedence, the report was not published until a year later. Problems of medical staffing and the pressure under which much hospital work takes place took their toll and, unfortunately, the oft-copied text of the annual hospital reports results in oft-repeated mistakes, so much care has to be taken in their use and interpretation.[22] What does seem to be reasonably certain is that a year before my first visit to Ha Popa in 1988 a permanent village health post had been built by local voluntary labour and a regular service established by village health workers. They were supported by medical staff from the hospital who were able by then in dry weather to reach Ha Popa in four-wheel-drive vehicles.

Surrounded by hundreds of acres (hectares) of grassland rolling away into the distance, with few other buildings in sight, it did look rather isolated. The whole treeless area was dominated by two massive conical, grass-covered hills that I was soon to call, with some difficulty, Moqhonoane and Maqhobeshane; despairingly, the Basotho soon forgave me the required clicks that the 'q' in both of those names requires from the competent Sesotho speaker. I was assured that the clinic served a population of around 10,000 Basotho, but where were they?

There was not much evidence of local habitation until I reached the overcrowded school that stood a short distance from the clinic along the single track. In relation to the few scattered rondavels it was in no particular position and apart from the clinic's corrugated-iron latrine (a 'nettie' to the Durham half of the LINK), the only other building I could see was a small, well-stocked, one-room store. From where would the patients come? They must be somewhere but this morning they were well camouflaged from my sight. The need for the school obviously meant there were families around even if I could not immediately see them. The road stopped at the clinic, beyond which there was no obvious pattern of footpaths coming from anywhere, but a maze of narrow tracks crept over nearby hills and disappeared round rocks, emerging to roll down slopes all determined to reach a small mountain stream from where women collected water. It was all rather bleak and desolate and, to European eyes, surreal.

The four of us sat in the brilliant sun, cooled by the mountain breeze, discussing at length what might be done to improve the medical services for 10,000 people I could not see but I knew were within walking distance of this small clinic. My notebook began to fill with sketches, my camera with pictures, my mind with ideas and my head with questions; predominately what could the LINK do here? I had no immediate answer but I did have enough information and personal experience to present to the medical group in Durham a clear picture of what was needed here at Ha Popa. Now I had to get back to Maseru as the next morning I had a meeting in the north of the country with the Chief of Ralehatsa, Morena Katiso Ramaisa, where the woodland group was hoping to start a tree nursery and to plant 1,000 trees.

But I wasn't going anywhere for the next couple of hours as we had received a message from a horseman that a man with severe abdominal pains was being brought round Moqhonoane. That gave me time to soak up more of the atmosphere, to wonder if the Durham-Lesotho LINK really could take on such a macro-project and to contemplate the prospects for the local people if it didn't! The sick man, probably about ten years younger than myself, eventually arrived on a stretcher made from old hessian sacks and two poles carried on the shoulders of four men of unequal heights; it must have been an uncomfortable journey. Paul, querying appendicitis, decided he should be admitted to St. James' Hospital so the poor man, in acute pain, was taken in the Land Cruiser on the rough, slow journey back to Mantšonyane. Presently I was to learn just a little of what he went through as fifteen days later I was admitted to Bloemfontein Hospital after a two-hour car journey from Maseru. Did I *really* have to be persuaded so spectacularly that medical facilities at Ha Popa had to be improved?

But that summer night, unaware of what was to come, Ha Popa dominated my thoughts as I drove across the mountains, arriving in Maseru just before midnight to make Ralehatsa the next morning, Bloemfontein two weeks later and then, on our thirty-third wedding anniversary, Durham just four days before Christmas Day, which is also Pam's birthday. With Edmund and Rachel we had a wonderful family celebration before entering 1989 with more questions than answers.

Encouraged by their success in responding to the financial crisis at St. James' Hospital, members of the medical group went into the new year wondering what would be the next call on their energies: they didn't have long to wait. Although Ha Popa was still very much in the forefront of my mind, I knew that I needed more time in which to prepare the ground for what would be a major commitment. The Durham ground, if it were to be productive, had to be properly tilled, fertilised with information, mulched with discussion and enriched with enthusiasm. Myself, I had to pray, to be challenged and questioned and Emmaus in Sunderland was where all that took place with Aelred Stubbs and the resident brethren of the Community of the Resurrection. I needed time to think about Ha Popa, so what was I to do with an enthusiastic medical group that had made such an excellent start with its early contributions to the work of the LINK? I concluded that maintained momentum would be the best preparation for what was to come at Ha Popa so I turned to drink.

Ever since my first visit to Mantšonyane in August 1976, when I saw cattle drinking from the same water source as that from which the hospital drew its supply, I was worried about the purity of the hospital's provision and when Paul Borgdorff raised the same concern with me during our first meeting I was prompted to do something about it. Back in England it was easy for members of the group to take potable water for granted. They turned on the taps in their operating theatres, wards and homes with an unthinking confidence that clean water would flow. There was never any doubt; they all lived within a few miles of the biggest, man-made, fresh-water reservoir in Europe[23] and even in the driest of summers there was never any danger to their water supply. How different it is in other parts of the world. I knew from my work on the other side of the continent, where I had been supervising the sinking of 296 groundwater wells in the Owamboland region of Namibia[24], that the supply of potable water is an enormous problem worldwide. I shared all this with the medical group and during the early part of 1989 it became clear that the water supply to the hospital was in serious danger of pollution. For what, to us, was a relatively small amount of money there was a solution to this problem.

In the Maluti Mountains technical help had become available as the husband of one of the Dutch doctors working at the hospital was a water engineer. He located a source of much safer water than the pond I saw animals using but it was on the other side of a mountain! We did have faith but, admittedly, we didn't say to the mountain 'move from here to there',[25] so I returned to Durham wondering whether we could we raise the £12,500 required to pipe water round this massive obstacle. In a letter from the hospital board dated May 1989 the secretary wrote, rather blandly, to the chairman of the medical group, '... it will make such a wonderful difference to the hospital to have a reliable, clean water supply'. To members of the medical group it seemed an essential need for any hospital and they resolved to provide it. Furthermore, for a group that began its life meeting in a hospital named Dryburn (a 'dry burn' in the north of England is an empty spring, stream or river), a water project seemed a most appropriate assignment. This was to be a tripartite effort. The group had shown in the previous year that it was an advantage to work closely with other charities, gaining their interest as well as their financial support; this year was to be no different.

The medical group set about raising its contribution of the required funds in Durham whilst I, literally, 'set in motion' arrangements to raise the balance through European co-funding. That 'motion' started on Friday, 28th April 1989 as I drove a representative of the European Union from Maseru to Mantšonyane; and what a motion it was. As we bumped our way up the Mountain Road the weather was appalling with heavy rain sleeting down from low clouds. Our progress slowed to such an extent that I considered turning back and abandoning the whole trip. I knew I had to be back in Maseru that same evening so the temptation to avoid the 160-mile (257 kms) round journey was considerable but, with a continuous supply of fresh water for the hospital at stake, the motivation to drive through the rain storm was mockingly stronger.

However, it was dangerous on the twisting mountain road that morning and reluctantly we decided to return, but just as I was trying to find a place on the narrow road to make the turn we drove up through the cloud into brighter weather at, appropriately, God Help Me Pass (Molimo-Nthuse) at 7,605 feet (2,318 m). We changed our minds and made St. James' Hospital and the site of the spring we wanted to cap and later that day, in the dark of the evening, I drove back to Maseru with £3,750 in my pocket, so to speak! Later that year, after Durham had raised its contribution, I was able to walk along Constitution Road in Maseru with some confidence on my way to talk to the third party in the triumvirate; a sharp left turn took me into Linare Road then, having greeted the security guard I had known for some years, down the slope into the British High Commission.

Producing a portfolio of technical drawings and notes that I didn't fully understand, a timetable that I did and a budget that I hoped for, I explained the need and the project we had designed to protect and cap the fresh water spring and take the water round the mountain to the hospital. The High Commissioner, John Edwards, was impressed that we had already raised 60 per cent of the cost and generously offered the remaining 40 per cent, so we were home and dry; perhaps, more appropriately, home and wet! The work was put in hand, and completed on time and within budget. The chairman of the medical group and his wife, who were on a private visit to South Africa in November of that same year, were able to make the long detour to Mantšonyane to see the water flowing from the spring, round the mountain and into St. James' Mission Hospital. We did not exactly tell the mountain to 'move from here to there' but we did get clean water to the hospital.

A heavily overcast sky on Saturday, 17th February 1990 did not lessen the rejoicing at St. James' Hospital. There was much to celebrate. The West German Ambassador opened a new extension to the buildings that his country had donated before we all drove to the site of the spring the LINK had capped on the other side of the mountain. There the suffragan bishop, Donald Nestor, said prayers of blessing and the European delegate, Achim Kratz, ceremoniously unlocked the gate into the compound surrounding the capped spring. Back in the grounds of the hospital there were more speeches during which the Minister of Health, Dr Makenete, thanked the Durham-Lesotho LINK, as did the medical superintendent of the hospital, Paul Borgdorff, and the representative of the British High Commission, Mary Tough.[26] I responded briefly; silently thanking Sister Matsoso that I could at least start in Sesotho even if I had to finish in English! Before lunch was served with traditional Basotho hospitality we were all entertained by the very non-traditional dancing of the Basotho Meso Theatre Group. Later in the day, as an ancient mariner resting during the second dogwatch, a heavy evening rain shower prompted me to modify the words of Samuel Coleridge: 'Water, water, everywhere, with many a drop to drink'.[27]

St. James' Hospital now had a clean water supply and could deal with all but the most serious medical conditions, but there were still thousands of people in the larger Maluti region who, when they required medical treatment, had to make long journeys on foot, often barefooted. The obvious answer was to take medical services to the people in the surrounding villages. Over the years, where that was feasible, St. James' had established small satellite outstation clinics[28] of which Ha Popa was one. For the next four years this rural health centre was to occupy much of the energy of the Durham-Lesotho LINK. My thoughts, ideas and suggestions were debated in Durham and Lesotho and then translated into plans that now had to be implemented. Lesotho had asked us, indeed had encouraged us, to go ahead with the project and the first formal move in that direction in Durham was a meeting between the medical and the development groups held on Monday, 19th June 1989. The chairman of the medical group reported on his visit to the site the previous November. He initiated a discussion covering the design, funding, building, staffing and operating of what the board of St. James' Hospital hoped would become a permanent medical facility that the LINK would finance and build and the hospital would operate.

The hospital had asked the LINK to provide for a residential nurse clinician, a maternity unit, primary health care facilities and an educational centre for village health workers in addition to dispensary, examination room, guest room and kitchens. After the meeting my right-hand man, Richard Briggs, drove me home and I remarked to him, 'That was a useful meeting but I am a little anxious about the fund-raising capabilities of both groups.' Being faced with raising somewhere in the region of £180,000 seemed to justify my anxiety but, as Richard pointed out, I had the prayerful backing of David Jenkins and Philip Mokuku, the support, development and medical groups, the encouragement of St. James' management board and the promise of help from many Durham parishes. What more could I want: apart from £180,000! At the end of 1989, just six months later, the accounts showed we had £1,345.86! Only £178,654.14 to go in just over two years – could it be done?

There were three years' hard work ahead. In Durham Frank White, as chairman of the medical group, was to be responsible for local fund-raising and, as chairman of the development group, I was to be responsible for raising funds from external sources, mainly the British government and the European Community, but there was much to be done before we could approach anyone. We had learned from the poultry unit project that thorough early preparation was essential so, with valuable help from the medical staff at St. James' Hospital, we set about preparing a comprehensive feasibility study, a carefully sculptured action plan, a detailed budget and a phased timetable. February 1992 was our target for the completion of fund-raising to enable the opening of the new clinic a year later. That was certainly an act of faith, but before then our faith was to be frequently tested as were the stamina, skill and dedication of the many people whom I brought in to help.

One of the most worrying features of the whole operation was to get each element in place at the correct time. The jigsaw pieces not only had to fit with each other, but they also had to fit at the appropriate moment; otherwise, I feared I might end up with a lot of money and no land on which to build, or no design for a building or, alternatively, plenty of land, contracts awarded with a faltering cash flow and hopes dashed. Early careful, detailed project-planning was crucial. I knew that I had to get the support of the European Union and the British government. What better way of doing that than to get their representatives to meet in Ha Popa to see the need for themselves and experience the eager support there was already from the Ha Popa chief, the medical superintendent and, most especially, the local people of Ha Popa.

So it was, after a logistical nightmare, that I found myself in Ha Popa on a beautiful summer January day standing under the gaze of the giant twin sentinels, Moqhonoane and Maqhobeshane, talking to the Chief, Morena Mafike Mahoa. Some distance from the clinic we sat together on a couple of rocks and there we went through the lengthy family preliminaries that, because of a combination of hesitant English and stumbling Sesotho, were more protracted than usual. After the scorching sun had travelled a considerable distance of its daily journey we reached the topic towards which all the organising of the day had been directed. Standing together, with the present crumbling clinic to our right, he pulled his brown blanket, decorated with pale blue graphic designs, round his slim frame and waved his thin, gaunt arm across a wide stretch of land in a generous gesture that gave the Durham-Lesotho LINK more than sufficient land on which to build a rural health clinic and surround it with trees. With a broad smile softening the angular features beneath his totally bald head, Morena Mahoa vigorously shook my hand, blessing the effort in which, in very different ways, we were both to be engaged over the next couple of years. I had the Chief on my side!

Meanwhile Paul Borgdorff, the medical superintendent, exercised his medical knowledge and diplomatic skill taking European delegate Achim Kratz and the British High Commissioner, John Edwards, round the present, poorly equipped, two-roomed clinic (which didn't take long), pausing effectively by the huge vertical crack in the end wall of one room. Unconsciously the people of the region also played their part. Once they had heard that there were three doctors at Ha Popa that morning (can you have a grapevine in the mountains?) they flocked in from all directions. They arrived with their aches, pains and injuries at just the right moment, so Paul and his two colleagues held an impromptu clinic which, as it progressed, attracted many pregnant women who had to sit around in the late-afternoon rain; even the weather helped our cause, highlighting what we wanted to avoid. Meanwhile I discussed our plans with the two men who would, sooner or later, be called upon to make their assessments of our plans and provide the international bureaucrats with their recommendations. As the wires buzzed between Maseru, London, Brussels, Johannesburg and Durham, where did those plans stand?

We had the support of many people but what exactly were they supporting? Shortly after my first introduction to Ha Popa about two years previously, I had gradually worked towards this moment, using the time to get professional advice for the completion of our feasibility study and preparing people in both Durham and Lesotho for the work ahead. I went to see the architect in Maseru used by the Anglican Church, Mr Moteane of HMH Architects and Planners, and he took my carefully worded briefing document and produced some sketches and a tentative budget. With the budget came the stark warning that it could be very difficult building at 8,000 feet (2,438 m) in a remote region where there were only makeshift access tracks and frequent bad weather with freezing temperatures in the winter months.

Journeys on horseback and in four-wheel-drive vehicles had prepared me for that comment but nevertheless it was all a bit discouraging, especially when I was so disappointed with his first sketch plans and began to wonder whether I should not have put the whole project out to competition. I wanted to set a new standard of design and building and I had hoped that something more imaginative would result than the first sketches indicated. Unfortunately this unsatisfactory sketch was all that was available for publication in the first edition of the LINK newsletter *'MOHO – Together*, where it appeared in November 1990,[29] but it didn't seem to trouble the Durham half of the LINK. I wondered if we were being too ambitious, so I discussed the matter with the representative of the European Community who I hoped would be the biggest donor and Achim Kratz agreed with me, thinking that the first design was unsuitable.

After more listening in Durham and Lesotho I brought all the varied strands together, gave the architect a further detailed briefing and waited for his interpretation of our requirements. It appeared that we were introducing some notions of environmental planning with which he was not familiar. Included in our thinking was the provision of tree-planting, roof-water conservation, secondary glazing and solar panels for electricity. More discussions led to more draft plans and a more suitable design resulted which Durham and Lesotho agreed would match the future needs of both the hospital and the people. To blend into the local environment the clinic was to be built in local uncut stone and would be set into the hillside with its front partly elevated. It would also be sensitive to all the hard work that had gone into the original building which would be repaired and incorporated into the new health clinic. Access for emergency vehicles was to be under cover and provision for a landing strip was to be considered if finance allowed. Fresh water would be brought from a local spring that also had to remain open to local inhabitants. The architects went out to tender and the contract was awarded to a well-regarded Basotho firm of builders. The LINK was operating on a budget within the region of £180,000: we were in business, hopefully the Lord's business, that David Jenkins referred to when the LINK first brought Durham and Lesotho together. Although surrounded by cement and stones it sometimes felt far from it but we were, after all, preparing to tend the sick.

All the many diverse elements were worked into a project proposal in the differing formats required by whichever funding agency we were approaching. I would formulate the first draft, Richard Briggs would take it away and produce the second, I would do the third and so on (Ha Popa went to five), until we were satisfied that it could be submitted to the Lesotho support group and St. James' Hospital board. In the days before email this all took a long time, but fortunately our experience of working with various funding agencies when financing the poultry unit project meant that we knew many of the people involved and, more importantly, they knew us. Where that was not so we made a point of making ourselves known to them. Richard and I travelled to East Kilbride to talk to officials of the Overseas Development Administration (as the British government's overseas aid department was then called). I also flew to Brussels where, once I had found (more precisely, once the taxi driver had found) the offices of the Commission of the European Communities and managed to get into them, I lost my way and sense of direction; perhaps I wasn't the first person to be thus afflicted by the building!

I eventually tracked down the torturously named Directorate-General for Development VIII-B-2 and then found (it really is worse than finding your way across the mountains of Lesotho) the very human personality of Carola Köster, who was dealing with our application for co-funding. We had extensive conversations, more officials joined us, paper flowed back and forth, calculators clicked, but it was all friendly, helpful and professional. But why did they, in January 1992, once again cast me in the role of explorer by moving their offices from rue de la Loi to rue de Genève? Oh yes, they also changed their name to the even more tortuous 'Non-Governmental Organisations Decentralised Cooperation Unit' but, as they had the money I wanted for Lesotho, we lived with those idiosyncrasies. I was becoming very familiar with the flights between Newcastle and Brussels, but it was worth the effort as the EU, having pared our proposal by only 4 per cent, backed us to the tune of £86,000. The journeys to Scotland were also productive: the ODA promised us £52,089,[30] so our external funding amounted to £138,089. Minor readjustments to the budget meant that we had to find another £30,000 and although I was still slightly anxious it was within our grasp.

One of the great advantages of the flexible organisation used by the LINK was the ability for many different things to happen concurrently. On the morning of Candlemas, Sunday, 3rd February, 1991, in the Anglican Cathedral in Maseru, I preached at the eucharist on 'The Light of the World at Ha Popa' after which, following a spontaneous appeal by a churchwarden, Bennett Khaketla,[31] an offering was made in a manner that is adopted in many Basotho churches with everyone, so it seemed, bringing their donation to the altar to make an authentic gift. No one was collecting: everyone was offering. The total was almost one hundred Maluti, a substantial amount in Lesotho but more importantly a cooperative gesture involving more Basotho in the project.

Six thousand miles to the north, on that same day, at the Church of St. John the Evangelist in the parish of Birtley, hundreds of people gathered for a special service to launch the Durham fund-raising for Ha Popa. The service, which was introduced with the words: 'A time for every matter under heaven; a time to build, equip and staff a Rural Health Centre at Ha Popa',[32] was led by the vicar, Frank White, who was also working tirelessly as the chairman of the medical group. A great deal of attention was attracted as the project was launched on a raft of prayer with every parish in the diocese receiving a supply of 'prayer-cards' listing topics and information leaflets about the project. No one could claim that they didn't know about Ha Popa.

Although Ha Popa seemed to dominate our work at this time the LINK was involved in much else including the provision of scholarships and one scholar, a senior cleric from the diocese of Lesotho, the Reverend Lebohang Kheekhe, travelled from Edinburgh to take part in the service so it was certainly a Durham-Lesotho coordinated act of worship. Although the service was to launch the fund-raising we had, by this time, received some £17,000 so with a pledged total of £155,000 we had only to raise another £17,000 but the last lap is always the most difficult. Many people throughout the county of Durham, and not just those associated with the Anglican Church, were fund-raising with the help of a group of speakers on call when needed. Ha Popa was a name that was to become almost commonplace in the vocabulary of the northern section of the LINK as people listened to the need, discussed plans and organised events to raise sufficient money 'to see this project become a living reality'.

Important though finance is Ha Popas are not built on money alone so, whilst the medical group was fund-raising in Durham, what else had been happening both in Durham and Lesotho that would bring the idea to life? Before the service at Birtley that launched the project much preparatory work had been done drafting the submissions we were to make to the British and European co-funding authorities and they, in turn, produced a whole range of questions. We were bombarded with advice that had to be assessed, questions that had to answered, enthusiasm that had to be tempered, lethargy that had to be countered. A hot-line triangle between London, Brussels and Durham was buzzing as officials, responsible for tax-payers' money, were ensuring that we were well prepared for almost every eventuality: their scrutiny of our ideas was quite impressive. Shortly before the launch in Birtley I had a temporary reprieve by flying back to Lesotho mid-January 1991.

I suspect to the amusement of the Devil, my temporary reprieve was to suffer a precarious ending. In airport jargon NCL, LHR and JNB were all behind me and flight QL333 was exactly half way to MSU when my relaxing relief was to be short-lived, not because of another intrusive telephone call but because of a disturbing tannoy announcement from the Lesotho Airways pilot. 'Ladies and Gentlemen, I have a problem with the port-side engine: it's not working.' (The propeller flapping in the wind was sufficient evidence to support that serene statement of fact!) 'But there is no danger (why then did we have to remove spectacles and practise sitting in the brace position?) as this aircraft is designed to fly using only one engine (there is only one more to go!). I now have to decide whether to go on to Maseru or return to Johannesburg.' (I admit I hoped for Jo'burg.) A few minutes later he was back again: 'Because of flying conditions I have decided to continue on to Maseru.' (Ah well, perhaps we should pray!)

There is in Lesotho a rather unkind saying that if you really do want to learn to pray you should fly Lesotho Airways! Sitting there at 8,000 feet (2,440 m) trying to focus on the rugged beauty of the mountains below but constantly being distracted by the swinging defunct propeller I was beginning to think there might be an element of practicality in that caustic advice. Fuelled by the prayers of all seven passengers (and, who knows, perhaps even those of the crew also) the one working engine took us to Maseru where we landed with a tremendous swerve between two fire engines and an ambulance in attendance on either side of the runway.

Composure restored, next day I was with the architect discussing his first design for Ha Popa Rural Health Centre. None of us were keen on his design so once again I went through the detail of what we required in the hope that something more creative would emerge from his pencil. Rather less tediously I arranged with the hospital superintendent to visit the site with the British High Commissioner and the European Delegate: I had to get them enthusiastic. This was an important visit as their assessment of the proposal and, perhaps more importantly, of the LINK's ability to conduct the project would be influential in the final co-funding decision. However, Ha Popa was not the only item on the long agenda waiting for me in Maseru after the alarming, prayer-promoting, flight.

The first group of young people to visit Lesotho from Durham had to be met; the slow progress of the poultry unit project had to be rectified; the British High Commissioner wanted us to 'raise the profile of the Durham-Lesotho LINK in Lesotho'; we had to advertise, interview and select someone for the academic scholarship; the writer-in-residence had to be appointed; additional woodland sites had to be chosen from the numerous requests received; planting had to be organised; there was a mass of forms (that must have destroyed scores of trees) requiring completion that would allow us to claim the hugely beneficial financial-rand exchange rate for all our building projects; the first stages of the Ha Mohatlane Community Education Centre were in progress; another container was on its way bringing with it problems of customs and excise duties to be paid. Ha Popa, nevertheless, took precedence: there were many more hurdles to jump; some we suspected, others we didn't even know existed.

At each stage we consulted widely in Lesotho and I met with the Permanent Secretary for Health and was greeted by a tired, dispirited lady with a croaky voice, a broken telephone and two silent 'advisers'. She excused her huskiness saying, 'Last night I slept with my mouth open and the fairies came and stole my voice!' Even so she made a courageous attempt to express her concern about the running costs of the health centre but I was able to reassure her that was a matter we had resolved some months previously with St. James' Hospital, which had agreed to take over the running costs after the LINK had agreed to be responsible for the first two years. She uttered a guttural sigh of relief before going on to wheeze about the more general problems of rural clinics. Meanwhile the drafting, criticism, modification and redrafting exercise continued until we were all satisfied that our project submission was the best we could offer. This, our second, co-funding macro-project was made public on Friday, 22nd March 1991.

Two months later, in the southern hemisphere, a serious political hurdle was in the offing. What none of us could have foreseen was the military *coup d'état* that took place on Thursday, 2nd May 1991 deposing General Justin Lekhanya as Chairman of the Military Council, to be replaced by General Elias Ramaema.[33] This dramatic event brought with it a collective feeling of uncertainty and insecurity and in a strange way brought the Durham and Lesotho elements of the LINK even closer together, feeling that we had a common adversary. There were widespread changes in government personnel and at all high-level discussions an armed member of the Military Council was also present. It was one of the few times (and the only time in Lesotho) that I have discussed professional matters with a Minister of Education whilst looking down the barrel of a gun! There were rapid policy changes and it was never clear who made the decisions that might determine the future of Ha Popa Rural Health Centre.

The morass of discussion circulating in a quagmire of decision-making led me, with the hospital superintendent, to seek advice from the secretary of the Private Hospitals Association of Lesotho.[34] Unfortunately the Association was unable to help us. It was also in a state of confusion and did not know which way to turn in its negotiations with Government: it was a time of total confusion. The Secretary said he would prefer us to suspend the start of the building until August which is about the worst possible time to start building in the mountains! In assessing that suggestion we had to take into account the effect of winter weather at

8,000 feet (2,440 m); the increase in costs as inflation was spiralling; difficulties in any suspension of fund-raising in Durham, Brussels and with the British government; the effect on the morale of all those involved including the people of Ha Popa who had begun to collect stones for building. The hurdles were uncomfortably close together: could they possibly be cleared in one leap?

A dejected Peter and Paul repaired to Maseru's oldest hotel, the Lancer's Inn, for a working lunch during which we decided to write to the Minister of Health, whoever that was at that moment in time, explaining the details of our concern at any delay in the project. With a draft of that letter weighing heavily in my pocket I returned to the Anglican Training Centre where I was not particularly receptive to the request from the suffragan bishop asking if the LINK would buy eight horses for rural clergy! What, at that time, was far more pressing was for me to contact Pam to ask her to get a message to the Mosotho priest holding the LINK scholarship at Edinburgh that he had just become father to a baby girl. Before taking to our beds that night we learned that the restrictive Order Four had been abolished by the new Military Council so we could now legally talk politics in Lesotho! What variety; what confusion; what perplexity; should we go ahead with Ha Popa? That night the words of the one whom we were seeking to serve were never clearer or more distinct: 'Come to me all you who are weary and burdened and I will give you rest'.[35] Having come thus far should the LINK not provide a place in the mountains where burdens could be laid aside and rest provided?

How far was 'thus far'? We had the land; we had essential local support; people in the north-east of England and Lesotho had been extremely generous; we had strong indications that we would be granted exemption from General Sales Tax; we had been able to negotiate a reduction in architect's and surveyor's fees; I had met with the British 'Health and Population Adviser' from Liliongwe, Malawi, who was very generous in her praise of the Ha Popa project, describing our submission as 'very good', adding it 'was one of the best of its kind'; we had successfully negotiated the financial rand exchange rate; informal hints from the British indicated that our co-funding request was being considered favourably; a chance meeting with Sir Leon Brittan, who was then a Commissioner of the European Commission, enabled me to talk about the LINK's work in Lesotho in which he expressed considerable interest and which he went on to describe as 'very imaginative', none of which did any harm to our European co-funding request; there was widespread prayerful support. 'Thus far' was a long way. Ha Popa would go ahead!

Having started with Biblical support[36] I had no intention now of looking back. Nevertheless four weeks after General Elias Ramaema had taken over, the political situation in Lesotho caused me to take more than one backward glance. Late one evening I was working in my Durham study when I received a telephone call from David Wells, the hospital treasurer, telling me that on Wednesday, 29th May 1991, there had been riots in Maseru, Leribe, Teyateyaneng and Mafeteng directed against the Indian and Chinese populations. The government had imposed a general curfew from six o'clock in the evening until six o'clock in the morning but not before some thirty people had been killed and ninety-three injured. He then added something that affected the LINK more directly. Not for the first time St. James' Mission Hospital faced imminent closure and now the military-controlled Government of Lesotho was not honouring an agreement to pay salaries in full and had remitted only half the necessary amount. There were serious implications for the whole of independent medical provision but also for the Ha Popa development. David was despondent as, from his many years of Lesotho experience, he cast doubt upon the future viability of independent medical provision. I was working in a turbulent island surrounded by the poisoning waters of apartheid. It was Philip Mokuku who once said to me: 'Peter, real friends are those that visit you in times of trouble,' but I did begin to wonder, to waver and to wilt, so I went to bed.

I waited: my patience was tested for a couple of relatively calm weeks that strengthened my resolve to continue, but then another blow. The estimate submitted by our preferred builder, Monahali Construction, was R140,000 (£28,000) over budget. What were we to do? There was no way in which I could ask an already generous north-eastern population to give more and I knew the diocese of Durham itself was in serious financial difficulties. A Durham LINK meeting had chairmen and treasurers poring over plans and scrutinising figures to suggest where possible savings might be made without sacrificing quality. I was greatly relieved when their ideas were well received by the hospital, architect and potential builder amongst whom a similar sort of exercise had been taking place.

Aware of the way 'estimates' can escalate we now moved into discussions aimed to reach agreement on a fixed 'quotation' figure within a contract that included fairly stringent penalty and dilapidations clauses. My insistence that these elements were to be in place before any signing of the contract was to cause some dissension between the hospital authorities and myself but since the LINK had the ultimate responsibility, and the money, I felt justified in maintaining my position. It was difficult for those in Lesotho to understand, and therefore to accept, that the British and European money was to be given to the LINK and not to the hospital. In any case any move to sign a contract would have been premature as we hadn't yet raised sufficient money to cover the construction costs: we were still in the faith mode! Somewhat later faith was justified and we moved again! It was now Wednesday, 26th June 1991, and the move was to accept formally £52,089 from the British taxpayer. I am not sure how we managed to get the odd £89.00 but every pound was acceptable.

I was back in Lesotho the following month with a former member of my college staff, Ewan Anderson, a geographer who was to conduct the feasibility study for our next big project, the Ha Mohatlane Community Education Centre. That promised to be a larger project but, as it would be in the lowlands on a conveniently accessible site, hopefully it would be somewhat easier to undertake. Equipped with my brief Ewan and Steven Molokeng researched happily together in the Berea District for three weeks, leaving me free to concentrate on the Ha Popa development and three other visitors.

At the end of July, at Moshoeshoe airport, I welcomed Pam who brought with her Richard and Elizabeth Briggs to experience something of the country and see the LINK projects, about which they had all heard so much and for which, in their distinctive ways, they had all worked very hard during the past few years. Within a couple of days of arriving they also became familiar with some of the difficulties of cross-culture working when, after strenuous pressure from the architect, again I had to refuse to sign the Ha Popa contract. There were still numerous pieces of the jigsaw missing and it would be another couple of months before the picture was complete and it was anywhere near acceptable.

It was now the beginning of August, although when the aim is to build a health centre in the mountains of Lesotho it is a time better, and more precisely, described as mid-winter. Snow capped the higher mountains as we drove slowly up the mountain road allowing everyone to soak up the beauty and grandeur of the constantly changing scenery. We were warmly greeted at St. James' Hospital where I met for the first time a second Dutch doctor and his wife, Paul and José Breedveld. Paul was taking over as medical superintendent from Paul Borgdorff who was returning to Holland later in the year after marrying his Mosotho fiancée, 'Mamolepa, on Saturday, 19th October 1991. It had been a tiring journey and breathing became more laboured as we climbed higher, so we rested during the evening of Monday, 5th August. The next day I showed Pam, Richard and Elizabeth around the hospital site, pointing in the distance to the place from which it was all generated, Ha Chooko. After they had admired all the babies in the maternity ward (dangerous to miss one out), we drove to Ha Popa.

The village health worker, 'Mè 'Maetšabi, was there to meet us and as we all tried to picture what the LINK building would look like two years hence, we munched our way through a picnic lunch José had prepared for us. It wasn't easy to translate the two-dimensional drawing into a three-dimensional building set into the hillside. We argued over the details, we waved our arms around, we walked from one corner, (or at least where we imagined one corner would be), to another. We turned the paper design this way and that way as the mountain breeze tried to capture it from us; all the time we were targeted with a querulous, penetrating stare. An old man, well he looked old, sat on a large rock watching us from afar so I took him some of the meat sandwiches that had been prepared for us. That seemed to please him and his stare softened only to harden again when I made an attempt to speak to him in Sesotho; we didn't get very far. I just could not understand a word he uttered (he was doubtless saying the same about me) so I excused myself thinking it must be a local dialect not unlike Geordie. As we drove back to the hospital our adventures for the day had not finished. On the return journey the clutch of the truck started slipping and as we made a sharp left-hand turn on the side of a hill we rolled backwards causing Pam and me (we were sitting in the open rear end), to abandon the vehicle sideways with the utmost speed. It was a long, slow, intermittent, uncomfortable journey back to the hospital before another slow, relatively comfortable drive from there to Maseru.

A day later found Pam and me flying over Lesotho to Swaziland where I had to advise a European co-funded project that was being conducted by a British charity. That left us little time to prepare our sermons for the next day so we used a long wait and such facilities as there were in Matsapa Airport, Manzini, before a bumpy flight back to Moshoeshoe Airport, Lesotho. Pam, who is also a Reader in the Church, was ready to preach at the eight o'clock morning service and I followed at the 09.30 and then wondered if this was the first time a married couple had preached in the cathedral on the same morning? Later when I introduced Pam as my wife to Bennett Makalo Khaketla he, ever the gracious politician, expressed surprise claiming that he thought she was my daughter! Did that compliment her or insult me? I could not spend too long on coming to a conclusion as there was much work to do on the LINK's micro-projects before I left. At a meeting of the Lesotho Support Group we dealt with arrangements for 1993; academic scholarships; a youth visit to Durham; a Mosotho writer-in-residence in Durham Cathedral; the next container; a day of prayer in both cathedrals at the same time; the gift of a Lesotho wall-hanging to Durham Cathedral to celebrate its nine hundredth anniversary; the appointment of a full-time executive officer in Lesotho; the poultry unit project; the community woodland project; the possibility of a large-scale forestry project; the suggestion of one-year delay in the Ha Mohatlane Community Education Centre and then, of course, Ha Popa. Disappointed at the lack of progress with Ha Popa I gave Paul Borgdorff a letter authorising him to sign the contract on behalf of the Durham-Lesotho LINK providing supporting documents had been received from the Ministry of Health; the fixed contract figure did not exceed R450,000 and General Sales Tax exemption had been granted.

There was quite a run around on our last day in Lesotho. The course included the Ministry of Education where I left some important research papers concerning Ha Mohatlane with a secretary in a small office heated by the traditional electric fire with a tin of water balanced precariously on its flat but dented top. Our conversation was brief and precise:

'Is Charles in?'
'No.' (She slides her comic into the top drawer of her desk and continues to lean over the fire.)
'Is Isaac in?' (There must be somebody 'in'.)
'No.' (Continues to lean over the fire.)
'So you're working hard?"'
'No.' (She must have been in the cathedral last Sunday when I was preaching on 'truth')
'Please make sure Charles is given this envelope when he comes in. It contains a very important study.'
'My diary will remind me!' (Noting it at the bottom of a long diary list.)
'Don't forget to look at your diary!'

None of which helped to lift me out of a pit of despondency when Pam and I left Lesotho on Friday, 16th August 1991. I felt I had advanced Ha Popa very little during the four weeks I had been there but perhaps that delay concealed a benefit as it ensured more of the winter had passed and better weather was closer.

A brief holiday in the home of a Kruger Park ranger with his energetic mother revitalised us both and we reached Durham at the beginning of September much refreshed and invigorated, a state enhanced by the Lesotho Tax Commissioners. Amongst the mail was the official notification that we had been granted exemption from General Sales Tax (akin to the Value Added Tax of Great Britain) but only at the cost of more time. We had to submit an inventory of all the materials used in the construction of the building! In Durham the chairman of the medical group continued to be encouraged by the fund-raising that was still continuing to attract donations large and small but despite his optimism I was worried by the effect of inflation in Lesotho running somewhere in the region of 17.5 per cent per year. Any delay in building had serious consequences for funding. For the LINK some of this concern was balanced in the contract but it would, nevertheless, have a detrimental effect on the construction company. Nevertheless by the end of September I felt we had everything in place and gave the go-ahead for the contract to be initialled. 'The pit of despondency' had not been that deep and at the end of the next month, October, I returned to Lesotho via two preaching engagements in St. Michael and All Angels' Church in Pretoria that, indirectly, led to substantial funding from the Anglo-American Corporation for our next macro-project.

Immediately I arrived in Lesotho I received a message to contact the hospital urgently. What had happened now? Could I not have a couple of hours to unpack and settle in? In these days before telephones had reached Mantšonyane it was often difficult to get radio contact to function but today it was loud and clear as was Paul Breedveld's troublesome message. The people of Ha Popa wanted to be paid for collecting the stones and rocks that were to be used for the building and they had gone on strike! It was crucially important to the project that the local Basotho collected stones and rocks, not just for building material but so they became personally involved through their contribution, in a co-operative effort. The District Secretary and the Ha Popa chief had called a *pitso*[37] for tomorrow morning in the hope that I could be there.

The long drive up the mountain road to St. James' gave me time to think about how to handle this new experience. Although I had been to a *pitso* in the lowlands I had never before addressed such a gathering of Basotho anywhere. When I first discussed the Popa project with Chief Mahoa he had assured me the people of Ha Popa would be willing to collect stones and rocks and payment was not mentioned; perhaps it should have been! Now, on this last day of October 1991, what did I find? Recent rains had made the 'road' unusable in places and we had to find alternative tracks, prolonging our journey but still arriving for the ten o'clock start. Morena Mahao greeted me with a prolonged handshake, a big smile and a gesture to sit on a large rock around which a score or so people were gathered. I adjusted my blanket to keep out the chilling mountain breeze, looking round to see that no building had started; a few stones had been collected and some sand had been brought by donkey up the steep slope from the riverbed. Not much to show for a month's work!

As the ten o'clock *pitso* did not start until shortly after midday I had plenty of time to engage in all the usual preliminaries with Morena Mahao, changing down a few gears to adapt to a consensus political mode. By the time we started, so I was told later, there were nine village chiefs present from thirteen villages and about 120 people had gathered, not a large number to represent the 10,000 for whom the centre was being built to serve. The District Secretary acted as chairman opening up the discussion with a warm welcome to everyone on a chilly, dismal day (I just hoped the rain would hold off). As the talking progressed a few voices, noticeably all male, were raised expressing the view that payment should be made for the collection of stones and one man, a schoolteacher, asked for food, '... because we are hungry'. Interestingly he spoke in English; was it so I could understand?

Then the hospital matron, 'Mè Khali, spoke at some length explaining that money was limited and Ntate Peter had come from England to 'see how high is the wall'. It hadn't even started to grow but I knew I had to be careful with what I said, to speak slowly and at length, to gradually get everyone supporting the project. So, speaking last, I began in Sesotho, which was greeted with applause, hesitantly telling them how and when I received my Sesotho name, Ramosa. With many a grammatical slip (much to the amusement of the crowd) and with frequent prompting by 'Mè Khali (with which some in the crowd occasionally disagreed), I reviewed my long connection with Lesotho and talked about the work of the LINK, the woodlands, the feeding project, the water project 'just over the hill': I knew I must not get to the point of my being there too quickly. By now my request to speak in English, 'so I could live tomorrow', had been granted by Morena Mahao (applied psychology) and the district secretary then translated my long talk. I didn't quite end with an account of how people in Durham were giving money to pay the builders and how the Chief had given us the land but I did end, at long last, by asking them to give by collecting stones. We would work together, Durham would collect money, Basotho would collect stones. No woman had spoken as yet; I must involve everyone.

'Do you want a clinic?' I asked.

'*E ntate!*' (Yes father!) men and women yelled.

'Will you collect stones to build it?'

'*E ntate!*' they shouted.

That was the note on which to end so I offered a short prayer and then a blessing before we all joined in the traditional conclusion.

'*KHOTSO – PULA – NALA*' (peace – rain – prosperity).

As it was necessary to leave immediately to get back to Maseru I had to decline the Chief's offer of hospitality. In a strange sort of way I was encouraged as I said to a very sad Morena Mahao, '*Sala hantle, morena*' (stay well, Chief) and he responded, rather dismally, '*Tsamaea hantle, ntate*' (Go well, father). He could have been glad to see the back of me but that clearly was not the case; he was sorry to see me go.

In Maseru I met with the Lesotho Support Group the next day when Steven Molokeng made the useful suggestion that we should try to support the efforts of the local people to collect stones by going to help the following weekend. In a splendid reinforcement of the talk I gave at the *pitso* five members of the group travelled to Ha Popa with Steven who spent five days there getting many people mobilised collecting huge quantities of stones and rocks. Shortly after this Trojan effort I had a glowing account from the architect that the stone collection was continuing to go well and building work was about to begin.

I had a break from the pressures of Ha Popa making the nine-hour journey to Ha Moshebi in the south-east of the country not far from the Sehlabathebe National Park. During our long journeys both before and after taking services and preaching Philip and I had plenty of uninterrupted time to talk about the mission of the LINK. Until this time all the work for the Durham-Lesotho LINK, in both places, had been done voluntarily but it was becoming increasingly obvious that we needed more labour hours than were available to us on a part-time unpaid basis. When we returned to Maseru we spoke with Steven Molokeng and on Monday, 11th November 1991, Steven started work as the LINK's first full-time paid executive officer thanks to generous 'pump-priming' initial funding by the Charities Aid Foundation in England. That was not the only generous contribution; there was also one from Lesotho. When he began working for the LINK Steven graciously accepted a reduction of one third in his remuneration: we just did not have the money to match his government-funded previous salary as diocesan schools' secretary. This was a turning point in the LINK's work and would have a great impact on Ha Popa. The Ha Popa Rural Health Centre designed by Basotho, being built by Basotho now had continuing LINK supervision by a Mosotho. Things were going in the direction I had hoped for when I started the LINK. With no weight of despondency this time the small plane lifted off for Johannesburg much, much easier, or so it seemed!

In Durham Ha Popa became less time consuming for me; Steven was able to make many decisions locally and building was taking place during the southern summer months. Money continued to flow in and I received regular reports through our newly acquired fax machine that the building was progressing satisfactorily. This gave me time to concentrate on our next big project, the building of Ha Mohatlane Community Education Centre; to visit Brussels; to talk with Stephen Hughes, the Member of the European Parliament for the north-east and to get his support both for Mohatlane and a large forestry project. I also had time to calculate that during 1991 I had spent just over 40 per cent of my time in Africa and to reflect on a question asked of me by a Mosotho man, '*Ntate* Peter, have you been to Durham recently?' For our double celebration at Christmas we were joined by the Mosotho scholar from Edinburgh University so during our rejoicing Lesotho was never far away.

By mid-January I was on my way back to Lesotho but the day before I left I received a letter from Aelred Stubbs with the sad news that the Community of the Resurrection was to close Emmaus in Sunderland. This affected me more than I suspected at the time but the trials and tribulations of international travel soon took over my attention. I was told in Johannesburg that I was on the 'stand-by' list for Maseru but when I did eventually get a seat I found the plane was only half full! That was not the only peculiar event. Shortly after arriving in Maseru I wanted to post a letter to friends in Rustenberg, South Africa, and I was asked if it was to go 'air-mail or surface?'. As Rustenberg is landlocked within South Africa and Maseru is surrounded by it I questioned the question to be told it would go by ship if I sent it surface: I did, at considerably less expense; and it arrived promptly!

This visit my personal luggage included a very heavy cold that confined me to my bed for three days where I was dosed with various concoctions. Steven Molokeng brought me a thick, dark brown liquid in a bottle on which the instructions read: 'take thrice each day and do not leave your blanket'! I didn't even leave my bed. Whilst I was feeling sorry for myself in the sweltering heat of 42° Celsius (108° Fahrenheit) Steven brought me the news that the drought, through which the whole of southern Africa was passing, might have serious implications for building Ha Popa. The Government had published a list of priority uses of water: human consumption, animal consumption, crop irrigation, personal washing, building and construction. It seemed that we might soon be stopped from building especially as the Ha Popa region did not have an excess supply of water. Would I ever get this health centre built?

Feeling slightly better on Sunday, 2nd February 1992, I went to the cathedral to take part in the 8.00 a.m. eucharist where I felt rather disorientated as we sang the hymn *The Day Thou Gavest Lord is Ended!* It was pleasant to be back in circulation even if a few hot days later I had to suggest gently, to two elderly ladies (one was over 70 and the other was 84 years) on a private visit from Durham, that it would be more tactful to refer to local people as 'the Basotho' rather than 'the natives'. Although, of course, we were all natives of our respective homelands, such a description could be misinterpreted and, because of misuse, it now has derogatory connotations. I did not need reminding (but my notebook does so), that the work of the LINK was a many-faceted service in which we can all make mistakes as I was to discover.

Steven Molokeng and I were going to the woodland site at Sekameng. As we left the tarred road and weaved our way along the track past Masite a huge bank of heavy clouds built up over our destination where we expected groups of school children to plant the saplings we had in the bakkie. Looking upwards and thinking ahead I said, 'Oh! Steven, that looks threatening,' to which he dryly replied, 'Oh! Peter, that looks promising,' but it didn't rain! We had to wait another two days for that to happen and then there was widespread rejoicing.

By this time the LINK had begun publishing its biannual newsletter, *'MOHO – Together* and Ha Popa was headline news in the first four issues of what was a widely circulating publication in Durham, Lesotho and elsewhere. I was constantly surprised and humbled by the magnificent response Ha Popa was receiving from near and far. Not only had the poor of Lesotho given but so did the old lady in Canada who sent a large donation and the friend in the west of England who phoned and started talking about 'this Ha Popa project' only to end the conversation by pledging five hundred pounds. So it went on until one year after the opening service at Birtley the medical group was able to hold a Celebration Service at St. Cuthbert's Church, Darlington on Friday, 21st February 1992. Appropriately that date is designated in the Anglican Church calendar for the remembrance of the Saints and Martyrs of Africa.[38] It was also the day on which I returned from Lesotho bringing with me, not only an up-to-date account of progress at Ha Popa, but also the voice of Philip Mokuku thanking the people gathered in Darlington that evening. He said:

> This is bishop Philip of Lesotho greeting our brothers and sisters in Christ in Durham: we feel very close to you all in spite of the 6,000 miles which physically separate us. We all know that the Holy Spirit, that binding power amongst Christians, takes no notice of boundaries. The Holy Spirit does not have a passport. The Holy Spirit does not have to fill in immigration forms. The Holy Spirit can travel across, around and within the world and the link between Lesotho and Durham is living proof of this truth. Let us thank God for the LINK as we bring our resources together in common tasks for the benefit of all God's people.
>
> As we have worked together for almost six years the Holy Spirit has been practically demonstrated in the community woodlands, the youth exchange, the poultry unit project and many other activities in both Durham and Lesotho. We thank God for all our work together but today we rejoice especially for the planning and building of Ha Popa Rural Health Centre. At Ha Popa, high up in the mountains, people have worked long hours preparing the beautiful site and

> collecting stones for the building. Very soon, when the rains come again, they will be planting trees on the site.
>
> The architect, contractor and workers, all Basotho, have made their special contributions. They have had to contend with many difficulties. Building high in the mountains of Lesotho is not easy: last October and November unusually heavy rains washed away part of the mountain track which was the only access to Ha Popa and that had to be repaired before equipment and building materials could be got to the site. But God has continued to bless us all and the work is progressing well.
>
> Whilst all the building activity is going on around them the medical staff of St. James' Mission Hospital continue to hold regular clinics in the old building; the task of caring must go on uninterrupted. Elsewhere the preparation and training of medical staff for the new Health Centre is being organised.
>
> None of this work – surely true missionary work for Christ – none of this would be possible without the varied contributions of many, many people. As skills, hopes and prayers are brought together with money, planning and organising we humbly thank God for whatever your contribution has been. We look ahead, with the confidence of Christ's people, to the day when the building is complete and the Centre is operating, when it is caring for those who are sick. But tonight, in Lesotho and Durham, let us rejoice that the LINK has brought us together in His Royal Service to demonstrate our love for each other, and of Him, in our many activities. Especially, let us celebrate with joy and thanksgiving for the development of the Ha Popa Rural Health Centre and ask God for His continued blessing.
>
> May God bless you all – *Molimo a ke a le hlohonolofatse bohle.*

Shortly afterwards the chairman of the medical working party wrote:

> It was a night to appreciate the sense of togetherness which is growing in our Dioceses through the Durham-Lesotho LINK.

It was a night when the worship was lively; the choir sang beautifully; the organisation was first-class and the refreshments unequalled; all so very distant from the tough environment of Ha Popa. Nevertheless that evening, after much sharing of experiences, those who had worked so hard for Ha Popa left with the news ringing in their ears that the fund now stood at a magnificent £183,237. It was difficult to believe that such a large amount had been raised in just fifty-five weeks but great blessings can be hugely difficult to comprehend. We had been wonderfully blessed and now we could go forward confident that the project would be fully funded. I had left Lesotho forty hours previously and now Pam drove a very tired, happy husband home to a bed that he desperately needed. As I got into the car I said, 'You know there is still a lot to do,' then fell asleep.

I returned to Lesotho in April 1992 and rode out to Ha Popa the following month. I was thrilled with what I saw. The so-long-delayed building had risen to window level with the irregular, uncut stones (each one laboriously faced by hand chiselling) blending in to the surrounding environment. The people of Ha Popa had collected literally tons of rock and stone from the surrounding mountains and now much of it was buried, unseen, deep within the foundations or underneath the floor levelling out the slope of the hillside. That in itself was a magnificent achievement: we were now building on their strenuous effort and sufficient stone had been collected to finish the building. As I watched the hive of activity with men facing stones, others laying them, some climbing over insecure-looking scaffolding, others mixing cement, donkeys bringing sand in sacks up from the river valley, it occurred to me that the LINK was not only bringing a medical facility to Ha Popa it was, in the process, bringing much-needed work and money to an impoverished local population. There must have been about twenty men engaged on the site, some of whom were just about to take a lunch break as I walked around among them joking and laughing at my poor attempt to speak and work with them.

My camera clicked away: I had a responsibility to share all this with people in Durham who had contributed so much, but before riding back to St. James' Hospital I took a long, careful, look at the old clinic. I wanted it incorporated into the new building because I reckoned that there was a lot of hard work and emotional investment in its construction and I did not want to be seen as the person who destroyed it. However, the ominous crack in the end wall seemed to be bigger and I did not see how my ideas could be put into practice, and so I resolved to speak again to the architect about how it could be preserved. Four strong legs took me back to Mantšonyane then four wheels to Maseru. Philip took me to the airport where we sat and discussed what he thought would be two very critical weeks in Lesotho. King Moshoeshoe II was about to go to Swaziland at a time when politics, drought and inflation were all adding their particular stressful influence to the increasing social tension. I assured him of the prayers of the people of Durham: it was all a long, long way from Ha Popa.

After ten weeks at home I was in the Lesotho field again with the architect and the medical superintendent tackling the problems of building in the mountains of Lesotho. By mid-May the building had grown to roof level but now there was a hitch with the delivery of the roof trusses; getting them over and around mountains proved to be exceptionally difficult. Rather more serious was the dispute between the village chief and the builders and hospital over the use of the meagre water supply in the current drought. The architect assured me that it would be possible to concentrate on those building tasks that did not require water and the Chief seemed happy with that. I was less than happy when I was told that the old clinic had 'fallen down'; perhaps I was being too sensitive as no one else seemed concerned at its loss. I then asked Morena Mahao if he were pleased with the clinic to which he replied in his hesitant English: 'We don't know how to express ourselves because sometimes we think this (pointing to the building) is a photograph which may blow away in the wind; it's so wonderful.' I hoped his pleasure would be justified. As I walked around during the lunch break some men were playing Moraba-raba, the intricacies of which I have never quite worked out in which ever African country I have seen it being played. Hoping that I might be further educated I paused to watch but came away confused both by the speed with which it is played and its purpose.

I didn't go to Ha Popa again during this visit but it continued to occupy much of my time as I tried to get money transferred for an accurate amount into the right account at the correct exchange rate at the proper time! We had made careful provision enabling us to finance the cash-flow and the system and its controls were working effectively in Durham. I was, however, beginning to question the arrangement and ability of the Lesotho diocese to handle our financial bookkeeping in the south. As a practical contribution to the LINK their help was welcome when we started but they had monumental time-consuming financial problems of their own. That, coupled with their lack of experience in dealing with the intricate banking arrangements of our relatively large funds, was a problem that was eventually solved by the LINK appointing its own financial officer and assuming full financial accounting. Streams of pounds, euros, rands and dollars all had to flow into the maloti river at the right time to keep the project ships afloat. It wasn't easy in the banking environment of the early 1990s and I spent much time that I could ill afford talking with bank officials when our biggest project, the

Ha Mohatlane Community Education Centre, was being launched into the river. Perhaps this was one of the causes that resulted in my now infrequent visits to Ha Popa although that was not to be regretted as it began to move the onus for decisions on to the Basotho which was all part of the LINK's long-term strategy.

In September 1992 Mantšonyane came to Durham. Paul, José and eight-month old Eva Breedveld stayed with Pam and me and met the Durham medical group during a reception when everyone was able to get to know each other; useful connections were being established. It was during this visit that one of our less successful ideas came to nothing. Previously the medical group had talked with dentists about the possibility of providing a dentistry service at the hospital and Ha Popa but, for a variety of reasons, it was never put into practice. What was more successful was the provision of an autoclave that Paul thought would be useful; it was available to us and was sent in the next container. He also attended a meeting of the development group and gave a very encouraging report on the design and quality of building at Ha Popa. Three weeks later when I was in Maseru that was to be confirmed by the architect although he was not so buoyant about progress and introduced the less welcome fact that building was some ten weeks behind schedule and, under the terms of the contract, the LINK could impose penalties up to R23,000 (£4,500). What a dilemma! There was a wealth of conflicting advice but eventually it was decided not to exercise this option providing the building was ready by Saturday, 13th February 1993, the date we had decided to have its official opening. Secretly, I left wondering if it would ever be ready.

The journey to Durham was relatively uneventful except for an incident that broke the monotony on the Heathrow to Newcastle sector. I was struggling with a cardboard box containing the architect's rather fragile, but very useful model of his design for the Ha Mohatlane Community Education Centre. When I was about to place it in the overhead locker, a lady sitting in the window seat to which I had been allocated said, in a stringent, domineering voice, 'Don't put that on my coat, that cost five thousand dollars!'

I didn't. I took off my fifteen-dollar (£10.00) jacket, sat down and said to her, in my most serious intonation, 'Your coat must be a dreadful worry to you!'

Ignoring my comment she didn't speak to me again until, unable to constrain herself when flying over Newcastle, she said, 'Is that Newcastle?'

'Yes.'

'I thought it was a city.'

'Madam, it is!'

I was glad to get home; perhaps, even fortunate!

Early next year I was back in Lesotho where heavy rains had broken the drought with a devastating violence, washing away tracks, making mountain journeys more difficult than ever and some even treacherous with displaced boulders and others precariously balanced. Rainwater had rushed through *dongas*, across roads and over causeways and the track to Ha Popa had not escaped attack. After an attempt to get through to the Health Centre in a four-wheel-drive vehicle the hospital driver came back with frightening tales of what he had experienced and the opening was just one day away! His report was substantiated by a forecast of bad weather from the reliable Missionary Aviation Fellowship in Maseru so I took the reluctant decision to postpone the opening until my next visit in May. This would also provide some extra time to get the building finished as the builder and men had also been affected by the consequences of the broken drought. It also gave me more time to think about whom I might ask to perform the official opening.

Earlier there had been many competing arguments about who should perform the opening throughout which I made it quite clear that I would prefer it to be someone from the local area. Someone said the Chief should open it, but which chief? Someone said the bishop should open it, but which bishop? Someone said ... and so it went on but there was never any spark of originality. The selection of one would inevitably cause friction among the others! It was during a late-evening chat at St. James that the answer came to me. We were talking about the old clinic and how I had hoped it would have been incorporated into the new building, a wish that proved impracticable as it had fallen down before it could be used as I had wanted. The conversation went on about the facilities it had provided including maternity services and then someone asked who had been the first child to be born in, what was then, the newly built clinic? Whoever it was would probably now be twelve years old. Got it! He or she would open the new Ha Popa Health Centre! But could we discover who it was? Could we find him or her? We did and tracked down 12-year-old Joalane Mokeretla, the first baby to be born in the original Ha Popa clinic and now, thirteen years later, on Saturday, 1st May 1993, for just one day, the first lady of Ha Popa.

The sun-drenched autumn day started at the hospital with an emergency delaying our departure for Ha Popa whilst a two-day-old baby with a life-threatening condition was transferred to Queen Elizabeth II Hospital in Maseru for an operation that could not be performed at Mantšonyane. A quick switch of vehicles took the LINK's new bakkie loaded with equipment and overloaded with people to swell the 800-plus Basotho, an uncounted number of Netherlanders and four English gathered for the opening in glorious weather.[39] Also there was the

Mosotho priest, Lebohang Kheekhe, who was at the launching service at Birtley, Durham, two years previously, in February 1991. He now led a short eucharistic service of thanksgiving and dedication. Welcoming everyone the Chief, Morena Mahao, thanked the LINK and all involved in the building of the Health Centre where medical services would be available to everyone in the region. I presented the Chief with a framed photograph of himself, thanking him for the allocation of land on which to build and speaking about the combined efforts of many people that had made the building possible. A rather diminutive Joalane, looking very smart in her brightly multi-coloured dress, black-and-white woollen jacket, grey woollen stockings and, I suspect, newly-bought-for-the-occasion black shoes, led the huge crowd the short distance to the main door decorated with balloons and fastened, most appropriately, with a bandage. Looking rather solemn Joalane ceremoniously cut the bandage with a pair of surgical scissors declaring that the health centre was now open!

Whilst an Anglican priest, Martin Mkwibiso, blessed each room in turn that they might be used effectively in the Christian mission to heal the sick and care for the infirm, and amid much cheering and dancing, Joalane led the crowd through the entrance hall, dispensary, treatment room and examination room into the large education room behind which lay the kitchens. The crowds poured through as Joalane continued on to the guest room, delivery-room, the ward and the Nurse-clinician's residential wing, leading them outside along the covered walkway, past the stables to the feast that had been prepared for whoever cared to join in the celebration. The joyful noise was almost overpowering rising to a crescendo of decibels to greet each dance, song or speech of which there were many, from all ages, to last well beyond a nightfall that eventually brought the rejoicing to an end.

People, conscious of the cold evening mountain breeze, thankful for their warm Basotho blankets, drifted away across the mountain tracks, their singing becoming quieter with every footstep. It was over: Ha Popa Rural Health Centre stood there, fully equipped, ready to serve whoever might need the medical attention it could now provide. Above all it stood there at 8,000 feet (2,440 m), nestled between Moqhonoane and Maqhobeshane, in the remoteness of Lesotho, as a symbol of what can be achieved by the prayerful labour of countless people working irrespective of colour, class or country, but simply as 'One Body in Christ'.

---

1. Luke 9:1–2 (NIV).
2. Chief Petrose Lekolomi went on to live another twelve years, dying at the age of 83 years (1880–1963).

3. Bishop John Maund was enthroned in the Cathedral of St. Mary and St. James, Maseru, on Sunday, 14th January 1951.
4. The Society for the Propagation of the Gospel in Foreign Parts (SPG), which was formed in 1701, merged in 1965 with the Universities' Mission to Central Africa (UMCA) when it took the title of the United Society for the Propagation of the Gospel (USPG).
5. Luckman, Kenneth, *Place of Compassion* (Hertford, UK: Authors OnLine Ltd, 2001) provides a full account of the founding of St. James' Mission Hospital, Lesotho, and of the outstation clinics.
6. See Chapter Four: In the Jungle (p. 81). Neil Yeats is Charles Yeats' uncle on his father's side of the family.
7. See Prologue: Before the Beginning? (p. xix).
8. Keith Dumbell retired living in Cape Town, Don Jefferies of St. Mary's Hospital, Paddington and Dick Madeley of the Royal Victoria Infirmary, Newcastle-upon-Tyne.
9. Equipment that was surplus to requirements or had been superseded by other products came from Durham Health Authority and Bishop Auckland General Hospital.
10. Most notably from Searle Pharmaceuticals (incorporated in 2003 into Pfizer UK) who supplied free-of-charge heart drugs and anti-diarrhoeal treatments, both urgently needed at St. James' Hospital.
11. Dr Barbara Castree and her husband Mr Colin Chandler from Newcastle.
12. Mrs Wendy Broderick, Winlaton, Tyne and Wear.
13. Makro, Washington, County Durham.
14. The LINK was fortunate to have a personal connection with Safmarine (when it was registered as a South African company before it became a UK company in 1996 and then, three years later, part of the Danish Maersk Group). Through its charitable programme it has donated in excess of 8,000 containers to poor communities in Africa for conversion into clinics and classrooms. The LINK was an early beneficiary of this company's generosity.
15. Health centres were at Marakabei; Methalaneng; Likalaneng; Ha Popa and St. James' Hospital, Mantšonyane with clinics at Ha Lephoi; Montmartre; Auray; Ha Mafa. St. James'Mission Hospital 'annual' report for 1993 and 1994 (pp. 38–48).
16. Since this meeting the hospital has been rebuilt and renamed, much less succinctly, The University Hospital of North Durham.
17. Luckman, Kenneth, *Place of Compassion* (Hertford: Authors OnLine, 2001) p. 80.
18. Including the Lesotho Diocesan Association; the Diocese of Durham; United Society for the Propagation of the Gospel; and, in welcome interdenominational cooperation, the Catholic Agency for Overseas Development (CAFOD).
19. For much of this information I am indebted to Frank White's annual report for 1988.
20. With me were Dutch medics Paul Borgdorff, Suzanne Vlier and Desirée Cleuren, the latter two from Maastricht, a small town in the south of Holland where Pam and I had close friends.
21. Luckman, Kenneth, *Place of Compassion* (Hertford, UK: Authors OnLine, 2001). Ha Popa Rural Health Centre (p. 110). There are some minor inaccuracies in this otherwise useful

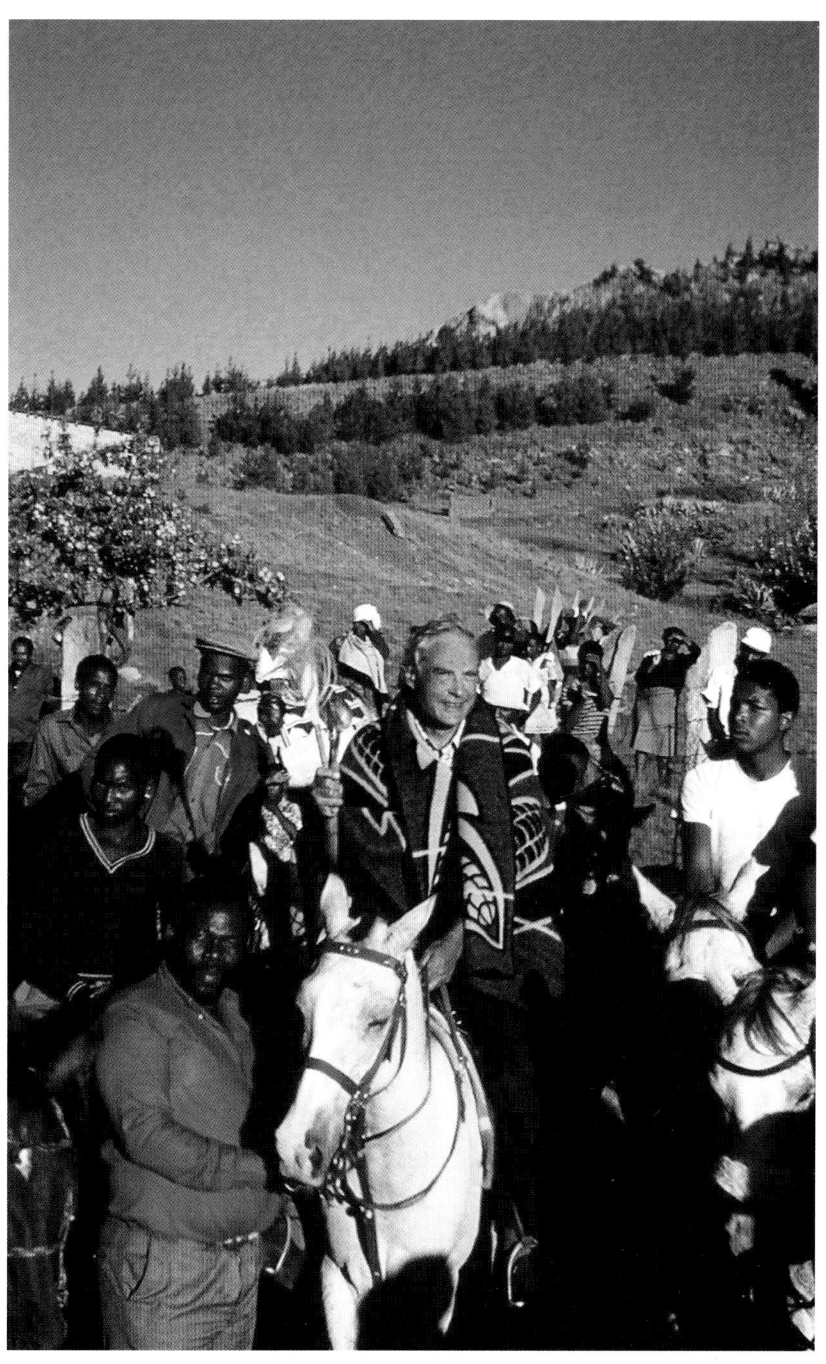

Ramosa is welcomed by All Saint's Church Hlajoane

Dongas carve their relentless way through Lesotho ...

... taking away its scarce valuable soil

A donga, starting in the foreground, under arrest by a LINK Community Woodland

Them + Us = We

Lay and episcopal energy
pump up essential spirit

Awe inspiring mountains make
mountain journeys hazardous

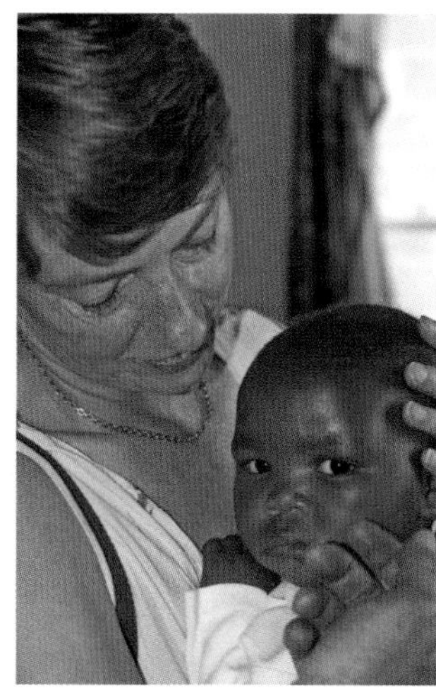

'I'm not too sure about
these exchange visits ...'

Africa comes to Europe: Basotho youth witness to Durham with their joyful singing and dancing

A new challenge for the Basotho: the Katse Dam where the LINK provided training in water skills

Lesotho is a small country with long distances

The LINK site by the Maqalika Dam, Maseru

Ha Popa Rural Health Centre ready to receive its first patients and trees

Isa Browns made a significant contribution to school learning ...

... and feeding

Durham hangs-out in Lesotho ...

... and Lesotho hangs-out in Durham (thanks to cathedral tapestry weavers 'Mafefa – 'Makeletso – 'Mamoakonyane – 'Mantsapi)

Micro-enterprises assisted many Basotho in business ventures

Philip and Peter link Lesotho and Durham for the people of All Saints Church, Ha Mikia

Holy Cross Church, Thaba-Tseka

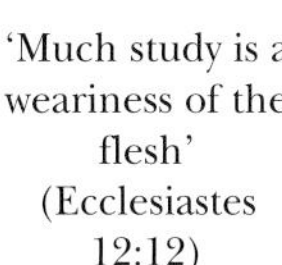

'Much study is a weariness of the flesh' (Ecclesiastes 12:12)

Planning for tomorrow (a school tree nursery)

A spiral aloe undisturbed by the floral link

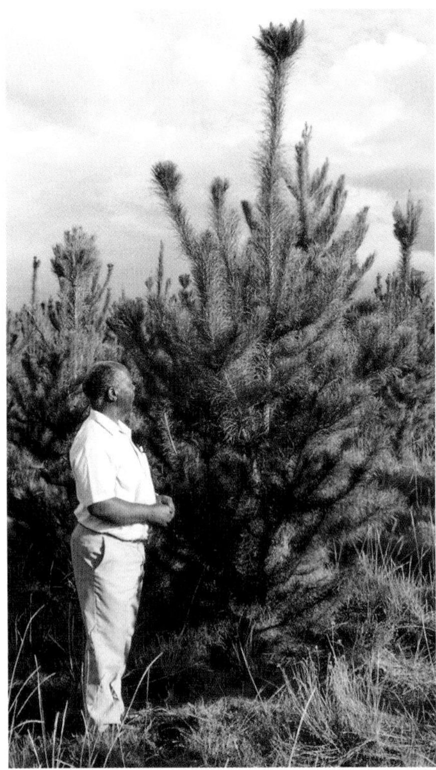

Steven Molokeng prefers to be in front of a tree than behind a desk

Breakfast in the making

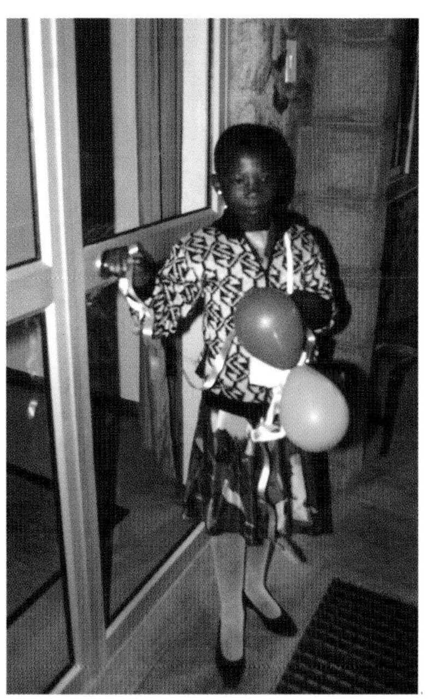
Joalane Mokeretla, the first lady of Ha Popa, as she opens the Rural Health Centre

Container contents have now helped to make this a rare sight

'Young people, enjoy your youth' ... (Ecclesiastes 11:9)

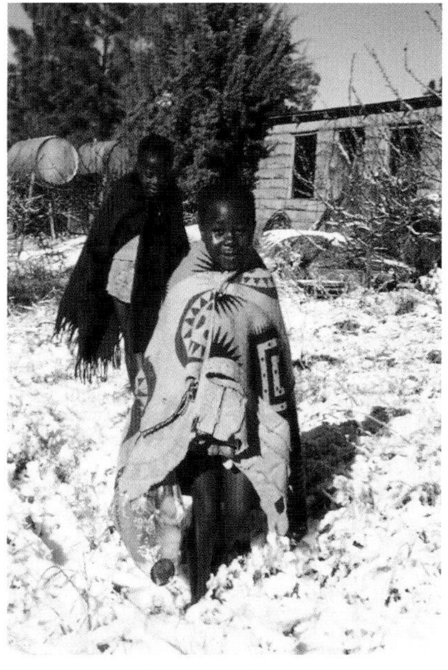
... and the mountain snow as you walk to school – without shoes

Architect's model of Ha Mohatlane Community Education Centre ...

... for which Lesotho collected stones whilst Durham collected pounds ...

... to convert the vision into reality

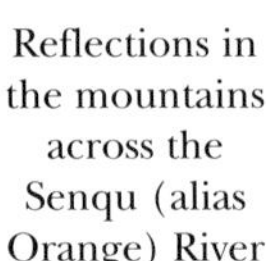

Reflections in the mountains across the Senqu (alias Orange) River

account. The building was not, as stated, blessed by a bishop as there was not a bishop present at the opening.

22. The 1993 report of St. James' Hospital describes the Ha Popa Rural Health Centre built by the Durham-Lesotho LINK as 'this beautiful new health centre' – a euphemism repeated in every 'annual' report until at least 2001. There are also errors and omissions in the description of how the project was financed and further mistakes within the accounts.
23. Kielder Reservoir in Northumberland is the largest capacity artificial lake in Europe, of about 70,397,852,000 imperial gallons (200 million cubic metres or 200 billion litres) covering an area of 3.86 square miles (10 square kms). Rutland Water is a larger surface area but with less capacity.
24. Green, Peter, 'Evaluation Review & Report on Namibian Development Projects', Appendix 4. EU (October 1993).
25. Matthew 17:20 (NIV): I tell you the truth, if you have faith as small as a mustard seed, you can say to this mountain, 'move from here to there' and it will move. Nothing will be impossible for you.
26. Mary Tough (pronounced Took).
27. Coleridge, Samuel (1772–1834), *The Ancient Mariner*, pt. 1, 'Water, water, everywhere, nor any drop to drink'.
28. In 2002 there were outstation clinics at Marakabei; Ha Lephoi; Methalaneng; Likalaneng; Ha Popa; Auray; Ha Mafa; Montmartre, and St. James.
29. *'MOHO – Together*, No. 1 (November 1990) p. 3.
30. At the Overseas Development Administration we negotiated with Robin Russell and Anna Turner. The decision to fund Ha Popa Rural Health Centre was taken during the afternoon of Monday, 17th June 1991.
31. Bennett Makalo Khaketla was born in 1913. When he was forty-five he was elected to the Executive Committee of the Basutoland African Congress from which he resigned in 1960 to form the Basutoland Freedom Party. Five years later he became Privy Councillor to King Moshoeshoe II. In May 1987, during a visit to Durham by the Lesotho Mothers' Union, his wife, 'Masechele, stayed with Pam and me. He was then Minister of Justice. At the cathedral he was notable for his role in maintaining the rhythm of hymns and the speed of singing by banging a copy of the prayer book on to his left hand! He died on Sunday, 9th January 2000 aged 86 years. A comprehensive account of his life can be found in Ambrose, David, Summary of Events in Lesotho; Vol. 7; No.1; First quarter, 2000. He wrote *Lesotho 1970* (London: Hurst & Co, 1971).
32. A paraphrase of Ecclesiastes 3:1-8 with special reference to verse 3b: *(He sets) the time for tearing down and the time for building.*
33. During this period the political leadership of Lesotho was very unstable. When the LINK started the leadership was in the control of a Military Council under the Chairmanship of General Justin Metsing Lekhanya who held office for just over five years from 24th January 1986 to 2nd May 1991. He was deposed by General Elias Phisoana Ramaema who was Chairman for just under two years until 2nd April 1993 during which period he made a

pledge to return political power to civilian leadership when Ntsu Mokhehle (see page 70) leader of the Basotho Congress Party became Prime Minister. He fulfilled his pledge.

34. At this time the Secretary of the Private Hospital Association of Lesotho (PHAL) was Mr. Makara.
35. Matthew 11:28 (NIV): Come to me, all you who are weary and burdened, and I will give you rest.
36. Luke 9:62 (NIV): Jesus replied, 'No-one who puts his hand to the plough and looks back is fit for service in the kingdom of God.'
37. A '*pitso*' is a meeting of all residents in a village.
38. February 21st is the date designated 'Saints and Martyrs of Africa' in the Anglican calendar as given in *The Alternative Service Book*, 1980 but it does not appear in *Common Worship* 20 years later in 2000.
39. A detailed account of the opening of Ha Popa Rural Health Centre as seen through the eyes of a Mosotho, Florence Tseko, can be found in *'MOHO – Together*, No. 6 (May 1993).

Chapter Seven

Sing a New Song

See, the former things have taken place,
and new things I declare;
before they spring into being
I announce them to you."[1]

"Sing to the Lord a new song,
his praise from the ends of the earth,
you who go down to the sea, and all that is in it,
you islands, and all who live in them.[2]

At their worst diocesan overseas links, wherever you happen to be standing and in whichever direction you are looking, are little more than an excuse for, and a means of, episcopal escape. Nevertheless, I was always sorry that circumstances worked against David Jenkins making just one visit to Lesotho but he graciously maintained that I could represent him when and where necessary, which I was willing to do even if I couldn't always explain him![3] Philip Mokuku did visit Durham but always with a specific, substantial and predetermined purpose. Since we were trying to be 'One Body in Christ' it was the bodies, not just the heads, that needed to be brought together and this concentrated our efforts and dominated our thinking. I was determined that the effort, energy and enterprise of the scores of people engaged in the LINK would not be episcopally self-indulgent but would allow the body of people to engage in mission as close to the action as possible. They would be welcomed for themselves not their money: they were the stakeholders.

When I started the Durham-Lesotho LINK I hoped it would be a manifestation of Isaiah's servant songs[4] and although, when celebrating the twenty-fifth anniversary of the LINK, 'the former things have taken place' and, therefore, I am unable to declare them 'before they spring into being' I can, at least retrospectively, 'announce them to you'! Of course, that was not the case at the beginning of the LINK and the start of its subsequent projects, when a strenuous effort was made to discuss new things 'before they (sprang) into being'. Durham was not the first. Other dioceses around the world had established connections, such as Lesotho and Johannesburg, with varying degrees of success (however that is measured) but there was really not much to show for the effort and the expense. I wanted to declare something new and in the process expand the concept of Christian development beyond the mere physical and material, important though that is, especially when actively woven into the faith of the Christian. Quoting Moses' discourse to the people of Israel[5] when they were in exile in Moab, Jesus said to the Devil, 'It is written: 'Man does not live on bread alone'.[6] The LINK could not flourish on its health centre, its school, its woodlands, its poultry unit project; it would not live on eggs alone. None of those were sufficient by themselves or, for that matter, collectively: another dimension had to be introduced. I had a large measure of freedom so why not use it? What new things should I declare?

Recognising that it is often small, intimate personal things that bring people closer together I wondered how the LINK could help the early bonding process of individuals. What would grip people within Durham and within Lesotho then bridge the gap between Durham and Lesotho? One answer came during a church service in Durham. It was June 1991.[7] I had just preached a sermon on the life of my Christian namesake when, during the hymn that followed, resting my voice, I listened to the large congregation singing in unison. It was then that I realised the immense psychological power of music; everyone was singing the same words to the same music in the same place. There was harmony; harmony of the hymn expressed a harmony of purpose. When I reflected further (after the service!) it occurred to me that this powerful medium spread across cultures, countries and creeds from church pews to football terraces, from sea shanty to opera oratorio, from herdboy to virtuoso. We needed a LINK song.

We are One Body in Christ – Re 'mele o le mong ho Kreste.

If we were to 'sing to the Lord a new song' then we needed a new song that would bind us together in the same tune and the same words and, hopefully, the same motive. A lively, easily remembered LINK song with a catchy tune was what we needed and, thanks to Chris Wagstaffe, that is what we achieved. I had known Chris for many years as an accomplished musician and talented actor so two days before I left for Lesotho in April 1992 we spent a late hour together[8] during which I set out what I was hoping for and gave him some fairly wide guidelines. I left him with a small collection of Basotho music and songs that I had recorded on tape over many years. Respecting that artistic people need time and space within which to exercise their creativity I did little more in the next seven or eight months other than make the occasional enquiry about progress. It took time but I was content to wait because I thought the result would be worth the wait.

It was on Sunday, 10th January 1993 that Chris returned my music tapes plus one! What that extra one contained was Chris leading a music group singing what he had composed: *We are One Body in Christ.* It was a simple, memorable and tuneful composition expressing just the right tone and, as the guitars strummed away, sending out just the right message. It was captivating. Before it went to general release I played it to half a dozen musicians more adept than myself in assessing its quality and received unanimous approval. Its first public performance was in the evening of Friday, 5th February 1993 at a LINK service held in the Chapel of St. Peter in Auckland Castle to launch the Ha Mohatlane Community Education project.[9] It was published in May 1993:[10] we had our new song and we sang with great gusto to the Lord:

(Chorus)

We are one body in Christ.
Re 'mele o le mong ho Kreste.
One body in Christ,
One in word and work.

Christ has gone before us,
showing us the way.
Follow in his footsteps,
serve him every day – for

Looking back through history,
he has guided us.
So, as we go forward,
in him we place our trust – for

Christ is at our side now,
His spirit lives within.
His transforming power
makes us more like him – for

We are one body in Christ
(Re 'mele o le mong ho Kreste)

The new song soon became popular beyond the confines of the LINK's activities and it could be heard in many a school assembly. It's swinging tune quickly went beyond the boundaries of Durham. Chris was helping at a summer Pathfinder camp at Sandsend, near Whitby, North Yorkshire when, during a music session, a young boy said he had learned a song at school which he liked very much and could they sing it?

'What's it called?' asked Chris.

'*One Body in Christ*,' replied the small boy excitedly, adding, 'Do you know it?'

'Do I know it? I wrote it!' exclaimed Chris.

With youthful scepticism the little boy wouldn't believe that he was face-to-face with the composer until Chris sang it to him from memory. There is no reliable record as to which of the two was the most amazed at this coming together of creator and devotee singer but it was an indication of the pervasive power of the song that increased with the years.

One Body in Christ was written to be played by contemporary music groups led by guitars and loses some of its vitality when played on a church organ so, knowing that not all congregations had access to guitar players and modern-day music groups, I thought it would be helpful to have something specially written for the organ. Those whom I approached were not interested and the idea never did hear the sound of its music. The nearest we came to it was when the melody of the South African anthem *Nkosi Sikelel' iAfrika*[11] was incorporated into the voluntary played before a service in Durham Cathedral at which Philip Mokuku was preaching.[12] I had hoped for something similar for the LINK but it has never been forthcoming, at least, not in Durham. In Lesotho, however, in March 1994,[13] during a holy communion service in Maseru Cathedral at which twelve people from Durham were present, a choir from Mafeteng sang two specially composed songs that were 'dedicated to the Durham-Lesotho LINK'. Sadly, despite extensive researching, no record can be found of either song.

During its third phase the LINK has promoted a variety of successful musical contributions. After seeing a slide show about the LINK at the beginning of 2005,[14] and after a great deal of planning and preparation, four young people[15] set off for Lesotho with the aim of conducting a two-week music school in Maseru for a group of young Basotho with musical potential. The second-hand musical instruments sent from Durham did not include a harp or a lyre but the hearts of the quartet certainly contained an enthusiasm to 'sing and make music'. Supporting the psalmist[16] with the more modern instruments of keyboard, recorder, guitar and drums they 'awoke the morn' with tuition groups and woke the afternoons with large band rehearsals and jam sessions. Before the end of the music school the Basotho, many of whom had never previously touched a musical instrument, were performing as a fifteen-strong orchestra playing in churches, at public concerts and at a youth rally. The LINK had shown that music really does break the barriers of oral language and entrenched culture.

Not all music is, of course, instrumental. Carrying forward the work of earlier years girls from Durham High School have tunefully shown that music can help to promote other ideas. Girls from the junior house, although only aged between four and eleven, managed to sing all day on Friday, 24th March 2006. when they raised £4,000 to help finance the building of accommodation at the LINK centre by the Maqalika Dam. The primary purpose of the building was to provide residential accommodation for young people from distant parts of Lesotho attending for education programmes, especially those connected to the peer teaching AIDS course.[17] The first association the school had with Lesotho was over twenty years earlier when I discussed with its then head teacher, Barbara Stephenson, a possible relationship between Durham High School and St. Catherine's School, Maseru. How that might develop we had no idea but it started by raising money to refurbish the chapel, library and computer centre of St. Catherine's School. I did not encourage school-to-school links (or, for that matter, church-to-church links) and, in many ways, did what I could to discourage them. My experience demonstrated that in most cases they damaged rather than enhanced relationships but here were two Anglican Foundation schools between which I thought a relationship might endure, which it has.

It doesn't require a deep excursion into the Bible to realise that music plays an important place in Hebrew culture. By the time the fourth chapter of the first book is reached it is announced that Jubal 'was the father of all who play the harp and flute'[18] and there follow scores of references to music right into Jewish culture. Music was used in rejoicing and, indeed, in times of sadness.[19] Music and dancing seem to have moved from the secular to the religious world with comparative ease as may be evidenced by the huge amount of music employed in religious services and worship. Not so drama whose transition has been much more tentative and faltering but that did not inhibit the LINK.

Drama

The curtain goes up on Act 1: scene i displaying a setting somewhere in Durham during 1989. Bill Hall, senior chaplain of the Arts and Recreation Chaplaincy, enters centre stage to announce that it might be possible to obtain funding from the government-sponsored Arts Council to finance the appointment of a residential literary Fellow. On stage is the education working party of the Durham-Lesotho LINK, and hearing this, it becomes interested and announces that it would like to arrange for a Mosotho to hold this new appointment 'if Peter Green could find a suitable person'. Scene ii moves the action forward to mid-January[20] the following year into the dining room of my house where I am lunching with Aelred Stubbs of the Community of the Resurrection and explaining that I didn't know where to start the search for a literary Fellow. The telephone rings; we hear the voice of Bill Hall saying that he has received a firm assurance from Northern Arts that it would finance the LINK's nomination for the post: would I find one? Yes, but I am not sure where. During our dessert Aelred suggests I go to see a friend of his, Dr. Ndebele, the pro-vice-Chancellor of the National University of Lesotho.

Act 2: scene i is set in Lesotho in the office of the pro-vice-Chancellor at the Roma campus of the National University of Lesotho on the last day of February 1990. There, after conveying the greetings of Aelred, talking about the LINK and my family, and his, I describe what we have in mind and the sort of individual I thought should occupy the Fellowship. He has just the right person; a senior lecturer in the University's English and Drama Department, Dr. Zanemvula Mda, whom I was so glad to learn everyone calls Zakes! Scene ii, the evening of the same day at the home of Philip and Matšepo Mokuku: enter Zakes Mda with his wife Adel. After the usual preliminaries we discuss the concept of a literary Fellow and I study his academic profile which looks impressive. He assures me that as a Roman Catholic he is willing to join in worship with Anglicans and would support the LINK's principle of crossing denominational boundaries. He leaves some of his publications including his latest book *When People Play People.* This is about the use of theatre as a medium for communication in development strategies, a notion that the LINK might be able to employ in its future work. He and Adel depart with no promise other than the idea would be pursued in Durham.

Act 3: scene i, in the Lesotho LINK office almost one year later:[21] me with a fax message from the chairman of the education working party that is angrily read aloud: 'Northern Arts has *still* not made a final decision about the Literary Fellowship for Zakes Mda'! Scene ii: is set in the British Council office in Maseru on a cold autumn day when its Director, David Bates, agrees to fund the travel costs and we make the final (?) arrangements for Mda's departure. Scene iii: is set in St. Chad's College, Durham, on an early summer's day in mid-June when Zakes Mda arrives[22] after flying overnight from Johannesburg almost two years after the Literary Fellowship at Durham Cathedral was first mooted. The LINK's transition of drama from the secular to the religious arena had certainly 'been much more tentative and faltering' than that of music. It had taken over two years to get Zakes Mda to Durham: he lost no time in getting to work.

During his residency Zakes wrote numerous poems, articles and plays contributing to a variety of events throughout the diocese. *Mother of all Eating* was a humorous, but in the end tragic, exposé of a human battle with principles in the administration of a developing country, with a message for all tempted by the corruption of high office. It was a powerful projection of ideals. No less powerful *By Way of the Rock* wove together poetry and prose to tell the story of the Basotho and the coming of Christianity to their nation, in the context of the history and contemporary experience of Durham. The hill on which Durham Cathedral stands became, for a brief time, the 'Hill of Destiny'[23] and our lives became richer through the promotion of Zakes' creative work by the Durham-Lesotho LINK.

It was a very sad Zakes Mda that I drove to Newcastle Airport on Tuesday, 24th September 1991. Because of very serious health problems in his family Zakes had to return to Lesotho much earlier than anticipated. The sadness of his departure was lightened somewhat by the announcement that a play he had written whilst in residence in Durham, *The Nun's Romantic Story,* had won, in a field of sixty-four competitors, the main award in the 1991 Amstel Playwright Competition of South Africa. Before leaving us he wrote:

> Coming to Durham has been a refreshing change. This city does not give one the slightest opportunity to have a writer's block. Everything about it is so inspiring that every single day I am able to write either a whole poem, or a few lines to be developed into a poem later.[24]

The written play, as Zakes readily concedes, is only the first step of a communication process to translate thoughts and ideas into a living message and that requires a sensitive and talented actor who is able to interpret and project the writer's thoughts and emotions. Another Mosotho did this splendidly for the LINK. I first met Gonzales Scout in the Victoria Hotel, Maseru, on Sunday, 2nd May 1993, where he was performing Zakes Mda's *Mother of all Eating.* I had been invited to one of his solo presentations which was well produced and staged. I pondered; if I could get him to Durham, how would it come across in the cathedral? It was first-class in the small hotel hall but a massive cathedral would require a different technique. We met after his one-man performance and I learned that he was going to perform at the 'fringe' Edinburgh Festival in three months' time. Things then moved very rapidly. The LINK organisation worked efficiently so the next time I met Gonzales was in my home before the dress rehearsal of two of Zakes plays that had been written in Durham, *By Way of the Rock* and *Mother of all Eating,* which he performed that evening, Saturday, 7th August 1993. Talking to a lady in Durham seventeen years after she had seen that performance she was still able to recall in some detail the storyline of *Mother of all Eating*: it was a powerful message and a commanding presentation.

Drama presentations did not stop with the departure of Gonzales and their attractive durability continued until many years later seven drama students[25] from Sunderland University decided not to leave all the dramatic presentations to the Basotho. After making the 'Kingdom in the Sky' their home for two weeks in early 2009 they returned to Durham and wrote and performed a play, *Shared Lives*, that illustrated their experiences and the impact the visit had on them. The result of their study was presented in Sunderland Minster to a small audience on Thursday, 28th May 2009. Each performer spoke of why they went to Lesotho; the drama workshops that they conducted; the fun and laughter; the sadness and tears they experienced; the huge disparities of life both within and between Lesotho and Durham; the experience of a different culture; how their concept of Lesotho had changed through their experience. Particularly they enacted how they had grown close to a fifty-one-year-old Mosotho woman, Mamotsamai Ranneileng. 'She made us laugh and sometimes cry.' It was all very moving. To link Durham and Lesotho through drama had been worth the effort.

Poetry

The Bible is full of poetry but not of poets. Poems, whether referred to as songs, hymns or psalms, dirges or laments, are spread throughout the Bible, so it does seem rather strange that poets, as such, get very scant attention with just one mentioned in the Old Testament[26] and another, who quotes from Greek legend,[27] in the New. It is Paul's close companion, Luke, who states explicitly[28] that God wants us all to seek Him and reach out and find Him even though He is never far from each one of us, and a poet was used to express and emphasize this wish. Because words do not carry meaning by themselves (it is the hearer who invests them with meaning), Luke saw the importance of using words to arouse, convey and encourage feelings and emotions through their skilful use in poetry. The LINK has encouraged two poets, one Mosotho, one English Zakes Mda and David Grieve.

When he had to leave Durham prematurely Zakes Mda left us with a poem that he wrote whilst in residence as the LINK's literary Fellow:

Not a Single Plaque

In the Cathedral Church
Of Christ and Blessed Mary
The Virgin:
Remember before God
The Durham miners who have
Given their lives in the pits
Of this country
And those who work in darkness
And danger
In those pits today

It is comforting to know
That even before our time
People
Have been dying

And back in Lesotho
We have not seen a single plaque
Fondly remembering
The hundreds who die every year
In the gilded pits
To make South Africa
And America
And Britain
Great

David Grieve, in Durham, has given us a small book[29] of sensitive poems inspired by a two-week sojourn in Lesotho in 1998 as a member of the LINK's adult exchange visit that year. The sub-title of David's book *Light and Love in a High Place* clearly expresses that Lesotho, and the Basotho, made a deep impression upon him which he effectively encapsulates and shares in his poetry. Although the Old Testament poet speaks to a single people, the Amorites, when he cries out: 'Let Heshbon be rebuilt', in his book, David addresses Durham and Lesotho, drawing them close together into one with pictures and thoughts, in Word and Work. The LINK is more than bricks and cement, chickens and trees as David portrays in his poem, *Keep Us in Easter*.

In the day and the night
In the heat and the shade
In the light and the dark
Keep us in Easter

In the birthing of spring
In the dying of winter
In the earth's rest and awakening
Keep us in Easter

In the long miles between us
In the faith that unites us
In the service that calls us
Keep us in Easter

In each fear that confronts us
In each pain that assaults us
In each sorrow that hurts us
Keep us in Easter

In Lesotho and Durham
In mountain and lowland
In earth as it is in heaven
Keep us in Easter

Books

As the tenets of our faith have been handed down through history stone, wood, ivory, clay, papyrus, leather, parchment and ostraca have all provided the ancient scribe with a durable writing surface since which time it has been difficult to overstate the importance of books in Hebrew and European culture. The first book to be printed in the English language was the translation by Caxton of a French text[30] which he completed on 9th September 1471 although the first dated printing of an English text was finished two and a half years later on 31st March 1474.[31] Thereafter, numerous printed versions of the Bible became available in English but, as it was 1822 before Moshoeshoe I brought the founding tribes together as Basotho, it was much later when the Bible appeared in written form in Sesotho.

It was not until 1836 that Eugene Casalis and Samuel Rolland, both of the Paris Evangelical Missionary Society, started their translation of the Bible into Sesotho. They published the gospels according to Mark and John three years later. By 1878 a printing works had been established in the lowlands at Morija and a complete version of the Bible appeared in one volume in 1881. How widespread its distribution was in Lesotho doesn't seem to be recorded but it is reasonable to suppose it was severely restricted as education was limited and an oral tradition dominated communication.[32]

The literacy rate in Lesotho is now high with an estimated 75 per cent of males and 91 per cent of females between the ages of 15 and 24 years able to read.[33] If the age is extended to 49 years there is only a slight decline to 69 per cent and 90 per cent respectively[34] so literacy levels seem to be well established with a slight improvement gradually taking place. Nevertheless, these high figures are challenged when the quality of literacy is questioned; cultural oral patterns still remain a strong influence. Although there is obviously wide literacy ability there is no evidence that Basotho read extensively and there is some evidence suggesting that cultural habits remain a strong influence on reading and communication patterns.

Many years before the Durham-Lesotho LINK started the Education Officer of the Mokhotlong District asked me if I would help him establish a small library in his remote high administrative district. This was an interesting development I was pleased to help with because in Lesotho at the time there was no national library service and, in Maseru, only three small lending libraries, two of which were attached to the British and American cultural centres. The other was a private enterprise. In Mokhotlong a building had been obtained and now had to be stocked.

With the splendid help of what was then known in England as the Ranfurly Library Service[35] I arranged for the gift of 10,000 good quality second-hand books to be sent to Lesotho via Durban, South Africa, where they were all stolen! Experience is an effective teacher so I did not start a LINK book working party without some hesitancy but we could not ignore the desperate need for books in Lesotho and members of the group responded magnificently. Many individuals and schools, plus the medics at St. James' Hospital, Mantšonyane, were asking for books and the community education centre at Ha Mohatlane contained a small library facility, perhaps the first outside Maseru. Under the leadership of the former Durham Diocesan Secretary, Phyllis Carter, and later Colin Tonks, the book working party appealed, collected, stored, sorted, selected, counted, packed, transported and shipped 42,500 books that still give much pleasure to hundreds of people of all ages in Lesotho. When they were not doing this they raised money to pay for it all and for the library at Mohatlane.

Money was needed for another aspect of their work. I was keen to provide the people of Durham with a reference library of books about

Lesotho and to establish a repository for papers, journals and the theses of LINK scholars. I hoped these would inform those who were visiting or just wished to learn more about Lesotho. Once it became established and more widely known I anticipated it would be used by research students of Lesotho and the Basotho beyond the boundaries of Durham. The book working party was eager to help so raised money to help me purchase books in Lesotho, stagger back to Durham with them in my already bulging over-weight suitcase and pass them on to a member of the group, John Lumsden, a university librarian, who then reviewed them, writing an article for the 'book corner' in each issue of *'MOHO*. The Durham diocesan resource centre, housed appropriately in 'Carter House', provided an easily accessible library facility in the centre of Durham.

It was tough work with long hours but here was a group of Christians helping others across the difficult divide into the twenty-first century: cultures are malleable.

Scholarships

When the LINK introduced scholarships into its programme of work there was nothing new in the idea of Durham providing courses of study for selected Basotho. St. Hild's College was the forerunner providing scholarships each year from 1966 to 1975 for two or three outstanding Basotho teachers selected from Lesotho-based courses. The aim was to improve their qualifications and to take their subject disciplines to an advanced level through specially designed courses. So, against that background, I was delighted when the Reverend Jim Francis, who was Anglican chaplain at what was then Sunderland Polytechnic, spoke to me about his idea of recruiting a scholar from Lesotho to read for a Master's degree. He suggested a 'tripartite' scholarship that would be supported by the World Council of Churches, the Polytechnic and the LINK, a proposal that I greeted as an excellent example of the type of co-operation I had always hoped the LINK would generate. We agreed the details; all I had to do was to find a suitable student in Lesotho, get them to Durham and hope they would work diligently, justifying their selection. In Maseru there was no shortage of applicants; we were almost overwhelmed.

Moleboheng (all Europeans found it much easier to use her diminutive Ntebo!) Ngozwana graduated from the National University of Lesotho with a degree in biology which was followed by two years' practical experience in a public health laboratory. Now at Sunderland in 1989 she started a two-year Master in Philosophy research degree in life sciences specialising in methods of testing for contamination in food. One of the strengths of her original application was her vision of how she would apply the knowledge gained from her study to the desperate needs of Lesotho in this specialised field. Ntebo's tutor described her research 'as an excellent piece of work' and she returned to Lesotho enthusiastic about the practical application of her study. How sorry we all were when she was unable to get an appointment in Lesotho! She had let none of us down but now her home country was not able to employ someone who would have made a significant difference to its food hygiene and therefore its health. Many lines of enquiry were pursued but to no avail. Apartheid South Africa snapped her up to lecture in Pretoria.[36]

We did not despair. Instead we also crossed a border, that between England and Scotland, taking Lebohang Kheekee, an Anglican priest, to Edinburgh University to study for a Master's Degree in Development and Theology which, given these twin elements of the LINK, we successfully argued with the British Council in Maseru was an appropriate and potentially useful area of study. The higher education front was becoming more and more active in the LINK's work. Another student from the small village of Peka, overlooking the north-west boundary between Lesotho and South Africa, arrived at Teesside. Paul Mohobela studied public-sector engineering and, spreading the academic net wider, Lomile Putsoa was selected as the second Mosotho LINK scholar for Sunderland. In the academic year 1993–94 she took a one-year Master's degree course in Human Resource Management and, on her return, was able to apply her learning in a publishing house in Lesotho. In Sunderland the Polytechnic was now a University and was going through the turmoil of massive educational change[37] and the LINK had to adapt to those changes. Although it was committed to assisting in the provision of advanced study courses in Durham it now responded to another specific request.

In the early 1990s Philip Mokuku had asked me if I could find some help for the theological teaching at Lelapa la Jesu, the Anglican seminary at Roma, the campus of the National University of Lesotho. St. John's College,[38] Durham, together with its theological 'wing' Cranmer Hall, has always been willing to support the LINK's requests to provide specialised courses of study and residence for many of its visitors. Philip Mokuku studied there in 1983 and many have followed since. It wasn't surprising then that I found there an enthusiastic response to Philip's request for help with the academic work at Lalapa la Jesu. Teaching New Testament studies at Cranmer Hall, Bruce Longenecker said he would consider visiting Lesotho. Having explained to Bruce what was required I flew off to Lesotho where I was pleased to receive a fax shortly after I arrived telling me that Bruce had agreed to give three weeks' teaching in August. The chairman of the education working party made the final arrangements and I next met Bruce on the Roma campus on Thursday, 15th August 1991 with Ian Corbett, the seminary warden. When he was in

England the next year he and Bruce came to see me on Saturday, 22nd February 1992 when the three of us spent two hours discussing the seminary and its work in the Diocese of Lesotho. Even though the LINK did what it could to assist, the future of the seminary was doubtful then, and it finally closed in 1994.

However, there was an appropriate and positive corollary to Bruce's brief visit to Lesotho. When, in the mid-1990s, St. John's College, Durham, was actively raising funds to establish three international scholarships it was encouraging to find that Lesotho was one of those countries chosen to benefit from this initiative. When I was consulted about setting up this fund I suggested that the minimum amount required to sustain one annual scholarship was £250,000 but that was considered to be too high to be attainable, so the target was lowered to £150,000 but that was not reached either – academic zeal was tempered by fiscal reality. Nevertheless the project did raise a substantial amount of money from the college alumni and beyond with a large anonymous donation coming from South Africa and a five-digit sum from a Durham diocesan parish so a decision was made to admit the first scholar for the academic year 1999–2000.

This was the head teacher of St. Catherine's High School, Maseru, Atwell Ntokwenzani Xana, who had, for many years, been actively supporting the work and witness of the LINK. Now that he sought ordination in the Anglican Church it was pleasing that he was chosen to benefit from this branch of the LINK's missionary activity. After a year studying in Durham he returned to Lesotho where, bridging the spiritual-secular divide, he now works in the Ministry of Education whilst, additionally, ministering at Botšabelo on the outskirts of Maseru. Atwell was followed by two ordained male priests[39] and in 2010–11 the Mohapi scholarship was awarded to a Obed Sebapalo from Thaba-Tšeka. Although the scholarship is open to both men and women it has still to be awarded to a lady. As available finance is well below what is required to maintain an annual scholarship it is now available only when the fund has been replenished sufficiently to cover the costs involved.

Alphonce Mohapi, after whom the scholarship is named, visited Durham as a member of the first adult exchange visit in August and September 1993, but I had known him, his wife, Thakane, and their family for many years before the start of the LINK. He was an undertaker and Thakane was employed by the Diocese of Lesotho but seconded to work with the Lesotho Scripture Union. They were energetic workers for the LINK so it was with very deep regret and much sadness that we learned of his untimely death at the early age of forty-five, on Tuesday, 17th September 1996 after a short illness had failed to respond to treatment.[40] In his younger years he represented Lesotho in athletics at the 1976 XXI Olympic Games in Canada. When his name was proposed as a title for the scholarship it was a fitting tribute to a man who was sufficiently humble to spend many hours collecting stones for the building of Ha Popa Rural Health Centre and later Ha Mohatlane Community Education Centre.

The scholarships provided for the Basotho by the former College of St. Hild started in 1966 and came to an end ten years later. British government changes in higher education took the college through a decade of turbulence and it was the Durham-Lesotho LINK that resurrected the scholarship notion in 1986. This kept alive, with the intermittent support of the Alphonce Mohapi Scholarship, an ethos that encouraged Durham University Department of Education to pursue, with the continuing assistance of the LINK, the provision of scholarships.[41] With funding from the British Council (less euphemistically the British taxpayer) the department ran a three-year project from September 2007 to August 2010 aimed at assisting the work of the National University of Lesotho and the Lesotho College of Education.

During those three years fifteen Basotho teachers have spent two weeks in Durham and five Durham lecturers visited Lesotho replicating much of what had been introduced many years previously. The professional benefits of this project have been enhanced by a developing relationship between participants as expressed in the official report to the British Council which reads:

> ... team members from both countries have sometimes resided in colleagues' homes for several days and visits to team members' homes to meet family members and share meals have also been a notable and highly enjoyable means of enhancing our collaboration.[42]

Just as the LINK inherited my thirteen years' experience of working with the Basotho so, in turn, Durham University has benefited, professionally, from twenty-five years of the LINK's presence in Lesotho.[43]

The number of Basotho to benefit, directly or indirectly, from the LINK's contribution to the overall scholarship programme is not recorded anywhere but must be considerable. Hundreds of scholarships have made a huge contribution to the Basotho in many varied ways but, whilst rejoicing in that, what must not be overlooked is the contribution of the Basotho to the people of Durham. Many Basotho gifts are less tangible than scholarships but are nonetheless significant in the development of people in the northern part of the LINK. Those expressed by the Basotho, although not immediately obvious, need to be recognised, in the Christian context, as genuine gifts to Durham. That many Basotho have given generously of their friendship has been apparent whilst studying during the succession of scholarship programmes, thus providing solid evidence that it is possible to become One through Word and Work. This supports the notion of equality expressed by Paul to the Corinthians when eliciting support for Christians in Judea:

> At the present time your plenty will supply what they need, so that in turn their plenty will supply what you need. Then there will be equality.[44]

Big Boxes

Shipping containers come in just two sizes: ‘big’ and ‘enormous’. The first two from Durham were in the ‘big’ category measuring 20x8x8 feet (6.1x2.4x2.4 m) although there was strong pressure from some powerful voices to send two ‘enormous’ containers measuring 40x8x8 feet (12.2x2.4x2.4 m). I resisted because I doubted the ability to fill them in Durham and to empty them in Lesotho, plus the problem there of distributing the contents. These first two ‘big boxes’ contained Durham’s response to the requests we had received for books, clothes, hand tools, school furniture, blankets and medical and dental equipment, all of which were sent to the appropriate working party. It all came together and the big boxes were sent in 1990 and 1992. Having set the trend other containers followed at irregular intervals throughout the LINK’s twenty-five years as and when required. The books started and stocked the libraries at Ha Mohatlane Community Education Centre and the long established Sekameng High School. The tools started many small enterprises. The blankets kept many Basotho warm.

Shortly after the arrival of the first ‘big box’ (without its key to gain entry but it’s surprising what can be done with bolt-cutters) there was much talk in Maseru about what Durham had given Lesotho. That was a notion I was anxious to modify and to bring thinking more into harmony with Paul’s concept of ‘equality’ that he expressed to the Corinthians.[45] In a cathedral sermon on the Sunday after the arrival of the first ‘big box’, almost within its shadow, I stressed that:

> ... if the people of Lesotho and Durham are ‘One Body in Christ’ then this is not a gift but a reallocation of resources within the one Christian community for the one Christian purpose of helping all people.

This notion was to become the over-arching motive for sending numerous containers to Lesotho the contents of which, from dental chairs to mountain bikes, from school desks to hospital beds, have been graciously shared as a distribution of our common resources.

Floral Link

One of the new things I have to declare is that Mike Hirst, a botanist from the local agricultural college, had been to see me in early January 1994,[46] to discuss an original and attractive idea. Five years earlier, thanks to the generous co-operation of Durham County Council, I had taken the Principal of the college, Alan Hethrington, to Lesotho to advise me about the woodland and poultry projects and he had returned full of enthusiasm for the LINK and its potential. Back in college Alan spoke to his staff about his visit and obviously enthused others because after that Mike came up with the idea of collecting seeds and plants in Lesotho and returning to Houghall College where he would establish a small garden of Lesotho plants. The imaginative idea appealed to me: it was different. Possibly it would capture the interest of other people, spreading the message of the LINK, knowledge of Lesotho and the beauty of God's creation in a new ingenious way.

As seeds and plants would be coming from Lesotho's fragile ecosystem Mike argued that his project could also provide an important means of conservation, more especially as the Lesotho Highlands Water Project had started. In Lesotho I knew there was a great variety of plants that would interest a professional botanist and I could imagine the tragedy of those being washed into the Senqu as future soil erosion took its inexorable toll. One of the plants I saw for the first time and was shown, with much pride by its owner, was the Sesotho-named *lekhalakhare* or the spiral aloe[47] which is endemic to Lesotho and is a protected species in both its clockwise and anticlockwise spiral form. We were entering a sensitive area of operations and we had to make careful enquiries about protection laws as care had to be exercised not to damage what we were trying to protect, God's creation.

This led me into detailed discussions with many officials in various Government departments where I found unexpectedly positive and precise support. Yes, the Durham-Lesotho LINK could undertake the proposal provided we stayed strictly within the boundaries of the regulations and yes, export licences would be granted for the specimens to be taken to the United Kingdom. Mike and a colleague from Kew Gardens, Darren Webster, overcame transport difficulties, searched, collected, catalogued, packed and, when they found the arum lily[48] which is a wild flower in Lesotho, they were able to observe 'how the lilies grow.

They do not labour or spin. Yet I tell you, not even Solomon in all his splendour was dressed like one of these'.[49]

By the end of March 1994 our two intrepid botanists, who had travelled far and wide, high and low, returned to Durham with no less than 470 specimens of plants and seeds with which to establish the Lesotho Garden. With keen foresight specimens were also deposited with Durham University's Botanic Garden and the Royal Botanic Garden, Edinburgh which, in 2010, was still propagating from seed collected during this project. Darren returned to the Royal Botanic Gardens, Kew, London, with useful specimens for its seed bank. One of the plants collected, *Glumicalyx flanaganii*, was awarded a preliminary Commendation by the Royal Horticultural Society. Three years after collection it was made available[50] to gardening supporters of the LINK in Durham bringing a colourful piece of Lesotho into the gardens of Durham to display its unusual white tubular flowers opening into bright orange petals.

The floral link expanded. Mike returned to Lesotho in 1996 to pursue his innovative idea and develop it into a practical reality to bring Lesotho and Durham closer together and to safeguard some beautiful elements of God's creation. Many specimens of Lesotho's flora at present in botanical gardens in England originated from this initiative that the LINK implemented.

National flag

Compared to the lofty mountains of Lesotho the 217 feet (66 m) of Durham Cathedral's central tower is but a molehill. Nevertheless the 325 steps it contains are a challenge even to the fittest verger who, on special occasions, now has to climb them on behalf of the LINK. In 1998, the dean and chapter accepted the unusual permission granted to the LINK to fly the national flag of Lesotho from the cathedral on certain days, such as Lesotho's Independence Day.[51] The abnormal, perhaps to some troublesome, sight of St. George succumbing to the crocodile of Lesotho as its national flag flies over a famous English cathedral, prompts some strange questions, and even stranger answers, but it does get people talking and hopefully stimulates some accurate responses about the Durham-Lesotho LINK and its mission.

When Lesotho gained independence from the United Kingdom on Tuesday, 4th October 1966 its first national flag displayed as its emblem the traditional Basotho hat and that design was flown until replaced, almost twenty-one years later, on Tuesday, 20th January 1987. That change was prompted by a military coup. On this second flag the Basotho hat was replaced by a traditional Basotho shield behind which there were crossed *assegai* (spear) and *knobkerrie* (fighting club). This emblem, in turn, was superseded at the 40th anniversary of independence in 2006 by the return, once again, of the Basotho hat. It was a flag of that design that was presented to Durham Cathedral's succentor in November 2006 during a visit she made to Lesotho with a group from Durham. The colours employed in this Lesotho flag, white, green, blue and black, are linked to the traditional Basotho national motto: *khotso* (peace – white); *pula* (rain – blue); *nala* (prosperity – green) with the black hat representing the people themselves. It was these four symbolic elements that the dean of Durham Cathedral wove into the prayer of dedication on Sunday, 30th September 2007 when he asked God 'to grant to the Basotho people his blessings of peace, prosperity and plenteous water'.[52]

The new flag, now in the safe custody of Durham Cathedral, is a small gesture within the LINK but one that can be seen across the city symbolising dynamic connotations that exemplify confidence, trust and oneness. It is an outstanding symbolic, and much-valued, gift from the Basotho.

'MOHO – Together

During the first phase of the LINK's work and witness it was spending, or planned to spend, hundreds of thousands of pounds of public money. By whatever means it came to the LINK it was money given by the public, either in the form of taxes or voluntary donations, so the LINK had a responsibility to keep donors informed of how it was being used. We were also very conscious that, with over seventy people in our Durham working parties plus an indeterminate number working in Lesotho, we lacked an effective means of communication, not only with our financial supporters, but also with a work force that was dispersed over two countries six thousand miles (9,656 kms) apart. So, after discussing various possibilities over a one-year period, we published a twice-yearly newsletter that proved to be one of the most valuable stimulants to our work. It provoked, informed, challenged, inspired in both English and, from May 1992 under a Mosotho co-editor, in Sesotho. However, before we published the first issue what we had to resolve was what to call it. The answer takes us across southern Africa to Windhoek, the capital of Namibia.

From there, early in the morning of Friday, 2nd November 1990, I had a long telephone conversation across the continent with Steven Molokeng, the LINK's executive officer in Lesotho. We had lots of decisions to make and much work to discuss because, on this visit to southern Africa, I was not going to Lesotho; I had more than enough work to do within the Diocese of Namibia. Nevertheless, as the first issue of the LINK's newsletter was ready for publication we did have to decide on its name. In September I had left him with the problem and now he came up with three answers! They were: *Thuso* meaning 'to assist'; *O'eso* meaning 'my brother'; *'Moho,* meaning 'together'. I spoke next to Richard Briggs in

Durham, who was to be editor for seven years, telling him that of the three possibilities Steven and I much preferred *'Moho* as that seemed to express a major principle of the LINK. Richard agreed adding that he would like to include its meaning on the title page so, after some leg-pulling about the initial apostrophe, the complete title became *'MOHO – Together* although everyday speech inevitably shortened it to *'Moho.*

'MOHO served the LINK admirably for almost eleven years, never missing any of its twenty-two issues from November 1990 to May 2001 by which time the cost of production and difficulties over editorship caused its demise.[53] During its early life it was a high-quality production with bold pictures and succinct descriptions of the LINK's work and activities. It kept donors up to date with the progress of projects in which they had an interest. It was available free of charge to parishes and all those interested in Lesotho and Durham. It was distributed to other influential outlets such as the Lesotho High Commission in London and the British High Commission and the British Council in Lesotho; the people with whom we dealt in Brussels, London and East Kilbride. Copies were also lodged in the archives of Lesotho maintained by Professor David Ambrose formerly of the National University of Lesotho and in three American Universities that had academic departments with an interest in Lesotho.

Unfortunately the late 1990s saw a decline in the quality of the written articles and editorship including the most extraordinary repetition of one article a year after it first appeared![54] The new millennium saw no improvement and an attempt to levy a copy charge was unsuccessful so its passing was inevitable especially as at that time there was an explosion in the use of the internet as a means of communication. Thus the LINK lost one of its considerable benefits: a distinctive, independent contact with each parish church, its parishioners and its visitors, and with supporters around the world.

As a second best *'MOHO – Together* was superseded by regular contributions to the Durham diocesan newspaper but as that contains no articles in Sesotho it is inappropriate to send to Lesotho. As the LINK's news became submerged in the wider Durham diocesan news the newspaper form was also unsuitable to distribute to the wider body of the LINK's supporters. There is strong anecdotal evidence to suggest that, in its heyday, *'MOHO – Together* was far more popular than the more frequently published Durham diocesan newspaper. An active mission LINK needs to be in active contact, not only with its supporters, but with those it is trying to influence in its missionary endeavour. The demise of *'MOHO – Together* lost the Durham-Lesotho LINK a lively and independent contact with the people of Durham, thus weakening its influence within a major target of the earlier criticism that was itself a major factor in its founding: the mission field of Durham.

Logo

The LINK was not very many weeks old when I began to think about how we should project its concept with a simple symbol that would represent its main features. From experience in the commercial world I knew that one of the most powerful publicity signs was a logo that was simple, quickly recognisable, easily interpreted and associated with the organisation it represented. In the early days of the LINK there was little money so it was out of the question to employ a professional graphic artist. As I enjoyed artistic expression myself, I set aside my easel, oils and an almost finished painting of an old lady at Soko in the southern mountains of Lesotho, to have a go at designing a logo for the LINK. The three elements I wanted to embody were Lesotho, Durham and LINK plus, if possible, a visual representation of 'linkage'. After a few wasted sheets of paper I took a piece of card from which I then cut three letters, two Ls and a D spending an hour sliding them around on my desk. After rejecting dozens of permutations I realised that the two Ls could be held together by weaving them through the centre of the D linking all three letters into one: that was just the message I wanted to convey: we had our logo. This first effort appeared on the 40,000 bookmarkers we had printed in the first year of the LINK but it wasn't until some months later that a simple yet startling breakthrough occurred. Why, oh why, had I not seen it before?

I was attending a committee meeting that was proving to be rather more boring than I could bear so I took to doodling on the agenda paper and as we moved laboriously from one item to the next I began thinking about the LINK. As I squiggled away, the logo came into view and I began to experiment with its proportions, about which I had never been completely satisfied: then I saw it! There, bang in the centre of the logo was the Cross of Christ, just where it should be seen at the centre of all the LINK's activities. What a wonderful revelation. It was there all the time, not because I so designed it but because it emerged out of the linkage between Lesotho and Durham. I don't easily get excited: but now I was! So much so that I had to forcibly remind myself that I was in a boring meeting which is no place to become excited! I had to remain quiet. I couldn't wait to get to 'any other business'. I had masses; but not for that meeting. Reaching home I drew the second version of the logo, blocking in the Cross. This was used for four years until early 1991 when a professional graphic artist looked at my effort and simply added a few serifs. The logo has been used for almost twenty-five years and is so well established that it is readily associated with the mission of the LINK in both Lesotho and Durham.

A logo is a small, easily recognised and related symbol. Other small visual features are just as psychologically important as they are also related to personal negative and positive experiences. We used two very effectively. In the early days the rather unimaginative description 'the link' was adopted by default. By the consistent use of upper-case contrasting letters it became distinctive as the 'LINK' and was easily recognised amidst its surrounding script.

When I was clarifying some elements of the LINK to an eager, questioning, senior South African cleric he asked me to explain my insistence that the words Lesotho and Durham should be joined together by a hyphen (Durham-Lesotho LINK) and not separated by an oblique stroke (Durham/Lesotho LINK). I explained that our visual perception and cognitive understanding of the hyphen is rather like the mortar that holds together the bricks of a wall while, at the same time, keeping them apart with the whole gaining strength. That type of bonding is not apparent with an oblique stroke that is perceived as dividing and separating two constituent elements one on each side of a dividing line. We talked for some time on the strong influence of these small details when he commented: 'Ah well; it will need a man of some dash to achieve that!' I left his study, inwardly smiling at his pun. It was then I noticed that the shelf above his desk ironically displayed a copy of George Carey's little book *The Church in the Market Place.*[55] I was vividly reminded of where I thought the LINK started and realised, with a flicker of foreboding, that the Market Place in which I was working was somewhat larger and certainly would require some dash to match its size.

Volunteers

During its first phase (1986–1994) the LINK relied heavily upon volunteer help which enabled it to keep its expense:income ratio at an exceptionally low level. During this initial eight-year period no one in Durham was remunerated by the LINK and in the first seven years in Lesotho never more than three people were paid by the LINK for their work. That was a very distinctive category but one other group of volunteers also contributed extensively to the success of the LINK which benefited from its close contact with local Universities.

We never used a press gang nor did we advertise for volunteers but, nevertheless, we did receive a great number of spontaneous offers that, at one time, threatened to overwhelm our ability to provide work for them in Lesotho. Although many people freely offered their services to the LINK, for its part the LINK had an obligation to provide a satisfying and fulfilling activity for those whose services it accepted. The LINK could be a noteworthy factor particularly in a young person's continuing education and development; not that all volunteers were young people. Far from it; we had offers from almost every age range from the post-graduate to the post-retired. In those cases where volunteers wanted to work in Lesotho they were, generally, responsible for providing their air-fares, insurance and upkeep but the LINK would provide accommodation where possible. Lesotho assisted in this process when St. Catherine's School provided lodging in a disused house in the grounds of the school. It became known for some years as LINK House and although not exactly four-star accommodation it was adequate after some refurbishment. Each person would volunteer for an agreed period and for a specific task that sometimes changed in the course of time and events.

By the early 1990s volunteers were undertaking a multitude of tasks as varied as dental inspections to unloading and distributing the contents of containers; from planting trees to helping with the accounts in the LINK office; from surveying tree-planting locations to researching the viability of new project proposals. One man walked two miles (3 kms) across the mountains carrying spades and saplings to plant trees at Ha Popa Health Centre when the four-wheel-drive vehicle could not get there! Families have also volunteered. Sponsored by St. Thomas' Church, Crookes, Sheffield, Paul and Cathy Middleton with their nine-year-old son, Matthew, spent three years working with our Youth Activities Project.[56] Help has also come from further afield: America, Ireland, the Netherlands. For one 1993 post-graduate volunteer it was a return to Lesotho as eleven years earlier she had lived for six months on the Roma campus with her parents and younger sister[57] as pioneers of the LINK. Clare Joy, now in her early twenties, reflected after her voluntary work:

> As a Peace Studies student at Bradford University, it was a privilege to experience Lesotho, firstly, because of the unusually peaceful transition to democracy last March and, secondly, to learn what is really happening at grassroots level in southern Africa.
>
> I was the second volunteer to 'really' experience the comforts of the renovated LINK House, part of an ex-convent in the grounds of St. Catherine's High School. Living there was important as I was able to share valued friendships with the Basotho living on the campus.
>
> I worked partly in the LINK office and also taught 'Conversational English' at St. Catherine's High School which meant being with the students during library periods and sharing ideas, cultures and thoughts. I was accepted with such warmth at both places and made to feel very much a part of

> Basotho life. The LINK work involved keeping the poultry-project accounts, visiting various sites and providing a smiling presence! It was a pleasure to work with Ntate Steven Molokeng who kept me busy, while doubting my driving capabilities (driving in Lesotho is a very different ball game; there seems to be no rules, all that matters is a successful and speedy ride from A to B!!). I also got to know the staff at the Diocesan office where the atmosphere of love and friendship is tremendous. I feel that the hospitality my friends in Lesotho gave me has been an integral aspect of the LINK, emphasized by my Basotho friends, on their return from the Exchange Visit, who told me how wonderful it had been (and how unlucky I was to be in Lesotho missing all the beautiful rain in Durham)!
>
> A huge thank you to all who enabled me to go and to those who made my time in Lesotho so special. I will be back again (but not during the dust season wearing contact lenses!).[58]

That letter is worthy of lengthy quotation not only because it highlights many aspects of the volunteer's life and work in Lesotho but because it also reveals the effect that our provision of this type of experience can have on the young about to start their careers. Clare took her experience into many years' work with the World Development Movement.

Many scores of volunteers have continued, throughout the past twenty-five years, to make their personal contributions to the LINK's work and to be influenced by it. In admiring that, what must not be overlooked is that some short-term volunteers are Basotho which is, perhaps, more surprising because in Lesotho there is little custom of voluntary work and to engage in unpaid work demands a much greater effort and sacrifice. Despite this many scores of people have been engaged in helping with the structure of the health centre, the education centre and with planting trees. Help to Durham from Lesotho has been provided by the placement and supervision of Durham ordinands whose selectors believe they would benefit by a broadening of their experience of the Church, its people and the world.

The work of the LINK has benefited not only from the voluntary help of individuals but also, as already recognised, from the freely given financial assistance of other charities such as CAFOD and CD. In a country where travelling by road is hazardous and unreliable we have also been grateful for the help of the Mission Aviation Fellowship.[59] This extensive Christian service has been of immense practical help to the LINK over many years giving a new, more peaceful, meaning to the adage 'on a wing and a prayer'.[60] It was in 1996 in a MAF aircraft that Paul

Jefferson, the LINK's Durham executive officer, found himself acting as midwife at the birth of a baby to a Mosotho woman. After prolonged labour she was being flown from Nohana to Maseru but the baby decided to arrive over the mountain, Thaba-Telle![61] The pilot of the MAF plane was American Dave Bacon, so after such an incident it was not surprising the baby was named Dave Paul. Throughout Lesotho small makeshift airstrips which from the air seem so frightenly small, have been carved out of its rugged terrain to open remote regions to facilities, particularly medical, in the wider world. Surrounded by cruel, vicious-looking mountains that appear to be protecting the tiny landing strips from intrusion the highly skilled pilots nurse their small planes to land most often in times of emergency. The danger that accompanies such work resulted in the death of Dave Bacon, on Wednesday, 1st October 1997 shortly after he had taken off from a tiny airstrip that served the rural health centre at Methalaneng.[62] As the plane flies this remote clinic lies just five miles (8 kms) to the south-east of Ha Popa across two major rivers that flow relentlessly through two huge gorges cut into mountain ranges that unmercifully took their toll.

Not only has the LINK brought hundreds of people together as One in Word and Work but also as One in Sadness and Sorrow.

School study kits

By the end of its fourth year, 1990, the LINK was well established in Durham where most people were aware of its existence if not of its presence. There were bi-monthly articles in the diocesan newsletter 'The Durham Lamp' that was widely distributed and was a convenient format to share with those in Lesotho who could read English. A small, not very adventurous, publicity working party met regularly and kept its finger on the pulse of Durham diocese taking opportunities as they arose to promote the LINK. We were all conscious that publicity is a continuous process, otherwise, however good the organisation's administration and however exciting its work, all of that can soon get swamped and forgotten in the continuous competition for the public's attention. Nevertheless, with projects well supported we felt this area of the work was going along smoothly except for one category that had been relatively ignored: children. I visited schools throughout the county and diocese to speak about our work and about Lesotho but something more permanent was required. The answer was found by responding to frequent requests from primary school teachers for project materials. The teachers' working party was charged to do something to satisfy the demand.

This resulted in Steven Molokeng returning with me from Lesotho on Thursday, 20th September 1990 heavily laden with children's Basotho blankets and hats plus cases full of artefacts so we could stock three school study kits. Before leaving for Lesotho seven weeks earlier I had met, in Durham, with the County Director of Education who suggested that on my return I held a two-day training session for a group of teachers and so Steven and I found ourselves working with about fifteen teachers. The teachers' working party had arranged for three storage boxes and Steven spoke about all the contents we included. Blankets led to art work on patterns; hats introduced weaving; maps of Lesotho prompted Steven to talk about the mountains, foothills and lowlands; a mounted collection of stamps stimulated discussion about how post was collected and delivered which inevitably introduced the topic of communication; a small set of coins was displayed on cards; flash cards of simple Sesotho words were made; large coloured pictures were included that inspired creative writing; guidance notes for teachers were written by teachers – it was a hive of activity.

So that the group had a sound background knowledge I showed a selection of slides of Lesotho to which Steven gave the commentary. It was two days of encouraging activity resulting in a group of enthused and well-informed teachers plus three school study kits and two specially designed teaching packs for use by church groups. The study kits were all lodged in the Durham diocesan resource centre where the collection of books on Lesotho was kept. Any teacher, in school or church, now had ready access to professionally produced study kits should they wish to mount a project about Lesotho and introduce a flavour of the country into their Durham classroom or church.

St. Agnes Primary School in Teyateyaneng, was one of the very best schools in Lesotho when Steven Molokeng was its head-teacher in the 1970s. Unfortunately for the school and its pupils he was promoted out of the classroom but, after then, he would always take every opportunity to return to what he really enjoyed: teaching children. Benefiting from 'Steven's delight' we needed to exert no pressure to get him to test out the study kits and he happily spent the rest of his time in Durham touring schools talking about the kits, the LINK and his country. He would come back from each school visit with new ideas on how the kits might be improved so the teachers' working party had a bank of information on which to work for many months. I already felt the excess weight of my luggage for many trips ahead.

Nothing that is alive is constant and if education is to be a live activity it, too, has to change, so we find in the third phase of the LINK's life a refurbishment of the school study kits taking place. Artefacts needed replacing and replenishing and by this time, for better or worse, politicians in England had imposed the National Curriculum[63] so the study kits had to be adapted to meet the new demands of 'Key Stages' in the current curriculum. LINK study kits allow children to gain a small amount of very valuable primary experience. To wear a Basotho blanket, to feel its weight, to experience its warmth, to know how difficult it is to wear it in a classroom and then to put up your hand to answer a question: how do you do it?! How do you stop the blanket from falling off so you don't get cold? This is good-quality learning and preferable to secondary experiences even though they are vital in the learning process. The LINK had gone some way to implanting knowledge of its work into the minds of the young. It brought Lesotho into Durham.

Small things in life

What, according to scripture, do all the following things have in common: seed, states, provinces, cattle, baskets, particles, boxes, grains, kingdoms, voices, coins? Answer: smallness. The numerous writers of the Old and New Testaments, somewhere or other in their writings, refer to this varied collection as 'small' so, we may safely conclude, that despite their small size they are, nonetheless, important. Certainly, Jesus did not pour scorn on smallness[64] so in 'singing a new song' the LINK felt justified in the attention paid to the small things in its life, giving them a status in its mission to match its much larger features.

In the LINK few things were smaller, or for that matter more important, than a communion wafer but it wasn't until 2005 that those made by the sisters of The Community of the Holy Name in their convent in Hlotse found their way to Durham. After a visit in 2005 to Lesotho by three staff of the Venerable Bede School in Sunderland, they imported communion wafers, selling 30,000 over the next two years. This was an excellent example of a local community becoming involved in a small activity springing out of the work of the LINK. However, it went further. The association between wafers and teddy bears is somewhat tenuous but, thanks to this initiative, does exist!

Basotho children are very ingenious and creative when it comes to making their own toys using whatever scrap materials are available. This is especially so in the production of moving toys like wire tractors, lorries and cars that can be pushed on the ground whilst their owners steer it as they, usually, walk alongside. Another favourite is the cardboard model of a human figure suspended on a wall or tree with its limbs linked by string and moved by pulling a connecting string. Nimble fingers, usually girls', plait ropes from grass before nimble feet skip as friends turn the rope. Meanwhile brother is sitting in an old cardboard box that becomes, in his imaginative mind as it is pulled over a bumpy surface (perhaps using sister's skipping rope), a boat in a rough sea where, amid much hilarity, it capsizes.

School playground games vary little from what may be found in Durham although it is somewhat easier to scratch a hopscotch course in dirt than on tarmac. With all this active participation there are few Basotho examples of 'static' toys. It was then something of a surprise when, during a visit of the Basotho Youth Mission to the Venerable Bede School in January 2008, its members were asked what the local community could do for children in Lesotho, to have it suggested that knitted toys would be welcome. Perhaps it was a variable of age. Surprise or not knitting needles clicked away in Sunderland and by the time a group of the school's students visited the Insured Salvation Orphanage in Maseru later in the year they had a few score of small bears to give away to delighted children. Smallness can have a large impact.

Most postage stamps are even smaller than the wafers imported from Hlotse so when keen Durham philatelist David Williams found himself there in the late 1960's it was they that captured his interest. David subsequently recruited me to help increase his collection of stamps and of postal cancellation marks from some of the approximately 350 remote post offices scattered throughout the country. It was some years later that he and I addressed the question as to how his large pre-1979 collection might be used in the service of the LINK. The publicity working party agreed with his suggestion to mount his collection as an exhibition and then set about trying to find a suitable public display area. The most obvious was the main post office in Durham City. It had a secure and safe window facing on to the main street that took hundreds of pedestrian passers-by each hour: it would have been an ideal safe and secure display area. The foreign stamps would have attracted attention to the LINK's work, illustrated as a secondary display. It was all to no avail; we could not get the manager interested. Perhaps it was not completely pointless as many exhibitions were mounted within private meetings around the county and diocese.

Smallness is not to be despised:

> He prayeth best, who loveth best
> All things both great and small;
> For the dear God who loveth us,
> He made and loveth all.[65]

Hospitality

It might well be argued that the Link hospitality working party had more Biblical support for its brief than any other group working on behalf of the LINK. Indeed, so important is care of the traveller in the Old Testament that it is almost taken for granted. The generous courtesy of Abraham[66] is used to advocate the provision, not just of shelter, but also of food and drink. Furthermore, once the host has provided for the traveller he is invested with responsibility for his guest's welfare[67] (not unlike the present-day responsibility that accompanies the sponsorship of a visa application). Isaiah goes one stage further[68] citing hospitality as an indication of true fasting and religion a position that leads to its acceptance as a duty to everyone but especially so to fellow believers. Jesus expects hospitality to be extended to his disciples and when it is not that then becomes a rejection of the gospel itself.[69] Little wonder then that hospitality is one qualification of a church leader or bishop[70] and an important aspect of mission.

In addition to providing hospitality to Basotho who were in Durham under the auspices of the LINK, we maintained close contact with the British Council and were notified of those Basotho who were in the north-east on bursaries mainly in the Overseas Department of Newcastle University. Modern interpretation of scripture took us on frequent trips around the fells of Durham, journeys to Lindisfarne (Holy Island) and visits to Auckland Castle. Our hospitality was more than providing shelter, food and drink; it also provided homeliness, relaxation and often a sympathetic ear, although it was advice, or where to get advice, that was most warmly received. For a quarter of a century the LINK has been faithful in its provision of hospitality echoing, for both Basotho and Dunelmian, the words of Job that 'no stranger (has) had to spend a night in the street for my door was always open to the traveller'.[71]

In the southern hemisphere the LINK has arranged and provided many hundreds of days and nights of generous hospitality to scores of people out of which has grown some long-lasting, firm friendships. At the start of the LINK it wasn't easy as there was no pattern or example on which the Basotho could base their hospitality as few had ever acted as hosts to Europeans. The LINK was entering new and sensitive territory. Basotho are a very generous people but it was all a bit daunting to have other people, even fellow Christians, from 6,000 miles (9,656 kms) away staying in their homes. What did they eat? Can they speak Sesotho? How did they behave? What are the cultural differences? Do they really have dogs in their houses? As we got started there was much hesitation but given time the response was magnificent, helped by previous visits to Durham of some Basotho hosts. We were all learning how to be welcoming hosts and, equally importantly, how to be acceptable guests. The LINK, both in the north and in the south, has become a living witness to the fact that Christian hospitality is not a grudging duty but the loving action of a cheerful giver.[72]

Banners

In the north-east of England, perhaps more than anywhere else in the country, miners' lodges, clubs and church congregations use banners to display their respective messages in a colourful and prominent manner. They are an accepted, colourful means of communication going back in history when they were the standards of kings, ensigns of knights and symbols of an army second only to the national flag. They carried emblems and slogans of guilds and cities expressing the principles the group upheld. So, why not the LINK? It had a message to project: what better way than the traditional banner.

When Philip Mokuku was in Durham in 1988 he preached in Durham Cathedral on Wednesday, 13th July, during a celebration eucharist attended by LINK workers and supporters. It was a splendid occasion made especially colourful by a collection of banners, each one symbolising the LINK between Durham and Lesotho. One of these banners was made in a Church of England school at Seaton Carew. It was one of two identical banners made by the children of the school so that one could hang in the school and the other in the LINK office in Lesotho as a reminder of the LINK between the two places. In addition to the large banner made for the cathedral in Maseru[73] six other banners made by children in Durham schools were taken to Lesotho for display there in churches and schools.

Prayer

From before its beginning the LINK has been strongly upheld with both the personal and public prayers of Basotho and Dunelmians. When Sisters of the Community of the Holy Name had a small house in West Auckland, Durham, in the late 1980's they produced and distributed a prayer schedule covering topics suggested by those most close to the LINK's mission. We also had a slot on the same day each week in the Durham diocesan 'Cycle of Prayer' which, being regular, had the advantage in Lesotho of people there knowing when the LINK was the subject of prayer in Durham so we could all engage in prayer at the same time. During its second phase a small number of people met to pray for the LINK, its witness and work whilst inclusion in the 'Cycle of Prayer' continued to motivate intercessions around Durham diocese. Attempts by the LINK in its later years to encourage monthly prayer meetings in Durham Cathedral have not flourished as they are generally poorly attended, relying on the assurance of Jesus that 'where two or three come together in my name, there I am with them'.[74]

In the southern hemisphere, for eleven months of the year the LINK is remembered in the Lesotho diocese on the thirtieth day in its monthly intercession cycle. Without putting too much emphasis on the numbers of people at public prayer it might be that we have not been adventurous enough in our prayer life. It is a matter of balance because for many people innovation is dangerous, as it seemed to be in Durham when I returned with a new suggestion namely that, throughout each diocese in the eucharist, the intercession for the bishop should include bishops of both Lesotho and Durham. In Durham this fell on deaf (or frightened?) ears!

Singing a new song

Singing a new song was not easy. Not everyone liked the tune. It has not always been comfortable. I wanted the LINK to avoid the established mould of the conventional; to branch out in creative faith; to sing new words to a new tune, to produce a new harmony for an old purpose! I faced criticism from those who thought some of the 'verses' were not what constituted a Christian mission activity. In that I rejoiced as it was evidence of a challenge to the conformist just as Jesus challenged the conventional when he sang a new song of many 'verses' to his disciples: we call them the Beatitudes.[75]

> Blessed are the poor in spirit, for theirs is the kingdom of heaven.
>
> Blessed are those who mourn, for they will be comforted.
>
> Blessed are the meek, for they will inherit the earth.
>
> Blessed are those who hunger and thirst for righteousness,
> for they will be filled.
>
> Blessed are the merciful, for they will be shown mercy.
>
> Blessed are the pure in heart, for they will see God.
>
> Blessed are the peacemakers, for they will be called sons of God.
>
> Blessed are those who are persecuted because of righteousness,
> for theirs is the kingdom of heaven.
>
> Blessed are you when people insult you, persecute you and
> falsely say all kinds of evil against you because of me.
>
> Rejoice and be glad, because great is your reward in heaven,
> for in the same way they persecuted the prophets
> who were before you.

---

1. Isaiah 42:9 (NIV).

2. Isaiah 42:10 (NIV).

3. David Jenkins was the controversial Bishop of Durham appointed in 1984 from his post as Professor of Theology at the University of Leeds. In Lesotho small transistor radios widely broadcast, often out of context, his most contentious interpretations of scripture. These were extensively discussed and I was often asked to interpret his interpretation. After discussions on 26th September 1989 when David was in Canada we nearly agreed an eight-day visit in August 1990 but then his suffragan bishop was moved from Durham and I had to be in Namibia so, disappointingly, it became impossible.
4. Servant passages (Isaiah 42:1–9) (Isaiah 49:1–6) (Isaiah 50:4–9) (Isaiah 52:13 to 53:12).
5. Deuteronomy 8:3 (NIV): He humbled you, causing you to hunger and then feeding you with manna, which neither you nor your fathers had known, to teach you that man does not live on bread alone but on every word that comes from the mouth of the LORD.
6. Luke 4:4 (NIV).
7. Sunday, 30th June 1991 during a service of holy communion after I had preached in Durham on Matthew 16: 13–20. (Jesus) asked, 'Who do you say I am?' Simon Peter answered, 'You are the Christ, the Son of the living God.'
8. In the home of Chris and Sally Wagstaffe, Monday, 27th April 1992.
9. See Chapter Nine: Ha Mohatlane (p. 239).
10. We are One Body in Christ: *'MOHO – Together* (May 1993) p.3.
11. *Nkosi Sikelel' iAfrika* was composed in 1897 by Methodist schoolteacher Enoch Sontonga but has since gone through a number of adaptations. Its second stanza is now sung in Sesotho.
12. In Durham Cathedral, Wednesday, 13th July 1988.
13. Sunday, 27th March 1994.
14. I am indebted to Alison Beck for much of this information which comes from an article that first appeared in the Durham-Lesotho LINK news in *Durham Newslink*, March–April 2005: p.9.
15. Sam and Leanna Williamson, Alison Beck and Alistair Bianchi.
16. Psalm 57:7–8 (NIV): My heart is steadfast, O God, my heart is steadfast; I will sing and make music. Awake, my soul! Awake, harp and lyre! I will awaken the dawn.
17. See Chapter Eleven: Yap! Yap! Yap! (p. 317).
18. Genesis 4:21 (NIV): His brother's name was Jubal; he was the father of all who play the harp and flute.
19. Matthew 9:23–24 (NIV): When Jesus entered the ruler's house and saw the flute players and the noisy crowd, he said, 'Go away. The girl is not dead but asleep.' But they laughed at him.
20. Friday, 19th January 1990, at 12, Gilesgate, Durham.
21. Tuesday, 5th February 1991: still no decision from Northern Arts about funding the Literary Fellowship.
22. Wednesday, 19th June 1991: Zakes Mda arrived in Durham staying in St. Chad's College.
23. Becker, Peter, *Hill of Destiny* (Granada Publishing and Panther Books, 1972). This is the story of Moshoeshoe and the founding of the Basotho nation.

24. Quoted from *One in Word and Work*: 1992: p. 16.
25. Amy Watt: Catherine Perrio: Cheri Mayell Davies: Jennifer Goudie: Melanie Freeman: Sarah Keveney: and Sophie Stanger with their tutor Nigel Watson.
26. Numbers 21:26–27 (NIV): Heshbon was the city of Sihon king of the Amorites, who had fought against the former king of Moab and had taken from him all his land as far as the Arnon. That is why the poets say: 'Come to Heshbon and let it be rebuilt; let Sihon's city be restored.'
27. Epimenides, the 6th century BC Greek philosopher and poet, when he addresses the supreme being, Zeus.
28. Acts 17:27–29 (NIV): God did this so that men would seek him and perhaps reach out for him and find him, though he is not far from each one of us. 'For in him we live and move and have our being.' As some of your own poets have said, 'We are his offspring.'
29. Grieve, David, *Keep us in Easter: Light and Love in a High Place* (Thambos Books: Phantom Hacker Publications 2005).
30. Lefèvre, Raoul, *The Recuyell of the Histories of Troy*. Caxton began the translation in 1469 and completed it in September 1471. This was the first book to be printed in English.
31. de Vignay, Jean, *The Play of Chess*, translated from French by Caxton: the first dated printing in English was 31st March 1474.
32. Coplan, David, *In the Time of Cannibals: The Word Music of South African Basotho Migrants* (Chicago: Aldine). This is a study of Basotho aural art conducted in Lesotho.
33. UNICEF Educational Statistics: 2010. See www.unicef.org.
34. Huebler, Friedrich, International Education Statistics: Demographic and Health Surveys 2003–2006.
35. The Ranfurly Library Service was a charity founded in 1954. In recognition of its increasing worldwide activity it changed its name on Saturday, 1st January 1994 to Book Aid International.
36. Where my wife and I met her again on Tuesday, 11th November 1997 happily teaching at Pretoria Teknikon but still regretting that her scientific knowledge was not being used by Lesotho.
37. Sunderland Polytechnic gained University status in 1992.
38. St. John's College, Durham, was founded as an Anglican theological college in 1909 becoming an independent college of Durham University in 1919. In 1958 Cranmer Hall, within the college, became responsible for theological education with the remaining part of St. John's College admitting non-theological students.
39. The second Alphonce Mohapi scholar was Solomon Lebona and the third Tanki Mofana, SSM.
40. An obituary appears in *'MOHO – Together*, No. 13 (November 1996) p.4.
41. Under the leadership of Tony Harries (member of the newly constituted educational working party).
42. Monitoring and Evaluation of DELPHE Project: Curriculum Development for Effective and Relevant Teacher Education in Lesotho: A Report for the British Council: February, 2010.

43. The project sought to improve: '(1) the teaching of literacy in English and numeracy at the primary level; (2) teacher education for special educational needs and (3) education for sustainable development.'
44. 2 Corinthians 8:14 (NIV).
45. 2 Corinthians 8:14 (NIV).
46. Mike Hirst first shared his idea with me on Saturday, 8th January 1994.
47. Talukdar, Sumitra, In *Molepe*: Vol.2: nos.4 & 6 and Vol.3 no. 9. I acknowledge these three articles as the source of this botanical information and refer the reader to the detailed information given there. The spiral aloe's scientific name is *Aloe polyphylla*.
48. The Lesotho lily is known scientifically as *Zantedeschia* and, in Sesotho, as *mohalalitsoe*.
49. Luke 2:27 (NIV).
50. See *'MOHO – Together*, No. 14 (April 1997) p.4. 'Lesotho in Your Garden!'
51. See *'MOHO – Together*, No. 16 (April 1988) p.6. Lesotho gained Independence on Tuesday, 4th October 1966.
52. Fully reported with photograph in: *Durham Newslink*: November-December 2007: p.7.
53. *'MOHO – Together*, No. 17 (November 1998) p.5 carried a major article under the misspelled title: 'The Alphonce Maphafi Mohapi Scolarship' (sic).
54. *'MOHO – Together*, No. 18 (June 1999) p.2 carried an article '*Youth Activities on the Move*' that was repeated one year later under the same heading in *'MOHO – Together* No 20 (June 2000) p.2.
55. George Carey: *The Church in the Market Place* (Kingsway Publications Ltd. 1984).
56. See Chapter Eleven: Yap! Yap! Yap! (p. 317).
57. See Chapter One: 'In the Beginning was the Word' (p. 1).
58. The full text can be found in *'MOHO – Together*, No. 7 (November 1993) p.4.
59. Mission Aviation Fellowship (MAF) was started after the Second World War. The first flight was made by Betty Greene in 1946. Sixty years later MAF works in 55 countries flying over 130 aircraft.
60. Michael Quinion: *World Wide Words: 1996–2010*: 'on a wing and a prayer' comes from a famous American World War Two patriotic song, with words by Harold Adamson and music by Jimmy McHugh. It tells the tale of a plane struggling home after a bombing raid.
61. A full account of this incident may be found in *'MOHO – Together*, No. 12 (May 1996) p.3.
62. An obituary appears in *'MOHO – Together*: No. 15 (November 1997) p.5.
63. *The National Curriculum* (Qualifications and Curriculum Authority, 1999). See also www.nc.uk.net.
64. Mark 12:42 (NIV); Matthew 7:5 (NIV).
65. Coleridge, Samuel Taylor, *The Rime of the Ancient Mariner*: part VII.
66. Genesis 18:3–5 (NIV): If I have found favour in your eyes, my lord, do not pass your servant by. Let a little water be brought, and then you may all wash your feet and rest under this tree. Let me get you something to eat, so you can be refreshed and then go on your way now that you have come to your servant. 'Very well,' they answered, 'do as you say.'

67. Judges 19:23 (NIV): The owner of the house went outside and said to them, 'No, my friends, don't be so vile. Since this man is my guest, don't do this disgraceful thing.'
68. Isaiah 58:7 (NIV): Is it not to share your food with the hungry and to provide the poor wanderer with shelter: when you see the naked, to clothe him, and not to turn away from your own flesh and blood?
69. Matthew 10:12–14 (NIV): As you enter the home, give it your greeting. If the home is deserving, let your peace rest on it; if it is not, let your peace return to you. If anyone will not welcome you or listen to your words, shake the dust off your feet when you leave that home or town.
70. 1 Timothy 3:2 (NIV): Now the overseer must be above reproach, the husband of but one wife, temperate, self controlled, respectable, hospitable, able to teach.
71. Job 31:32 (NIV).
72. 1 Peter 4:9 (NIV): Offer hospitality to one another without grumbling.
73. See Chapter One: In the Beginning (p. 1) for a description of the banner made by Martha Bissett.
74. Matthew 18:20 (NIV).
75. Matthew 5:3–16 (NIV): with a shortened version in Luke 6:20–23 (NIV).

Chapter Eight

Suffering Little Children

... if (your son) asks for an egg will (you) give him a scorpion?
If you then, though you are evil, know how to give good gifts
to your children, how much more will your
Father in heaven give the Holy Spirit to those who ask him![1]

Contradictory weather of brilliant sun and low temperature at 7,500 feet (2,286 m) is not as unusual as the lowland dweller may assume but fine sunny, cold weather at the beginning of December 1988 is what Philip Mokuku and I experienced as we spent many energetic days going from parish to parish in the rugged mountain region of Ha Pakiso to the east of Semonkong. As we neared the end of our parish visits I left him to his episcopal duties and went on horseback with a Mosotho guide to Ha Mohloka where we met later.[2] Using our small four-wheel-drive Suzuki truck we were both very weary and relieved by the time we reached Maseru, getting there just in time and with just sufficient energy to do a very un-Mosotho thing: we celebrated Philip's birthday. It was a calm commemoration not only of his birthday but of half a lifetime spent in the service of the Anglican Church in Lesotho. As we made our way to early bedtime rest I was given a message asking me to visit the European Delegate urgently. Oh dear! What had I done?

The next day,[3] still tired and not a little sore, I walked somewhat tenderly and apprehensively into Achim Kratz's small office to be reassured by his warm welcome. After recounting the mountain adventures of the past week I relaxed for a brief while to listen with considerable surprise as he told me that the World Food Programme was, unexpectedly, going to phase out its support for meals in secondary schools. We talked about the problem for an hour or so and tossed ideas around as to what might be done to prevent the widespread hunger the decision would undoubtedly cause. Then the bombshell: could the Durham-Lesotho LINK propose a project to relieve the situation in at least some of the Anglican Secondary Schools but, he added quickly, I should be warned, there wasn't much time. If I could come up with a project and get it written up and delivered to Brussels by the 15th of next month then the EEC,[4] as it then was, would most likely agree to fund it. That was only five weeks away including Christmastide! What a challenge to focus my prayers and thoughts. How big the challenge was I didn't appreciate at the time. What we had no way of knowing during our talk was that I was just a week away from lying in a South African hospital bed in Bloemfontein quite seriously ill! This, with Christmas rapidly approaching, reduced the time available to less than three weeks in which to formulate a project, discuss it in Lesotho and Durham, write up a proposal and calculate a budget.

Confined to a hospital bed with everyone around me speaking Afrikaans, which I don't understand, gave me time to pray, to think, to plan and mentally to organise what we might do to help satisfy thousands of empty stomachs, but it became increasingly obvious we were not going to make the closing date. Very weak, I arrived back in Durham just forty-eight hours before Christmas Day which is a double celebration in our household of faith as it also happens to be Pam's birthday, but this year the celebrations were somewhat subdued. In the mornings I worked from my bed (on the insistence of Pam: the bed not the work). Most afternoons in the early days of the New Year I met with Richard Briggs bringing together ideas and possibilities to help with the feeding of pupils in twenty secondary schools with the built-in hope that others might copy the model. I explained to Carola Köster, our contact in the non-governmental organisation section in Brussels, what had happened and managed to get an extension beyond 15th January 1989, 'because the matter is so urgent'. I accepted, with some hesitancy, that we should get our suggestions to Brussels by the end of the month and she agreed to delay decisions until our submission was received. We worked very hard and that made some Church decisions extremely disappointing. It was a frustrating period during which we were encouraged by the secular and discouraged by the religious!

During lunch together mid-January[5] I shared with David Jenkins what I had in mind and he expressed concern about the parlous state of the Durham diocesan finances and, although he said that he believed people would only give to what genuinely attracted them, it would help if I did not appeal directly to the diocese for funding. That was quite a blow, not because it cut off a funding channel but because it cut off Durham diocese from becoming involved in a Christian mission activity. It seemed that the notion of Lesotho and Durham being One Body in Christ was in danger of disintegrating because Durham was fearful of its own financial safety.

When later he and the Diocesan Secretary declined to write supporting letters to accompany our submission to Brussels and the Diocesan Treasurer refused to assist with charitable giving I knew I was on my own. If you have been 'in the jungle'[6] with us you will appreciate our frustration.

But, I had made a mistake: I had underestimated the widespread support the LINK attracted. Had we achieved what I hoped for and gained assistance from diocesan authoritities it may even have been a handicap. I learned from this experience so after this rebuff we never again, during the first phase of the LINK, approached Durham diocesan authorities for their support of any of our projects. That does not mean it wasn't forthcoming but it does mean it was given spontaneously which, perhaps, made it more effective than if we had actively sought it. Despite those refusals we continued to work for the diocese although clearly we were not part of it. For its part the Durham diocesan organisation seemed pleased that we did so and even asked me to write an article for 'The Durham Lamp', the monthly diocesan leaflet, which I did under the title of 'Hungry Anglicans'. Significantly, the diocesan organisation has made sizeable financial contributions to the LINK over the past twenty-five years but 1989 must have seen the Devil smirking.

David spelled out his quandary and I recognised that I had to be sensitive to the problems of the diocesan finances but whilst he was dealing with only one diocese I was dealing with two, both of which had serious fiscal difficulties. The real dilemma I faced was empty coffers in the north and empty stomachs in the south. Caught between the two what was I to do? Could I somehow accommodate both? Within the LINK we tried to do just that. I agreed not to appeal directly to the diocese but to concentrate our fund-raising on the general public as the larger constituency which, of course, was partly made up of Church members. We both accepted that neither of us could prevent the public from appeasing Basotho appetites rather than replenishing Durham reserves. I suspected that suffering little children would have the greater appeal. It certainly carried weight in some of the least expected places. One ironical outcome of all this was that, whilst we had no donation from the Anglican Church as such for the feeding project, the (Roman) Catholic Agency for Overseas Development supported the LINK's interdenominational stance by giving us a handsome four-digit sum. I had always wanted the LINK to be interdenominational and this was an excellent step in that direction.

The poultry unit project which, for convenience, we were all by now calling the 'PUP', assumed precedence in the LINK's work. We had been told there was a desperate need to get it into action before the World Food Programme's phasing out of provision was complete, probably by the end of 1991 and, also, we knew bureaucracy took a long time. Furthermore, although Brussels had told us that our submission was 'well presented', as our first big co-financed project we wanted to make sure our submission was acceptable. We sent it by courier on Monday, 30th January 1989, one day before the newly agreed closing date (recent events in Bloemfontein made that a rather less emotive description than the usual 'deadline')!

We had made it! The next phone call[7] from Brussels encouragingly asked for more details. That was only ten days after receiving our proposal so something was happening pretty quickly for the EEC, indicating the veracity of the urgency that had been frequently expressed. This was very heartening but there was much more work ahead. Having made the case with Brussels for half the money required we now had to start the next submission to the Overseas Development Administration[8] of the British government. From them we were seeking its support to the tune of 35 per cent of the budget but aggravatingly both agencies required slightly different information in largely different formats. However intense the pressures there was one other thing I was anxious to do before February's twenty-eight days had left us for ever. I was very conscious that we were relatively unknown in Brussels and understanding how valuable personal data can be in the socio-political field I thought it wise to pay a visit to our Member of the European Parliament. As newcomers to the Brussels scene, seeking a large sum of taxpayers' money, surely someone in the funding department of the DGVIII's NGO (non-governmental organisation of which the LINK was one) office would enquire about us. So, I argued to myself, it was important that our Member of the European Parliament, Stephen Hughes, knew who we were and I should go and introduce the LINK and myself to him and his wife who carried out research on his behalf. One other reason for making this contact was particularly active in my mind at this time. I had always hoped, as shown in the community woodland project, to work closely with secular authorities showing that Christians could exercise their mission in co-operation with others who were not aligned closely with the Christian faith. In this way I hoped that something of our faith would 'rub off' on others less committed to mission.

So it was that Stephen Hughes and I spent the morning of Monday, 20th February 1989 talking about Lesotho during which I sought his support for the LINK in general and the poultry unit project in particular. I found there was a ready willingness to talk about the Christian faith as he openly revealed that he was a practising Roman Catholic and welcomed the basis of our mission. Stephen praised our initiatives and promised to represent our interests in Brussels starting with enquiries about the poultry-unit funding. I found him an easy person to work with that morning and over the next four or five years when his support of the LINK was to prove invaluable, particularly for the community forestry,[9] Ha

Mohatlane[10] and Ha Popa[11] projects when even larger sums of money were being considered. The establishment of these formal contacts gave us a useful presence in Brussels beyond the current project and provided officials there with a ready contact to whom they, in turn, could refer. A similar meeting with the then Durham Member of Parliament, Gerry Steinberg, served a similar purpose in Westminster. During the first phase of the LINK I met regularly with them both.

So, what were we proposing to Brussels in response to this urgent request from the European Delegate in Lesotho? He was asking us to try to alleviate hunger amongst Basotho schoolchildren attending Anglican secondary and high schools but clearly the national problem was too large for an immediate response from a relatively small organisation like the Durham-Lesotho LINK. The recognition of our limitations was probably a sound starting point so whatever we proposed should be able to be replicated or, in the jargon of the day, should be a model that others could copy. The second influence on our thinking was the possibility of failure and how to contain it. In many of the countries in which I had worked, especially in Africa, I had seen the frequent failure of feeding programmes so I knew we were starting an operation that could easily go wrong. We took the precaution, therefore, of adopting the unit structure that had already been successfully used in our community woodland project where the failure of one small component does not bring down the whole project.

The third consideration in planning our submission was that, although its major target was the alleviation of hunger amongst schoolchildren, were there any subsidiary objectives that could be incorporated without detracting from, perhaps even enhancing, the work necessary to achieve the target? We found the answer to that by incorporating in the project curriculum support for the government of Lesotho's policy of what was known as 'Education for Production'. It was argued that by putting the means of production within the school this would provide first-hand support for agricultural education. Furthermore, we hoped that by being close to the means of production those who benefited would exercise care of the unit knowing that it produced food for their own meals. Fourthly: bearing in mind my conversations with David Jenkins and with possible funding problems ahead I put a maximum figure on the budget within which to plan and set that at a faith-testing £150,000. Provided all the pledges were honoured this would require us to raise something in the region of an additional £14,000 in covenanted giving which, optimistically, we considered to be within our scope. To provide a firm financial base we included in the budget the provision of the first-year running costs in order to finance an annual cash-flow for each unit. Our preliminary thinking concluded by reflecting on how, and for how long, any project we proposed might be sustained which we answered by reference to many feeding programmes in other parts of Africa, arbitrarily setting a period for our project of five years.

That was the skeleton that we now set out to clothe: the parameters within which to work. After many temptations to alter the self-imposed boundaries, particularly the budget, we spent hours in Durham and Lesotho drafting and redrafting within the guidelines which resisted any changes! The result was a decision to build twenty deep-litter poultry units at twenty Anglican secondary and high schools in the most densely populated areas of the lowlands provided that no school had any denominational barriers to admission. Each unit would house 250 laying chickens and would be professionally constructed of concrete blocks, with corrugated-iron roofs, large enough to provide adequate space for the birds. Also included was a store room for eggs and food plus a small room for other equipment such as tools, feeders and water troughs together with provision of space in which to keep records. To encourage roof-water conservation and provide a convenient on-site supply of water especially in periods of drought the design also included the installation of two water tanks each of 40 gallons (180 litres). Although people and chiefs were consulted because each unit was built within the boundary of each school no long discussions to obtain land or permission to build were required.

One further advantage of the unit structure, whether it is applied to trees or eggs, is that the start of any project need not await the completion of full project funding before a start is made. As we had frequently been told of the urgency of a feeding programme we responded by starting to build five poultry houses before we had achieved the full project funding for the target twenty chicken units. This gave an impetus to raising money because potential donors were able to see pictures of what they were giving to achieve: happy, well-fed children. By May 1990 we had raised sufficient money to fund the building of the first five units, to stock them and provide sufficient funds for a year's running costs. At a cost of £21,860 we built the units at five reasonably accessible places: Tsikoane, Hlotse, Motšoane, Sekameng (that was the furthest from a tarred road) and Masapong, stocking each deep-litter unit with 250 hens.

After the units had become established it was reported that at Sekameng the production was around 170 eggs a day which, twice a week, supplemented the school diet. Surplus eggs were sold to the public or to the government-organised 'egg circle' thus providing cash for the poultry feed which was ordered centrally. To pay for this, cash from the sale of eggs had to be submitted to our office in Maseru, but even that had built-in difficulties especially for some units that were in isolated regions. To most Europeans this was a simple procedure but not so in Lesotho. Eggs were sold to local people, often one at a time; the transaction recorded in the unit's books; the teacher-in-charge would then have to keep the money safely for perhaps a week then, having completed the paying-in slip, walk some miles to pay in the money at the local office, rondavel or separate room of the Lesotho Bank and walk back to school. It consumed a lot of time and energy but most schools thought it all worthwhile. As an appreciative article from the headmaster of Sekameng High School comments: 'It is very difficult, almost impossible, to teach students with empty stomachs,'[12] so, now that the students 'went to work on an egg'[13] the poultry unit project improved the educational environment for many children during a very difficult period.

One difficulty was the turmoil over teachers' pay prompting a three-month-long strike. We did wonder why none of the poultry units were adversely affected and how production continued normally, but perhaps that query was answered by one head teacher in the south of the country who said that before entering the chicken unit he always first knocked on the door and whilst feeding the hens he spoke to them all the time! There is no record of what he actually said to them and such practical sensitivity cannot be attributed to Basotho superstition: the headmaster was English! There is also no record of how widely this behaviour was practised but I do have evidence to support the claim that this unit, in Mohale's Hoek, had the best production rate when all twenty units were operating!

Early problems didn't stop with striking teachers returning to work nor were they solved by conversations with chickens. Constructing a building to house chickens seemed to be more difficult than building a house for human habitation, certainly in Lesotho where rondavels seem to rise from the ground easily and rapidly! None of the places in which we proposed to build the first five units were isolated or remote but there was, nevertheless, some considerable difficulty in finding builders. There were no advertising channels other than word of mouth. We had to go in person to the areas in which we wanted to build, walk around and ask around the villagers, in order to find builders willing to take on such a small job. To make matters more complicated there was a mini-building boom in Lesotho at the time so there was great demand for good builders. Parish priests were useful sources of information but we did not want to be accused of denominational bias! When we did find a builder whom we thought might be suitable we often wondered how genuine the recommendation was from other people. Which relative was recommending which relative? If possible, which it wasn't always, we inspected some of the builder's previous work to try and assess the quality of workmanship.

Once someone had been identified it was then often difficult to get a satisfactory quotation. Steven Molokeng skilfully guided us through that quagmire spending many hours with prospective builders, showing them how to calculate and draft an estimate before turning it into a fixed-figure quotation. This was an educational by-product we hadn't foreseen. Amongst small builders written quotations were not a cultural norm but a European demand. That was also the case with the concept of staggered payments according to progress: damp course, roof level and completed unit payments. It took much patience. It was something of a relief when the supply of building materials presented no difficulty and only once did we have to drive into South Africa to obtain what was required. What was far more difficult was the supply of hens for which, sometimes, we had to wait weeks beyond the promised delivery date despite giving the supplier ample warning of our needs.

A massive amount of activity was taking place in Lesotho but what was happening in a different sort of field 6,000 miles (9,655 kms) away in the north? Taking care not to appeal directly to church congregations the 40,000 'Chickens for Children' leaflets we had printed were widely distributed in the county. With the help of the British government's Department of Overseas Development which had also accepted our proposed project for funding, the money rolled in, so by May 1991 we were able to announce the target figure of £154,300 had been achieved. People had given generously 'to what genuinely attracted them'. Our faith and optimism had been justified and there was more than one amazed Dunelmian at the financial result of our first big co-funded project. Of course we have no way of knowing if the Durham diocese suffered financially from our success but for our part we kept faith with David Jenkins' request not to appeal directly to the diocese and to my certain knowledge large sums came from outside that constituency so I feel justified in believing that the LINK's poultry unit project had very little adverse financial effect on the diocese of Durham. Hopefully the project acted as a stimulant to the mission activity of both dioceses but, again, we have no way of telling whether such a positive reaction took place. It seems likely that was the case as there followed some large-scale funding and widespread interest in the future, as yet unrevealed projects to build the rural health centre at Ha Popa in the mountains and a community education centre at Ha Mohatlane in the lowlands.

Funding was helped by many varied events, people and organisations. The project captured the imagination of hundreds of people. One fifty-year-old man set himself a target of running four miles in thirty minutes and although he missed his target by just three seconds he sent a cheque for a substantial amount that covered the cost of equipping a unit.[14] We were grateful for that sort of giving which helped to offset the hindrance caused by the international banks who managed to 'misplace' £15,000[15] of our funds! In spite of that hiccup by the end of 1991 we had ten units running relatively smoothly even though the difficulties we had in obtaining laying pullets delayed the stocking of some units. These short delays were turned to good use as they gave us the opportunity to implement the training aspect of the project which arguably we should have introduced at an earlier stage. This involved bringing into Maseru the head teachers and agricultural teachers from all the participating schools for a short training course for which we had obtained the assistance of staff from the Lesotho Agricultural College.

It was fortunate that we started our project promptly because early in 1992 the Lesotho government declared a state of emergency because of the prevailing devastating drought and its effect on food supplies. Lesotho was hit very hard indeed.[16] The LINK had a head start on many other agencies having already established fifteen poultry units and we had people praying for us in both south and north. Records suggest[17] that the six-month period over the summer of 1992 was probably the worst drought in southern Africa since 1926; it was exceptionally serious with livestock and humans dying. Using a six-month time scale researchers calculate that this was a worse disaster than the drought of 1933 which, at that time, was the most devastating experienced since reliable records started in 1921. Between 1933 and 1992 five other six-month periods of severe drought have been officially declared. They occurred in 1945, 1949, 1952, 1970 and 1983 so we were now working on the front line. Our insistence that all the PUP units should incorporate roof-water conservation was now being seen as a wise move especially when 80 gallons (360 litres) seemed so precious but so very little. Nevertheless, it proved to be sufficient in all of the units then functioning for none of the birds to suffer from lack of water during this distressing period. How distressing is difficult to convey.

When I left Lesotho at the end of May that year it was widely accepted, even if it were only gossip, that the Maqalika Dam serving the capital Maseru had just twenty-nine days of water left! I had never, during twenty years visiting Lesotho, seen it lower. Whether that was an accurate measure is irrelevant when you don't know when, or perhaps even if, it's going to rain again! When it hasn't rained for the previous six months, twenty-nine days' water isn't all that much! The whole population was suffering from acute anxiety. People were becoming tense and brittle. Emotional stress was expressed in community tension.

I did ponder, somewhat later, if my interpretation of the psalm written by David when he was in the Desert of Judah, would now be radically different because I had experienced serious drought and seen its disastrous consequences. Can someone who has had no experience of drought really understand what David is saying? What degree of intensity would they employ when seeking God? Would it be different to someone who has had to live through really long drought? Experience, either physical or spiritual, actual or symbolic, provides a realistic and intensive meaning to the one who has lived 'in a dry and weary land where there is no water'.[18] When the Maqalika Dam was down to twenty-six days' supply 'a beautiful rain that we all enjoyed' relieved the strain as the heavens opened. People stood outside thankfully getting saturated and danced under the wonderful gift of water, rejoicing at being soaked to the skin! They surely knew how Elijah felt when, after three and a half years without rain, 'he prayed, and the heavens gave rain'.[19] Drought is no new problem and is destined to become more severe.[20]

In Lesotho there were serious repercussions to this prolonged period without rain. Inevitably those who suffered most were the poor, the infirm, the old and the young. Food production was at rock-bottom and animals died in their hundreds. A couple of days before I left Lesotho I had discussed the aftermath of the drought with Paul O'Conner who was in charge of the British aid programme at the British High Commission. He told me that the British government had allocated 2.5 million pounds sterling to drought relief in the smaller sub-Sahara countries and went on to ask if the LINK would submit proposals for a drought-relief programme. I responded by saying that as a small organisation we did not have the resources. He countered my diffidence by saying that the LINK had gained a reputation for being a 'well-organised and efficiently managed NGO' and in the present circumstances the High Commission would like us to make a submission. After an exhausting visit, when things did not seem to be going particularly well for the LINK, that was pleasing to hear even if I felt the accolade was not entirely deserved. I left for Durham agreeing to produce a proposal within the next six weeks.

This time we were well within the self-imposed schedule. After putting in some long hours we managed to send a comprehensive proposal to the Overseas Development Administration on Wednesday, 3rd June 1992 copying it to the British High Commission and the Lesotho office of the LINK. In my discussions in Maseru it became increasingly clear that, whatever the commodity, one of the major difficulties in running an efficient relief programme in Lesotho was the lack of reliable field information. The government of Lesotho had set up a Drought Relief Implementation Group (or DRIG for short) and John Skinner, a retired British Army officer, was supervising the distribution of the emergency food that the World Food Programme was now importing!

In the circumstances I thought the LINK's mnemonic DRIP (Drought Relief Implementation Project) was much more appropriate but we had more urgent matters to argue over than that! Because the LINK was working closely with the Anglican Church with its priests spread, albeit thinly, across most of the country at every level there was, I argued, the nucleus of an information-gathering network that it would be possible to mobilise and use as the basis for a reliable communication system. I also thought, privately, it would be a valuable Christian mission activity that would be welcomed by those most affected by the drought. As many of the priests worked in remote mountains areas we knew they would be in touch with those who could be suffering mostly in silence. John Skinner's work was being handicapped by the lack of an information-gathering system. Was the food getting through? Were those in most need getting it?

I was in Durham for most of August 1992 but far removed from the north-east of England. I was over the ditch in Durham, North Carolina, U.S.A. An invitation to talk to clergy and church congregations about the LINK was welcome as I had long wondered if I could get them involved in our work. In the event it was a poorly organised visit and the result was disappointing, producing a lot of individual interest but little collective action. A quick visit to Durham, UK, then back to Lesotho at the end of September when I met with Roy Cowling, then the High Commissioner. We went through our DRIP proposal which I fear was too closely associated to, and too reliant upon, priests in the Anglican Church to be completely acceptable. It was patently obvious during the LINK's first phase that one of its great strengths was its distance from the organised Church: although it was working for the Anglican Church in Lesotho and Durham it was not part of it.[21] Now, as soon as secular authority suspected a closing of the gap doubt arose and there was a reluctance to become involved however urgent the need being addressed. Nevertheless, I was asked to join forces whenever possible with John Skinner's group and the LINK was able to provide some useful help to the Drought Relief Implementation Group through local detailed information many Anglican priests passed on to me at frequent intervals.

Although we had taken seriously the insistence that the hunger situation was critical it nevertheless took almost two years to get all twenty poultry units fully operational. We could have done it quicker but I wanted to phase the work so we could learn from any mistakes made in the preceding phases. Using additional contractors on different sites it would have been possible to build all twenty units at the same time but far less efficiently. Despite the building inflation rate in Lesotho of a massive cumulative 2 per cent per month we worked within our building budget. By September 1994 we were able to report to Brussels, London, Durham and Maseru that, as one wit put it, in 'The Pup Final' that, '16 units are operating at a level enabling them to be self-sustaining in the foreseeable future'.

The money was in the treasury: the hens were in the chicken house; the children were in the school. So, how did they operate? The LINK could not, of course, replace all the food that had been withdrawn from secondary and high schools by the phasing out of the World Food Programme but we did add a substantial supplement to the children's very basic diet. Our aim was to provide a stable source of eggs throughout the year and when all twenty units were operating the 5,000 hens were producing in the region of 3,800 to 4,000 eggs a day. The agricultural teacher was responsible for the care of the unit and its use within the curriculum as a practical aid to teaching. The LINK's administrator arranged centrally for delivery of feed to each school each quarter. At the end of the school year in early December, before the long summer holiday, the hens were culled and sold for meat, the unit cleaned and in January restocked for the following school year to continue the annual cycle. We suffered some delays that occurred as a result of difficulties in obtaining hens for stocking new units and restocking of the first-phase units after the annual cull. As the project was using the deep litter system of production it needed a supply of wood chippings with which to cover the floors of the units and these proved unexpectedly difficult to obtain in either Lesotho or South Africa but dried grass was used successfully as an alternative.

An assessment of the PUP was carried out during September 1992 by Steven Molokeng, the LINK's executive officer, with a representative of the poultry division of the Ministry of Agriculture, Molapo Hlasoa. They were accompanied by either Rob Bianchi who, at the time, was on his first visit to Lesotho from Durham, or myself. The quality of construction of the units was found to be generally high and the design effective although there were some suggestions on how the ventilation might be improved in any future expansion of the project. Of the twenty units in operation at this time it was considered that twelve were well managed and sustainable within the adopted guidelines; six were requiring assistance to improve; two were considered to be badly managed. If those that were failing to come up to the standards required by the LINK could be improved with help the report expected them to be self-financing within the following twelve months. By the end of 1992 all units were operating satisfactorily and providing not only eggs and meat but first-hand experience for the government's agricultural production curriculum. What was disappointing was the lack of interest shown by other schools in doing something similar so the idea that these units might be 'models' for other schools to copy was not realised.

The impact of the serious drought upon the PUP was most evident in the sharp increase in the cost of feed. Although this was contained within the project budget those units in the first phase that had reached the stage of self-financing saw a dramatic drop in their cash-flow which was not corrected until higher egg prices filtered through to compensate. With the benefit of hindsight it would have been prudent to establish a reserve fund to cover this type of unpredictable situation over which we had no control. Not surprisingly the supply of feed was also affected but fortunately we had transport available and our executive officer was able to make deliveries to those most seriously in need. On reflection it might have been a useful idea also to have a reserve store of food available.

Another problem over which we had no control also seriously affected the PUP. It is a dilemma that casts its shadow over much of education in Lesotho, namely, the mobility of teachers. This is an old unsolved problem in Lesotho, largely provoked by the low salaries of teachers. It manifests itself in one of two ways. There is a type of professional mobility that is apparent within the educational system as teachers who seek a higher status move from classroom teaching to a higher position in the sector. Others, moving out of the educational system altogether, engage in a social mobility resulting in the loss of expensively qualified teachers who seek higher salaries in other professions. The problem for the LINK was similar. Some teachers left their posts shortly after attending our training courses leaving a shortage of qualified personnel to care for the poultry units. The training programme was revised to provide more frequent, shorter courses at several centres around the country and this helped to increase the number of teachers attending by reduced travelling distances and costs.

I don't know if a chicken has an Achilles' heel or not but, despite all the minds that had considered the proposal, the project had a vulnerable spot that no one had exposed and to which the LINK gave insufficient attention in its training programme. The project was sufficiently resilient to withstand drought, teachers' strikes, escalation of chicken-feed prices, Newcastle disease[22] and small scale theft but there was inadequate local supervision to protect against dishonesty with money. Whilst most of those involved with the project dealt honestly with the cash involved there was a gradual weakening of the central revolving fund that indicated a persistent loss of funds. However distressing we found this it had to be seen in the context of the poverty that surrounded teachers and other workers who were supervising the units. For some, poor and hungry as they were, handling cash and food was too big a temptation when both were immediately and conveniently available. Money and eggs gradually seeped out of some units because we had no way of locally supervising record-keeping. Too much reliance had been placed on agricultural and head teachers and both categories were as mobile as any other. Many were disillusioned with an education system that barely paid them a living wage. For our part, we had to understand that the centralisation of finance exercised a degree of control but it also probably introduced a measure of local misgiving and undermined local responsibility. It may be that the local labour force did not trust the centre to which they had to submit cash they received from sales.

Whatever the situation in the handling of money there was nothing we could do about the eggs: were too many broken? Were correct charges being levied? Were some just given away to the hungry and poor? Where the established system operated honestly it worked well, providing eggs and meat, not only in the schools, but also within the villages. In those units where things had gone wrong it sometimes helped to change from egg production to other types of food production. In some cases it was thought that pigs would be better suited for the school and villagers. We had no objection to a unit-building being adapted to this type of change if the objective of the project, better-fed children, was still achieved. One other school also changed from keeping chickens to keeping rabbits although that did not prove to be productive. The only alteration I stopped was the request to change to the battery production of eggs. There were objections to this because, in its most intensive form, many people felt this was an inhumane method of production. In Durham, David Jenkins had received a complaining letter from one lady who accused me of animal cruelty by employing this method of egg production. Her information was wrong as was her accusation.

At the best-managed units, despite drought, teacher mobility, rising prices of poultry feed, unreliable deliveries and their varied consequences, egg production continued successfully for many years. Even though scorpions can be found in Lesotho they are now outnumbered by eggs so 'if your son or daughter, pupil or friend asks for an egg, will you give any one of them a scorpion?' Suffering little children might find some relief in the knowledge that eggs are now available.

---

1. Luke 11:12–13 (NIV) is the only place in the New Testament where an egg is mentioned.
2. See Chapter Ten: Saddle-Sore (p. 281).
3. Thursday, 8th December 1988.
4. The European Economic Community (EEC) became the European Union (EU) on Monday, 1st November 1993.
5. David Jenkins and I lunched together at my house on Friday, 13th January 1989.
6. See Chapter Four: In the Jungle (p. 81).
7. Saturday, 11th February 1989 via a recorded message left the previous day.

8. In 1997 the Overseas Development Administration (ODA) of the British Government became the Department for International Development (DfID).
9. See Chapter Five: Trees of the Field (p. 109).
10. See Chapter Nine: Ha Mohatlane (p. 239).
11. See Chapter Six: Ha Popa (p. 147).
12. Joshua Hlakoane: The LINK in Action: *'MOHO – Together* No. 4 (May 1992) p. 1.
13. 'Go to work on an egg' was an advertising slogan used in the UK during the 1950s. It is attributed to Michael Twogood, an advertising agent who left the UK advertising industry to become a minister of religion.
14. See *'MOHO – Together*, No. 3 (November 1991) p.4. 'Fowl Deeds at BT Research'.
15. Chapter Four: In the Jungle (p. 81) recounts the full story of the lost £15,000 and its recovery.
16. Mitigation of the Devastating Drought Effects in Lesotho: *Work for Justice*: No. 34: September 1992: p. 7. This is a quarterly newsletter published by the ecumenical Transformation Resource Centre, Maseru.
17. Rouault, M. and Richard, Y., *Intensity and Spatial Extension of Drought in South Africa at Different Time Scales*: Oceanography Department, University of Cape Town: Water Research Commission. (Undated.) CAB International at <www.cababstractsplus.org>.
18. Psalms 63:1 (NIV): A psalm of David when he was in the Desert of Judah. 'O God, you are my God, earnestly I seek you; my soul thirsts for you, my body longs for you, in a dry and weary land where there is no water.'
19. James 5:17–18 (NIV): Elijah was a man just like us. He prayed earnestly that it would not rain, and it did not rain on the land for three and a half years. Again he prayed, and the heavens gave rain, and the earth produced its crops.
20. Gommes, R. and Petrassi, F., *Rainfall Variability and Drought in Sub-Saharan Africa.* Section 5 refers to Lesotho. See <http://www.fao.org/sd/eidirect/Elan0004.htm>. *Sustainable Development Department, Food and Agricultural Organization of the United Nations (FAO)*: May 1996.
21. See Chapter Four: In the Jungle (p. 81).
22. Newcastle disease is a contagious condition that can affect chickens but presents no major hazard to humans. In 1926 it was discovered 'just up the road' from Durham in Newcastle-upon- Tyne. In 1999 it was reported that a strain of the virus had been used successfully to attack some cancerous cells in humans.

Chapter Nine

Ha Mohatlane

It was (Christ) who gave some to be apostles, some to be prophets,
some to be evangelists, and some to be pastors and teachers,
to prepare God's people for works of service,
so that the body of Christ may be built up until we all reach unity
in the faith and in the knowledge of the Son of God and become mature,
attaining to the whole measure of the fullness of Christ.[1]

Encouraged by biblical support and motivated by our desire to see an improvement in the provision of education in Lesotho and Durham Steven Molokeng and I often used to talk about the development of education in our respective countries. Before I started the LINK Steven had worked with me for fourteen years as teacher, headmaster, lecturer and educational administrator so it was no accident of conversation that our talking frequently brought together his experience and mine. We had many mutual friends involved in the national administration of education in Lesotho so, now that he was seriously considering my offer to become the LINK's first salaried administrator,[2] we discussed ways in which the LINK might assist the work of education. His home, which he had largely built by himself at Teyateyaneng, was always open to me and his wife, Fabia, always graciously welcomed me there. It was a sanctuary in a busy life where we had long, productive talks and where the idea of a community education centre was thrashed out. By mid-1988 the preparatory outline planning for Ha Popa Rural Health Centre[3] had been formulated and, knowing how much time is required for ideas to germinate, I was keen to consider what the LINK's next large project might be. There was also a lot of energy and interest in Durham that I needed to capture before it found other outlets in which to engage.

I cannot claim to have been struck by a brilliant vision but I did find my thoughts increasingly converging upon the possibility of starting a high-quality school. Six months earlier in Zambia I had teamed up with three farmers who wanted to start a Christian school and, although the context in Lesotho was hugely different, I was wondering if something similar might be possible.[4] During one of our long talks I described the Zambian enterprise to Steven and, enthused, he told me about an outstation of St. Agnes' Church, Teyateyaneng, where there was a long-established small church building that served also as a school for a village called Ha Mohatlane and the surrounding region. It sounded interesting and he drove me there to view the church, the school and immediate area.

As we walked around we noted that a women's workshop was operating in the building; we called in the well-stocked local store to chat with the owner and spoke with the people who had been attracted by our presence. Although the church building occupied a tiny plot it was only part of a larger site that, if we could obtain it, would make an excellent location for a school. Footpaths converged towards the adjacent store and the land was alongside a tar-surfaced road. Over the excellent meal Fabia had prepared for us we eagerly discussed the possibility of starting a school at Ha Mohatlane. That was a name that would become a regular feature of conversation in Durham in the years ahead but now there were scores of questions to ponder, ask and answer, the first being could we find any Biblical support for education?

That was difficult. Education is not a word that appears in any major translation of the Bible. Nevertheless, a collection of the familiar words of the day such as training, instruction and teaching do appear in both Old and New Testaments. These associated words describing very different styles and patterns of tuition support the present-day, more sophisticated, notion of education. So it seems reasonable to suppose that teaching and learning were considered to be crucial activities of the Biblical idea of faith. Support is also evident in the Book of Proverbs that states if we 'train a child in the way he should go and when he is old he will not turn from it';[5] although some commentators, sensitive to contemporary negative aspects of training, substitute the word 'start' for 'train'. Paul, when writing to the Corinthians, seemed to be aware of the delicate distinctions contained within the broader concept of education. He avoids the use of that notion and recounts that some people are given 'the message of wisdom' whereas others are given 'the message of knowledge.'[6]

Later, in his same letter, he emphasises the importance of teaching when he describes it as an appointment of God.[7] Even though the word 'education' is not used in the Bible support for the modern-day concept is strong and extensive. Present-day effective education, where it exists, is not the conditioning of children as it appears to have been in Biblical times, although the lack of highly qualified teachers and limited material resources in some countries may inflict processes akin to training. This is one of the major factors in the field of education causing the achievement of laudable aspirations to remain frustratingly out of reach. The language and semantics used by government and educational officials around the world can be admirable whilst the practices remain deplorable, the resources inadequate and the prospects pitifully inadequate for the twenty-first-century needs of the host society. But where was the likely 'host society' to be found?

Escaping from the hustle and bustle of Lesotho's capital city by driving northwards the first big 'camp' that is reached is Teyateyaneng. Shortly after entering the built-up area a sharp right turn and another eight-mile (13 kms) drive eastward along a well surfaced tarmac road leads to the village of Ha Mohatlane. The collection of generally well-cared-for huts, kraals and stores is the focus of a region that rises gently, compared to most of Lesotho's terrain, from 5,250 feet (1,600 m) to just over 6,235 feet (1,900 m). This lowland village is situated on a ridge running north-west to south-east that separates three river basins: Tebetebeng; Tejatejane and Phuthiatsana. As Dr Anderson emphasises in his feasibility study[8] for the LINK the significance of this Ha Mohatlane drainage system is its strong influence upon the siting of surrounding villages and physical communication between them by tracks and their associated footbridges. With an estimated population in 1991 of 537[9] Ha Mohatlane was not the largest of the twenty-four villages surveyed in the area[10] but it was the most strategically accessible to local populations given the high cost of public transport.[11] Travel costs in the area were carefully considered especially as the authors of another study, when describing the Malimong census sub-area in which Ha Mohatlane is situated, observed that this is: 'a poor area ranging from the lowlands to the foothills, with a serious shortage of school facilities and employment. It has fields and livestock, but agricultural productivity is low'.[12]

It was not an area of the country I knew well so during the last six months of 1988, whether I was in Lesotho or Durham, I took every opportunity to talk with those who did. This wide, time-consuming consultation process was an essential early feature of any large-scale development project or programme to inform myself and gain the support of others. I found this direct approach more effective than asking people to speak at meetings (*lipitso*) where some, especially women in the foothills and mountains, were often inhibited in their contributions. With Philip Mokuku in Durham during July 1988 we had ample opportunity to discuss the ideas that I was beginning to assemble and I was able to return to Lesotho in November that same year with a raft of ideas, possibilities and suggestions to place before my support group there. It was on this trip I was accompanied by the principal of Durham County Council's Agricultural College[13] who was also a member of the LINK's development group. Although he was there to advise on agricultural matters I was able to engage him in discussions about a possible future school so he not only challenged me in discussion but also took back to Durham some first-hand impressions of the tentative proposal to build a school. It so happened that the treasurer[14] of the Durham development group was also able to visit the site as he and his wife were making a private visit to southern Africa at the time and I was able to take them to Ha Mohatlane. In addition, when preaching in nearby outstations,[15] villagers, teachers and priests contributed their comments until I had a large portfolio of ideas ranging from the obtuse and incredible to the just about possible. If nothing else was achieved we had, at least, stimulated creative thinking!

I was *not* proposing, as some voices advocated, to build a cinema, a hospital or a swimming pool; clearly we needed time for some cherished hopes to mature and others to die. That time became available as other events, projects and responsibilities in the LINK and elsewhere gave me some ten months or so to switch into a realistic mode of thinking. This resulted in the gradual emergence of the concept of a community education centre which was, in my thinking, to be planned as a place that would become the centre of village life, open and attractive to anybody in the region. Perhaps not a cinema but a place where films could be viewed: perhaps not a hospital but a clinic: a swimming pool presented a bigger problem that we never did resolve.

One of many useful lessons I had learned at Ha Popa was how important it was to be sensitive to what was already established on any site that may be allocated to us for future development. At Ha Popa the villagers had worked long and hard building the mud-and-stone clinic there and I knew that I mustn't alienate their support by destroying their clinic. If I were to attract their future labour it was essential to incorporate their invested labour into the new development. So at Ha Mohatlane we took careful account of the established buildings and gardens fortunately clustered toward one end of the site. At this stage, May 1989, we had no idea whether or not the land would be made available to us.

There was a small rectangular concrete-block building with a pitched corrugated-iron roof without guttering about 50 feet (15 m) long and 20 feet (6 m) wide with a single metal door in the middle of one side. Inside on the earthen floor there was a collection of chairs and benches in various stages of collapse. The many broken panes of glass in the large windows were evidence, not only of the lack of repairs, but also of the very high cost of glass. For five days a week this inhospitable building was a school classroom accommodating some seventy children[16] (although it has also been reported[17] that three hundred children in four classes worked together in the one room). On Saturdays or, more frequently, Sundays it was converted into an Anglican church for a congregation of an indeterminate number of worshippers. Not far away was a ramshackle teachers' house with a small kitchen next to a vegetable garden. This, then, is what somebody's hard work had provided, together with a distant mud-and-stone deep-pit latrine with a single sloping corrugated-iron roof held down with masses of large stones and boulders.

During 1989 the LINK's community woodlands, poultry units, rural health centre, forestry, exchange visits, books and tools projects were making great demands upon what time was available so Ha Mohatlane became more of a cognitive exercise than a physical development. This was a considerable benefit. It gave me the opportunity to organise, to encourage and cajole, to assess support, to think ahead. The primary notion of a community education centre that developed from my conversations with Steven Molokeng and others included provision for a primary school, for an adult training centre, ladies' workshop, crèche, clinic, library, church and a multi-purpose hall open to the community. Outside there would be a woodland site, poultry unit and a sports field. Provision would also have to be made for teacher housing and a house for the warden of the centre. This was the picture we had in mind as we began thinking and talking about support.

Unit-financing was not an idea of economists but it was one I hoped to utilise for what was to be the LINK's largest building project so far. It involves dividing up a large project into its constituent parts and seeking funding for each according to the ability and financial size of the donor who thus has a specific responsibility within the larger enterprise. The skill is bringing all the separate individual support into the one project. I tested the idea when I was with a representative of the Canadian International Development Agency[18] and asked if it would be interested in funding part of the development. The request to provide finance for the latrine block was not rejected 'provided (their) help (was) recognised in a clear visual way'. When I suggested that could be done by painting a maple leaf on each toilet seat the idea was not greeted enthusiastically.

The preparatory work for what we were increasingly thinking of as a community education centre continued throughout 1989 but I became more and more concerned about the potential size of the project. Although we had not received a definite decision about the land we had been given a clear indication from the Chief of Ha Mohatlane that he supported the development. In spite of all the positive comments we were receiving I found myself asking whether it was all necessary or was it simply a mammoth status symbol through which local people would express their superior position in the region? This nagging question needed serious attention and in Durham I discussed it with the development group and specifically with a former academic colleague, Ewan Anderson, who had wide experience of overseas development and had offered his help to the LINK.

I wrote a short briefing document for Ewan who agreed to research our proposal and prepare a detailed feasibility study, but before then I wanted some reassurance that we would be able to raise the necessary finance which by this time I estimated would be upwards of £280,000, a huge amount for the LINK to find in the early 1990s. Also in Durham there was as yet no working party that had the ability to undertake a responsibility of this magnitude. I knew who I wanted but could I persuade him? As part of the early planning at the beginning of the year another colleague whose work I greatly respected agreed to help, but not yet. He was about to start a six-month sabbatical. So, we waited. Ten months later, the Rev'd Dr Jeff Astley, who was, at this time, Director of the North of England Institute for Christian Education, agreed to be chairman of the LINK's education working party that we had recruited. The year ended discussing our ideas with officials at the Lesotho Ministry of Education, the British High Commission and the European Commission. Without exception we were encouraged to pursue the idea of a community education centre and I had a clear indication that a well-presented, carefully budgeted enterprise would be welcomed.

At this time, early 1990, the LINK was obviously being talked about elsewhere for on Wednesday, 3rd January I received a telephone call from Hilary Armstrong, Member of Parliament for North West Durham, during which she questioned me about three of our major projects the poultry units, Ha Popa Rural Health Centre and the proposed community education centre. It was a short talk that she wanted to pursue in more detail so she came to see me three months later on Friday, 6th April 1990 when we spent the late afternoon together talking about the LINK, education, development and Ha Mohatlane in particular. After an interesting talk she left my study quite enthusiastic about the LINK, saying that she would see the Minister for Overseas Development, Lynda Chalker, to encourage positive action in respect of our projects and proposals.[19] She did. Five years and many thousands of pounds later, in September 1995, Baroness Lynda Chalker arrived by helicopter at Ha Mohatlane Community Education Centre to see how British and European taxpayers' money had been used. One unexpected telephone conversation can have interesting consequences but much work was undertaken by the LINK during the intervening five years before her visit.

It was time for me to switch from a Westminster politician to a Mosotho chief. I needed to meet Chief Likoata Mohatlane to obtain the land so essential to our proposal. We had already made a large investment of time and energy on the basis of an assumption that we now had to put to a practical test. Would the LINK be given the land it required? By now I had negotiated with other Basotho chiefs when I needed support for the poultry units, when I required land and labour for the community woodlands and when building Ha Popa Rural Health Centre. The LINK had been allocated land at Malealea by Chief Setlakotlako, at Ralehlatsa by Morena Katiso Ramaisa and at Ha Popa by Chief Mahoa so, with that experience and Steven Molokeng's comprehensive knowledge of Basotho custom, we were quietly hopeful as we arrived for the site meeting that he had arranged. Conscious that this really should have been a hurdle close to the starting line and not one halfway through the course, my confidence was more than a little fragile: what would happen if the Chief failed to arrive or, if he did have a change of mind, said 'no'?!

He was not there when Steven and I arrived; had he already decided against the centre? We walked around the site trying to picture where each part of the centre would be constructed if we were ever to reach that stage. We occupied ourselves waiting, then, when we were at the most distant spot from the entrance to the land we hoped the LINK would be given, Chief Likoata Mohatlane arrived. Overjoyed, to an extent that showed we had both really doubted if he would ever come to see us, we hurried across to meet him and engage in the usual preliminary introductions which Steven skilfully conducted in the blazing heat of the day. Chief Likoata Mohatlane was a short, wizened, slightly bent man who looked older than the years Steven attributed to him. His Sesotho flowed at such great speed I was only able to gather the gist of what was being said which may have been fortunate even if a trifle annoying. He said that he was pleased I knew the Basotho well (what had Steven told him?) and he was pleased to welcome me to Mohatlane.

So far, so good; what now? After thirty minutes or so of social exchange Chief Likoata indicated that we should all sit in the shade of the small clump of trees that were growing on the site. Steven broke a twig off the tree. Scratching diagrams in the dust he outlined what we had in mind. Without going into great detail he explained our ideas and soon moved on to the larger question of the buildings and the need for land, translating the Chief's questions for my responses. It all took a long time which I welcomed because I knew that in this culture to hurry is to waste time. I felt he was keenly interested in the proposal which gave me some optimism which his next question inflated almost to bursting point and for which I was unprepared. 'How much land did we want?' From my very first viewing of the site I had always thought in terms of the area that had some natural boundaries, in all about seven acres (2.8 hectares),[20] and was, with two small indents, roughly rectangular in shape, level in surface contour and adjacent to a tarred road. Access to the site and building there would be so simple contrasted to mountainous, barely accessible, Ha Popa. But the question still remained, 'How much land did we want?'

By now I had the '... true knowledge ...' that Paul advocated (I knew the Chief was willing to help us and I knew the size and shape of the land we had been hoping he would allocate to us) but I had not anticipated we would be offered considerably more land. Now I had to exercise '... perfect judgement, so that (I would) be able to choose what (was) best'.[21] This was much more difficult. More land would enable us to plant another woodland site but fencing costs would rise considerably. If we asked for more, and it were granted, the local community might become angry and fail to cooperate with the building of the centre especially if they had been refused land as we knew some had. I very much wanted to involve them in the work, knowing that the place in which they had invested their labour would become special to them. Steven carried on talking to the Chief whilst I carefully considered how to respond without offending either the Chief or the local people. My response was to request the land for which we had originally hoped and to be grateful that it would be given without any cost to the LINK. I shall never know whether or not that was '...perfect judgement ...' or whether I chose 'what (was) best ...' but I do know that Chief Likoata slowly unwound from sitting on the ground, rising to inflict a bone-shattering handshake tempered, slightly, by a smile that split his weathered face from cheek to cheek as he gave us permission to use the site for a community education centre. I stuttered a *'Kea leboha, morena'* ('Thank you, Chief') the inadequacy of which Steven diplomatically alleviated in the flood of Sesotho that followed. Clasping two fingers of my almost crushed right hand Chief Likoata led me around the site with Steven interpreting the deluge of excited conversation as I explained where and what we planned to build. We now had to stake our claim.

Meanwhile in Durham the eight members of the education working party under Jeff Astley's chairmanship worked well, undertaking small projects such as compiling the teaching project boxes for use in Durham schools and supervising the assembling of project boxes for use with children in parish churches. Rob Bianchi, who led the first Durham youth visit to Lesotho in January of the following year, was responsible to this working party and took a group of young people to Mohatlane on Tuesday, 22nd January 1991. Much was happening but more was to follow and the working party was ready for bigger things when the time came. In a strange, very unusual, reversal of emphasis the Durham end of the LINK was under strong pressure from the Basotho to work toward a 1992 completion date for the community education centre. I thought this was unrealistic especially as at that stage we had virtually no money for such a centre and we were just about to experience a financial setback. Six months after the Overseas Development Administration had agreed to pay[22] for a feasibility study it, unusually, reneged on the agreement on 18th June 1991 but since, at the same meeting, it approved a grant of £52,000 for Ha Popa Rural Health Centre, I did not complain too strongly.

The LINK had a contingency fund that had been financed by private donations which covered the travel costs of Ewan Anderson, who was working voluntarily, so he was with me when I left for Lesotho on Monday, 15th July 1991. In addition to voluntary work one other feature of the LINK that I strongly encouraged from its very beginning was interdenominational cooperation, so I was particularly pleased to be working with Ewan who is a practising Roman Catholic. During its first phase the LINK also had an excellent working relationship with the Catholic Agency for Overseas Development (better known as CAFOD). Despite financial constraints at the time it had already made substantial donations to the poultry unit project and Ha Popa Rural Health Centre so three of our major development projects had benefited from interdenominational contributions. As Ewan Anderson's contribution demonstrated not all donations to our work from other denominations were financial. 'One in Word and Work' was an illustrated account of the LINK's work during the first six years of its life and this benefited also from the professional advice and voluntary work of a Roman Catholic, John Bailey, who with a colleague, Dick Colquhoun, advised on the layout and design.[23] Denominational boundaries were proving to be no more restrictive to the LINK than geographical borders.

The stated aim of the feasibility study was 'to provide a comprehensive set of appropriate data' on which we could make a decision as to whether the LINK should go ahead with the provision of a community education centre at Ha Mohatlane. We asked that the study should clearly indicate if Ha Mohatlane was a suitable location and what facilities the local population would wish to be available. I was very keen to have documented the needs and requests of the people in the region so, although we had suggested what might be possible, the end product was what the local population wished to have available. I did not want the LINK to be accused of imposing any project, least of all one of this size, on the villagers. Ewan Anderson, accompanied by Steven Molokeng, spent three weeks in the field conducting his study which resulted in a professional 58-page document being delivered one month later. Face-to-face interviews were held with over 600 people constituting an 8.5 per cent sample of the population in twenty-four villages in the catchment area. The main requirements mentioned by the villagers were close to those we had earlier identified: we had been well briefed. Ewan reported that each village chief was asked to arrange a *pitso* with, as far as possible, a cross-section of the community attending.[24–25]

After a welcoming ceremony and prayers Steven provided an eloquent prologue to the actual interview, translating the questions on village services and requirements. A group photograph was taken before coloured picture postcards of Durham Cathedral were distributed which Steven described 'with some exaggeration as fifty times larger than the Roman Catholic Cathedral in Maseru!' Even if that was unfathomable to most Basotho the fact that Durham Cathedral was 900 years old was incomprehensible given it was only 158 years previously that the first religious missionaries arrived in Lesotho in 1833. The village meetings ended with something much more understandable; dancing and singing. The results of the enquiries indicated that a major preoccupation was with 'adult training, particularly in such skills as knitting, sewing, building, carpentry and car mechanics'. At this time, in the first half of the 1990s, there was a sharp decline in employment opportunities in the Republic of South Africa for Basotho men and therefore a potential increase in the demand for training was likely to occur.[26] There was a very strong request for clinic facilities mainly because some pregnant women had to walk up to four hours for medical attention. Some irregular and unreliable transport was available but at a high cost.

Ha Mohatlane occupies about one third of the Malimong area east of Teyateyaneng and by using some of the poverty indicators selected from the *Poverty in Lesotho*[27] study Anderson gives an interesting picture of what the Ha Mohatlane region was like in 1991. As with any development project it was important to know the economic context of its work and the social factors we had to accommodate. For those people in the northern section of the LINK some details could act as a gentle reminder that certain aspects of living that are taken for granted in Durham may be absent in Mohatlane. I live in Durham in a medium-sized house that has three inside toilets: 77 per cent of households in the Mohatlane region have no toilet. In my house there are nine-cold water taps and nine-hot water taps: 25 per cent of households in Mohatlane have no piped water, hot or cold. I have a savings account: 68 per cent of people in Mohatlane have no savings account which is probably because 61 per cent have an income of less than M20 (£2.00) per month. All teachers in Durham schools are qualified: in Mohatlane only 44 per cent of teachers hold that status. Every school in Durham is connected to a water supply: in 67 per cent of the schools in Mohatlane there is no water tap. No school in Durham is without toilet facilities: there are no latrines in 64 per cent of schools in the Mohatlane region. When the LINK was working in Mohatlane in 1991 school attendance was complusory for all Basotho children between the ages of six and fifteen but 37 per cent of children in that age range were not in school. Although there is no strictly comparable figure available for Durham an indication of the difference that exists between regions can be grasped by reference to 7 per cent unauthorised absences within the complulsory age range of 5 to 16 years for the year 2004.[28] Durham schools provide desks or tables and chairs for every pupil: 19 per cent of children in Mohatlane had no seating of any description.

It was also important to establish the significance of Ha Mohatlane in the normal life of the region because if it could be shown that it occupied a central position on which people normally converged then enhanced facilities in the proposed community education centre were more likely to be welcomed and used more effectively. In each village surveyed the only commercial service generally available was that supplied by the café and two villages did not have even this provision. In total the region had forty-nine cafés and two general all-purpose stores, one of which was at Ha Mohatlane where there is also a postal agency and a maize mill. With people from twenty villages claiming to use its stores and the mill, which is considered to be the most reliable in the region, Ha Mohatlane seems to be a centre of activity. Its function as a service centre is greatly enhanced not only by the postal agency but also by the presence of a bus stop for nine other villages. It was against this background that the survey investigated each of the six facilities the LINK suggested might be incorporated into the development plan. In order of preference stated by the local population they were:

Adult training centre

In a region with a declining number of employment opportunities the population expressed much enthusiasm for the possibility of adults acquiring skills that could be marketed. The feasibility study showed clearly that men and women would be prepared to travel from every village within the Mohatlane area and perhaps even beyond. Helpfully, drawing attention to the need for local instructors, the study identified a group of ten people who had teaching abilities that could be utilised in a wide variety of skills. Another 107 were categorised from those possessing very good skills to those having low-level skills that were rarely used. The highest demand from women was for sewing and knitting skills and from men for building skills although, in total, twenty disparate trade skills were requested covering both hand and mechanical use.

During the survey it was found that 213 people in the sample required skill training which, at that time, extrapolated to the total population of the region, produced a figure of 2,520 adults who would be likely to seek adult training at several levels. That figure almost certainly increased substantially following the end of the apartheid regime when the recruitment of Basotho as miners for the gold mines declined rapidly. 'The mining industry peaked at about 130,000 Basotho employed in 1989, and by 2006 had declined to 45,000'.[29] The unemployment data contained in the LINK study was convincing when analysed in 1991. The use of that evidence to establish an adult training centre at Ha Mohatlane was fully justified as was the forecast that it would be intensively used. The LINK was well ahead of others in providing retraining for retrenched mine workers.

Crèche

In Basotho society, because of the close and immediate availability of the extended family, the idea of a crèche is not widely established. However, it does tend to be more acceptable in those areas where women are employed or are hoping to learn skills that will assist them in finding employment. Our preliminary discussions had suggested that this would be a welcome facility at Ha Mohatlane so it was included in the briefing document for further investigation. The study produced some interesting findings. Of all the potential facilities discussed this was found to have the smallest catchment attracting interest only from women living in three adjacent villages. Clearly travelling distance was a major consideration for those mothers who were working as they could be confronted with two double journeys between their home and the centre, so not only would it be physically tiring but also a time-consuming exercise.

There was a small nucleus to whom the idea had no appeal but despite that our enquiry showed that private crèches were established in seven villages, six of them without any trained supervision. We obviously had to be sensitive to the negative reactions expressed but without the provision of a crèche mothers with young children would be severely restricted in the training courses they could undertake at the proposed education centre. At most village meetings a crèche was accepted as being an intrinsic part of an adult training centre. When the idea of a crèche was expanded to include pre-school activities the study revealed the presence of a much greater enthusiasm within eighteen of the twenty-four villages in the enquiry. We had a lot of data containing much useful information that would have to be considered carefully and guide our decisions.

Clinic

Medical services were available in the hospital at Teyateyaneng but travelling problems of one sort or another made them inaccessible to many villagers so there was a high reliance on local clinics. At the time of the study three clinics were available, the most popular of which was the government-run facility at Pilot village which was the only one actually in the region of Ha Mohatlane. Of the three that were used this was probably the most attractive because the fees were lower than at the other two which were run by Roman Catholic missions. They were all of similar design with waiting area, examination room, dispensary and limited dormitory accommodation. The LINK study found that the biggest problem was not the service that was available but the distances to be travelled, generally on foot, often carrying a baby in one form or another. Evidence was collected of some women who walked three hours from the village of Ha Sello, lying to the north-west of the clinic at Pilot, when they themselves were unwell. The researcher was left in no doubt during all village meetings to the west of Ha Mohatlane that the establishment of a clinic as part of a community centre would be very welcome. To the east the clinic at Pilot would still be accessible. This 'traffic-flow' is clearly shown in the feasibility study.[8]

Library and recreation facilities

The school-cum-church building on the site was used, occasionally and irregularly, for public film shows and concerts but if a suitable building could be designed it was suggested that this type of cultural provision might be expanded to incorporate a library. Other ideas that were floated included a games facility, fitness training and drama. The enquiry therefore included an investigation into what facilities currently existed and what future use would be made of those that might be included. All the villages in the research sample were equally poorly provided in terms of leisure facilities. The most commonly available was a football pitch although six villages did not have this basic provision. Apart from schools and their limited facilities, there was only one hall in the region and that was a privately owned establishment at Ha Moholobela.

As a result of this limited accommodation only six villages showed the occasional film or video, although there was a stated demand for such entertainment. People occasionally watched television at Pilot village clinic. During the group interviews in the villages a strong demand was expressed for improved sporting facilities such as the provision of tennis, basketball, volleyball and cycling. However, by far the most important additional feature was considered to be a library and learning resources centre in which books and learning aids should be in Sesotho. The research data indicate that people would be willing to travel long distances to avail themselves of any facility of this nature especially if they were available during daylight hours.

School improvement

The low priority given to the provision of a new school and upgrading of the church facilities can be partly explained by the fact that both a school and a church existed on the site. The fact that the single building in which the school and the church were housed was, by Lesotho standards, in a fair state of repair also had to be recognised. Why replace it? The suggestion for a new school did not have the novelty of a new adult training centre, crèche, clinic or library and leisure facilities. Nevertheless, important information was forthcoming about the influence a new school might have, especially on the pattern of school attendance in the region.

At the time of the research the majority of the children were drawn from three neighbouring villages plus a few from three others further afield. There was a strong expression of opinion that a new school building at Ha Mohatlane would attract increased attendance. The children from the twenty-four villages surveyed attended fifteen primary schools of which only four offered the full primary curriculum, and of those, three were located on the periphery of the region entailing long walks.[30] In his report Ewan Anderson comments, 'The pattern reveals the fact that many long journeys of up to one and a half hours on foot are made to (and from) school each day.' To what extent that inhibits school attendance is difficult to judge but the central position that Ha Mohatlane occupies was seen as attractive and the survey indicated that there were several good reasons for upgrading the formal educational facilities there.

The most important seemed to be the poor conditions at the school but there was concern also over the lack of primary schools for children from Anglican families there being only one other in the region. Additionally, children at Ha Mohatlane primary school had to transfer for their last year (grade seven) to Ha Nkalimeng which entails a walk, at the age of ten or eleven, of one and a half hours each way, much of it along a busy road. More significantly, educationally it involved adaptation to another school, different teachers and another style of discipline and work. One further aspect the researcher was asked to investigate was the effect an upgrading of the school would be likely to have on other schools in the region. From the comments that were forthcoming regarding this aspect there was sound evidence that indicated there would be some readjustment of attendance patterns in favour of a new, better-equipped school at Ha Mohatlane but not at a level that would seriously disadvantage any other regional school.

During the time when the study was being conducted school fees were being charged and this was a strong influence on where, and indeed if, a child attended school. Fees tended to reflect facilities in the school such as the provision of midday meals, extracurricular activities and the number of 'private' teachers employed in addition to those paid for by the government. The annual charges levied at the Anglican primary school at Ha Mohatlane were: Standard One M25.20 (£125); Standards two to four M27.20 (£135); Standards five and six M30.20 (£150).[31] Sending one child to this school, assuming there were no increases in fees during their six years attendance, would cost a family the considerable sum of M167.20 (£830).

Following the lead given by the United Nations Millennium Development Goal to achieve universal primary education by 2015 Lesotho began to phase out school fees in 2000 when, with the help of international aid, it also began to build many new schools. The LINK was about twelve years ahead of the international community that, in 2006, funded the building of seventeen new schools in Lesotho. Since the national population at the time of our study was increasing at the rate of 2.6 per cent annually there were strong reasons to believe that Ha Mohatlane school could increase in size without adversely affecting other nearby schools. Furthermore, all the school buildings in the region were overcrowded so new building was required to accommodate the expected increase within the primary school range. That was a genuine expectation in the mid-1990s that could not forsee the effect of the HIV/AIDS pandemic so there may be surplus school places in the future.

Church improvement

As we might have expected, and as we discovered with the proposal to upgrade the primary school, there was greater support for the introduction of new facilities than for the improvement or replacement of those that already existed. Nevertheless, it was discouraging to find that on every variable the researcher investigated (age, gender, location, social status) church improvement occupied the lowest position in the priority scale. If it came to assessing and deciding on development priorities the LINK had to be sensitive to this reluctance of the local community to invest resources in the refurbishment of the church building. Since church attendance is relatively fixed by denominational adherence any changes in attendance were likely to be relatively minor. The research brief included a request for this to be investigated as preliminary conversations had included a consideration of the influence of developing ecumenical services and the use of the facilities by denominations other than Anglican.

There was little hard evidence that either an improvement in the buildings or a more inclusive form of religious service would have much effect on attendance. We had no data relating to church attendances but the study revealed that the Anglican church at Ha Mohatlane drew its congregation from twelve villages several of which are at least an hour's walk away. Within three other denominations (Roman Catholic, Lesotho Evangelical Church, Apostolic) for which data is available people seem to be willing to walk for up to three hours to attend the church of their choice. The suggestion of ecumenical services was welcomed by respondents as was the possibility of sharing any church provision between denominations.

Based on the accumulated objective evidence of his study Ewan Anderson made the following recommendation:

> It has been demonstrated clearly that Ha Mohatlane is the most suitable village for the development of a community centre. Furthermore, there is support, varying from strong to solid, for the facilities envisaged and there is hard evidence that they would be well used. Most importantly, there is a substantial number of trained people available to ensure that such provision would be sustained and, indeed, developed. Therefore, it is strongly recommended that the Development Group accepts the establishment of a community centre at Ha Mohatlane as a worthwhile and viable project.[32]

That recommendation contained in the researcher's report concealed a less formal suggestion he made in an article in *'MOHO – Together*:

> Perhaps, in your prayers, you might think of the enthusiastic and lively people with their great sense of humour but diminishing employment opportunities; of the young man who had raised an orchard from peach stones and had designed his own fuel-efficient stove; of the blind ex-miner who had lost the use of his fingertips through years of underground drilling and was only 42 years old; of the young woman in one of the poorest villages who assured us that, if she were involved, the project would indeed work.[33]

These were some of the people the LINK was trying to minister to so, confronted with that weight of evidence and knowing there was already strong institutional support, the development group entered into a long detailed discussion, finally accepting the Anderson Report and so initiating the next phase.

With a large, complex development, as Ha Mohatlane was becoming, it was necessary to organise things concurrently rather than consecutively. This was, in part, caused by the wish of the Basotho to have the centre up and running by 1992 but the in-built danger of this form of organising is that if one component changes or collapses it affects all the others within the process. In the last quarter of 1991 I was running many lines of enquiry simultaneously with education and church officials, architects and quantity surveyors, charitable and personal donors, high commissioners and the European Delegate and, inevitably, the bankers. In Durham the development working party had agreed to submit the proposal for a 1992 joint-funded project so when I was exchanging the summer heat of Lesotho for the winter cold of Durham the 'flight-work' was a first draft of the proposal. As soon as I reached home Richard Briggs was on my doorstep to take my draft and type a second, soon returning with it to discuss the budget which I wanted to keep at a maximum of £200,000. That was not practical given the many imponderables, not least the rate of inflation in eighteen months' time.[34] With some anxiety I agreed to a total of £280,000. Many drafts followed and then, with only nine days to go before the papers were due to be completed, we realised that, amid all the activity, I had failed to return with any technical information about electricity supplies to the area. I made a rare telephone call to Steven who replied with one of his calm, characteristic responses: 'Peter, do I know?' which, being interpreted, means 'Peter, I have no idea!'

It was a frenetic period during which everyone worked hard and, although it was sometimes a close thing, no deadline was ever missed. By now it had been accepted in Lesotho, albeit with a degree of reluctance, that 1992 was an unrealistic target date partly because of the weight of work caused by many other LINK activities. Ha Popa was in the final stages of completion; our largest development programme, the forestry project, was in the submission stage; an adult exchange programme was being organised; I was searching in Johannesburg for £15,000 that the banks had 'misplaced'; the education working party was gearing up to launch the public appeal in Durham; the budget, which we had to get through London and Brussels, of £280,000 was a figure that frightened some but motivated others. The biggest challenge yet might still lie ahead.

Unit-financing was a great strength in the LINK's organisation and financial strategy. In Durham the development group was, hopefully, raising money from the European Commission and the British government; the book working party set itself a target of £10,000 to provide the Sesotho library books; the woodland working party were paying for trees around the site; the medical working party undertook to finance the equipment of the clinic; the container group collected sewing and knitting machines for the ladies' workshop; the British High Commission paid for fencing. Lest contributions seemed only to flow from north to south the Basotho had already given the land; we had valuable exemption from Lesotho General Sales Tax (described in Durham as Value Added Tax); South African banks were providing limited funding at hugely beneficial financial rand exchange rates. One of the most vital contributions to the overall cost would be the collection by local people in Ha Mohatlane of gigantic piles of rocks and stone for building. It was time for me to see the Chief again, not this time for land but for labour. What I had to do then was to bring all the contributions together at the right time in the right place.

In Durham we despatched our submissions to meet the 28th November deadline and 1991 slipped quietly into history as offers from volunteers continued to arrive. I visited the Durham members of the Westminster and European parliaments to gain their support for our proposals in London and Brussels and then flew back to Lesotho mid-January to find it parched by the serious drought that ravaged the country in 1992. Because trees take much longer to grow than buildings Steven had already mobilised voluntary labour to plant two rows around its 337-yard (308-m) perimeter. That back-breaking labour was not rewarded as most of the trees died in the persistent drought. The King asked that prayers for rain should be offered in every church: that was done in the Anglican cathedral on Sunday, 26th January 1992 when the recorded temperature was a blistering 108° Fahrenheit (42° Celsius).

When the prayers of thousands of Basotho were answered the tree planting was completed to provide in the years ahead a naturally graceful surrounding of the building and site. As Steven attended to the arboriculture in Mohatlane I concentrated on the political in Maseru as personnel there were changing and new contacts had to be established in the essential interaction with those leaders whose voice could determine the future of the project. The European Delegate who had been so supportive of the LINK's work, Achim Kratz, had been replaced by a Netherlander, Mr Joachim Zuidberg, and there was also a new British High Commissioner, Roy Cowling. One person still occupying his post in the High Commission, and with whom we had a good working relationship, was Second Secretary Paul O'Connor. He was responsible for the British aid programme and had already received our Mohatlane submission from the Overseas Development Administration in London. Things were moving.

The reception of our ideas was positive so I went to see another newcomer to Maseru, Kubilay Esenbel, the Director of the World Food Programme in Lesotho. I asked if they would supply food for us to allocate to those people who collected stones and rocks for the building, explaining that the use of local labour was an essential feature of our strategy to encourage local responsibility. The idea was not received with any enthusiasm and I left empty-handed. So, what about the Canadians who, much earlier, had expressed strong interest provided we recognised their contribution with a visual acknowledgement (about which I was not keen)? In yet another change of personnel the official with whom I had originally talked had been replaced[35] as had her earlier enthusiasm as they now rejected our request for the funding of one element of the centre. They did not have the confidence that we could pull the components into a coherent entity.

Encouraged by the major funding agencies but disheartened by their smaller counterparts I went back to Durham for a couple of months. European Commission officials soon tracked me down. A phone call from Carola Köster, our contact in the Directorate-General for Development office, asked for more detailed costings of the building which were more easily provided than was her second request. The assessors required a sketch and diagram of the buildings. But the potent sting was in the bureaucratic tail! They were meeting again in three days' time and needed the information by then. Richard Briggs dealt with the figures whilst I dealt with the building plans. I knew what I wanted but, not being an architect, I had to spend hours translating it on to graph paper. I sketched, threw away, sketched again, became frustrated, paused (but there wasn't much time for that luxury), sketched again, and again, and again. Eventually my design emerged as a central octagonal hall with a conical roof (relating to the surrounding village rondavels); four 'faces' of the octagon were extended outwards to form four classrooms; one 'face' provided the main entrance to the centre's main hall with one 'face' on either side of the entrance to be extended as a clinic and, opposite, a warden's office plus a kitchen and storeroom. The remaining 'face' of the octagon across the hall, directly opposite the main entrance, would provide the library and staff room with a small space facing the central hall to be used as a 'sanctuary' for church service requirements. The adult training centre was a simple rectangular design and, as a separate entity, located some distance from the school to lessen the effect of noise. Ewan Anderson and Richard Briggs came in to take a critical look before we sent everything to Carola Köster in Brussels.

The British Overseas Development Administration was the next major interruption with its questions about the sustainability of the community education centre which I answered in a letter dated 27th March 1992. I was beginning to feel over-questioned but I had to remind myself that we had requested a large sum of taxpayers' money for which others were initially responsible. Back in Lesotho in May I learned that London officials had been in touch with the High Commission asking similar questions and checking our credentials as an organisation. There was obviously a lot of behind-the-scenes activity so we were confident that our submission was being considered seriously and actively, as indeed it was because on Thursday, 4th June 1992, I received a letter from the Overseas Development Administration saying that the LINK had been awarded £82,246 towards the cost of the community education centre. All our 'spadework' was paying dividends. Now we awaited the response from Europe but that required much more patience. Discussions with Brussels about 'sustainability' went on for some weeks and were eventually resolved by adding another budget line to distinguish two areas of expenditure. At the beginning of July, during a telephone conversation with the Head of the Director-General's office,[36] I was told that our application would be approved but we had to wait ten anxious weeks before we received the contract awarding us £117,500.

Escaping from Durham and Lesotho during August 1992 Pam and I visited our son, Edmund, in America where he was undertaking post-doctoral research in the University of Louisiana at the mouth of the Mississippi. We had planned a quiet break so we could spend a little more time together but a vicious attack by Hurricane Andrew and two speeches about the LINK defeated our hoped-for isolation. After a brief stay in Durham to bring essential administration up to date I returned to the southern hemisphere at the end of the following month with the Rev'd Rob Bianchi who was to investigate the setting up of a LINK youth activities project.[37] It was Wednesday, 23rd September when I flew to Lesotho with a metaphorical £200,000 in my pocket for Mohatlane but, as Jeff Astley cautiously pointed out,[38] that would only become a reality if the education working party raised their contribution of £35,000. Nevertheless I knew that because that amount had been underwritten by generous donations and excellent financial management within the LINK I could now confidently negotiate and plan for the whole development as I was assured of financial viability. Maintaining our principle of using local labour whenever possible I briefed three Basotho architects using as a basis for our discussions the design I had already submitted to the European Commission.

The architects were invited to a site meeting that Steven arranged for the morning of Monday, 5th October 1992 when we hoped the Chief would be present, but he sent his deputy instead. Despite that it was a useful, constructive meeting with the village development committee, three church representatives, architects, the head teacher of the primary school, and two other LINK workers from Durham.[39] In all there were seventeen people present. The discussion incorporated questions and comments about the use of the building by the Church, where it would be built on the site, its availability to children, noise in the hall disturbing pupils in the classrooms, the need to build a secondary school, teachers' housing and who would run the proposed clinic. Nobody asked where the money was coming from: that was a problem that Ntate Ramosa had to solve. Nevertheless, it was a useful meeting in a friendly atmosphere but I wished the Chief had been there because although he had already given us the necessary land I also wanted the labour of his villagers which he had the social standing to encourage.

However, I was not despondent and, after being described inaptly by one Durham clergyman as 'a modern-day Paul', gained some comfort from my Bible reading[40] that morning which was written by Paul to the first church he established in Europe. Was the establishment of an out-station church, school, crèche, clinic, library in Lesotho so very different? It was, to the extent that I had to deal with architects, each one of them having been asked to submit their plans, if they so wished based on my design, before I left Lesotho on Tuesday, 20th October 1992. They all made the deadline with one providing a very impressive model of his proposal. It was a delicate mock-up that I knew would be very useful to the education working party if only I could get it back to Durham in one piece. Someone packed it carefully so despite the squash of a long-haul flight and crowds in four airports the journey was achieved without damage to anything except my composure.

The first three weeks of October 1992 was a defining period for the LINK in Lesotho during which many decisions were taken that would influence its work for years ahead. Rob Bianchi's investigation into the viability of a youth activities programme produced a positive result that the British Council in Maseru was willing to support. To the benefit of the work at Ha Mohatlane many hours of negotiating with officials at the Central Bank of Lesotho resulted in the LINK being granted the exchange of £150,000 at financial rand rate. This concession led me to review our financial control and administration in Lesotho. Since 1986 this work had been handled by the diocesan treasurer as a helpful contribution to the LINK's work but now our operations were becoming too large and complex for the fragile infrastructure of the diocese to support. A series of errors, all of which had been corrected, led me to become increasing apprehensive about the manner in which our accounts were being handled so the decision was taken to establish our own financial accounts and controls for which the LINK would be entirely responsible. Also during this period we were under considerable pressure to mount an increasing number of projects most of which we resisted because we just did not have the necessary staff. I was also concerned that the central tenet of the LINK might become submerged in the increased amount of work: we decided not to expand but it was not an easy decision. One suggestion we were to pursue was that of the European Delegate, Joachim Zuidberg, and his assistant, Paddy Gallagher, who suggested the LINK might submit a proposal to conduct a small-scale enterprise project .[41]

All these influential issues paled into insignificance compared to what happened at 10.30 on the morning of Thursday, 8th October 1992. It was that moment when drought succumbed to rain when we listened intently with unbelieving ears to the musical symphony played on the metal roof. We gazed at each other in wonderment at the assault; some ran outside to test its reality. It was not an illusion: light showers turned into a beautifully moderate downpour before heavy rain dripped its way through the roof and ceiling of the house into strategically placed buckets and bowls. Ironically it was only a few days previously that the LINK had presented its Drought Relief Implementation Programme or, for linguistic convenience, DRIP! The opening clouds gave an elated sense of relief and refreshment even if the only scorpion I ever saw in Lesotho chose just that moment to take a devilish walk along the hallway to remind me that there were lurking dangers other than drought but nothing so widespread and devastating to so many people. None of that did anything to distract from the pertinent quotation my Bible reading provided that morning to open my journal entry on this wonderful day: 'Don't worry about anything, but in all your prayers ask God for what you need, always asking him with a thankful heart'.[42]

As memorable 1992 turned into momentous 1993 the development and education working parties studied the proposals of the three Basotho architectural firms that had been invited to make recommendations for the community education centre. That submitted by Paul Croce Associates stood out as an exceptionally well-formulated tender and, after our choice was strongly supported by professional advice received in Durham, agreement was reached that we should retain this firm for the contract to build the centre. The Mosotho architect was Ntate Theodore Ntlatlapa who had studied architecture at the Australian Institute of Technology and had an excellent command of English and a wide experience of professional assignments. He was sensitive to the charitable aims of the LINK and its Christian foundation, quickly grasping the needs of the Mohatlane project, and related well to members of our team.

It was Friday, 5th February 1993 when I met with Theodore in his office in the southern hemisphere on a brilliantly sunny summer day. Later that same day in Durham some two hundred people gathered on a dark, wet, cold winter evening for the launch of the project appeal. At what was reported to be a wonderfully vibrant service in the Chapel of St. Peter in Auckland Castle the appeal was launched after two months of prayer stimulated throughout Durham by attractive prayer-cards. It was at this service that the LINK song *We are One Body in Christ* was sung publicly for the first time.[43] A couple of days later, on what in Durham was 'Education Sunday', the revised plans were displayed, as you can in the summers of Lesotho, outside the Anglican Cathedral in Maseru thus enabling more comments to be recorded as congregations left and arrived for the three services. The architect had incorporated our observations on his first interpretation of my design and produced a second set of plans which Steven Molokeng also used to consult widely with the Basotho.

At the beginning of the year, officials in Brussels were insisting that we showed two budget lines to distinguish two areas of expenditure but it might also have been appropriate to show two areas of income because, as a local Mosotho writer described the situation, Durham was collecting pounds whilst the Basotho were collecting stones:

> Sunday 7th February was hot; very hot. The crowd was large; very large. Mohatlane hadn't seen anything quite like it before. Hundreds of people of all ages, some of whom had walked many miles, gathered in the field where the community education centre is to be built by the LINK. There was an air of excitement. For many this was the beginning and what a beginning! We worshipped God and joined with our fellow Christians in Durham to ask his blessing upon the venture which brought us together. Father Bernard Duma, our parish priest, presided at the Eucharist, after which Ntate Steven Molokeng described the Project. Some 30 miles away in the Cathedral in Maseru people were praying for the work. As they left they saw an exhibition of the plans of the Centre. Much further away 6,000 miles away (but nevertheless very close), in the parish churches of Durham, people were praying for the project and planning money raising efforts ...
>
> ... and so the third and final set of plans were drawn up. Meanwhile, quantity surveyors, bankers, government officials and water diviners were all working for the project. But perhaps the biggest task for us still lies ahead: collecting –

> pounds in Durham, stones in Lesotho! An immense task for people in Mohatlane and in Durham, but a task, which, together, we will tackle with the same excitement which was present at the Eucharist when we all affirmed "We who are many, are one body."[44] (sic)

That we were effectively bridging the distance between Lesotho and Durham was further demonstrated a week later when the preacher at the Maseru cathedral was Maurice Simmons, a retired priest from Durham who had offered his help to the LINK organising the successful adult-exchange programme. He and his wife, Sheila, were in Lesotho on a self-financed fact-finding trip.

The first Mosotho I worked with professionally in Lesotho in 1973 was Charles Bohloko who, during his career, rose to be Principal Secretary for Education and knew more about education in Lesotho than, perhaps, anyone else. We had developed a sound working relationship over many years so I took the plans for the community education centre to him as, having inspected schools all over the country, I knew he would be constructively critical. Meanwhile, whilst Charles and I were poring over the plans, the architect had instigated a site survey and three men could be found walking criss-cross over the site with twigs poised and fingers crossed hoping to indicate the presence of water if it existed! Back and forth they went until they discovered that ground-water was there and they were able to locate it accurately.

For our part the LINK had consulted far and wide and now it was time to collate the comments for the architect to make his third, and possibly last, set of drawings. Whilst that was happening I was receiving spontaneous expressions of interest in the post of warden, organising more tree-planting, arranging bank accounts and reorganising our own financial arrangements before returning to Durham via Sebokeng, an apartheid South African township. I had been invited to undertake a five-day preaching tour in the diocese of Christ the King and in Sebokeng managed to avoid any serious clashes with the oppressive tyrannical apartheid regime or, for that matter, with the deep bitterness so brutally embedded during the massacre at adjacent Sharpville.[45] This I found graphically expressed in the graffiti under which, unwittingly, I stood talking with a black colleague before he gently drew me aside out of the range of the message that demanded the reader should 'Kill a White'. Since I was the only white around perhaps it *was* wise to move away.

In Durham Mohatlane dominated my time. Interest was high, there were talks to give, visits to make, leaflets to distribute; Lesotho was not the only place where hard work had been taking place. In the north there was an eagerness for up-to-date information. Exactly six weeks after the launch service Jeff Astley was able to announce to the education working party that the community education centre fund had reached a magnificent £218,985 but tempered the elation with the warning that the last lap, in this case measured as £16,015, is always the hardest. The day after the meeting my friend George Carey was in Durham when I was able to share with him something of what had happened since our disagreement precipitated the founding of the LINK.[46] It was a story of great blessing not centred just on the community education centre but on much that had happened in the previous seven years. Conversely, since Mohatlane was in the forefront of the LINK's activity my anxiety about the effect of the rampant inflation within Lesotho must have made me seem ungrateful and, even worse, unfaithful.

As we had already experienced, being One Body in Christ demands a sharing not only of joys but also of sorrows and mid-March 1993 brought deep sorrow to many of us. Steven Molokeng's wife Fabia died after a long period of suffering.[47] She had made a significant 'backroom' contribution to the development at Ha Mohatlane in the hospitality she extended to Ewan Anderson for the three weeks he was engaged in the feasibility study of the region. On the morning[48] of her funeral at St. Agnes' Church, Teyateyaneng, I was able to talk by telephone with Steven when, in response to my condolences, he made another of his profound comments: 'Thank you, Peter; we all accept she has now fully recovered.' One of the saddest things about living this period of my life in two countries six thousand miles apart was that I was often in the wrong place at the wrong time: I certainly was today.

By the end of the month I was back 'in the southern field' making the first contact with the then designated Minister for Water, Monyane Moleleki,[49] and receiving permission for the LINK to use the Maqalika Dam for water sports. Although plans for youth activities took most of the day I was able to meet with the architect to pass on the comments from our consultations so he could make the final adjustments to his plans. From politician to architect, then to banker to discuss, in constantly changing language, FinRand and ComRand, Sterling and Maloti, retentions and bonds: the twenty-first-century missionary needs a twenty-first-century vocabulary. Work at the end of April *for* Mohatlane was a long way *from* Mohatlane but very influential on what would eventually take shape there.

Much closer to the site was Steven's mobilisation of the local community to clear the site and start stone collection from a nearby quarry, a task that would go on for the next five months. It was to make a constructive contribution to the psychological framework around which the community education centre was built and, perhaps more importantly, organised: but there were problems. We had to be careful when balancing voluntary help with the contractually paid work especially when holding the contractor responsible for any defects. It was a matter for some delicate diplomacy about which our architect expressed some anxiety and which tended to delay the initial planning. I very much wanted the villagers to invest in the construction as others had already done so successfully at Ha Popa. The villagers had little money but plenty of muscle and this was their treasure that they could, and should be allowed to, contribute: 'for where (their) treasure (was), (their) heart (would) be also'.[50] Leaving Lesotho with plenty of work to do I returned to Durham via Zambia where Chengelo School was officially opened on Saturday, 15th May 1993 by Brigadier General Godfrey Miyanda, later to become Minister of Education.[51]

Ten days later a fax arrived in Durham from the Central Bank of Lesotho confirming that we had been granted financial rand for Mohatlane which was worth to us about £80,000. We should have been excited but our emotions were immediately subdued by an estimate for the adult workshop that was considerably higher than budget which was an indicator of what was to come. By that time we had twelve Basotho adults in Durham for an exchange visit at the end of August when my desk was covered with excessively high tenders for the Mohatlane main building. Those figures occupied me and my calculator for the next twenty-four hours. The following day we decided to try and negotiate a figure nearer to our budget but in any event to go ahead with the adult workshop and main building. We would then fund the warden's house, clinic and equipment separately thus demonstrating the strength of our unit-funding. After many faxes and telephone calls the main fixed-priced contract was signed and awarded to J. B. Construction on the recommendation of our architect. The company made a prompt start on the adult workshop so it could be used as a secure site store.

My first full week back in Lesotho mid-September 1993 was an interesting mix of LINK activity. It began with a gathering of those who had recently returned from the Durham section of the adult exchange. It 'was a huge success' in the lives of the Basotho because 'we felt at home'. One member of the group, the manageress of a Maseru bank, when introduced to her counterpart in Darlington was delighted to be presented with an 1833 one-pound note, Barclay's Bank providing the bridge. The cherished note is now framed and proudly displayed in Lesotho. It was then that sadness again descended upon the LINK when Vincent Makosholo, who accompanied Philip Mokuku and me during our preaching trip in the Maluti mountains seven years previously when the LINK was launched, died after a short illness.

The LINK was growing up encompassing a wide span of poignant conditions and attracting many varied demands. As the artistic contributions of Zakes Mda, Gonzales Scout and David Grieve[52] had already demonstrated we were not only using stone, cement and gravel to link Lesotho and Durham in the word and work of the gospel but were also engaging in literary, musical and academic contributions. I had an excellent opportunity at the National University of Lesotho to reinforce our commitment to the gospel of Christ when I was invited to give a lecture there on 'Christianity and Politics'. Just before all this activity another small piece of Durham had been established at Masite just 36 miles (58 kms) from Mohatlane. I had taken Aelred Stubbs there, to the Priory of our Lady of Mercy, after his arrival from Emmaus, the retreat house of the Community of the Resurrection in Sunderland.[53] Aelred was making a nostalgic visit to Masite recalling his four years there following his banning from apartheid South Africa.

By now the community education centre loomed large and was growing larger by the day. In September the site was a hive of activity with some fifty men working vigorously in the hot but overcast conditions supervised by a Mosotho foreman.[54] As the managing director of J. B. Construction, Johnny Chen, took me around the site explaining some of the technicalities it occurred to me that, whatever else it was promoting in Lesotho, the LINK was making a valuable contribution to the national economy by providing so many jobs especially as they were being financed by money that we were bringing into the country. I walked round inspecting the cores of the bore that had been drilled following the work of the diviners; the concrete-block-making by hand; the huge piles of rock and stone local people had collected; the almost finished adult workshop; the staking out of the main building (that looked bigger than I had envisaged); the provisions we had made for roof-water conservation and the solar panels for pumping and electricity.

Translation from design to reality was rapidly taking place. Trekking round the site, admiring the growth of the perimeter trees that had had such a struggle to get established, Durham seemed a long way off but it was from there that the whole operation had to be financed through the organisation the LINK had established. So, satisfied with what I had seen in Ha Mohatlane, I returned to Maseru to check our financial administration, before leaving for four days in Johannesburg to try and raise more money so we had some to administer! Across the continent in Namibia building in Lesotho (plus many other things) was replaced by building in the Kalahari Desert where the construction of a clinic at Tamtam, specially for bushmen and women to use when their nomadic life style allowed, presented some peculiar difficulties not experienced at Ha Mohatlane. Lesotho had to assume a back seat for two weeks as I concentrated on Namibian water, small-scale businesses and forestry. Back in Durham community education was the subject of a first interim report for Brussels.

We were encouraged at the start of January 1994, by the progress being made, to think it really would be 'a happy new year'. The architect, structural engineers and quantity surveyors were all sounding optimistic and reporting satisfactory progress at Mohatlane. My four days in Johannesburg had ended with the Chairman's Fund of the Anglo-American Corporation promising enough money to build the warden's house which we promptly reinstated. Things seemed to be going smoothly. Then, in Maseru, the shooting began. Everyone became tense and nervous as soldiers began to capture politicians and control the movement of people and goods by numerous roadblocks. Although it was worrying at the time fortunately the army mutiny did not last long and social and individual composure was regained, although there was a cost to building at Mohatlane which was about four weeks behind schedule. Nevertheless, even if the immigration officer would only grant me 72 hours to stay in the country for my next visit, we were often encouraged not only with cash but also comment.

At the end of January the British High Commission combined the two when an unsolicited offer of £8,000 towards the cost of classroom equipment at Mohatlane was accompanied by the observation that the money was 'unlikely to be spent by other NGOs' and could come to us 'as one of the most efficient NGOs in Lesotho'.[55] Both the accolade and the money were gratefully accepted as an encouragement at a time when problems were coming to the surface. Four days later the builder was reporting trouble in obtaining roofing material as suppliers in South Africa were anxiously assessing the effects of the military uprising and were reluctant to deliver and reduced the availability of credit. There was also an unforeseen need to recalculate our recurrent budget in the light of reductions in school fees being made by neighbouring Roman Catholic schools. It was difficult to quantify what effect this would have on our enrolment but our projections assumed a minimum of 120 pupils.

That was the visible surface of the project but what lay behind the facade? One day when I was working in the LINK office in Maseru Johnny Chen arrived in an agitated state. After describing the progress of the building he asked me to engage in a most extraordinary act of contrived accounting that would save him money by avoiding the payment of taxes. I listened carefully to his scheme so I was justified in refusing to involve the LINK in any part of what would be a highly dubious financial process. Preoccupied with responding correctly to this modern challenge that has been around since the Pharisee's confrontation of Jesus,[56] what I did not do, and what I should have done, was to question why such an insidious proposal was obviously so important to his company. Had I done so I might have been less surprised when the architect told me a couple of months later that the company had gone into receivership and we would have to appoint another contractor. This was a setback but not as serious as it might have been if the initial contract had failed to include the lodging of an agreed bank bond and a ten per cent retention clause.

Before turning our attention to finding a new contractor we spent a lot of time trying to put the High Commission grant to the best possible use and Steven, maintaining another of the LINK's principles to keep as much money as possible within Lesotho, was visiting a long list of local manufacturers. We knew what we wanted but it was difficult finding the quality we required. Steven sought the help of the Basotho Enterprises Development Corporation (BEDCO) who directed him to a manufacturer that grasped our needs and produced very strong school furniture that would withstand the vigorous use of a six-year-old Mosotho boy or girl, stack in a small space, and not ruin the flooring each time chairs were dragged over its surface. Steven was not exactly bullet-dodging but they and shells were criss-crossing Maseru at the end of January. It was then that I drove out to Mohatlane with Paul O'Connor who was responsible for the British government's aid programme in Lesotho. He wanted to see how the LINK was using British taxpayers' money and I was pleased to drive with him out of the battle zone. As the troops in the mountains surrounding Maseru withdrew and weapons were surrendered during the day the environment became a little calmer.[57] An eventful day in a relatively peaceful zone ended with Paul expressing his satisfaction at our efforts at Ha Mohatlane.

The community education centre was not, by any means, the only item on the LINK's varied agenda at this time. As the diversity of the LINK's activities demonstrates we were determined not to slip into a rut of mundane diocesan inert 'partnership or companionship'. We were forging a different style of association with our southern-hemisphere diocese for a specific purpose and at this time Mohatlane was at the top of the agenda, but what else was in the concurrent programme? Firstly, there were eighteen hopeful applicants for the two scholarships at Sunderland University that Jim Francis had arranged in conjunction with the World Council of Churches, the Overseas Development Administration and the LINK: Steven Molokeng and Richard Briggs were out of harm's way in the south of the country launching the community forestry project[59] in and around Quthing and Mohale's Hoek: in Maseru I met with the group of Basotho adults who had been to Durham for an exchange visit when my patience was tested as the chairman for the meeting arrived ten minutes before its 'backend' (as people in Durham Diocese would say, that is, its finish).

At her request I met with Dr Patricia Rojas of the World Health Organisation to discuss their suggestion that the LINK should consider mounting a TB awareness, education and treatment project which I found an attractive proposition given my personal battle with the *tuberculli bacilli.* More telephone conversations with the Minister of Natural Resources about the use of the Maqalika Dam for the proposed youth activities project (YAP) was immediately followed by driving up the mountain road to St. James' Hospital, Mantšonyane on my way to try and open the LINK's Ha Popa Rural Health Centre.[60] That was a frustrated journey as the road from Mantšonyane to Ha Popa was completely impassable, so leaving our four-wheel-drive vehicle we walked the remaining distance carrying the tools and 120 saplings which we then planted round the clinic. It was during this visit we made arrangements for the visit of botanists Mike Hirst and Darren Webster[61] and for the cancellation of a preaching engagement that would have involved me in a five-hour cross-mountain journey to Phamong. I returned from Ha Popa to St. James' Hospital on horseback so going on to Masite in our bakkie was a welcome relief.

There I drafted the job description for the appointment of a community forestry officer; received exorbitant quotations for fencing land allocated to the LINK at Ha Mokoati; took delivery of a bright red Toyota 4x4 and resisted the suggestion to paint the LINK's logo on its side; interviewed a shortlist of six for the Sunderland scholarship selecting one lady; after all the planning it seemed that the adult visit to Durham was in doubt as some people were having second (late) thoughts. Back to Durham, changing my watch by one hour on the journey leaving me unsure if I am in time credit, debit or balance; at home remembered to thank the many people who prayed for me whilst I was under fire in Maseru at a time when the LINK personnel arrived and the United Nations withdrew. It had been a long agenda and we had reached any other business. By now I had announced my intention to relinquish the leadership of the LINK and the Trustees had received forty-one applications; the person selected must be adaptable to many differing and quickly changing scenarios.

Many of those different scenarios required a huge leap from conventional to creative, from stagnant to stimulating. I had just taken a bodily leap from the rural village of Ha Mohatlane to the urban metropolis of London before taking a conceptual one from the LINK to that of the office of the Anglican Partners in World Mission organisation where I was meeting[62] with its secretary. He wanted to talk about a comment I had appended to a recent questionnaire from him in which I had tried to explain (probably inadequately) the unique concept of the Durham-Lesotho LINK. After explaining that the LINK was not a 'partnership' nor a 'companion diocese' (which was a huge leap for him) but an attempt to be One Body in Christ through Word and Work his delayed response was a muted, 'interesting,' which meant that he didn't really understand what I was saying. What neither of us could foresee in 1994 was that, sixteen years later, at its 2010 Conference, his organisation would:

> '... look afresh at Partnership – sharpening the issues and speaking honestly with each other. One part of the question is about our relationships with the rest of the World Church: we often talk about being in partnership, but what does that really mean and what does it feel like to be on the other side? The other part of the question is about relationships here at home: when it comes to resourcing and finances.'[63]

Although the content of our discussion took sixteen years to find its way into a Mission conference perhaps more was understood during our meeting than I assumed at the time. These were questions that the LINK was asking and responding to, and living and working within those responses, twenty-four years before the formal structures of the Anglican Church got round to considering them at a conference. Perhaps we were encouraging other people and organisations to think more critically about twenty-first-century mission.

Mission is a continuous process so I returned to Lesotho in time to greet the twelve people from Durham on the first stage of the adult exchange visit. During the first phase of the LINK's work a lot of attention was given to these visits as I felt strongly this was an important feature of being One Body in Christ, and David Jenkins, when writing a foreword to *One in Word and Work,* stated, 'I particularly hope that exchange visits will develop further,'[64] concluding with 'I am sure it (the LINK) will help to deepen our sense of belonging to one another in the one Church for the one Gospel.' The Durham Dozen, as they came to be called, included Mohatlane in their schedule of visits and arrived to a rapturous welcome and a white-iced celebration cake made by the school manager, Alina Pholosi.

Alina, with whom I had worked in both Durham and Lesotho for twenty-two years, had been very influential in planning the centre and was now greeting fellow Christians with her infectiously broad smile.[65] Accompanied by Chief Likoata Mohatlane the Durham Dozen, avoiding cement mixers, spades, bricks and pipes, buckets and ladders, toured the partly finished central hall and classrooms, adult workshop, clinic, sewing room, library and sports field, in the process experiencing how the hard work of their fellow Christians in Durham and Lesotho, working as One Body in Christ, had turned vision into reality.[66] In his speech to the group the Chief said how pleased the community was with the building and how he hoped the LINK would now develop a high school on the site; at which point it wasn't only the heat of the sun that made us wilt.

It took seven days and one phone call to turn wilting into despondency. The phone call came from an unusually sad Alina and the despondency from her message that the solar pumping system had been stolen. In all our projects, in addition to providing for the conservation of roof water, we stressed the environmental benefits of solar and installed an extensive system at Ha Popa but never once had any problems of theft although we were well aware how attractive the panels were to potential thieves. Perhaps with ground-level installation for pumping we had made it too easy for panels to be stolen from Ha Mohatlane.

Before the end of April we were confronted with more building delays; it seemed that with the end in sight completion drew further and further away. May was a very unproductive month at Ha Mohatlane although other advances in the LINK were strong and robust. We had everything ready for the clinic to open; agreement had been reached with the Minister of Health that the clinic would be run by staff from the hospital at Teyateyaneng; school furniture had been ordered and was being held for delivery as soon as the building of the centre was completed.

On Wednesday 15th June I left Newcastle on the first leg of my final visit as leader of the LINK's activities, flew to Brussels, and took SN0551 to Johannesburg. There I had arranged to collect a return flight ticket to Maseru and back to Johanneburg on Wednesday 15th July but when collecting my ticket in Jan Smuts Airport I was issued with a single one-way ticket only: as I sat alone in the small 'Otter' aircraft, I wondered, was someone trying to tell me something? That question didn't occupy much serious thought for very long as I had to get a new contractor working at Ha Mohatlane. Theodore Ntlatlapa recommended a fixed-fee contract should be awarded to EFS Construction with which I agreed, and the company made excellent progress with high-quality building that despite one or two small setbacks was almost finished as the LINK entered its second phase in the latter part of 1994. I pressed hard for a hand over date hoping to conclude that process and see the centre finished before I passed over the responsibility to my successor, but despite a work schedule that unusually included Saturdays, that was just a step too far too quickly.

Paul Jefferson, who was to lead the LINK through its second phase, and I had a three-month overlap period which wasn't a day too long to visit the LINK's forty sites across the country on which it now managed its projects. The two most northerly sites were at Ha Sefako where we were heartened by the sight of magnificent eucalyptus and fir trees gently sighing as they gracefully swayed in the mountain breeze coming off the Mafatle Range in the Republic of South Africa. I wouldn't exchange any one of my whispering giants for Wordsworth's crowd of fluttering and dancing daffodils:[67] what's more he didn't plant any of them!

The woodland sites within the grounds of the primary and secondary schools had obviously been carefully nurtured and I hoped the children's work as a partner in God's creation would be recognised by themselves as well as by others, not least their parents and teachers. As we left the trees my sorrow in bidding them farewell was tempered by the sight of their sturdy growth. At the call of Mohatlane we left Sefako and drove south to find the site seething with men and materials even though it was a Saturday when builders in Lesotho do not usually work. The building that I had first designed in Durham in such haste two years earlier in two dimensions was now taking its three-dimensional shape in Ha Mohatlane. Five of the 'fingers' jutting out from the main hall were almost finished. It all looked functional and the stonework was visually attractive.

After the successful conclusion of another series of discussions resulted in the award of a further tranche of financial rand the financial future of the centre was secured. As I walked round the site with Paul I went through my ideas for its use in the knowledge that what went on inside would be more important than the building itself: nevertheless, I hoped a sound purpose-built structure would help. Although I wanted to hand over a completed building I was content with what I saw and returned to Maseru for an afternoon of protracted, and sad, 'farewells': I've had to say 'good-bye' too many times and it comes no easier with repetition. But, for me, the 'backend' had come after twenty poultry units had been built to feed hundreds of children and give a practical dimension to their agricultural education; Ha Popa Rural Health Centre was sitting up there in the mountains providing care for some 10,000 Basotho and now Ha Mohatlane had a community education centre that was almost ready to serve the people that had worked so hard to bring it into being; around the country many hundreds of thousands of trees were gracing what previously were barren hillsides or sparse scrubland. Their proximity to villages was saving scores of women the drudgery of walking miles with heavy loads of firewood balanced on their heads and their families had not been overlooked as the youth activities project had been successfully launched and discussed with King Letsie III during my last full working day in his kingdom. Most importantly hundreds of people in both Durham and Lesotho had been introduced to each other and had come to a deeper understanding of what it means to be One Body in Christ through Word and Work. They have come into direct contact with a practical working example of the Gospel of Christ, experiencing, perhaps for the first time, the reality of His love and care for them whatever skin colour or social status they have inherited. Jesus is for everyone.

Sufficient progress had been made with the main building of the community education centre to enable the school, equipped with its brand-new furniture, to open in November 1994, just under six years since I first visited the site at Mohatlane. As so often happens the 'official' opening took place later on Saturday, 4th February 1995 just one day short of the second anniversary of the fund-raising launch in Durham. Quite a lot had been packed into those years. By that time Mrs Rose Sebeta had been appointed the first warden of the centre and a local management committee had been formed under the guidance of the regional manager of schools, Alina Pholosi. All units of the original plan had by now been reinstated and the contractors were able to hand over to the LINK the completed community education centre as originally planned plus an additional poultry unit and a piggery that provided a small income to offset the recurrent costs. The government provided and paid for all the qualified schoolteachers but the LINK was responsible for any additional recurrent costs which were met from a substantial reserve fund that had been established. The clinic was fully equipped with basic furniture plus medical and surgical equipment bought by the Durham medical working party. I had negotiated with authorities at the government hospital at Teyateyaneng that it would staff the clinic on behalf of the LINK but later the Ministry of Health went one stage further and agreed to supply all surgical stores and medicines. It was reported in 1996[69] that the clinic was fully operational each day of the week which was a great benefit to very many people in the region.

By the middle of 1995 all building was complete and the contractors moved off the site leaving it to become a living entity motivating the local population to become a learning community. With the primary school roll now totalling 260 children (and rising to over 400 two years later in 1997) our earlier fears of a decline in numbers because other providers had lower fees were unfounded. The evidence seemed to suggest that parents were willing, when able, to pay for the better-quality facilities now being provided by the LINK. Children attended the school throughout the week whilst 120 ladies went to instructional courses in sewing and forty others on courses in knitting. Of these 160 ladies many were mothers of children in the school so, with fathers retraining in the workshop, Ha Mohatlane Community Education Centre really did become a centre of education for the whole family that, on Sundays, worshipped within their weekday learning environment bringing the word of their faith closer to their sustaining work. Overcoming a false, artificial division, worship was becoming an integral element of work. The main hall was being used, as originally designed, as a regular place of religious worship but also during weekdays as a place for meetings and social community events. It was reported that, at this time, people from 'over twenty villages (were) participating in activities at the centre'[70] so it also acted as a meeting place for the convergence of a dispersed population.

As 1995 became 1996 the warden continued to lead a lively enterprise and was able to bring the adult training centre into full operation with the start of men's training courses in metalwork, welding and carpentry thanks to the assistance of a volunteer from the American Peace Corps, Mr Jerry Densmore. He had travelled from Hemet, a small town in southern California, United States of America,[71] leaving his wife and daughter there, to arrive in Mohatlane on Friday, 11th July 1997. The centre was infected by his enthusiasm and energy which in no small measure was responsible for the expansion of the workshop's training programme to offer welding, arc-welding, soldering, brazing and gas-cutting. There were twenty-four men registered for the carpentry course and fifteen for bricklaying.

Whole families could now engage in holistic learning especially as another Peace Corps volunteer, Colin Powel, had made a strong impact on the library that had brought a steady stream of borrowers into the centre.[72] During the early planning of the centre seven years previously it was essential to promote the notion of self-help so, in addition to the collection of stones, one of the first pieces of equipment bought when building started was a hand-operated concrete-block-making machine. This was now facing an increased demand for its products with a recorded 25,496 blocks being sold. Also in demand were the products of the poultry unit with a recorded sale in 1996 of 179 broilers and 96,945 eggs.

As the years changed so did the centre's activities and a schools' choir competition was one of the highlights of 1997, which also saw the accommodation of a three-day teachers' conference. Mohatlane was becoming known as rather more than a dot on the map of Lesotho. The LINK's community education centre was chosen as the workshop venue of The Lesotho Society of the Mentally Handicapped. At this stage of its life expansion was being discussed and three extra classrooms were planned and were eventually built at the side of the main building. The original unique design of the centre had allowed for extra space to be added at the end of each 'finger' but no record seems to exist as to why the new classrooms were not built as intended but separated at the side of the main building. The Lesotho Ministry of Education supported this expansion by providing three more full-time professional teachers thus relieving the LINK of the burden of having to pay for private teachers. With over 400 children in the primary school, and the possibility of that number increasing in response to the United Nation's Second Millennium Development Goal to achieve universal primary education for all children by 2015, the demand for space looked assured for some years to come.

Charity shops are a familiar sight in most towns and cities in County Durham and in 1997 the idea was exported to Ha Mohatlane where a shop was opened at the centre. Durham received a request for nearly-new clothes and materials to stock the shop, the proceeds of which were used to help with the running costs of the centre. Thanks to the continued support of the British High Commission, the labour of many volunteers in Durham and the gifts of many people, a forty-foot container was despatched in April, 1997 to arrive in time for the clothes to protect many a Mosotho from the bitter cold of Lesotho's winter months. Not all clothes were sold as, trying to maintain the notion of cooperation, some were donated to the Lesotho Disaster Management Unit and to a local shelter for young people. The shop also acts as a retail outlet for many high-quality garments made during the sewing and knitting training courses. The standards reached were impressive and in no small measure due to another US Peace Corps Volunteer, Mrs. Mary Levander.[73] At the National Agricultural Show entries from the Ha Mohatlane knitting training courses gained the major award.

What was less encouraging was the threat posed to the clinic despite its intensive use by the local population. Heavy demands were made upon this facility during 1997 when 9,780 patients were treated or referred but despite, or perhaps because of, this heavy use the Ministry of Health decided to reopen the government clinic at Pilot about three miles (5 kms) from the centre. This put additional strain on arrangements with the Teyateyaneng Hospital to run the centre's clinic on behalf of the LINK and from this point onwards long-term planning and organising has been difficult. The LINK had responded to a local request that the attendance figures show was strongly justified. It was reported that in 1998[74] the clinic was open five days each week with a recorded demand for the year of 8,263 general patients; 1,374 pregnancy advice; 1,046 under-five clinic; and 1,212 family planning[75] attendances. In addition sixty-six village health workers had been trained. Such an active use made all the hard work seem very worthwhile but it also made the lingering doubts about the future of the clinic more intense.

During this year, 1998, Lesotho experienced social violence on an unprecedented scale with serious looting, arson, riots and violence.[76] None of the LINK's personnel or property was seriously affected but inevitably there followed a period of social instability and widespread tension amongst the population. Maseru was extensively damaged taking some years to rebuild and return to its former condition. This was the febrile atmosphere surrounding all the LINK's work at this time. It was not a happy period for the LINK as that year, following a decision to increase the number of classrooms, there were the first hints of financial difficulties at the centre with repeated references to the difficulty of covering recurrent costs. These additional classrooms were paid for by the British High Commission but there are times when the attraction of a large donation can lead to impetuous decisions resulting in financial difficulties and it is better to remain small and be able to cover recurrent expenditure. It is difficult for enthusiasts to resist the temptation of funding for expansion and to understand that any capital expenditure incurs a running cost. In recognition of this, as a 'rule-of-thumb' guideline, it is wise to set aside at least one per cent per annum of any capital expenditure to cover recurrent costs that spending will inevitably incur. This was a principle that guided the funding of all our projects during the LINK's first phase but now, after a vigorous beginning, the clinic itself has had an uncertain existence before its story moves on to 2010.

At some indeterminate point a local group attempted, unsuccessfully, to run the clinic. The lack of success was not surprising as within the group there were some dubious practices and clinic services for the region were moved by the Ministry of Health, much to the annoyance of the local population, to a less accessible place which is when the LINK resumed control of the clinic at the end of 2009. Shortly afterwards, in an unsolicited approach to the LINK's executive officers, a group of doctors at the Royal Free Hospital, London,[77] explained they were undertaking a fund-raising run to buy medical equipment for the Maluti Hospital, which lies to the north-west of Mapoteng, some 23 miles (37 kms) by road from the Ha Mohatlane Community Education Centre. No doubt the good tarred road that connects the two places encouraged the LINK once again to cross denominational boundaries to reach agreement with the Adventist Maluti Hospital, considered to be one of the best in Lesotho, to run the clinic at Mohatlane for one day every week. In addition to providing essential medical services requested by the local people this reopening of the clinic will help to restore something of the comprehensiveness of the community education centre.

Eight years after I first began to think seriously about building a community education centre at Ha Mohatlane, and four years after it opened, the warden, Rose Sebeta, was able to report[78] continuing progress 'to prepare God's people for works of service', some to be welders, some to be carpenters, some to be builders, some to be teachers, all of whom were able to worship together in the centre, whatever their religious denomination, 'so that the body of Christ may be built up until we all reach unity'. Unity has been exemplified as we drew together disparate agencies; British government aid, Irish aid, United States Peace

Corps volunteers, South African financial support, the European Union, the Lesotho Ministries of Health, Education and Finance, the skills and qualifications of numerous Christians, irrespective of their denomination allegiance, plus the financial and prayerful support of hundreds of people who have donated thousands of pounds in addition to their taxes dispensed by statutory agencies.

At Ha Mohatlane Community Education Centre children are now being educated in comfortable conditions so that in the knowledge of the Son of God they may become mature, and, with their parents working in well-equipped workshops and reading in a well-stocked library, or worshipping together in the main hall as One Body in Christ, they may, especially when benefiting from the comfort, care and advice of the clinic, all 'attain to the whole measure of the fullness of Christ'.[79]

---

1. Ephesians 4:11–13 (NIV).
2. During discussions with Philip Mokuku and Peter Green on Friday, 8th November 1991, Steven Molokeng accepted the offer of appointment as the LINK's administrator in Lesotho. To accept the post Steven was willing to take a reduction of one third in the salary he was then receiving as Anglican Schools' Secretary. This appointment, variously called 'Administrator' or 'Executive Officer', was originally funded by a grant from the UK Charities Aid Foundation. It was the LINK's first full-time salaried post.
3. See Chapter Six: Ha Popa (p. 147).
4. Collingwood, Jeremy, *As a Witness to the Light: the story of Chengelo School in Zambia* (Terra Nova Publications, International, Bradford on Avon, Wiltshire, UK. 2006).
5. Proverbs 22:6 (NIV).
6. 1 Corinthians 12:8 (NIV): To one there is given through the Spirit the message of wisdom, to another the message of knowledge by means of the same spirit.
7. 1 Corinthians 12:28 (NIV): And in the church God has appointed first of all apostles, second prophets, third teachers, then workers of miracles, also those having gifts of healing, those able to help others, those with gifts of administration, and those speaking in different kinds of tongues.
8. Anderson, Ewan, 'Ha Mohatlane Community Education Centre: Feasibility Study', report to Durham-Lesotho Diocesan LINK: September 1991: p. 9.
9. The 1991 estimate is based on the 1986 census figure enhanced by an assumed population growth of 2.6 per cent.
10. The largest population was found at Ha Libehampaba with a 1991 estimate of 1,133 assuming a population increase of 2.6 per cent. Anderson: Op. cit. Annex 3: p.45.

11. See Anderson, Ewan, op. cit. as above: Annex 4.
12. Gay, John et al., *Poverty in Lesotho: A Mapping Exercise* (Sechaba Consultants, Maseru, Lesotho. June 1991).
13. Alan Hethrington's visit was another example of the practical support the LINK received from Durham County Council which gave him leave of absence and paid the travel expenses for his visit.
14. This visit took place on Monday, 12th December 1988. At this time the Treasurer was Dr David Gregory-Smith who handled all the complex issues involved in co-funding and the transmission of large sums of money through the international financial system.
15. See Chapter Ten: Saddle-Sore (p. 281).
16. Anderson, Ewan, Ha Mohatlane Community Education Centre: Feasibility Study: Annex 8: p.50.
17. Durham-Lesotho LINK Annual Report 1989: p.17. No reliable evidence can be found for the figure of 300 pupils given in this report nor for the description of a 'mud and stone church building'.
18. Jill Sharp of the Canadian International Development Agency on Tuesday, 9th May 1989.
19. Lynda Chalker served as Minister of State for Overseas Development at the Foreign Office in the Conservative government from 1989 to 1997.
20. Based on Ewan Anderson's survey measurements on p.58 of his study: September 1991.
21. Philippians 1:9–10a (GNB).
22. During a telephone conversation with Guy Mustard on Friday, 12th December 1990.
23. John Bailey and Dick Colquhoun were professional journalists from The Sunderland Echo. John Bailey also edited the Roman Catholic journal *The Northern Cross.*
24. *'MOHO – Together,* No. 3 (November 1991) p. 3. I acknowledge with thanks the quotations used from this article.
25. Anderson, Ewan, Ha Mohatlane Community Education Centre: Feasibility Study, report to Durham-Lesotho Diocesan LINK: September 1991. The names of the villages and the Chiefs are listed in Annex 2 of the Report: p. 43.
26. The President of South Africa F. W. de Klerk announced, in February 1990, the dismantling of the apartheid system and this had a noticeable impact, lessening the demand for Basotho men to work, mainly as hewers, in the gold mines. It was against this background our study was conducted. The first democratic non-racial elections took place in South Africa on Wednesday, 27th April 1994.
27. Gay, John et al., *Poverty in Lesotho: A Mapping Exercise* (Sechaba Consultants, Maseru. Lesotho. June 1991).
28. National Audit Office 2005 Press Release – Improving School Attendance in England. See www.nao.org.uk.
29. Ambrose David, *Summary of Events in Lesotho*: Volume 17, No. 1, First Quarter 2010: p. 8.
30. Anderson, Ewan, op.cit.: see p. 27a for mapping of primary school attendance.

31. At the beginning of the school year in 1991 (when data was collected) the exchange rate for the Maluti against the Great Britain Pound was M0.2016 to £1.00. Assuming there were no increases in fees during the child's primary school education at the Anglican Church's Ha Mohatlane School it would cost £830 (M167.20) for each child to pass through Standards one to six (before going on to Standard seven, at an additional fee, at Mesapela school at Ha Nkalimeng).
32. Anderson, Ewan W., op. cit.: p. 40.
33. *'MOHO – Together.* No. 3 (November 1991) p. 3. 'A New Community Education Centre'.
34. Our information was that during November 1991 inflation was running at 17½ per cent per annum.
35. Pippa Moore had replaced Jill Sharp at the Canadian International Development Agency when I renewed our request for funding on Wednesday, 19th February 1992.
36. At this time, Wednesday, 1st July 1992, this was Bernard Ryelandt.
37. See Chapter Eleven: Yap! Yap! Yap! (p. 317).
38. Astley, Jeff, *'MOHO – Together* (November 1992) p. 1: 'The Ha Mohatlane Project'.
39. Among those present were Steven Molokeng (LINK executive officer); Alina Pholosi (schools' manager for Teyateyaneng); 'Mè Motopi (primary school head teacher); Bernard Duma (parish priest); Mr. Moteane (architect); Rob Bianchi (who was investigating the possibilities for the LINK Youth Activities Project); Colin Griffiths (a LINK volunteer).
40. Philippians 1:9–10a (GNB).
41. At a meeting in the European Delegation building on Wednesday, 7th October 1992.
42. Philippians 4:6 (NEB).
43. See Chapter Seven: Sing a New Song (p. 187).
44. I am indebted to the anonymous writer of this extract from *'MOHO – Together*, No. 6 (May 1993) p. 5.
45. Sharpville was an apartheid township adjacent to Sebokeng near Johannesburg. The Sharpeville Massacre took place on Monday, 21st March 1960. Sixty-nine black residents were killed when South African police opened fire on the crowd leaving an indelible hatred that this graffiti spectacularly expressed.
46. See Chapter One: In the beginning was the Word (p. 1).
47. An obituary was published in *'MOHO – Together*, No. 6 (May 1993) p. 4.
48. Saturday, 3rd April 1993.
49. Our first meeting was on Saturday, 24th April 1993 to be followed by a second longer, more detailed discussion, two days later on Monday, 26th April 1993 when he approved our suggestion that the dam might be used for young people's water activities as part of our proposed youth activities project.
50. Luke 12:34 (NIV): For where your treasure is, there your heart will be also.
51. The Hon. Brigadier General Godfrey Miyanda was representing the President who was leading a ten-day period of national mourning following the aeroplane crash in which the Zambian national football team was killed.

52. See chapter 7: Sing a New Song (p. 187).
53. Aelred and I met frequently at my home in Durham and at Emmaus, Sunderland, a Retreat House of the Community of the Resurrection, Sunderland. He was a monk of the Community and worked in South Africa from 1960 when he became a close friend of Steve Biko. After visiting the UK for his mother's funeral in 1977 he was banned from returning to apartheid South Africa but went instead to Lesotho and lived at Masite for four years. He stayed in touch with Steve Biko's mother through letters that I smuggled through to her. He died at Mirfield, West Yorkshire, on Sunday, 17th October 2004 aged 81 years.
54. Friday, 24th September 1993. See Volume 15 of Peter Green's photographic records.
55. Telephone message from the Second Secretary, Mr. Paul O'Connor, Thursday, 27th January 1994.
56. Matthew 22:17–22 (NIV): Is it right to pay taxes to Caesar or not? But Jesus, knowing their evil intent, said, 'You hypocrites, why are you trying to trap me? Show me the coin used for paying the tax.' They brought him a denarius, and he asked them, 'Whose portrait is this? And whose inscription?' 'Caesar's,' they replied. Then he said to them, 'Give to Caesar what is Caesar's, and to God what is God's.' When they heard this, they were amazed. So they left him and went away.
57. Green, Peter, 'Personal Daily Journal' (Tuesday, 1st February 1994).
58. See Chapter Seven: Sing a new Song (p. 187).
59. See Chapter Five: Trees of the field (p. 109).
60. See Chapter Six: Ha Popa (p. 147).
61. See Chapter Seven: Sing a new Song (p. 187).
62. I met with John Clark on Wednesday, 16th March 1994 in his office at Partnership House, Waterloo Road.
63. Partnership for World Mission website <http//www.pwm-web.org.uk/>.
64. Jenkins, David, In *One in Word and Work* (1992) p. 3.
65. 'The First 10 years Durham-Lesotho LINK' anniversary celebration brochure 1996: p. 1.
66. Wednesday, 30th March 1994.
67. Wordsworth, William, (1770–1850): *I wandered Lonely as a Cloud.*
68. *Durham Network*: The Newspaper of the Diocese of Durham: No. 8: Lent, 1995: p. 16. See also *'MOHO – Together*, No. 10 (May 1995) pp. 2–4 (although some of the figures given there are inaccurate). The school children opened the centre in November 1994 and Philip Mokuku opened it 'officially' on Saturday, 4th February 1995.
69. Durham-Lesotho LINK: Annual Report, 1996: p. 4 (section 6.1).
70. Durham-Lesotho LINK: Annual Report, 1995: p. 5 (section 2.4.2).
71. *'MOHO – Together*, No. 15 (November 1997) p. 2. 'Letter from America' by Jerry Densmore.
72. *'MOHO – Together*, No. 24 (January 2003) p. 3.
73. *'MOHO – Together*, No. 18 (June 1999) p. 6. 'Ha Mohatlane Community Education Centre satisfies its communities' in which Mary Levander is inaccurately described as 'A second US Peace Corps volunteer'. She was, in fact, the third.

74. Durham-Lesotho LINK: Annual Report, 1998: p. 5 (section 5.1).

75. These figures taken from *'MOHO – Together*, No. 18 (June 1999) p. 6 are quoted only as a guide to the extent the clinic was being used at this time and not as an accurate statement of numbers receiving treatment because they disagree with those stated in the earlier issue for May 1998: No. 16: p. 3.

76. After a failed lawsuit challenging the legality of the March 1998 election vote in which the Lesotho Congress for Democracy won 79 of the 80 seats, rioting broke out across Lesotho. To quell the uprising the ANC government of South Africa led by Nelson Mandela sent South African troops into Lesotho on Tuesday, 22nd September 1998. The 700 South Africans were later joined by troops from Botswana but it was not until May of the following year that all foreign troops had withdrawn. It is variously reported that between 60 and 70 people were killed in the rioting and the subsequent invasion that was code-named Operation Boleas.

77. The Royal Free Hospital was founded in 1828 by a surgeon, William Marsden, to provide free treatment to the poor. It is a large teaching hospital and is now part of the Royal Free Hampstead National Health Service Trust.

78. *'MOHO – Together*, No. 16 (May 1998) p. 3. 'New Projects are born at Ha Mohatlane Community Education Centre'.

79. Ephesians 4:13 (NIV): so, as Paul envisaged, they 'will no longer be infants, tossed back and forth by the waves, and blown here and there by every wind of teaching and by the cunning and craftiness of men in their deceitful scheming. Instead speaking the truth in love, we will in all things grow up into him who is the Head, that is, Christ.'

Chapter Ten

Saddle-Sore

I (Paul) pray that you may be active in sharing your faith,
so that you[1] will have a full understanding
of every good thing we have in Christ.[2]

As a disciple of Christ, Paul was anxious that the wealthy churchman Philemon should share his Christian faith with the poor slave Onesimus who, by this time, was also a Christian. But why? They were both Christians so what more was there to share? Paul goes on to give a most extraordinary reason which is also surprising given the social context in which the incident takes place. Before he absconded Onesimus was Philemon's slave and now he, Philemon, was being told to share his faith so that he, the wealthy slave-owning churchman, 'will have a full understanding of every good thing we have in Christ'. It's rather like telling the Bishop of Lesotho and the Bishop of Durham to share their faith with a retired servant to improve episcopal understanding of the good things we enjoy as Christians! Therein lies a powerful lesson for the LINK most particularly for the relatively wealthy northern sector.

If Christians in Lesotho and Durham were to be bound together as One Body in Christ then it would only come about if people from both dioceses learned from each other through active sharing and participating in common experiences, accepting the consequences whether they are successes or failures. The LINK, if it were seriously striving to accomplish this relationship, had to make provision for Paul's edict and become 'active in sharing (our) faith' with each other. Only then would people of both dioceses learn what is involved in having 'a full understanding' of that sort of relationship with each other and with Christ. From its beginning the LINK had provided for people to share their faith through its development projects and programmes, including the bringing together of people through its programme of individual and group exchange visits. Whilst the LINK was in its infancy (although at the time we didn't know that it was, as its strength to survive into its mid-twenties was then unknown) we experimented with visits by clergy, youth and adults. We built into the programme an active exchange of visitors between the two dioceses but that would, we all recognised, involve only a very small number of people. Furthermore, those Basotho that could travel to Durham in the late 1980s, even with generous subsidies, would be unlikely to come from the poor, remote mountain areas of Lesotho where people live in comparative isolation and poverty and who were likely to remain isolated from Durham Christians visiting Lesotho.

So, how was Paul's teaching implemented? What did 'sharing your faith' imply for the LINK? By the close association of development strategies to the Christian faith it has actively promoted the teaching of the gospel, not only telling of the Good News but practising it so that joy and sorrow are common experiences; so that the discipline of the gospel permeates throughout all its activities involving the participation of both north and south; by accepting that not all sharing results in equal division; recognising that sharing of the abstract is as important as contributing to the concrete; that sharing involves participating and, therefore, responsibility; above all knowing that our mutual faith is the embodiment of Basotho and Dunelmian and Christ.

The teaching of our faith, by its application to projects and programmes, has been supported throughout the twenty-five-year life of the LINK by a second component of spreading the gospel message: preaching. Most importantly this has been done in both dioceses by lay and ordained representatives from the other diocese preaching the same message thus showing that no matter what shade of brown or white we were born, or whether we reside in Lesotho or Durham, in Christ we all live by the same principles. In the beginning was the word and we lost no time in putting that into action. Until we brought more people into the orbit of the LINK this task inevitably fell on the leadership and just two days after the 'official' start of the LINK it was Pentecost and I was speaking at St. Agnes Church, Teyateyaneng, the first big 'camp' north of Maseru. The Holy Spirit is not the easiest of notions to convey and I was thankful for my education as a teacher as I was surrounded by scores of school children. Then at the parish communion service I preached to the adults on 'Jesus is for everyone' before a quick change to attend a *pitso* to be a listener to none other than General Lekhanya, then military dictator of Lesotho, as he tried to convince his sceptics that Lekhanya was for everyone.

But it wasn't all happening in Lesotho. The next month, June 1986, the Suffragan Bishop of Lesotho, Donald Nestor, visited Durham diocese to promote the LINK. Without getting saddle-sore but no less travel weary, he covered many miles in Durham carrying out an active programme of visits to working parties, parishes and people. Within a couple of days of arriving he was preaching a sermon in Durham Cathedral on Sunday, 22nd June 1986 on 'Christian Mission'. Wanting to make full use of his presence we arranged, with the help of Newcastle Polytechnic (as it then was), for Donald to record a video interview and message. That film was shown to the Durham diocesan synod on Saturday, 1st November 1986, a year after the synod had first given its support to the formation of the LINK.[3] The Synod started with a recorded greeting from Philip Mokuku after which David Jenkins started his presidential address by saying:

> The most important item on our Synod agenda today is, I believe, the presentation about our developing diocesan link with the Diocese of Lesotho. It is important because it invites us to develop our thinking and praying and acting about being members of a worldwide church. This is a church that is worshipping, living and suffering in all sorts of places and under all sorts of circumstances, many of them different from our own, many of them with surprising echoes of our own.
>
> … we want, and we need, to have our ways of seeing things and our ways of doing things constantly challenged and expanded … So I look forward to the presentation and I expect that it will provide us with much food for thought, reflection and prayer …[4]

I then took a series of questions about the first year of the LINK's life and future prospects. During that first year we got off to an active start. Although, in the past twenty-five years, there have been a few gaps in our formal preaching the LINK has expounded the gospel widely in both dioceses, demonstrating a unity of purpose in a common faith. This was spectacularly demonstrated in January 2008 when ten young, enthusiastic, and two not-so-young but equally enthusiastic, Basotho conducted an evangelistic mission in Durham. Africa came to Europe: but it very nearly didn't happen. It was 'touch' (down at Dubai) and 'go' (back to Johannesburg). Fearful of British immigration law the airline on which they were travelling tried to prevent the group from coming to the United Kingdom and, having flown them to Dubai, then took them back to Johannesburg. After much prayer and high-level parliamentary protest they were flown back by the same airline using the same immigration documentation and the same tickets. Nothing was achieved by this erroneous and intrusive officialdom except to heighten public interest in the mission and increase the Devil's concern at what was going on. William Cooper[5] was correct, not for the first time, in his poem-turned-hymn: *God moves in a mysterious way, His wonders to perform.* In the context of this airline confusion the original title of the poem was equally relevant: *Conflict: Light Shining out of Darkness.*

The Basotho brought us the blinding light of Christ as they moved around the northern diocese of the LINK singing, dancing, speaking and acting, in twenty-six schools where 4,300 pupils benefited from their youthful enthusiasm; in churches that echoed with their testimonies of faith; in the market place where shoppers paused to listen to the gospel that is so often imprisoned in a church building for the benefit of those who already believe. It very nearly didn't happen but when it did it was greatly blessed.[6] The LINK has now lived through a full generation. None of those young Christian Basotho were even born when a pioneer of the LINK's preaching ministry in Durham made his impact twenty-eight years previously. Ignatius Malebo, the rector of St. Matthias Church, Peka, north of Maseru, was a popular figure who toured Durham diocese in late 1980 and early 1981 when he did much to prepare the northern ground for the growing of the first shoots of the LINK before it blossomed in 1986.

The southern ground was also prepared years before my April 1986 preaching tour with Philip Mokuku although it was then that it came to life in the mountainous Thaba-Tseka district of Lesotho.[7] That work expanded as I continued to promote the LINK and exercise my ministry throughout the dioceses of Lesotho and Durham, drawing us all closer to Paul's charge: 'be active in sharing your faith, so that you will have a full understanding of every good thing we have in Christ'.

It was exhausting work that gave me a sympathetic admiration for those who had spent many saddle-hours as exponents of the faith in the years before ladies' nylon tights became available to the tough adventurer! It was a member of the Society of the Sacred Mission who first introduced me to this splendid garment for the horse rider. Australian David Wells, who gave many years of his life to serving the Basotho, was concerned at the long hours I was spending in a variety of saddles on a variety of horses and passed on this valuable information that led to my occasionally using this rarely acknowledged article of equestrian gear. My wife looked askance when I asked her to buy me two pairs of ladies' tights and, as someone who is only just over five feet (1.5 m) tall, received her share of peculiar looks as I am over six feet (1.8 m) tall! It was worth the embarrassment as for some long rides they did prevent chafing of the inside of the legs but I always questioned whether the struggle to get into them, and out of them when nature demanded, was worth the effort. I became hardened and, without nylon tights, made frequent comfortable rides as I toured the country with Philip Mokuku and Donald Nestor, living a three-dimensional life, north, south, east, west, in lowlands, foothills and mountains. Believing that Jesus is for everyone we made sure that the LINK, with the gospel message it carried, was denied to no one.

The first half of 1987 brought Lesotho to Durham in many different forms. The LINK was in its first year so people were anxious to learn more about this distant diocese with which they were working. The LINK was strengthened in Durham with a heavy programme of talks, sermons and speeches to synods, churches, special meetings and displays. Every week there was someone to satisfy. Curiosity produced a remarkably vigorous demand for information. Everyone seemed to be enjoying the adventure even if, at this time for most people, it was only of the armchair variety. There was little excuse for anyone in Durham not knowing how to pronounce 'Lesotho', or where it was, or what the LINK was aiming to achieve. A former Bishop of Lesotho, Desmond Tutu, timed his visit perfectly when he arrived to receive the Honorary Freedom of the City of Durham on Tuesday, 10th March 1987 and, later, to preach in Durham Cathedral, packed to standing room only. A couple of months later the Lesotho Mothers' Union were not far behind with a representative group that travelled round Durham diocese supporting their witness with their singing and dancing and in the process capturing much more than people's attention.

These events kept the LINK alive in front of the people of Durham but their enthusiasm had to be contained as it was to be October 1987 before I was available to pursue the work again in Lesotho. It wasn't only time that was at a premium. There was little money for travelling which was perhaps fortunate at this stage as it allowed the notion of the LINK, and the ideas it incorporated, to become soundly embedded in those who would form the bedrock of its development. After an adventurous journey, for which tickets only became available at the last minute via Harare, Zimbabwe, Friday, 2nd October 1987 dawned for me over the Zambezi and ended in Lesotho without any luggage. Since I had suffered this loss many times around the world I went comfortably to bed in pyjamas that, with my notebooks, journal and passport, I always carry in my hand baggage. Despite my lack of possessions how could I but be cheerful after reading a greeting left for me by Philip Mokuku written in his own inimitable style: 'Welcome to Lesotho and thank you for giving us and the country your enriching presence once again'!

I must confess I didn't feel qualified for Philip's complimentary welcome as, with the minimum of clothing, I wondered quite how I was going to cope on a planned five-day trek in the south of the country. In Maseru everyone was being kind, spontaneously offering me money from their meagre budgets to re-equip myself. Then the weather came to the rescue making difficult decisions easier to take. Rain fell extensively, flooding the Nohana region where, with Philip, I was to have taken the message of the LINK to parishes and schools. Roads became impassable; cattle were drowning so the trek had to be cancelled much to my disappointment as it would have been a return for me to the remote southern region in which I started my educational work in July 1973. For those people who had prepared for confirmation the cancellation of the Bishop's visit was of greater disappointment as they would now have to wait for many months before his next opportunity to visit the region. Back in Maseru that which was lost was found, after a ten-day search, and how pleased I was. If this is what it feels like to be reunited with your luggage how excited the father must have been to be reunited with his profligate son.[8]

Not far off the main road to the south of Lesotho the 6,820-foot (2,080 m) Masite Mountain towers over the Priory of Our Lady of Mercy, the Lesotho home of the Society of the Precious Blood.[9] This is an oasis of calm and a haven of peace where the Sisters' careful attention often revived my flagging spirit and revitalized my dwindling energy. It was from Masite, mid-October 1987, that Donald Nestor and I set out to reinforce the message of the gospel and spread news of the LINK, firstly in and around Makoetje. After driving on tar to Morija, then through the village of the King's country home, Matsieng, we followed a dirt track that took us to Mosoang, where new driving and navigation skills had to be employed as we followed a line of large stones marking the direction to our destination. They were difficult to see. The recent heavy rain had caused the grass to grow rapidly, disguising them from all but trained eyes so we were pleased to have with us the local priest, Willie Andrews, telling us when to turn at points that seemed to mark no apparent direction. After an hour of this sort of driving it became all too obvious how, even in a practical context, the straight and narrow is to be preferred to the winding and broad.[10] We were all relieved, including Willie who by now thought he had us completely lost, to be met by twenty local horsemen at what to us was an indeterminate spot.

There was a noisy welcome for us as the mounted escort formed two columns, one either side of the Suzuki with the headman, waving his stick, leading the way into the foothills. The men, all dressed in traditional Basotho blankets, made a colourful and noisy display but in our vehicle it was stifling as eighty hooves stirred clouds of fine dust into the air. To get through narrow passes now that we were in the foothills the horses converged into touching distance from us so driving, which by now I had taken over from Donald, became increasingly difficult. I could barely see through the fog so it was with some relief that we changed from mechanical to natural horse power.

We left the vehicle in a small village and accompanied by the horsemen rode for a couple of hours up and down mountains, through rivers and round *dongas* but always through stunningly beautiful country: it was pleasant riding. Moments before the sun set we rode into the Makoetje valley to be greeted by much cheering, handshaking and laughter, mainly at two white men dressed in blankets and one, at least, with a saddle-sore rear end! It was all good-humoured. There was just enough light to see that this was a fertile valley with a few scattered mature trees. Very soon the sun had had enough for one day and went to bed as we went to our spacious rectangular hut close to the large Church of St. Mary built of local stone. It was then that bowls of hot water were produced for us to wash before tea, coffee and cakes appeared; this was a highly organised and welcoming community.

As the dusky quietness was only occasionally disturbed by animal noises, children playing and adults talking, Donald and I sat around the fire with the horsemen who had guided us here, watching the women prepare a meal. I was fascinated. They first boiled a whole chicken over a wood fire before frying it in a huge pan. It was then served on one metal plate and, in a greasy scrum, we all pulled pieces off the fowl to eat, which was when I discovered it contained all its innards including four small partly formed eggs that, rather strangely, made a pleasant addition. With only spoons to eat with it was either hunger or one's fingers. Well-cooked steamed bread, rice and carrots completed the first course which was followed by over-ripe bananas. And so to bed; it was cold so the five blankets I'd been given were carefully and usefully deployed.

Well rested and adequately fed the next morning, Thursday, 15th October 1987, Donald confirmed sixty candidates before celebrating communion to which people came in their hundreds, flocking in from surrounding villages not only to worship but also to socialise with friends and family. The service was enhanced by the powerful singing of a girls' choir that had been imported for the occasion from Matsieng, lying many miles away across a mountain range. They had had a long walk despite which each singer was smartly dressed in a sparklingly white blouse and black gymslip clasped at the waist with a black and white belt: how did they keep them so clean? It was when Donald and I were administering during this open-air celebration that, with drums banging and voices singing, hundreds of members of the African Zionist Church marched over a nearby hill in their ritual robes (rather like colourful academic gowns). These were but a few of the largest religious denomination in southern

Africa which is estimated to have some sixteen million adherents.[11] It looked like a 'takeover' but turned out to be nothing more than well-behaved, if boisterous, 'backing-music' to our celebration and also a timely reminder that others approach Christ by different routes.

After our service there were speeches, presentations and singing plus much bargaining and bartering in an impromptu market rather like the English 'car-boot sale'. This provided an excellent opportunity to bring Durham and Lesotho closely together as Willie Andrews and I walked among the Basotho displaying our collection of large coloured photographs, talking about the LINK and answering questions that came so thick and fast that I would have understood nothing without Willie's interpretation. In the excitement of the moment my *'butlè, butlè'* ('slowly, slowly') had little effect as we talked about school books, medical supplies and the provision of work that didn't take men away from home. Their interest in the gospel was at its most intense when its message related most closely to everyday living. They seemed to enjoy the close contact that our 'walkabout' allowed. 'Concentrate on the practical; don't try to explain everything but simplify something; promise only what you can produce' I kept telling myself and 'remember, the Basotho like stories'.

By lunch time I was beginning to wilt but that mattered little as by then almost everyone had found somewhere to sit and share their food. Willie and I staggered to the kitchen where we had another chicken, this time with *moroho* (spinach), potatoes, rice, beetroot and salad followed by dessert of home-grown peaches, jelly, hot custard and fresh fruit with masses of steamed bread. All of this was well shaken down in the saddle immediately after the last mouthful by a fast ride to Mosoang where we collected our vehicle to drive to Morutoang and then back to Masite. Once there, in the Chapel of Our Lady Mother of Mercy,[12] we commorated the thirtieth anniversary of Sister Diana's profession.

Spreading the message the next day was somewhat less enervating. Just ten miles (16 kms) due north of Masite lies the village of Rankhelepe in the lowlands below the Qeme Plateau which forms a natural barrier protecting it from Maseru. It is not the easiest of places to find so when we took a wrong turning near a primary school in which I had worked years previously we had to consult with the only other person in sight; a herd boy . He directed us with detailed accuracy to take us half an hour later to within five miles (8 kms) of St. John the Baptist Church. There we were met by the 'household cavalry' of fifteen donkeys. They were all being ridden bareback by young boys most wrapped in little more that a blanket held in place by a large blanket-pin. The boys, all of whom were 7 to 8 years old, rode without reins, clasping the animal's mane with both hands and their knees gripping the animal's belly with their feet underneath. At their head was the leader waving aloft his flag of office, a piece of off-white tattered cloth attached to a stick, and still remaining upright on the donkey's back. It was an impressive display especially as he was one of two boys wearing animal skins, the forerunner of the Basotho blanket. Animal skins were rarely seen in the late 1980s. It was a time when one distinctive ceremonial feature of herd boys was their thunderous whistles which on this day they blew indiscriminately, or apparently so: the noise was deafening.

As we neared the village of widely scattered rondavels a man on a fine grey horse took over the authority of the head boy, riding his horse zigzagging from side to side in advance of the two columns. It was quite difficult to avoid the rocks, gullies, donkeys and the horse whilst not stalling the engine. Much shouting urged the procession onwards and, in the lowest possible gear, we emerged out of a *donga* to see the village schoolgirls, dressed in white blouses and royal blue gymslips, gathered in two lines – but where were the boys? They couldn't all be on herd duty could they? By now we had been joined by more horses each decorated with strips of coloured cloth round their left foreleg. At breakneck speed they and the donkeys charged between the two ranks of girls and I was expected to drive at speed between the horses and wave my greetings at the same time.

After listening to the musical welcome of the Mothers' Union, smartly dressed in their blue uniforms, we started the service outside with no protection from the blazing sun which was intent on changing my colour to that of the Basotho. Ninety-three confirmations, one short talk from me and hundreds of communicants later the sun had almost succeeded. Everything was well organised and orderly even when one of the confirmation candidates decided it was time to breastfeed her baby; even that was accomplished with calm composure. It was not until the administration of communion that things began to go awry. Some of the girls, for this great day dressed in white bridal gowns, white gloves and white shoes, decided that they should remove their shoes. I don't quite know why but as a consequence the white gloves were no longer white and so they, too, had to be removed before receiving the bread and wine. Some order was restored before we began the back-breaking stooping to serve hundreds of communicants kneeling low on the ground. Ladies with bowed heads shielded in wide-brimmed hats made it particularly difficult to administer the chalice but it was their day and we survived the two very hot hours.

I then involved the children who seemed to enjoy walking around showing off the large pictures of Durham. I answered questions before singing, dancing and speeches followed with a strong appeal for the LINK to do something about providing a primary school and to help with the village development. Taking special note of the second of these two appeals I returned some years later to assist the Church and the school with the planting of many hundreds of trees which improved the stark and barren landscape.[13] To help with the school feeding programme the LINK also established a poultry unit at the secondary school[14] so this visit brought together both the word and the work of the gospel into a practical Christian development. However, that was to be some months away. Now, as I moved around, they wanted to know if people in Durham went to church, owned cows, had to pay to go to school, worked hard, had many children. Soon the time came for us to take our place amid the 'household cavalry' for a ceremonial departure with Donald driving behind a horse, the left rear leg of which we managed to hit when it suddenly stopped right in front of the Suzuki. Little damage was done to either animal or vehicle but a couple of miles further on we had another hold-up when one of the boys fell from his donkey which, like all the others, he was riding bareback. He was cared for by women who came out from a small group of huts to cheer us on our way. There the donkeys stopped and the horses turned back: we were on our own and at Masite we cleaned ourselves and rested. The day was almost complete. Compline[15] was peaceful and we went to bed relaxed.

Over the next three days visiting continued on much the same pattern at Emmanuel Church, Ngoatonyane; St. Barnabas Church, Masite (where, much to the silent consternation of Donald, someone slipped up with ecclesiastical titles introducing me as 'Bishop Peter'); and St. Stephen's High School, Mohale's Hoek. A quick switch the next day surrounded theology by forestry for four days (it was then more difficult to see the wood from the trees) after which a bumpy internal flight took Philip and me to Leribe for an even bumpier landing. Half an hour later as we took off from Leribe the pilot switched on the 'no-smoking' sign just moments before lighting a cigarette!

It was a smooth flight onward and upward over some dramatic mountain ranges to make a rather fearsome landing at Mokhotlong, the highest, coldest large 'camp' in Lesotho at 7,218 feet (2,200 m). The air strip[16] is at the top of an escarpment so, depending upon the wind direction at the time, it may be necessary, as it was for this visit, to fly directly toward the cliff positioning the altitude of the aircraft at just the right height so the undercarriage touches the runway at the edge of the cliff face. The door to the pilot's cockpit was still open so, through the smoke of his second cigarette, the rapidly approaching precipice suddenly looked precariously close as our altitude plummeted from thousands of feet to just a few. Never has the landing bump been more welcome. Was this a modern version of 'You of little faith, why are you so afraid?'[17] Perhaps, but I would rather deal with a Galilean storm any day.

Our destination the next day was the small village of Ha Senkoase that lies some three hours steady riding north-north-east of Mokhotlong. No one-day religion here. It was Saturday, 24th October 1987 when Michael Khang, the parish priest, led the way to the start of the wide, rock-strewn, gravel track that snaked away into the distant hills. The start of a trek is often the most difficult part. Once on the right track it is usually a matter of just following it but you have to find where it starts amid many converging pathways. Soon after we started there was an early problem with the swollen Mokhotlong River that recent rains had turned into a raging, noisy torrent which the horses did not like. Two of the five horsemen in the troop could not get their mounts near the river. Dismounted we led them all across the fragile concrete bridge which had no safety barriers. The rushing, foaming water, just a few inches from flooding over the bridge platform, and in some places coming through, looked very threatening. We were all aware of the danger of flash flooding in Lesotho's rivers, no one more so than myself, having lost a friend when he was caught in such a flood in this region during 1976.

Flash flooding at this time of year occurs after heavy falls of snow in the mountains are followed by a rapid thaw. Conditions in the Lesotho mountains during the first part of October 1987 were treacherous. An example of this atrocious weather and the cost to young lives was reported on Monday, 12th October 1987, in the South African newspaper *Evening Chronicle*, under the heading 'Frozen to Death':

> Eight herd boys frozen to death in freak blizzard which dumped snowdrifts up to nine feet deep on mountainous African kingdom of Lesotho. South African military planes and helicopters airlifted food to isolated villages.

The Mokhotlong mountain river was now swollen by the melting snow so as we crossed caution was not inappropriate. From the river valley the track rose steeply quickly taking us into a quiet valley where an energetic farmer had terraced a section of the steep hillside, something which is not frequently seen. Everywhere was colourless except for the unremitting shades of drab brown broken only by the dark shadows of hill upon hill. The track could not be seen directly underfoot but only as it stretched out in the distance before us as a lighter shade of brown. I wondered what lay beyond the hills around which it disappeared. I had no idea how long we would be in the saddle or what the conditions were likely to be. When you are already in the mountains to be told we were going 'into the hills' can be a little disconcerting.

Basotho horsemen hold both reins of their horse in one hand. One rein goes between the first and second fingers with the other between the third and fourth fingers of whichever hand is most convenient. This I mastered without too much trouble. Having, by now, spent many hours in the saddle one other small, useful skill I had managed to develop was riding for short periods across smooth ground without using the reins. This allowed me to take photographs from horseback. My present horse was going well and responding calmly to my riding so this was the first time I felt sufficiently confident to use my new ability to any extent. Philip was most concerned but my effort was short-lived as in the distance there was a large gathering of parishioners led by a formidable body of ladies in blue blouses, navy blue skirts and black hats. The Mothers' Union was on the march!

With their red banner flying high in the mountain breeze they processed out to meet us. Behind them was a group of eight men riding a motley troop of horses and, in this environment, looking very strange as none was wearing a blanket. They were all dressed in jackets and trousers with one man even sporting a tie. Was it, on this Saturday, their 'Sunday best' in respect for the bishop and his guest? I never did discover but it did look strange and, again, drab, dull and dreary in contrast to the colourful, enthusiastic and noisy welcome we received as the huge crowd led us to their small Church of St. Francis.

After the confirmation service and communion Philip spoke about the LINK and I talked about the woodland we hoped to plant at Mokhotlong (which we did eventually). Later I had to counter requests for the woodland to be in their village and it was then that I began to worry about building up false expectations and promoting jealousy. Some years later we sent school furniture.

Incongruous though it was, as we were about to leave the thirty-strong all-girl choir sang another song of welcome. This was followed by a second song during which they danced towards me with one girl holding a tin tray on which there were seven glass tumblers. The parish priest, Michael, translated for me. It was a song about recent hardships the community had experienced during the winter months and the tough life they lived in the mountains but, nevertheless, they asked their honoured guest to accept this gift. Knowing how little they had compared to how much I had it was all very touching and I wondered how much sacrifice there was in the gift; for me it would become my 'widow's mite'[18] story. But that was not the end. Philip insisted we could not take the gift on our horses and it should be delivered later to the Mokhotlong rectory where six of the seven glasses and the tin tray were delivered two days later by a lady who walked with them across the mountains; barefooted! They eventually arrived safely in Durham packed very carefully into my hand baggage.

Late afternoon we were back on our horses. We left to much cheering and handshaking for a quick ride, encouraged not to linger by a few drops of rain and the knowledge that the snow still on the peaks was not far away. The horse I'd ridden in the morning lived at Ha Senkoase so I now had to get used to another that lived in Mokhotlong. There is much horse-shuttling in the mountains. These frequent changes made me realise that riding in someone else's saddle is rather like wearing someone else's shoes; not very comfortable. I had hoped that at the end of the ride a small compensation might be the sighting of a flock of bald ibis, the bird from which the river takes its name, but we saw nothing as we returned over the wildly roaring Mokhotlong River, except a young woman collecting water in a battered metal can.

Next day we drove the short distance to Ha Mojakisane, a group of rondavels lying scattered just off the wide dirt track that continues south-east through the Kotisephola Pass at 10,630 feet (3,240 m). This pass is a mere 794 feet (242 m) below the grandeur of Thabana-Ntlenyana to the north-east which, at 11,424 feet (3,482 m), is the highest point in southern Africa. This massif lies about 16 miles (26 kms) south-east of Ha Mojakisane in a desolate region I explored eleven years previously in 1976 so now there was little incentive to ride beyond the village. Had we continued to follow the track we would have descended into the spectacular hairpin bends of the Sani Pass and across the border post with the Republic of South Africa. This time there was no question of continuing. The track was barred by a group of ferocious looking men, some mounted, others on foot, but all making a blood-curdling noise threateningly emphasized by flailing knobkerries.[19] Two undernourished white dogs prowled menacingly around snapping at men and horses alike as they advanced to surround the truck.

Even if the Sesotho was difficult to follow as it was submerged by the confused noise there was no doubt that Philip and Michael were ordered out of the truck to join the (welcome?) group. Just as I was thinking that they had been 'captured' and I had been left to drive the truck into the village, I was approached by half a dozen of the men wearing woollen hats, gum boots, shorts or trousers, with colourful blankets billowing. They made an awe-inspiring, even frightening, noise as I was ushered out of the truck and given a horse to mount. It may have been nothing more than a ceremonial welcome but I kept a wary eye on those treacherous knobkerries. A remarkable scene that, avoiding damage to myself and my camera, I failed to capture adequately. Nearer St. Peter's Church were some two hundred less aggressive-looking villagers who greeted us more calmly with songs and dances.

Philip conducted the confirmation service and the eucharist outside where wafers and words were in constant danger of being wafted away into the majestic hills and valleys that formed a commanding and formidable backdrop. A small copse of mature trees, an unusual sight in the harsh mountain climate, was growing near the stone-built church. I preached on cheating using the African story of people who went to a chief's feast pretending their gift of water was a celebration wine. After the services came the speeches. Philip and I spoke about the LINK and the Chief about relief supplies that were not getting through to the village of Mojakisane because someone was cheating![20]

Over lunch I was able to make closer contact with the people, meeting one man who attended the first educational course to be run in Lesotho's National University by St. Hild's College, Durham in 1966. During the twenty-one years that had since elapsed he had changed from being a teacher to a farmer but, he told me proudly, he still remembered the name of his tutor. He, Samuel Lemena, had the name, Mark Humphries, exactly right and on my return to Durham I was able to put them in touch again. Whilst ecclesiastic conversations were going on elsewhere I spoke with the schoolteachers and villagers learning that the school had a small tree nursery started at the behest of the nearby government nursery which was, in the years ahead, to supply the LINK. Like Ha Senkoase there was widespread poverty in the area declaring its austere presence in the uninhibited naked children running around with just one begging, in well-rehearsed English, 'twenty-cents please'. Little wonder that pneumonia is the second biggest killer of children in the Lesotho mountains.[21]

After a long session the next morning with the head teacher of St. Michael's Primary School we returned to the air strip where, in a small shed, we were weighed with our baggage. Since the weights on the ancient bar scales were a mixture of imperial and metric the accuracy of the recorded load was in some considerable doubt. The unexpected arrival of an army helicopter delivering emergency food and fuel supplies served to remind us how tough life can be at eight to ten thousand feet (2,440 to 3,000 m) and the swarms of people how great was the need. Two army salutes later we left on time after reading a crudely written poster inviting people to the home of the local German medic to read newspapers between two and four o'clock on Saturday afternoons. This was his effort to get people better informed of local and international news. Once in the air, despite the combining of metric and imperial measures, the flight arrived safely in Maseru.

Other LINK activities fully occupied me during the next four days but I then found an afternoon to research old parish records that whisked me back 111 years to 1876. It was a uniquely strange sensation to be reading the copperplate handwriting of the Rev'd John Widdicombe,[22] one of the first two Anglican ordained priests in Lesotho. It is often overlooked that in his early work in the Leribe district he was accompanied by a layman, Willie Lacy from London, about whom we know very little, but it is evidence of the groundbreaking presence of the laity from the start of evangelisation in Lesotho. Lacy and Widdicombe were based in Hlotse (Leribe) from 1876 to 1906 and it was to Leribe that I drove on Sunday, 1st November 1987, this time with a bishop visiting for a Partners in Mission conference, Daniel Omolo, from the diocese of Maseno West, Kenya. As we swung round a bend just outside Teyateyaneng we were confronted with a police road block and its supporting armed soldiers. This is one hazard with which Widdicombe and Lacy did not have to contend. We were stopped but as my papers and those of Daniel were complete and in order we were not delayed, questioned or arrested and we went on our way northward.

At Hlotse we made a short detour to pass Widdicombe's old house and the church he built which we found in a sad condition. On the opposite side of the tarred road was the Convent of the Holy Name, my northern sanctuary whenever I needed a safe haven. At Butha-Buthe we met Philip Mokuku in that Basotho centre of political intrigue, the Crocodile Inn, where we paused briefly before driving towards the Caledonspoort border post. We left the road to take a track to Mamazibuko where a large enthusiastic crowd of some five hundred people was singing, dancing, laughing and enjoying themselves. The immediate impression was of a happy Church: this was the Church enjoying itself as it gathered for the dedication of the new Church of St. Peter. Widdicombe and Lacy's church building may have been crumbling but the gospel they proclaimed was robust and lively. It was blazingly hot for the four-hour confirmation and communion service and many sought, contrary to its usual use, the shading-protection of their blanket. With most people sitting on the ground, and also contrary to their normal use, umbrellas seemed to sprout from the earth as refuge was sought from the blistering power of the sun. I had been asked to preach on the concept of persistence for which, after checking that frogs did actually live in Lesotho, I wound the life of two frogs into the comment by Jesus that anyone who starts to plough and then looks back is not fit for service.[23] It is rarely easy to get an accurate assessment of the contribution a sermon makes and for a genuine reaction to this one I had to wait for two years. It was 1989; I was walking along Kingsway, the main street in Maseru, when a small, thin, elderly man stopped me, calling excitedly: '*Ntate*! *Khotso*!' After the traditional preliminaries he said he had been at Mamazibuko two years ago. He had enjoyed the story of the two frogs which he clearly recounted in some detail! As we talked we recalled the use that Jesus made of stories and questioned why they have largely fallen into disuse. In the memory of one man the frog story had lasted for two years; I wondered if the message it conveyed had also stayed alive?

It was eleven months before I could go back to Lesotho. The LINK in Durham was making heavy demands on my time and since it was as much for Durham as it was for Lesotho I felt I had to respond to that need. The first preaching engagement didn't exactly make me saddle-sore. I only had to walk some two hundred yards (183 m) from my home to St. Antony's Priory, the Durham home of the Society of the Sacred Mission that has exercised an active ministry in Lesotho for the past one hundred and six years.[24] A not immediately obvious connection between Durham and Lesotho had now led to an invitation to preach at Evensong on Sunday, 21st February 1988. I had a free choice of topic so, given the date,[25] I spoke about 'Modern Saints and Martyrs of Africa – Don't Get Tired Tomorrow'. Not surprisingly the LINK was the topic of our supper conversation.

The Lambeth Conference of 1988 gave Philip Mokuku the chance to visit Durham where he found the seat of my car rather more comfortable than the saddle journeys that usually preceded his preaching in Lesotho. It was all so different: it was the 'culture shock' of the sociologist. After fifteen years working in both Lesotho and Durham it was a personal challenge I had to handle each time I changed location. Now Philip had to adapt to many very different venues. He has a splendid rapport with children and visited many schools so different from those in Lesotho. An early introduction to a television studio was a 'first' for him: together we made a recording about the LINK for the Independent Television programme *Inner Space*.[26] He couldn't escape from being filmed.

The LINK was given permission by the Dean of Durham Cathedral to video-film, it is thought for the first time ever, a celebration service on Wednesday, 13th July 1988. Throughout its nine hundred years Durham Cathedral has been the scene of many outstanding events but, for those in the huge congregation gathered this evening, this was perhaps one of the most memorable. Philip preached a powerful sermon in which he said that the Lord's work was being carried out as the LINK makes everyone 'look beyond their own horizons'. During his introduction he acknowledged the presence in the congregation of a short, white-haired, 78-year-old man on whose pioneering work in Lesotho the LINK had been built: John Maund, the first Bishop of Lesotho. He sat in the congregation, anonymous to most, as David Jenkins and Philip Mokuku presided over a joyful celebration with schoolchildren parading their specially made banners and Philip's wife, 'Matšepo, reading the collect.

Accompanied by Philip's broad beaming smile the choir sang, in Sesotho, a specially composed setting of the 'peace' (*khotso*) before everyone joined together in a brief act of commitment:

> In the name of God the Father whose children we are, we commit ourselves anew to the work of the Gospel ...[27]

The scene switches four months later from northern Durham to southern Maseru, from black bishop to white Reader, from huge cathedral to small church. St. John's Church in Kingsway, Maseru was built in 1912 and stands in the middle of the capital city as a constant reminder of the Church's presence amidst commercial and industrial activity. It was there, at the invitation of Clement Mullenger,[28] that I preached in November 1988 and I survived the high jinks of a young boy who, in the process of running around, knocked a lighted candle on to me as I sat next to the candle stick. I still carry the burn marks on my blue Reader's scarf as a permanent memento of the incident and of Lesotho. In calmer surroundings later that same day I was speaking in Lithoteng at a new church dedicated to Christ the Healer planted in the expanding sprawling suburbs of Maseru. Here, in close proximity to the capital city, life seemed to be much more sophisticated with only the occasional blanket to be seen and that, sometimes, lying on the back seat of a parked car. Questions about the LINK were also more direct, financially focused and time-orientated.

The next weekend I had to adapt again, this time to the distinctive sub-culture of the foothills, teaching and preaching in a small out-station of Masite, Setleketseng. It overlooks a river of the same name and lies to the east of the King's country home in Matsieng. Philip and I were met on the track by a dozen singing horsemen and led to St. Paul's Church, a modest building of cut stone with a pitched corrugated-iron roof: it was packed for the confirmation service. Rarely was a visit to a parish or out-station not characterised by some memorable incident or feature. We always had to be prepared for the unexpected. Today we were met by a schoolteacher, acting as the leader of this out-station, with the news that a catechist of the church had been struck and killed by lightning on his way to the service. Although not an unusual event in the mountains the nonchalant manner with which the news was received was uncanny but since, in this tough environment, the death of someone or something occurs almost daily perhaps calmness should be received not as a surprise but as a tribute.

The next day, Saturday, we were at Matsieng in St. Matthew's Church where I sat in the sanctuary surrounded by bags of maize, the practical offering of a local farmer. During the sermon and the LINK talk that followed, I found a persistent photographer in the congregation intrusive but since it seemed to trouble no one else I said nothing and wondered what Paul would have done had cameras been around in his day. The day after it was all change again. The day had been designated Education Sunday when hundreds of teachers from all over the country joined the Minister of Education and his colleagues, school managers and university professors in the cathedral in Maseru. As I had been actively involved with Lesotho education over the previous fifteen years it was quite a reunion marred, in my eyes, only by the lack of children in the congregation. The readings, from Paul's first letter to the Corinthians chapter two[29] and Proverbs chapter six,[30] provided the structure for my talk: Christ: the Master Teacher. During the service I presented to former Professor of Education, Mac Mohapeloa, one of the banners made by Seaton Carew School that was paraded at the Durham Cathedral service in May.

Four years before the great drought of 1992 I made my first visit to Semonkong, famous for its 656-foot (200-m) Maletsunyane waterfall which I have yet to see. I had yet to learn not to grumble at even the slightest shower of rain. I still saw clouds, even those as small as a man's hand,[31] as a threatening menace, rarely seeing beyond their power to make me wet, cold and miserable, whereas the Basotho, who rejoiced in the refreshment of water, saw them as a promise of better things to come and were overwhelmingly thankful. Now, as Philip Mokuku, Bernard Duma and I drove uncomfortably in the diocesan four-wheel-drive vehicle ever upward, there was a sky full of small hands mockingly waving at us from south to north. Elijah, 'at the top of' Carmel's 1,740 feet (530 m), would have been pleased. I was not quite at the top of Semonkong's 7,218 feet (2,200 m) and was not at all pleased. It had been a hard, frequently dangerous, four-hour drive for the 50 miles (80 kms) from Maseru and we were glad to see a familiar sight, one of Fraser's[32] many stores with its red corrugated-iron roof rusting away around one or two small, dirty skylights. Scattered around the treeless camp people, mostly men wrapped in blankets decorated with multi-coloured graphic designs, drifted about with, seemingly, no particular purpose other than talking. Half a dozen horses rested waiting for their next load. Thinking as an Englishman, I knew we had to get across the next nine or ten miles (15 kms) of mountain tracks so, with rain still expected, we changed from one twelve-horsepower engine to three one-horsepower animals. Conversely, thinking as a Mosotho, I thought it would take us what daylight remained. Distance, especially in the mountains, is often measured by time-span rather than length-span and Ha Pakiso was not far away because we could ride there in more or less a straight line before sundown. Expressing distance by time rather than by length is, if not a precise calculation, a very practical measure especially when travelling along a U-shaped track skirting a deep impenetrable gorge to reach a point that remains visible all the time across the cavernous divide.

At the camp Philip had to bargain hard for a little petrol as it was in short supply because the tanker had been unable to negotiate the road from Maseru. After an hour or so listening to, and occasionally talking with, the locals we left the comforting shade of the store with our Basotho guides, to ride slowly almost due east pushing into the interior toward Ha Pakiso at 6,500 feet (1,980 m). With the sun behind us anxious overhead glances were soon replaced by long admiring looks at the constantly changing shape of the hills as the slowly moving shadows transformed them from the rigid into the flexible. Even though the ground was parched and the stunted scrub was wilting it was uncannily beautiful. My horse was going well; it was so peaceful; even though it had been a long time since I had last eaten I wasn't aware of hunger; it all seemed so tranquil. Then, without warning, we came under the rapid fire of hailstones that were so ferocious we sought protection in a nearby house.

The owner invited us into the rectangular stone room that contained only one chair and a small table covered with a spotless white cloth on which lay an old newspaper. On the wall facing the door were three pictures one of which was a colour photograph of Queen Elizabeth II riding a horse. As we sat around on the floor I couldn't help but wonder, in this equestrian sub-culture of the mountains, whether the picture was there to exhibit the person or the horse! We rested in the room enduring the relentless noise of the hailstones attacking the corrugated-iron roof knowing that, when the noise stopped, we could safely leave the house.

A fast, quite easy, gentle ride enabled us to get to Ha Pakiso late afternoon before dark to be greeted quietly and almost sedately by both men and women. This was unusual but, nevertheless, very friendly with much hand-shaking and the offer of the occasional wrist when the hand was soiled in some way. One old lady, with a beaming smile, demurely dropped a perfect curtsy as we shook hands. Not being used to that type of regal greeting I was embarrassed. As we greeted each other I felt the leather-like texture of her hand and wondered what they had been through in her lifetime. Now they seemed unprepared for us. Philip wondered if there had been a breakdown in communication. Even if that were the case a drink of tea was produced from, so he told me, their only tea bag which, I suspect, had been used many times previously: it was almost dead. Philip drew attention to the just-about-coloured water so the lady brought along a tin of *milo* (for Dunelmians that is a drink powder similar to Ovaltine) with which to give it some colour! There followed a chipped tin plate full of fat-cakes (a type of ring doughnut) which filled a vacant space in our stomachs that lay beneath our thick blankets on this cold summer day.

Philip and I settled into a rondavel where he rested whilst I explored the surrounding area taking my notebook with me. It records that:

> I've now walked alone to a small hill above the rondavels of the village in which we are living. It is late evening and as the sun sets and the shadows on the mountains lengthen there is a constantly changing beauty in this quiet world. Only the cheerful voices of some Basotho children break an eerie mountain peacefulness. Smoke slowly rises from three or four cooking fires to scent the still air. Deep in the Maletsunyane gorge[33] in front of me, with its river snaking eagerly away to the Atlantic Ocean, men are finishing the day's ploughing on the few small, flat areas and herd boys drive home the cattle which, thanks to good rains in recent weeks, look in good condition. The horses on which we rode here are grazing and resting from the hard journey and heavy loads. As I write the temperature is falling rapidly at this 6,500-foot spot above a sea-level that is hundreds of miles away and which few, if any, of the Basotho who live here have ever seen. I'm cold. I must retrace my steps to the warmth of my *ntlo,* a stone-built, grass-thatched, hut. Found Phillip awake so by one candle light we spent a long time chatting about life in the mountains whilst we waited for supper to be taken from the open fire to the dining hut where we each ate an extremely tough chicken leg, *moroho* (spinach), rice with gravy and steamed bread for dessert and *milo* to drink.

Returning to our sleeping hut I noticed, probably because it is unusual, that the apex of the conical grass roof boasted a circular metal cap. The surrounding countryside was bleak; there wasn't a tree to be seen. Pushing open the ill-fitting wooden door we found that Basotho central heating had been installed: a fire of cow-dung had been put in the centre of the hut floor. This had been started outside in a large tin can with holes punched in the sides and then, when the dung is glowing red, it is placed in the hut with another tin open at both ends, standing on top of the original tin. This second tin, theoretically, acts as a chimney directing the smoke upwards towards the thatched roof through which it percolates. Reflecting that this visit to Lesotho started, exceptionally, in the four-star Lesotho Sun Hotel in Maseru this was quite an extraordinary experience. As we sat on the one available bed we talked about the diocese, the LINK, our respective ministries, our families and tomorrow's services. We were both feeling weary and equally reluctant to claim use of the one bed! As we reached the end of our agenda the fire was removed and a mattress appeared on which I slept soundly. The altitude was tiring.

Ostensibly the four services in St. Luke's Church, Ha Pakiso on the morning of Saturday, 3rd December 1988, were to begin at 9.15 a.m. but in this almost timeless society, in practice, they started when it was thought everybody was assembled and ready. Seemingly impervious to the mountain harshness they came in their scores shuffling along dusty tracks wrapped in distinctive blankets, some with French *fleur-de-lis* motifs and majestic crowns displayed on brilliant background colours. Even on this mid-summer day it was cold despite the body heat from the hundred or so Basotho men and boys crammed on the low benches plus an equal number of women, young children and girls seated on the floor. Everyone was tightly packed into the small church with those sitting on the floor occupying every conceivable spot and also some inconceivable ones.

We started with an adult baptism and then forty confirmations. Holy communion followed for about a hundred during which I preached briefly, remembering that translation doubles the length and the time. When making their offering this congregation adopted the practice of taking their gift to the altar, placing it there as a positive act of giving, thus avoiding the notion of a passive enforced collection. It is a custom that can be found in many churches in different African countries and is sometimes accompanied by dancing and singing to express the idea of a 'cheerful giver'.[34] Here in Ha Pakiso we concluded with a short service of healing for three people. It all went on for just over three hours without so much as a glance at a watch or clock but I am sure some, even if only those seated on the floor, noted where the shadows were and how far they moved during the succession of services.

After the services Philip and I, with the aid of large photographs, talked to the people about the LINK. Philip would introduce the topic, and me, with his usual humour and relaxed style but, nevertheless, I must have seemed a strange person. It was very rare for them to see a white person and certainly to have one sleeping in their village and eating the same food as they did. At the time it made me wonder what, for these people, the world was like beyond the surrounding all-embracing mountains. Does another world exist over the lofty horizon other than 'the mines' that takes men and sends money? Is it just the radio that penetrates this barrier reef? Our talk about the LINK was not helped by the untimely intrusion of 'unnatural' noises into the peaceful quietness of the village. The surreal sound of an aeroplane attracted everyone's attention and speculation and, later, that of a radio coming from the nearby cooking hut (*mokhoro*).

Outside this hut there were sacks of food aid labelled 'Gift of USA – Corn Soya Milk'. It was unlikely that the two herd boys asking for food could read the labelling but that didn't matter when any food would be welcomed. Dressed underneath torn, threadbare blankets, in tattered shorts, filthy singlet vests and over-large wellies 'imported' from Johannesburg they looked undernourished and so received the food they were given by the women in the cooking hut with obvious pleasure.

After our talk we sat on a rock outside our hut bizarrely contemplating our pre-lunch observations. Why, living in villages where the ground is rough, where it is strewn with large stones and boulders and having to walk many miles, do some Basotho women wear high-heeled shoes?! Is this a status symbol? Philip says the male status symbol is the number of animals he has and asks me what the status symbol of the man in Durham is. I plump for his car as it's mobile and travels with him. By now some people have gone, but where to? Where did they come from? There are few rondavels visible. There is a large group of people milling around; Church is a very social occasion because that may be the only time meetings take place. I recounted my boyhood visits to the property of my maternal grandfather: the hole-in-the-ground latrine; the closeness to nature as he had a large orchard, chickens and pigs; getting water from the hand pump in the kitchen; the smell of paraffin burning as there was no gas or electricity in the house. Philip told me of the time he was a herd boy and how outdoor life could be enjoyable if you stayed fit and well but brutally cruel if you are even slightly unwell.

Lunch stopped our reminiscing. It was very adequate but I never did quite work out the logic of the servings. Huge chunks of aged chicken served with biscuits and *milo* came at the start of the meal so I thought that was hors d'oeuvre. That would have been sufficient in itself but we were then given cabbage, *papa* (mealie pap), baked beans and more tough chicken. Over this substantial farewell meal Philip asked if I would be willing to ride with a Mosotho guide direct to our next stop, Ha Mohloka, whilst he took the vehicle by a longer route that would enable him to call on various people he needed to see. Not knowing exactly what my journey would entail I agreed, packing my few belongings into two plastic carrier bags that made ideal saddlebags. As we were preparing to leave about twenty women and girls gathered by our hut and started to sing (harmoniously but, I thought at the time, quite incongruously) Blake's poem *Jerusalem* to Parry's tune.[35] It was a kind gesture but 'England's mountains green' seemed a long way off and there were probably only two of us who had ever seen 'England's pleasant pastures'. In stark contrast, there were plenty of 'clouded hills' in view as I left Ha Pakiso on my white stallion alongside my Mosotho guide: the dark, heavy clouds certainly looked menacing.

Giving a final 'goodbye' wave as the cheering of the women died away we crossed the small plain, conserving our energy and I developing a silent rapport with my mount as a gentle trot took us into the hills rolling towards one of the surrounding mountains: it looked formidable and, even though I had a local guide, I felt very much on my own. He spoke no English and I spoke little Sesotho. I didn't know where I was going or how far it was. Was it really beyond this mountain? For the first ten minutes or so my white nameless horse gave me some trouble; it was in a frisky mood (was it trying to tell me something?) but as we left the plain and began to climb a barely visible track it settled down. I pulled my woollen hat over my ears and adjusted my blanket to keep out the bitingly cold wind.

As we climbed ever upwards, Blake's words came to mind: 'O clouds, unfold', and they did, with a violent vengeance the ferocity of which can only be fully understood when on horseback, wrapped in a blanket, on the side of a Lesotho mountain. In what was probably about thirty minutes I was soaked through, literally to the skin. My blanket became increasingly heavy and gradually began to drip water; my shoes were full of water. Everything in the plastic carrier bags was wet so perhaps, after all, they are not so useful as saddlebags but at least some water was escaping through the small safety 'breathing-holes'. Perhaps what was most uncomfortable was the wet saddle as that seemed to increase the chafe on the inside of my upper legs and round my bottom. Why had I not put on my tights? I think it was the singing women crowded around our hut that inhibited me. My poor horse was also having its problems as the track deteriorated and became increasingly broken and slippery as we zigzagged upward and slowly forward. By this time we should really have rested the horses but being soaked to the skin and standing still without any shelter defeated that wisdom and we did the next best thing.

We dismounted and led them through a particularly rough patch so gaining the benefit of being physically active thus generating a little warmth. Thunder rolled in with deafening explosions backed by distant flashes of lightning that fortunately kept their distance as they detonated more eruptions. At least we were on the leeward side of the mountain until we reached the ridge which we had to cross to get to Ha Mohloka. Saturated, but now also filthy and very weary, we neared the mountain ridge where the wind became stronger and its direction irregular, swirling its bone chilling attack into every crevice. But what a sight when we crossed the highest point, meeting the wind's full cruel blast that viciously objected to our intrusion and safe arrival. The valley below, in which Ha Mohloka nestled, was deeply covered in pure white hailstones. It was as if, in the dusk of the day, the village was trying to shrink into the icy landscape and then disguise its presence by wrapping itself in a white cloth the corner of which a few scattered horses were trying to lift to find some protection.

Refuge for us was still twenty minutes away as, mounted once again, we slipped and slithered now downhill into the village to be greeted by men and women, boys and girls just three hours after leaving Ha Pakiso. An elderly man, small in stature but big in kindness, took my plastic carrier bags and led me to a stone-built rondavel where I stripped, peeling off my skin-clinging saturated clothes that slopped with an audible slosh on to the mud floor. A small towel, that had suddenly been produced from somewhere by someone, made a valiant effort to get me dry enough to be comfortable before cocooning myself, stark naked, in a dry blanket to enjoy a hot sweet drink that defied description other than 'a loving gesture'. Alone I ate a meal untypical of a poor Mosotho before gratefully resting on a piece of thin foam rubber under another dry blanket that had arrived; three more blankets kept me warm through the night. Except for my shoes all my clothes, my guide and my horse had disappeared. It had been a journey I would remember for many a year: to be exact for twenty-three thus far! Now, in Ha Mahloka at almost 9,000 feet (2,700 m) in the mid-summer of December 1988, it was still very cold so my attentive host (whose name, to my shame, I never did record) made a star-fire in the centre of the hut. This *naleli* is a fire around which small logs are placed flat on the ground end-on to the central fire; as the ends burn they are gradually pushed in to the central fire thus keeping it going indefinitely.

As I rested the little old, wizened man crouched on his haunches by the fire murmuring to himself whilst my shoes steamed over its glowing embers. He held each shoe by a thick stick in each heel turning them as they roasted. Hoping he would not incinerate them I fell fast asleep. I don't know for how long I slept but I do know that when I woke my helper was still patiently turning my shoes and as I woke, perhaps wondering where on earth I was, in a low, gentle voice he said to me, *'khotso ntate; khotso, khotso ntate'* ('peace, father; peace, peace, father'). I was then conscious of him wrapping my feet in a knitted woollen blanket as if he were caring for a helpless baby. Relieved by the warmth I dozed and he left me to return a few minutes later with a 'carpet to stand on next to the bedside'. The fact that the carpet was an old sack in no way lessened the kindness of the old man's action, in fact, in a very real sense, its value was greater as that was probably all he had. It seemed that on rousing I was in some distress and he was trying to comfort me. He succeeded: I turned over and went back to sleep.

Again for how long I do not know, but I do know that I was learning what it was like to be a mountain Mosotho. Stark naked under my blanket I was about to learn another lesson. Fierce coughing had roused me. Dragging myself out of my stupor consciousness slowly returned and I sat up; that was my mistake. Except for an inch or so from the floor the hut was full of smoke. The fire had gone out and with no heat to raise the smoke upwards through the thatched roof it filled the hut so I should have kept my head low to avoid the asphyxiating effect of the falling smoke. I had obviously inhaled lots of smoke to cough; cough; cough: it was all rather unpleasant. The man who had been so helpful to me had gone to his bed elsewhere taking my shoes with him. As I had no means of lighting the fire I decided to sleep as I had seen many Basotho doing, completely submerged by blankets. I now know why. So with one of my precious blankets covering my head I claustrophobically snuggled down in the hope I would avoid the worst effects of the smoke.

I woke to eat a typical Mosotho breakfast whilst wrapped only in a blanket. Later a lady brought my clothes, smoke laden but dry, in time for me to attend the confirmation service in a small wattle-and-daub building; St. Joseph's Church where I spoke about being firm in the faith. It was packed to overflowing with about sixty people after which, sitting around wherever a space could be found, we ate mutton stew for lunch. During the post-lunch chat I discovered that the horse I rode yesterday was named 'Pilot', or was it, I wondered later, Pilate! The natural beauty of the scene in which it was now grazing was spoilt only by human rubbish and untidiness caused by bits of corrugated iron, firewood, broken boxes and wire dumped seemingly anywhere. The mood here was sombre; the living was pitiable; the prospects poor; the emotional impact severe. Perhaps personal development and action *is* conditioned by being told what we are: Ha Mohloka in Sesotho means 'In Need'.

I didn't know it at the time but I was to return to Ha Mohloka three years hence in August 1991 by which time little had changed. Now my carer and I exchanged farewells: '*tsamaea hantle, ntate*' (go well, father): '*sala hantle, ntate*' (stay well, father), and Philip and I left with women marching, dancing and singing around our vehicle to the parish boundary. It was to be the start of yet another horrendous journey. More hail and heavy rain, rocks and boulders reduced our speed to just over 3 miles an hour (5 kms per hour). As we both had to get out and push when not driving we were both wet with mud up to our knees. It was tough going but perhaps not quite as tough as for the woman to whom we gave a lift. To attend the service she had walked the ten miles (16 kms) each way from Semonkong to Ha Mohloka and was on her way back when we met her wet and bedraggled. At least her shoes were not wet: she didn't have any!

The next weekend we had an easier and more pleasant journey as we drove on Sunday, 11th December 1988 northwards on the tarred road for most of the way to St. Matthias Church, Peka. For me this was a return visit to Ignatius Malebo's parish. I had last been there seven years previously on Sunday, 18th October 1981 when I also spoke at a baptism service at an out-station church, Ha Musi. Today was a much bigger occasion as Philip Mokuku was to ordain as priest deacon Peter Letsie and there were, seeking whatever shade was available, hundreds of people and priests from all over the diocese. During the three-hour service I preached on the theme of priests as watchmen who are required to speak out avoiding the sin of silence.[36] A great party followed when I was able to talk for a long time about the LINK to a large number of influential people who would be able to take the message around the country.

It was to be another seven months before Phillip and I were on the Lesotho trail again beginning with a six-hour service at St. Barnabas Church, Masite for the induction of Thaele Mokhele who had just returned from political exile in Botswana. In four years time Thaele was, in a reciprocal gesture, to spend three months preaching in Durham diocese but now[37] he had to receive the welcome of some 800 Basotho at Masite. There were many hundreds of communicants of which, during the administration, I served wine to one who was reluctant to stop drinking; it was a difficult context within which to exercise muscle power. It was a wonderful celebration but it did test one's stamina. Being in the lowlands travel was comparatively easy although I drove back to Maseru with a 'bakkie' load of nine Mothers' Union ladies, all of very ample proportions, which, with two of them in the one passenger seat, made changing the manual gear exceedingly difficult.

During my visits over the next five years Philip and I were to travel the length, breadth and height of Lesotho visiting congregations in the lowland cathedral, the foothill churches and the mountain out-stations. To reinforce the word and work of the pioneers we carried the same message by foot, horse, four-wheel-drive truck, and aeroplane: Jesus is for everyone.[38] In addition, to spread news of the LINK and its work, we spoke not only through sermons, but by formal and informal talks to thousands: there could be few who were unaware of its active contribution to life in both Dioceses. During each parish visit, to church or out-station, there seemed to be one or more 'incidents', some serious, some humorous, but all distinctive. In May 1989, at St. Cyprian's Church, Molipa,[39] I was distracted by an adventurous mouse that had found its way beneath my alb[40] which reached floor level. I feared the mouse was about to explore further but then (miraculously?) a cat appeared and a chase ensued ending only when the mouse was caught and deposited at my feet. Until the cat appeared the congregation could see nothing of the cause of the strange antics of this Englishman but sat in wonderment as to what was going on in the sanctuary. As all became clear the congregation was convulsed with laughter at my expense!

The next day at Rantuba[41] my knowledge of Basotho tradition was discomfortingly expanded. After a baptism I took, with the mother's approval, a photograph of her with her baby, commenting what a beautiful little girl she had, an honest observation that was received with a peculiar silence. No less peculiar was the severe episcopal look that shot in my direction! Philip took me aside to explain that it was a grave mistake to make that sort of complimentary comment as tradition demanded that however beautiful the baby it must never be described as beautiful to protect it from the attention of the Devil who, doubtless, by this time was ecstatic at my error! Noticeably Philip went and spoke to the mother and I refrained, after that episode, from any further contact with mothers and their babies. How *does* an Englishman say 'what an ugly looking baby you have'?

In Lesotho the close relationship that the LINK was establishing between word and work had to be projected conceptually not just semantically. In English 'word' can easily be changed into 'work' by the alteration of just one letter: not so in Sesotho where '*lentsoe*' and '*mosebetsi*' are alphabets apart. Preaching and practice had to be brought together into one message that could be experienced by everyone so that what was said and what was done were indistinguishable in everyday living in Lesotho and Durham. We preached the gospel so that experiencing its message could be realised in the activities of the LINK. The extensive visits to parishes and their out-stations that Philip and I made together provided the opportunity to communicate the principle that our social actions can only be fully effective when conducted within a common value structure. Chiefs and people, for their part, were almost invariably supportive, one consequence of which was that the LINK had a substantial 'land bank' for tree-planting. Another was a large expansion of the 'ideas bank'; we knew what the people would like which was a sound starting point for the expansion of our work. Christians had to work to live the gospel.

Our next stop was a village due south of Teyateyaneng, Ha Senekane. It is situated on the edge of the Berea Plateau looking south into the valley of the River Thupa-Kubu. Lying a short distance from the gravel track it was easily accessible by vehicle. The church, clean and tidy, was the original stone-and-thatch building subsequently enlarged by a mud-and-wattle extension but still too small to accommodate the assembled crowd on Friday, 19th May 1989, so the services were held outside where a canopy had been erected to give some shade. Many of the people had travelled the day before and slept in the church at what was the start of a grand social occasion during which I found the conversation educationally centred, stressing the need for a new school which the LINK eventually built not far away to the north-east at Ha Mohatlane. The next day we made a rough four-wheel drive from 'Mamathe travelling due north to spend the day at Ha Phoofolo, which overlooks to the north the valley of the River Phuthiatsana. We were greeted by the usual horsemen, the usual raucous noise, the usual joyful enthusiasm but with an unusual mass of donkeys all decorated with red plastic and cloth ribbons. It was a happy open-air celebration during which we all enjoyed my 'stick' sermon with much fun and laughter, perhaps the result of a more relaxed easier life in the lowlands.

It was to be another seven months before I returned to my preaching and teaching role in Lesotho but, in the meantime the LINK gained strength with many Basotho coming to Durham before I was to go south again. It was very heartening to see the increase of these personal contacts filling our Visitors' Book with Basotho names from across a wide spectrum of the southern society; priests, the Lesotho Diocesan Registrar,[42] a head teacher, classroom teachers, a Ministry of Works official, students, the suffragan bishop.

At the end of January 1990 I again switched countries and cultures. After I had been back in Lesotho for ten days, the dean of the cathedral, Andrew Duma, suggested we should go to the Place of the Baboons, otherwise known as Majoe-a-Litšoene. After a brief time on tar we drove over some appalling tracks through a densely populated suburban region of Maseru, just below a distinctive opening in the surrounding mountains that can be seen from almost anywhere in Maseru, Lancers' Gap. It was so named after British troops in scarlet uniforms marched on Maseru with drums banging to be ambushed and routed by concealed Basotho warriors. Now in more peaceful times Andrew and I twisted our tortuous way between the closely packed houses and huts, home to the hundreds of children playing wherever space was available to them, but never quite arriving at the site which had been allocated to the diocese for the construction of a new Anglican church. At a junction, which we had negotiated twice in the previous ten minutes, Andrew stopped to consult a group of seven boys.

Amidst much laughter they claimed to know exactly where to find the site. They piled into the back of the truck with one, the navigator, in the highly privileged position in the front cab between Andrew and me. After two 'dead-ends' and one complete circle, Andrew realised that it was us that was being 'taken for a ride'! More enquiries and the ten o'clock open-air eucharist began an hour late after some consternation about the position of the imported chair I was to use. I was told it was over a 'live hole' in which, since I imagined that a hole can be neither dead nor alive, I began to take more interest. 'Why alive?' this innocent enquired: to be told 'it has a snake in it'! This resulted in sticks being pushed down the hole followed, why I don't know, by the right front leg of my chair! If there was, in fact, a snake down there the attack worked. We completed the service without further interruption but I did just wonder what answer I should give to my sermon question 'What does the Lord require of you?'[43] After lunch the LINK was asked if it would plant trees on the small site which we did with the aim of surrounding the proposed new building with trees. Since trees take longer to grow than buildings the people here were getting things in the proper order; it's certainly beneficial to plant trees before mixing concrete.

With the progress of five big projects in various stages of development my time for travel in the mountains of Lesotho was severely restricted so for the remainder of the year my preaching and speaking was confined largely to the cathedral and to churches in and around Maseru. Nevertheless, by meeting a request from Lincoln Theological College to arrange a pastoral placement for a Durham ordinand, Simon Mason, the LINK maintained an active church presence. Simon spent ten weeks with Andrew, visiting and speaking in many churches before preaching at the cathedral early in the morning of Sunday, 26th August 1990,[44] a day that saw a remarkable interdenominational service for those teachers engaged in what was, by then, a three-month-long teachers' strike. The service was called by the Heads of Churches to seek a just and peaceful resolution to their grievances. Pondering on whether this could have happened anywhere else Simon and I spent the afternoon discussing his experience of the placement. When we were joined by Caroline Wright, a Durham graduate whom the LINK had been able to assist with her enquiries into gender and migration in Lesotho, our talking focused on her work which eventually expanded into academic research for her doctorate.[45]

By mid-1990 the LINK was making a substantial contribution to academic studies in both Lesotho and Durham but it was 1991 before I was in the saddle again. On Saturday, 9th February Philip and I left Maseru later than we intended, which was not unusual, so we were pleased to make speedy progress on the newly tarred road to Mapoteng. At a rough cross-country track we met our guide who had been occupied waiting 'since early morning' to lead us southward to Ha Tšiame. It was fortunate he was with us as the track had no obvious existence where it crossed bare rock but even that was to be preferred to the mud in which we stuck. The guide and I pushed whilst Philip drove; it was a messy business. At its narrowest part the track was only just wide enough to accommodate the truck but with mere inches (cm) to spare we made Tsiame where we were greeted, not with horses, but tea and cakes. The village nestles in a fertile region of the lowlands which also supports a few trees that, because of their rarity, were particularly obvious. With a noticeable absence of men, everyone assembled in the stone-built church which served, during the week, as the school for 200 children in six classes in the one hall.

That morning the age range in church was huge! I faced a challenge to make my talk on being a 'Light in the World' suitable for young and old. After the service, with Philip 'as my voice', I spoke about the work of the LINK and felt sufficiently confident to test the people's reaction to the possible development of a community education centre at Ha Mohatlane. I did this because I knew the two places were within Basotho walking distance and there were connecting foot-tracks but my mistake was to do so in the absence of men in this masculine-dominated society! I should have spotted that at the outset for that was the reason I received virtually no response to the idea. What brought a much more animated response was the collection of large photographs of Durham that I passed round when talking about the LINK. Boys were particularly active in asking lots of questions and commenting on the pictures.

It was a relief on this very hot mid-summer day when, late morning, we were encouraged to rest on two beds in a thatched, and therefore cool, rondavel and I was asleep within a couple of minutes. Later, I was woken by a gentle calling of *'Lijo, ntate'* (food, father). It was a fine chicken lunch with, again, a dessert of jelly and hot custard. Speeches followed and then I was presented via the catechist, priest and bishop with fifteen maluti (which at that time was worth about three pounds sterling)![46] As Philip passed the money to me he whispered that I must take it and I should indicate how I would use it for myself because that would be the wish of the people. Receiving the gift, Basotho style with upturned palms so the money could be *given* into my hands and not *taken* by them, I made one of the most difficult 'thank-you' speeches I have ever had to make.

We left Ha Tsiame in the truck and arrived at All Saint's Church, Hlajoane[47] on horseback having taken a long detour to enable us to negotiate a swollen river that had swept away the wooden bridge. At the crossing we met scores of men and boys on horses and donkeys. My white horse took great care of me and after an easy ride, compared with those in the mountains, we were soon settled in the home of the priest.

Next morning I woke with the sun in a sparsely furnished room where, apart from the bed, there was one small chair, two tin trunks and a suitcase. There is no electricity or any water on tap so it is important to perform one's morning ablutions in the correct order. So what is 'the correct order'? First, use the inside toilet for which there is no flushing water; second, wash all over using as little water from the jug as possible making sure to use the plastic bowl and not the sink (as the waste pipe has not been connected and leads directly to the floor); next, use the same water to shave with before using it to flush the toilet (which is connected to a cesspit). Get one out of order and you are in a mess.

When I reached the final stage the church bell, a large metal can hanging by a cord from a tree branch, rang out but as the bishop was one stage behind the preacher still had time to reach the outside latrine some 100 yards (92 m) distant. People here must have a built-in early warning system; this may be my last opportunity for some hours. The services included the blessing of a fine new primary school, three baptisms, scores of confirmations plus the eucharist during which an over-enthusiastic young server, wildly swinging the censer, approached the seated bishop only to deposit its burning charcoal into his lap. A smouldering bishop in the sanctuary can be dangerous but Philip was unharmed and the disruption was short-lived.

During the same service my knowledge of Basotho behaviour, at least in this region, was unexpectedly enlarged. Unlike some other churches in which the offertory is taken by individuals to the altar at All Saint's it was collected in a tin. Why, I do not know, but this morning for some reason I was asked to take the offertory so I stood at the end of each row to discover that many of the women keep their 'collection' money in their bra between their, usually ample, cleavage! As hand after hand delved deeply beneath dresses, cardigans and blankets I thought this must be a very safe depository and an effective counter to the pickpocket.

Many places followed Tsiame and Hlajoane; Kolo, Tšakolo, Ha Mohloka for a second visit, Kingsway, the cathedral, Durham, Pretoria. Now, the last trek of the year, the nine hours it took Philip and me to drive from Maseru to Ha Moshebi on Saturday, 2nd November 1991 took us through a beautiful region of a beautiful country and, for some of that time, alongside the Senqu River as it roared its angry way around the water cycle. As we went through Mount Moorosi, with Bethel just across the river, it was, for me, a return to 1973 when, with an educational colleague[48] we had to ford this mighty river and climb its distant bank. Now Philip and I stayed on its eastern side driving below some enormous escarpments, feeling very vulnerable to rock falls the evidence of which lay all around.

Ha Moshebi lies a short distance south-west of the Sehlabathebe National Park alongside what the maps describe as 'a fair weather road' that, as it leaves the Senqu, follows the mountainous south-eastern border with South Africa. It was getting dark as we arrived but the villagers still greeted us with their singing and fed us around the warming fire before we gratefully collapsed into our beds in a rectangular stone hut that had a single sloping corrugated-iron roof. During the night rain lashed down, lightning stabbed through the darkness, thunder rolled and roared and wind howled around the mountains trying, unsuccessfully, to lift the roof from the walls. The danger is that the wind gets in through ill-fitting windows and doors, and under the eaves, and lifts the roof from the inside but the unknown builder had done his job well. We remained dry and comfortable but the noise was deafening: it was what one might imagine living in a drum to be like.

The day dawned bright and cheerful with the night-time noises being replaced by those of cockerels, hens, cows and humans. Breakfast took a long, long time, everything being served with a gentleness and care found among mountain people. Their clock still rises above the horizon each morning setting there in the evening but on the other side. Everything was spotlessly clean in the house and in the church where the services started forty minutes late, but did that really matter? There was no bus to catch; no television to watch; no one to meet as everyone was there; it didn't much matter whether you ate at one, two or three providing you ate; we left at four, but it wasn't pre-arranged, it just happened that was the time when we were ready to go. Stopping briefly at Rankakala secondary school for me to survey the site where the LINK might build a poultry unit we shared the two hours' driving to Qacha's Nek.

At St. Barnabas Mission, in the paraffin-lit guest room with my notebooks and journal acting as aide-mémoire, Philip and I took stock of the years during which we had travelled many hundreds of miles to expound the word of the gospel and explain the work of the LINK. The LINK grew out of 'a marriage'[49] between Lesotho and Durham so Paul's comment to his young Christian assistant, Timothy, who himself was the son of a Greek father and a Jewish mother, seemed to have a special relevance. Paul was anxious[50] that preachers and teachers should not be silenced any more than oxen should be muzzled when they are working.[51] In Lesotho, where oxen are still used to till the soil, the LINK did not allow its extensive development programme to muzzle its far-reaching contribution to preaching and teaching. To the Devil's chagrin the developments were being used as vehicles for the spread of the gospel.

The same was true for Durham as there the LINK was engaged in raising large sums of money to support the work. In parishes in both dioceses we showed how faith becomes stronger by bringing together in our lives the teaching of scripture and the toil of labour. By living with the people we had attempted to relate to them, to listen to them, to console them, to rejoice with them. Now, as we reflected on the past five years, many weeks of which we had spent in the saddle, we agreed that how we tackled the years ahead would largely depend on what time, and people, we had available for parish visiting. We knew this would be likely to be limited because I had five large co-funded development projects to launch and manage, and Philip was increasingly involved in the serious political upheavals that were shaking Lesotho at the time and needed the attention of his steadying counsel and perceptive wisdom. Nevertheless, we agreed that I would continue to accompany Philip whenever and wherever possible so during the next four years I was to draw closer to the Basotho, experience a wider variety of extraordinary 'incidents' and become more frequently saddle-sore as Bishop and Reader continued their respective ministries and the LINK's unifying work. We continued for many years to preach what we practiced.

This element of the LINK's contribution to the life of both dioceses has, inevitably, varied over the subsequent years as different personalities, attributes and qualities became available. Whichever phase of the LINK's existence is considered, hopefully it may continue to reflect, and answer, the apostle Paul's prayer:

> I pray that you may be active in sharing your faith,
> so that you will have a full understanding
> of every good thing we have in Christ.[52]

---

1. Douglas, J. D., (Editor): *The New Bible Dictionary* (Inter-Varsity Fellowship) 1963. p. 983: Walls, A. F., Epistle to Philemon. In Philemon the second person singular is used throughout, even for the greetings; the only exceptions are in verses 22 (the hoped-for visit) and 25 (the benediction). Therefore, here, Paul is addressing Philemon not Onesimus.
2. Philemon 1:6 (NIV).
3. Saturday, 2nd November 1985. See Chapter One: In the beginning was the word, (p. 1).
4. Jenkins, David, Durham Diocesan Synod, 1st November 1986 – Presidential Address.
5. Cooper, William (1731–1800), an 18th century poet who wrote the hymn *God moves in a mysterious way* / His wonders to perform; He plants His footsteps in the sea / And rides upon the storm. This hymn was originally a poem called *Conflict: Light Shining out of Darkness.*
6. Detailed accounts of this mission can be found in the newspaper: *Durham NEWSLINK*: March-April 2008, pp. 1 & 7.
7. See Chapter Two: Saddle Up! (p. 25).
8. Luke 15:22 (NIV): ... the father said to his servants, 'Quick! Bring the best robe and put it on him. Put a ring on his finger and sandals on his feet.'
9. The Mother house of the Society is at Maidenhead, Somerset, England. See website <www.burnhamabbey.org>.
10. Matthew 7:13–14 (NIV): Enter through the narrow gate. For wide is the gate and broad is the road that leads to destruction, and many enter through it. But small is the gate and narrow the road that leads to life, and only a few find it.

11. The Zionist Church is the largest religious denomination in southern Africa. Known also by the Zulu word '*amaZioni*' its adherents, many of whom wear ritual robes, play drums and carry staves at parades and services, are said to number up to sixteen million. They practise a blend of traditional African and Christian religions. The Zionist Church (not be confused with the Israeli Zionism political movement) was started about 1903 in South Africa by an Afrikaner, P. le Roux.
12. The Chapel of our Lady Mother of Mercy was designed by the Rev'd Maurice James who was a civil engineer before his ordination. There is some uncorroborated anecdotal evidence that he came from Sunderland in the Diocese of Durham. The chapel was dedicated by John Maund on Saturday, 19th September 1959.
13. See Chapter Five: Trees of the Field (p. 109),
14. See Chapter Eight: Suffering Little Children (p. 223).
15. Compline, from the Latin word *completorium* meaning completion, is the last service of the day after which silence is kept.
16. Opened in 1948 although a plane had landed at a makeshift runway in 1943 for a medical emergency.
17. Matthew 8:26 (NIV): 'You of little faith, why are you so afraid?' Then he got up and rebuked the winds and the waves, and it was completely calm.
18. Luke 21:2 (NIV): (Jesus) also saw a poor widow put in two very small copper coins. 'I tell you the truth,' he said, 'this poor widow has put in more than all the others.'
19. A strong stave about three feet (one metre) long with a heavy knob the size of a tennis ball at one end that is used as a fighting club.
20. Proverbs 20:17 (NIV): Food gained by fraud tastes sweet to a man, but he ends up with a mouth full of gravel.
21. Annual Report of St. James' Mission Hospital: 2001-2002. p. 11. See Chapter Two: Saddle Up (p. 25).
22. John Widdicombe was born in Devonshire in 1839 and went to South Africa in 1860 and was ordained as a priest in 1869. In 1876 he founded the mission at Hlotse (Leribe), Lesotho, which he left in 1906 returning very briefly in 1911. At the age of 88 years he died in South Africa in 1927. A more detailed account of his work can be found in: Dove, Reginald, *Anglican Pioneers in Lesotho* (No publisher acknowledged) 1975. pp. 13–14. The other priest, who worked in the south from Mohale's Hoek, was an Irishman, Edmund Stenson.
23. Luke 9:62 (NIV): Jesus replied, 'No-one who puts his hand to the plough and looks back is fit for service in the kingdom of God.'
24. Houghton, Michael, *SSM at TY (1904–1975)* (Morija Printing Works, 1976).
25. *The Alternative Service Book 1980*: jointly published by William Clowes; the Society for Promoting Christian Knowledge and Cambridge University Press: p. 18: *Lesser Festivals and Commemorations: 21st February: Saints and Martyrs of Africa.*
26. Recorded in Newcastle on Wednesday, 6th July 1988 and transmitted on the ITV Programme *Inner Space* Friday, 15th July 1988.

27. Transcript of the video-film produced by David Williams: Wednesday, 13th July 1988.
28. See Prologue: Before the beginning? (p. xix)
29. 1 Corinthians 2:1–10 (NIV): When I came to you, brothers, I did not come with eloquence or superior wisdom as I proclaimed to you the testimony about God. For I resolved to know nothing while I was with you except Jesus Christ and him crucified. I came to you in weakness and fear, and with much trembling. My message and my preaching were not with wise and persuasive words, but with a demonstration of the Spirit's power, so that your faith might not rest on men's wisdom, but on God's power.
30. Proverbs 3:1–7 (NIV): My son, do not forget my teaching, but keep my commands in your heart, for they will prolong your life many years and bring you prosperity. ... Trust in the LORD with all your heart and lean not on your own understanding; in all your ways acknowledge him, and he will make your paths straight. Do not be wise in your own eyes; fear the LORD and shun evil.
31. 1 Kings 18:44 (NIV): The seventh time the servant reported, a cloud as small as a man's hand is rising from the sea.
32. Fraser's is a chain of general stores scattered throughout Lesotho. The founders of the Company, Donald and Douglas Fraser, arrived in Lesotho in 1877 from the author's home town of Ipswich, Suffolk, England.
33. Schwager, Dirk and Collen. *LESOTHO* (Schwager Publications, Lesotho, 1986) p. 16. The caption reads: 'The Maletsunyane gorge at Semonkong. The falls at the head of this gorge are 200 metres (656 feet) high and are the second highest straight drop falls in the southern hemisphere.' This picture shows this magnificent gorge capturing the drama of the surrounding mountains.
34. 2 Corinthians 9:7 (NIV): Each man should give what he has decided in his heart to give, not reluctantly or under compulsion, for God loves a cheerful giver.
35. William Blake's poem of 1804 set to music by Sir Hubert Parry in 1916 and known as the hymn *Jerusalem.*
36. Ezekiel 33:5–7 (NIV): Since he heard the sound of the trumpet but did not take warning, his blood will be on his own head. If he had taken warning, he would have saved himself. But if the watchman sees the sword coming and does not blow the trumpet to warn the people and the sword comes and takes the life of one of them, that man will be taken away because of his sin, but I will hold the watchman accountable for his blood. Son of man, I have made you a watchman for the house of Israel; so hear the word I speak and give them warning from me.
37. Sunday, 30th April 1989. St. Barnabas Church, Masite.
38. Matthew 7:8 (NIV): Everyone who asks receives; he who seeks finds; and to him who knocks, the door will be opened.
39. Friday, 12th May 1989 at St. Cyprian's Church, Molipa which is to the west of the northern road between Kolonyama and Peka.
40. For those unfamiliar with ecclesiastical dress an 'alb' is a full-length, generally white, loose-fitting robe reaching to the feet.

41. Ha Rantuba, directly north of Peka, close to the Caledon or Mohokare River which is the border with South Africa on Saturday, 13th May 1989.
42. Winston Churchill Maqutu, Registrar of the Anglican Diocese of Lesotho.
43. Micah 6:8b (NIV): And what does the Lord require of you? To act justly and to love mercy and to walk humbly with your God.
44. Mason, Simon D., *Pastoral Placement: Lesotho, June-September 1990.* Simon arrived in Lesotho on Saturday, 16th June 1990 and left (for Bloemfontein because of flight cancellations) on Wednesday, 29th August 1990.
45. Wright, Caroline, 'Unemployment, Migration and Changing Gender Relations in Lesotho' (Ph.D. Leeds, 1994). She now teaches in the Department of Sociology, University of Warwick, England.
46. If this M15 is multiplied by the then current Gross National Product it was worth the enormous amount of around £60.00 sterling.
47. All Saints Church, Hlajoane. Sunday, 10th February 1991. The picture on page 19 of *One in Word and Work* gives the wrong date: the photograph was taken Saturday, 9th February 1991 not 1992.
48. Ray Benton, a mathematician with a sharp sense of humour.
49. See Chapter One: In the beginning was the Word. (p. 1). 'Members of synod (are) about to make a decision that would marry the Diocese of Durham to the Diocese of Lesotho: it's a lifetime commitment'.
50. 1 Timothy 1:17–18 (NIV): The elders who direct the affairs of the church well are worthy of double honour, especially those whose work is preaching and teaching. For the Scripture says, 'Do not muzzle the ox while it is treading out the grain.'
51. Deuteronomy 25:4 (NIV): Do not muzzle an ox while it is treading out the grain.
52. Philemon 1:6 (NIV).

Chapter Eleven

Yap! Yap! Yap!

My children, do not forget my teaching,
but keep my commands in your heart,
for they will prolong your life many years
and bring you prosperity.[1]

The playful puppy sound Yap! Yap! Yap! by which the LINK's Youth Activities Project became known has been heard in Lesotho and Durham for longer than any other acronym associated with the LINK. Interest in the YAP has, in fact, been around for longer than the LINK itself and since we now also have a PUP[2] the reader who has reached this stage of our history could be forgiven for thinking that we were being dogged by canine mnemonics. As a Christian endeavour our venture into youth activities cannot be Biblically justified as other projects have been. Although a whole chapter of the Book of Proverbs[3] is devoted to giving advice to young men, adolescence, as such, is not Biblically recognised. It seems to have been unknown as a distinguishing concept although its distinctive behaviour was experienced if not accepted. At the age of twelve years Jesus failed to accompany his parents when they left the temple. He stayed behind without telling his parents. Eventually finding him, no doubt somewhat relieved, Mary, like many mothers since, reprimanded her son: 'My son why have you done this to us? Your father and I have been terribly worried trying to find you.'[4]

Even though the notion of the family is frequently employed in scripture the distinction of youth and puberty is avoided. This feature was reflected in ancient Basotho society. In the process of growing up and being recognised in society the boy or girl was, starkly, either child or adult. There was no in-between period of adolescent uncertainty as to what you were or, consequently, how you should behave. Equally, and what is sometimes overlooked, there was no adult uncertainty about how the young person should be treated.[5] In ancient Basotho culture, to attain the status of an adult the young person was required to go through the rigours of a gruesome initiation ceremony after which, if they survived, they graduated and were received into society as adults.[6] Over the years as the Basotho have moved ever closer to an enlightened social order the physical elements of initiation have lessened but, although modified, cultural expectations remain and are still strongly abhorred by the Christian Church. One result of the Church's repugnance is the need for the Church itself to offer an acceptable alternative to smooth the transition from childhood to adulthood.

It was April 1985 when I first heard demanding yelps. I was just beginning to lay down the foundations of the LINK when I had a visit from Ntsebeng Mafereka. As the Lesotho diocesan youth officer she had responsibility for helping hundreds of young Basotho to journey through the bewildering teenage period of human development. It was no secret that things in the difficult world of youth activities were not going well in Lesotho. Everyone knew what was being discarded but no one knew what should take its place. It was a time of considerable uncertainty. Young lives were emerging into adulthood, not through a comparatively short initiation ceremony but through a protracted period of some five or six years. The Church, surrounded by the young of its flock grappling with their immature Christian faith, found itself unprepared. Ntsebeng wanted to know if the LINK could help, were it to be started. We discussed the possibility of the LINK engaging in an ambitious plan to stimulate youth work in Lesotho but came to the reluctant conclusion it was not the most effective way to start the LINK. There was plenty of enthusiasm, no money and few labourers, none of whom were experienced youth leaders.

Leading an organisation like the Durham-Lesotho LINK, especially in its early months, was very much like riding a bicycle: to proceed too fast risked crashing; to go too slowly risked collapsing. It was a question of maintaining just sufficient momentum to keep upright. So the youthful barking continued throughout the early months persisting as only over-enthusiastic yapping can. Ntsebeng, known more fluently to European tongues as Alice, was studying youth leadership at Westhill College, Birmingham,[7] so was able to remind me, frequently, that I had assured her[8] we would consider the possibility carefully. So, ten months after the LINK had officially started, when a Durham clergyman came to see me with a plan to take a youth group to Lesotho my thoughts were sufficiently well formulated to ensure we were not barking up the wrong tree.

I felt that the Rev'd Malcolm McNaughton[9] was doing just that. His plan was to take a group of young people to Lesotho in the following year, 1988.

I argued that if we were to become One Body in Christ we also had to open Durham to the Basotho. His proposal made no provision for that; it was a one-way visit. As visits can be a burden to the hosts the plan did not capture my enthusiasm especially as I also had to bear in mind the weak state of youth activities in Lesotho. I maintained that any visit, youth or adult, should be the basis for friendships to grow into maturity. How future contacts were to be encouraged was a question we all needed much more time to address. I did not want the LINK to become the vehicle or, as has regretably happened in some cases, the excuse, for tourist-trips. The LINK needed to make provision for two-way exchange visits within which learning about our other half was a crucial element in becoming One Body in Christ. Youth and adult visits during the early years would have a vital influence on the ultimate success of the LINK so we had to get them off to a sound start. Crucially, each region of the LINK had to be ready to receive. Although I began to emphasise the idea of exchange visits, both youth and adult, other LINK work was taking much of my time which had to be shared with other parts of Africa as Zambia had just come on my scene.[10]

The support groups in Durham and Lesotho continued to discuss the possibility of engaging in youth work but it took a long time before any scheme that was acceptable to north and south began to take shape. Whilst we were all exercising patience without destroying enthusiasm offers of help continued to arrive by one means or another. One such was in September 1987, sixteen months after the LINK started. Two young members[11] of the congregation of St. Nicholas Church, Durham, had listened to my frequent sermons and descriptions of what was happening in the church on the other side of the world. They had become enthused about the possibility of going to Lesotho to work with young people. Their enthusiasm was such that they came to discuss their ideas twice in two weeks. I was being difficult to convince that what was being proposed was what was required to enliven the work of the gospel amongst Basotho and Durham youth. Their offer to go and work in Lesotho was generous but, again, it was a one-way proposal: I was looking not for labour, of which there was plenty in Lesotho, but ideas that would have a practical application and would be attractive to young people, both boys and girls, in both Lesotho and Durham. Two genders, two cultures: one objective: it was not an easy brief.

Although I wanted to go fast enough to stay upright I recognised the wisdom in David Jenkins' words, '… it will take time to work things out and we must go slowly and faithfully and hopefully and with great friendship while we find out where we can go together, what we can do together, and how we can support one another in the Lord's business'.[12] So it was not until Thursday, 6th April 1989, that yapping made itself audible in my study once again. This was during a telephone call from Rob Bianchi, the vicar of St. Paul's Church, West Pelton, a small former mining village, in the north-west of County Durham now overshadowed by Beamish and the widespread fame of its spectacular open-air museum.[13] There is nothing very spectacular about the 19th-century West Pelton church building. For something extraordinarily impressive you have to look outside in the graveyard to reveal the story of a truly remarkable couple.

A son of the village, Jack Lawson, is buried there. Jack became a coal-miner at the age of 12 years working underground for ten hours a day. After twelve years hewing coal Jack was elected a Member of Parliament. He served as Secretary of State for War in 1945–46 and was later made a Baron before becoming the King's Honorary Representative in County Durham as Lord Lieutenant of the County. Concealed behind that remarkable social service was the unfailingly faithful support of his wife, Isabella, who took the job of a housemaid to supplement the scholarship awarded to Jack to study at Ruskin College, Oxford. Throughout an incredible joint career the two Lawsons consistently demonstrated Christian humility. They had no pretensions to grandeur; they continued their community service whilst living in their small, modest terraced house. Jack Lawson was also a Methodist lay preacher. How he came to be buried in an Anglican churchyard does not seem to be documented. What is documented, and in no doubt, is the husband and wife support that existed within the marriage of Jack and Isabella.

Mutual support seems to thrive in West Pelton with a nearby public house named The Shepherd and Shepherdess; although any reference to their actual relationship remains obscure. The joint application of skills and interests was further enhanced in the area by Rob and Margaret Bianchi who, as probably the first couple to be ordained after the ordination of women was permitted in the Anglican Church, exercised their joint ministry at St. Paul's Church, West Pelton. Continuing the joint application of skills, in September 2003 they were appointed as joint executive officers of the Durham-Lesotho LINK, a position they still held eight years later.

But that's leaping ahead: a lot was to happen before then. I recorded in my journal on Thursday, 6th April 1989 'Rob Bianchi phoned to discuss an idea for a youth visit to Lesotho in 1991; sounds good'. It did sound good: the exchange principle had been grasped. Nevertheless, I needed to launch a youth activities project on something much more substantial than just one phone call so I asked him to do something that he really did not enjoy. Because I thought it would help to clarify our thinking I asked him to write a description of his proposal. My request was not enthusiastically greeted; Rob is very much a man of action but the ideas on paper were as good as those on the phone. Yapping had been going on for almost four years: it had not been ignored but it had to be introduced with other LINK activities that were taking huge amounts of time, energy and money. The long delay had been a useful pause giving the necessary time to make preparations but now it was time to make progress. It was also helpful to have time for the new ideas to germinate and I wanted to allow for that to happen.

The proposal discussed with the Lesotho youth committee was for five boys and three girls between the ages of seventeen and twenty-one from churches in the Durham diocese,[14] to spend two weeks with a similar group in Lesotho at the end of January, 1991. The Basotho hosts would return to Durham for a two-week period in the summer of the same year so friendships made could be continued. During their visits they would be camping, walking, climbing and worshipping together and undertaking some light work, such as tree-planting, on LINK sites. In the process they would hopefully come to understand more about each other, their countries and cultures in addition to learning more about the LINK through which they would become increasingly aware of the Christian unity it was working to enhance. Rob and Margaret Bianchi would be leading the Durham group which accepted responsibility for raising the money to pay for their own costs and also to subsidise the Basotho visit to Durham.

Now resistance came from an unexpected source. In Lesotho the discussion went smoothly until climbing was mentioned as a possible activity. It was not the Basotho who had doubts but an Australian who worked for the diocese. For many days he voiced his genuine anxieties. At every possible moment there was a difficult question to answer. In a diocesan council meeting he asked what I proposed to do after the first climber had fallen to their death! He was a very worried man. I was eventually able to convince the sceptics and the Council (although, I suspect, not my antagonist) that adventure was an essential ingredient of youth activity; that we had excellent, well-qualified leaders; that assessing risk and taking appropriate precautions was an important element of youth training. In the twenty-five-year history of the LINK no climber has died but on Saturday, 4th September 2010 we did suffer a tragedy. Matsieli Manyane, a student from St. Barnabas High School, Masite, drowned in an accident that took place, ironically, during a Royal Lifesaving Society training exercise on the Maqalika Dam. All the normal safety precautions were in place and no explanation of the accident has revealed that anything untoward took place. In the complex mission and work of the LINK, exercised in a dangerous environment, we have had to cope with a number of accidents but none has been quite so distressing as the death of this young man.

Twenty years earlier as the new year of 1990 came alive it seemed to Pam and me that we should have swapped roles. She had been on an (in)famous Baker Day course[15] on 'Stress in Education' and I was feeling the considerable pressures of the LINK. The work in Durham was not without its difficulties especially when dealing with a large variety of personalities and abilities. Before Rob Bianchi arrived on the afternoon of Thursday, 11th January 1990 to discuss the YAP I had been annoyed to learn from the container working party that a twenty-foot container had been sent to Lesotho without the necessary papers from the Lesotho customs authority. Still troubled by that a request arrived from The Farmers' Third World Network to mount a display at its annual conference. What next? The chairman of the medical working party arrived with his wife to talk about their recent private visit to South Africa when they were able also to visit Ha Popa Rural Health Centre. We were interrupted by a phone call from a Mosotho studying at Leeds University; he wanted to come and stay.[16] It was a time when I, with others,[17] began to wonder if we should recruit more full-time help but now, with those things dealt with, it was time for me to attend to the yapping.

As yapping became 'barking' so exchanges became, in the language of youth, 'swaps' and the LINK was, once again, experiencing its strength in flexibility. It is difficult to know quite how to assess success or failure of an activity such as a youth exchange, sorry, swap; perhaps we shall never know. The words of one young Durham participant[18] are, perhaps, the nearest we can hope to get as they encapsulate a moment that she found significant and provide an insight into the value of such contacts:

> Passing through a village, the people emerge with welcoming smiles waving enthusiastically, children in bright ragged clothing sidle towards you, hide their eyes when you first acknowledge them, before timidly touching the hand you reach out to them. In short, it is a beautiful country with beautiful people.

Reporting when they returned, one of the leaders, focusing on a Sunday service in Butha-Buthe, wrote:

> The Durham-Lesotho LINK proved to be widely effective … and the majority of Basotho ... we met were delighted with the schemes active in their area. Thus our welcome was made even warmer. A certain Sunday service in Buthe-Butha (*sic*) here springs to mind, four hours of singing and praise that

> lingers in my memory as one of the most moving and breathtaking experiences of my life.[19]

Clearly, deep impressions were being rooted in the minds of the young and not-so-young alike as they carried out activities together ranging from tree-planting to conducting a survey on leisure activities in the Mohatlane district where the proposal for the LINK community education centre was being formulated and investigated.[20] With an exaggeration born of unbridled enthusiasm the writer continues:

> The whole fortnight was made up of a million indescribable moments that I feel privileged to have experienced. From tree-planting and hospital visiting to horse riding and Sunday worship, each and every activity was undertaken with an enthusiasm which slowly brought together the English and the Basotho groups.

These friendships were cemented when six months later the Basotho visited Durham to live with the families of the Durham group they had entertained earlier in the year during their January summer. The Basotho youngsters could not possibly afford the travel expenses involved so Durham subsidised their visit from a fund of £15,000 that had been raised before the Durham group left for Lesotho. They filled their fourteen Durham days camping at the Franciscan Friary at Alnmouth,[21] visiting Holy Island,[22] Auckland Castle, the tiny Saxon church at Escomb[23] and the huge Norman cathedral at Durham. They relaxed whilst dining with the chairman of Durham County Council, canoeing on the River Wear, abseiling down rock faces and living as adopted members of Durham families. Perhaps not quite so relaxing, but a new experience nonetheless, was to sing on Radio Newcastle and then to load 32,000 books into the next container to go to Lesotho.

After two enjoyable youth swaps, one in each direction, what then? The education working party, which was exercising the oversight of youth activities at this time, was planning an adult exchange visit in 1993 and another youth exchange in 1995, that is, one of each age range every four years. However, we all accepted that youth exchanges could only be part of a more comprehensive scheme of activities if the LINK was to maintain the continuing interest of young people. Interest would flag in a four-year gap so we needed some sort of continuing activity. Rob and I talked a lot and he again recorded his ideas on paper so we could see where they might be taking us and how. I wanted to determine the long-term strategy. By Thursday 13th June 1991, his useful paper 'Outdoor Pursuits in

Lesotho' was being critically analysed to enable a third paper to incorporate our joint thinking. He suggested that the LINK should train instructors in activities in which the Basotho would be interested, some of which should be structured within a commercial environment to provide an income to fund other youth activities.

We met for an hour in July 1991[24] to knock about some ideas but I was more than a little sceptical as I had seen so many 'self-sustaining' schemes go wrong in other places. 'Sustainability' is a much overused word and often misapplied with little conceptual rigour. In weak economies it is often difficult to sustain the income-producing venture let alone make sufficient profit to fund another additional project. It was October,[25] during a long telephone conversation, that we drew closer to agreement. Despite that it was another fourteen months before we met again during the morning of the last day[26] of what had been a very active year. We drew together all the disparate suggestions and thoughts into one coherent proposal from which Rob and I now produced a long-term strategy for a programme of youth activities that we felt would be attractive to the Basotho and to Durham's education working party.

After a long wait the ideas were put into practice in 1993 when two young Basotho men arrived in Durham. With three Durham young men they took part in a training course at the West Pelton Outdoor Activity Centre run by Rob Bianchi. Before the Basotho arrived the Lesotho youth officer had found it difficult to select two suitable candidates and asked if we would agree to the Lesotho Outward Bound Centre making the selection. It was not our first connection with this group. Five days after Lesotho had accepted the Durham proposal for a YAP I was with Philip Mokuku at the Roman Catholic retreat centre, Lelapa la Lerato (Family of Love), Mahobong in the Leribe District, attending a conference on 'conflict' being run by 'Transformation'.[27] Over our meals we discussed the sort of activities that a YAP might involve and he suggested visiting the Lesotho Outward Bound Centre,[28] 'just across the road' at the Lionel Collett Dam. There we talked with the senior tutor Colin Gordon-Davies about demand for the courses that made full use of the nearby Thaba Phatšoa, the Collett Dam and the inevitable *dongas* one of which was straddled by a monkey bridge. Colin explained that because of the high course fees most of the participants were from South Africa. The Basotho just could not afford the high charges.

As the LINK was working only with the Basotho we would not be in competition but now we were just about to experience for ourselves the 'high charges' when our comparatively minor request commanded a fee of £600.[29] That short visit convinced me that our attempt to establish a YAP for the Basotho and, in due time, run by them was the right way to proceed. The LINK's financial controls limited the fee to £200 which was accepted. They selected well. In the years ahead one of the two, Stephen Mabula, was to become the LINK's executive officer in Lesotho. Now he and Teboho Tlali who went, in due course, to work for Outward Bound, arrived in Durham to undertake a one-year training course. That started in October 1993, and was designed in three sections: to develop competence in leadership; to acquire outdoor activity skills for canoeing, climbing and general youth work;[30] and to provide employment and generate income[31] by training in glass-fibre construction. The participants also attended a course in Christian studies.

While future leaders were caving, climbing and canoeing in Durham a lot of yapping was taking place in Lesotho. I was conscious of the need to get a quick final decision to enable the project to use the Maqalika Dam for its water activities. It was urgent to bring this to a satisfactory conclusion because, although I had been assured by the Minister for Natural Resources we could use the dam and some land on the shore line for LINK youth activities, I was not convinced it was a definitive decision. Furthermore, I had been told that the Minister, Monyane Moleleki, was probably going to be moved from Natural Resources but, when I was given that information by a usually reliable source, I had no idea of the style of that removal. When I met with the Minister on Friday 8th April 1994 we made very little progress: his thinking was distracted. Also his Deputy Principal Secretary, Ntate Mohafa, who was dealing with the matter, was 'unavailable' so we agreed that the three of us should meet again on the following Tuesday, 12th April 1994.

Over the weekend the political atmosphere became increasingly tense. I was about to experience how unstable the Lesotho government was at this time. On the day of our rearranged meeting I received a telephone call asking me to meet again with Monyane Moleleki 'early next week' by which time soldiers[32] had kidnapped him with three other ministers, killing the Deputy Prime Minister, Selometsi Baholo. Clearly the need for the Durham-Lesotho LINK to use the Maqalika Dam for youth activities had slid down the priority list. Was the Devil smirking by now? 'Early next week' slipped to Wednesday, 20th and then Thursday, 21st April 1994 when I spoke by telephone to Ntate Mohafa who asked me to see him just minutes before I was due to be at the airport to return to Durham. We discussed the situation and concluded by agreeing that when I returned to Durham I would write to him about his Minister's decision. That letter was to be one of the most influential I ever wrote on behalf of the Durham-Lesotho LINK.

Now there was a lot to do before I left a turbulent Lesotho. It was not only the nation that was in turmoil and confused. The Church also had its problems which, in turn, affected the LINK. There were serious ructions within the medical staff at St. James' Hospital, Mantšonyane, that had repercussions across the mountains in our clinic at Ha Popa. There we expected a supporting strike of medics would, sooner or later, take place. Within the LINK we urgently needed to appoint someone to take over from Steven Molekeng who wished to retire and had been such a strength during the first phase of our development. He would be difficult to replace. Following a long announcement on Radio Lesotho about the LINK and its need for a project manager we had to deal with many enquiries. I was also beginning to wonder how much longer we could continue without a full-time secretary or administrator: we were at that difficult stage of being too big for one person but not big enough for two.

Not unusually the Church was grappling with its constant problem of poor administration and inadequate financial resources both of which generated an increased sense of frustration that began to confront the LINK. Our organisation was sound, our administration was effective, our finances were strong and the controls robust. The LINK also had the highly visual advantage of adequate transport and communication. All of this was in stark contrast to the processes of the Church within which our success was beginning to cause some resentment amongst more susceptible people. It was, indeed, a turbulent time for Philip and me so we decided to escape to the peace of the Community of the Holy Name at Hlotse where together we talked, prayed and rested. Tranquility was not to last!

Next day King Letsie III sent a message that we should return immediately to Maseru with the Roman Catholic bishop, Paul Khoarai, because of the instability caused by the kidnappings that had taken place (at that stage we knew nothing of the murder of the Deputy Prime Minister). Extracting Paul Khoarai from a clergy conference at St. Monica's Roman Catholic Mission we drove at high speed to Maseru, passing safely and quickly through a police road block at Teyateyaneng. Our dash was worth the effort as the two bishops were able to mediate on behalf of the captured four ministers and they were released later that same day Friday, 15th April 1994.

Before I escaped northward into calmer waters I drafted a submission for the YAP's glass-fibre unit requesting finance from the British High Commission's micro-project funding. It was submitted on Saturday, 16th April 1994 at the end of an astonishingly confused week that vividly reminded us all that we were working in an environment that could erupt at any time without warning. Not all the disorder and confusion was in the lowlands. There was more to come from the mountains! I had no warning at all that the burden of my psychological baggage for the flight next week was about to be dramatically increased. When Dr Lieisbeth Menwissen